# Teaching Mainstreamed Students
## Methods and Techniques

# Teaching Mainstreamed Students
## Methods and Techniques

Kathleen M. McCoy
*Arizona State University*

Herbert J. Prehm
*late of Council for Exceptional Children
and Arizona State University*

LOVE PUBLISHING COMPANY
Denver/London

Library of Congress Catalog Card Number 86-82893


Printed in the U.S.A.
ISBN 0-89108-131-3

# Preface

With the advent of a mainstreaming movement that is now well established and here to stay, special and regular educators alike are facing new challenges daily. There is a real need for a book to help teachers teach in the mainstream with more success and more satisfaction. *Teaching Mainstreamed Students* is intended to meet that need, by presenting workable, proven methods for the mainstreamed classroom.

Regular educators have to be knowledgeable of the individual needs of special students placed in their classrooms. They have to be able to choose, adapt, and modify materials and methods to maximize the educational growth of these students. At the same time, they are responsible for teaching 20 or more regular students of varying levels and competence and motivation and encouraging the educational growth of all.

Within a single classroom may be a highly gifted student who requires challenge and enrichment in learning and a slow learning child who may need repetition and practice to retain certain skills. The class also may contain an emotionally disturbed student whose need for attention disrupts the entire class. An assortment of other students with their own social, affective, and learning characteristics mingles with these others to create the unique chemistry of each class.

Special educators have their own responsibilities, first to identify and assess special needs in a student, and then to decide how these needs can be best met—in what setting, with which instructional methods and materials—for each subject area. They have a charge to monitor the progress of special students and be prepared to change the course and direction of the individualized education program in the student's best interests. They play a key role on the IEP team. Special educators are teachers, consultants, advisors, resource teachers, communicators, and support persons working toward smooth transitions and operations within a school system.

The authors of this book have extensive training and backgrounds in both regular and special classrooms, with both regular and special students. The educational experiences are real. With an emphasis on practical guidelines, strategies, and methods that work in the regular classroom, the premise of this book is that if the teacher's job is made easier, more time can be spent in productive teaching. The discussion covers the gamut from the sensory impaired to slow learners to the gifted. It encompasses subject area bases from reading to all the language arts to mathematics, with suggested evaluation tools and instructional ideas for each.

After providing a background of the mainstream movement, philosophy, and labeling practices, the book discusses the specific exceptionalities and proven methods that work with each of them—the learning disabled, mentally retarded, behavior disordered, and physically, visually, and hearing impaired. Then the book explains the concept and practice of the IEP, its components, and team involvement in its planning and implementation.

The next area of discussion revolves around classroom organization and classroom management—how to "reduce the extraneous," consolidate, manage time, schedule, and maintain a productive class day. It includes behavior management and the affective components of learning, attitudes, and how to communicate teacher expectations.

In the last section, the basic skill areas are addressed, with specific methods for assessing and teaching them. Reading instruction includes identification of problem areas, the related components of reading, and the major reading strategies, including methods developed specifically for slow learners. The language arts discussion covers oral and written language, spelling, and handwriting. Mathematics evaluation and instruction takes into account the assessment tools, instructional content, and specific techniques for helping children with special learning needs in math.

This book is intended to be understandable, readable, and applicable to classroom needs, giving as many examples and step-by-step suggestions as possible. As a text, it is suited for any course directed at teaching the handicapped child in the regular classroom, teaching mildly handicapped students, effective instruction of students in the mainstream, and the like. Whomever the reader, it is hoped that the ideas and concepts presented will lead to children's growth and fulfillment as students.

The authors, Kathleen McCoy and the late Herbert J. Prehm, wish to acknowledge all the people who have given us support throughout this writing venture, especially Jane Dowling, Renee Newman, and Francie Margolin.

# Contents

*To my parents,*
*Vi and R.E. McCoy*

# 1

# A Modern Fable

Once upon a time there was Ms. Smith and her class of 30 excited, happy, and eager students. Room 23—Ms. Smith's classroom—was reputed to be "laid back" but highly productive. Like all elementary classes, Room 23 had its predictable good and not-so-good moments. But, all things considered, the class was a very mellow place to be.

Ms. Smith, of course, made some special arrangements for some of her students. Sometimes Sammy got his letters—especially $b$'s and $d$'s—confused. Because $b$'s and $d$'s looked alike, Ms. Smith decided to change them a little. She marked all the $b$'s in Sammy's reader like this: $\overset{?}{B}$. She left all the $d$'s the way they were. Sometimes Ms. Smith forgot that the books were school property. She often modified the books for instructional purposes.

After Ms. Smith marked Sammy's book, Sammy never confused $\overset{?}{B}$ and $d$. Gradually Ms. Smith changed the $\overset{?}{B}$ to $\overset{?}{b}$ and then the $\overset{?}{b}$ to $\overset{.}{b}$. Even after Ms. Smith no longer marked $b$'s with special marks, Sammy never confused $b$ and $d$ again. Ms. Smith was pleased—and so was Sammy!

Alice, another student in Room 23, got some special help from Ms. Smith too. Alice could read the Dolch Sight Words when each word was presented on an individual card or when the words were listed vertically. But Alice couldn't seem to read the words when they were in her reader. Ms. Smith wondered a long time about what to do to help Alice read from her reader. She thought and thought and wondered what the difference was between reading the words in a vertical list and reading the same words from a reader.

After Ms. Smith thought about the difference for a while, the problem was obvious. The words in the list were separate items; they were in isolation

**Figure 1.1**
Vertical List of Words Taken from a Basal Reader

**What makes reading**

A brown and white dog barked.

**Different from reading**

A
brown
and
white
dog
barked.

from any other words or spaces. The words in the reader were beside each other. Ms. Smith, remembering that Alice could easily read words in isolation, decided to isolate the words in the reader too. She took each word and outlined its shape.

**Figure 1.2**
Outlined Words

Each outlined word was isolated but still with the other words in the reader. (Ms. Smith knew that Alice really wanted to read from her reader.) To be sure that Alice could follow the words in the correct order, Ms. Smith added an arrow at the beginning of each word. The arrows pointed in the direction that Alice was supposed to read.

**Figure 1.3**
Using an Arrow to Signal the Beginning of Words

The very first time Alice read in her specially marked book, she got all the words right! When Alice read her book that first day, she was so excited that her cheeks got all pink and her eyes couldn't stop laughing. Ms. Smith almost cried that day—she was so filled with Alice's joy at being able to read. Ms. Smith knew that she couldn't mark all of Alice's books forever. She gradually changed the words in the reader from "A brown and white dog barked" to "A brown and white dog barked." After that, Alice could read any book she wanted. In fact, Alice won a prize for reading 30 library books by the end of the school year.

And then there was Michael. He had more energy than "you know who" had pills. Some days it seemed like Michael had swallowed "Silly Putty." He bounced around the room so much that sometimes Ms. Smith was sure his head touched the ceiling. Energy like Michael's was wonderful to behold, but the intensity of the motion did seem to be a bit distracting to Michael, the other children, and Ms. Smith herself. Having Michael sit still all day seemed too confining. How could he move around and still learn his lessons and not disturb the other children? Michael and Ms. Smith talked the

**Figure 1.4**
A Series of Word Modifications Leading to Independent Reading

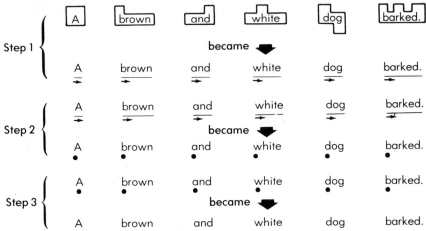

problem through and came up with an idea. Ms. Smith would provide three places where Michael could work: his desk, a study carrel, and a table in the back of the room. Whenever Michael felt the need to move around he could quietly take his work to one of these three places. Michael promised that once he arrived at his chosen place, he would work there for at least 10 minutes. Over a period of weeks, Michael and Ms. Smith lengthened the time spent at a work place from 10 minutes to 15 minutes and then to 30 minutes. Once Michael was able to sit in one place for 30 minutes, he and Ms. Smith didn't worry about extending the time. Actually, after he hit the 30-minute time, he sometimes went beyond the limit. In fact, there were whole days when Michael worked in only one place! He was still filled with electric energy, but he seemed to save his energy for use at recess.

Ms. Smith made program modifications for other children too. Johnny had special problems in math, Kari needed help with writing, and Chuck needed to bring his head out of the clouds. In fact, there really wasn't one child in the class whose educational program was identical with any other's. Each child worked at his or her own pace—sometimes in groups and sometimes individually. Some children had more problems than others; most of the problems had solutions. Life in the classroom flowed on.

As the years rolled by, Ms. Smith found many people who were willing to help her solve her students' problems. These people were specialists trained in the latest teaching technologies. Although they were always willing to help, they sometimes spoke in rather technical terms. Ms. Smith, being too polite to ask for clarification, found herself beginning to have problems communicating with the specialists. Their language was foreign to her. While she would often say their language was Greek to her, it was really Latin! The language was rather impressive and some of the terms—*dyslexia, acalculia, dysgraphia*—could even be found in a medical dictionary. Truly, these specialists must be scientists! They used such scientific terminology and impressive batteries of tests. Ms. Smith knew "only" how to teach reading, writing, and arithmetic. The specialists also began having problems talking with Ms. Smith. Communication is a two-way street but Ms. Smith rarely had anything to say.

In the true spirit of generosity, however, the specialists continued to observe the problems of the children in Ms. Smith's class and soon began to identify the problems for her. Sammy and Alice were called "learning disabled" (LD). They and other children like them were called learning disabled because they had average or above average intelligence but were not achieving academically at grade level. Some of the learning disabled children couldn't write their names very well, were having problems attending to instruction, and were a little clumsy and awkward. Ms. Smith felt terrible. She had always thought of these children as members of her class. She hadn't realized the depth of their problems!

Other children were also given labels. Some were called "educable mentally handicapped" (EMH). Not only were these children lagging behind in academics, but their intelligence quotients were low as well. Thank goodness the school psychologist had tested them or Ms. Smith would probably have never found out the exact number that defined each child. Instead, she would have probably kept on breaking her instruction into smaller and smaller steps. Some children would have learned a little more slowly than others but no one would have known about the officially defined problems.

All the "Michaels" in Ms. Smith's class were labeled "behavior disordered" or "emotionally handicapped" (BD or EH). Some children were called "hyperactive"; others were called "hypoactive." These official labels were very confusing to Ms. Smith because some of the behaviors that Michael showed could also be seen in Hank and Lori. But Lori was classed learning disabled and Hank was called normal. In fact, to Ms. Smith, Michael seemed a lot like Hank except that once in a while Michael got behind in his classwork.

Ms. Smith was much relieved that the specialists had come. She was feeling very guilty about her past classroom program. The specialists promised her that the LD's, EMH's, and EH's would all be fine. In fact, they offered to take them out of Ms. Smith's classroom and provide them with special programs—special programs to deal with special problems. Ms. Smith almost wept for joy! At last, after all these long years, her beloved students would get the education that she, in her naivete, was unable to give them. May the specialists be praised!

The years continued to roll by. More and more specialists came to Ms. Smith's school. Ms. Smith stopped solving classroom problems. When a child seemed to be different from the other children in some way, she sent for the specialist. The specialist would identify problems, diagnose, and officially label the child. Within weeks—well, sometimes months because there was a lot of diagnosing going on and not quite enough diagnosticians—the child would be placed in a special setting for part or all of the school day.

The only minor problem Ms. Smith had was not knowing what to do with an officially labeled child between the time of labeling and the child's placement in the special classroom. The specialists assured Ms. Smith that, though this situation caused her concern, it was really not her problem. It was the specialist's problem. Ms. Smith felt that there was very little that she could or should do to foster the academic or social growth of the child. As time passed, Ms. Smith gradually came to accept the fact that some of the children in her room were not her responsibility. Initially, acceptance of this fact was uncomfortable, but time—and specialists—heal all.

Meanwhile, the other children in the class began to notice that the Sammys and Alices were somehow different. (The children had always known that the Michaels were special.) The Sammys and Alices and Michaels all went to special classes. Sometimes they left and didn't join the regular class again. Sammy, Alice, and Michael were in the same building most of the time but were usually on a different schedule for recess and lunch. Because of the different schedules, the other children stopped playing with the Sammys and Alices. Since Alice and Sammy were no longer in the classroom, they didn't have much in common with the other children except their ride home on the school bus.

The other children also learned the official names for Sammy and Alice but chose to shorten them. When the other children got mad or wanted to tease one another—or Sammy or Alice or Michael—they called each other by the shortened version of the official label.

This kind of teasing made Michael and Alice and Sammy very sad. They wondered if being officially labeled and receiving special classes was such a good deal after all. Ms. Smith wondered about the special placement, too. The specialists assured her, however, that the special programs were the most beneficial option available to her former students.

At the same time, some parents were becoming concerned that their children were not receiving the special services given to some other children. Some parents demanded that more classrooms be built and that more specialists be trained. Being influential with elected officials, they got laws passed to ensure the spread of special services for their special children. Through legislative acts, money was made to train more specialists, identify more children, and open more classes.

Soon it seemed that almost every child could be given some sort of label. No matter how quickly new classes were opened, they were not opened quickly enough to keep pace with identification. Something had to be done!

Something was done! The official labels were made more restrictive. Many children who came from low socioeconomic environments were excluded from special classes. "Environmental deprivation" was not to be confused with "true" learning or social problems, said the supervisors of the specialists. Intelligence quotients that defined official categories were reduced by roughly 15 points, and then, a couple of years later, raised by roughly 5 points. As a result, many EMH students were no longer EMH students for a while. Of course, some of them simply switched labels and moved to the LD class. The special classes were still crowded, but fewer children were eligible for placement. The specialists began to sigh with relief.

In fact, the sound of sighing could be heard throughout the hallowed halls of the school. However, not all the sighs belonged to the specialists. Ms. Smith was also sighing, but not from relief. What was she supposed to do now that specialists would solve only some problems? Sammy did not qualify for service anymore, and neither did Alice or Michael! Many specialists secretly confided that these children did have special problems and expressed their sorrow that Sammy and Michael and Alice couldn't be officially labeled.

Ms. Smith didn't know what to do! She had forgotten how to solve problems for the special children. Worse, she wasn't sure that she should even try. She was trained to teach skills like math and reading; she did not know how to teach officially unlabeled LD's, EH's, and EMH's.

To compound matters for Ms. Smith, a new law was passed. This law, the Education for All Handicapped Children Act of 1975 (PL 94-142), said that all handicapped children had to be educated in the Least Restrictive Environment. Ms. Smith translated this to mean that some children who had been officially labeled would either never leave her classroom or would be coming back. Ms. Smith was now responsible for teaching some officially labeled children and all officially unlabeled children.

At first, Ms. Smith was petrified. She thought all labeled children would be returned to her room for all of the school day. However, she was reassured that only those children who could benefit from regular class placement would be in her classroom for part or all of the day. When she was also told that the specialists would give her support services, her heartbeat slowed down a bit and she unpacked her books. (She had seriously considered going to a remote region of the Yukon, opening a real estate business, and never looking at a child, labeled or not, again.)

So now it is the present. Ms. Smith is a little dazed, moderately concerned, but willing to try working with all the children in her room. She knows that, though support services have been promised to her, she will be the primary teacher for some officially labeled children. Ms. Smith is still a little anxious. But ... she remembers the laughter in Alice's eyes.

# 2
# The Mainstream

A small boy named Jeffrey sits slumped at his desk in a regular education classroom in Anytown, USA. The school day has just begun, marking the beginning of a new life for Jeff. Today is Jeff's first day away from his self-contained special class and his first day in Room 23. Jeff watches the freckles play leapfrog on the backs of his hands for what seems like hours. Gently, hands touch his shoulder. Jeff looks up and his eager brown eyes meet the warm, generous face of his new teacher, Ms. Smith. "Welcome, Jeff," says Ms. Smith. Jeff breathes an audible sigh of relief, produces a tenuous smile, and thinks "Maybe, just maybe, I'll make it through the day."

Scenes like this one occur every day in regular classrooms throughout the United States. Hundreds of special class pupils are returning to regular classroom or are entering regular classrooms for the first time. Officially, the exodus of many handicapped children from special classes began on November 29, 1975, with the passage of the Education for All Handicapped Children Act (PL 94-142). Through this act, Congress declared that every handicapped child has an inalienable right to be educated in the educational setting most appropriate for that child. Furthermore, Congress specified that the most appropriate setting is one that can be described as the "least restrictive environment."

Attempts to comply with this act form what is called the *mainstream* movement. Regular classes in which handicapped children participate are called *mainstream rooms*. A primary feature of a mainstream room is that the group of children taught in the room is intentionally heterogeneous. Physical, emotional, and intellectual differences are recognized and respected but are neither diminished nor emphasized.

Prior to 1975, more than half of the handicapped children in the United States were either institutionalized or did not receive appropriate educational services (Lance, 1976). Over time, most handicapped children will be integrated into regular classrooms, and these regular classrooms will become mainstream rooms.

## FACTORS CONTRIBUTING TO THE MAINSTREAM MOVEMENT

Impetus for the mainstream movement comes from the normalization principle, failure of special class placement, administrative concerns and dissatisfaction with the process by which children are identified and labeled as handicapped. Each factor has made a unique contribution to the mainstream movement.

## NORMALIZATION

### The Scandinavian Experience

Historically, the roots of PL 94-142 began in Scandinavia during the mid-1960s (Bank-Mikkelsen, 1969). A principle embodied in the term *normalization* emerged from the Scandinavian experience in providing services to mentally retarded people. The principle emphasized providing retarded children and adults with experiences that approximate, as closely as possible, the experiences of normal society. Living in community-based homes rather than large institutions, experiencing the normal rhythms of the year, complete with holidays, birthdays, and other special days of personal significance, and wearing age-appropriate clothing are examples of the application of the normalization principle.

### Individual Experiences

Normalization is both culture-specific and person-specific. Accordingly, the mainstream model is determined both interindividually and intraindividually (Thomas, 1980). While the celebration of holidays is universal, there may be many cultural differences in the manner in which the same holiday is observed. For example, in the United States, the New Year is met with confetti and paper hats, while in China the New Year is met with much pageantry and dignity. The normalization principle asserts that handicapped people should be allowed to celebrate the New Year in the manner common to the culture of their country or cultural group. Thus, a pupil in Akron, Ohio, should be granted a chance to blow horns and throw confetti and a pupil in China should be allowed to observe the dragon miracle.

### Goals of Normalization

The normalization principle also suggests that services and activities experienced by handicapped people be as integrated as possible in goals and methods of delivery (Wolfensberger, 1972). In addition, the principle suggests that, whenever possible, social, vocational, and life goals of the handicapped person should approximate the goals of the mainstream population. In general, handicapped persons must be integrated into society as well as possible. The physical context in which a handicapped person will receive services may be a sheltered workshop, a ward in a hospital, a public school classroom, or even the natural home. Choice of a setting is related to the nature and degree of the handicapping condition. Normalization also implies social acceptance of the handicapped person and stresses the value of human dignity for all persons, be they handicapped or not. The philosophical intent of the normalization principle is difficult to question. It has gained world-wide acceptance and provides the catalyst for the "least restrictive" service alternatives in educational settings, as mandated by PL 94-142 (Thurman & Fiorelli, 1980).

## FAILURE OF SPECIAL CLASS PLACEMENT

### Performance Results

A second factor contributing to the mainstream movement is the failure to show evidence that the academic and social skills of mildly handicapped pupils enrolled in special classes are superior to the skills of mildly handicapped pupils enrolled in regular classes. Special class placement is extremely expensive; yet it appears to make no educational difference (Larrivee & Cook, 1979; Madden & Slavin, 1983). Research that suggests that special class placement produces about the same degree of performance as regular class placement has been criticized for methodological flaws (Kaufman & Alberto, 1976). Nevertheless, "the advantage of special curricula and/or teaching strategies for such children has not been adequately documented" (Smart, Wilton, & Keeling, 1980, p. 219).

While academic performance is vital to school success, the quality of children's lives is also important. Opponents of mainstreaming have argued that a handicapped child's quality of life will be enhanced if the child is separated from nonhandicapped children. The argument is based on the belief that the unique needs of many handicapped children are not tolerable to the mainstream. Special classes are viewed as safe harbors or sanctuaries for handicapped children. Theoretically, if a handicapped child is given a supportive environment, which is supposed to be easier to provide in a segregated setting than in a regular setting, the child's self-concept will be more positive. It is argued that the more homogeneous the classroom, the better will be the child's self-concept. Thus, it is assumed that handicapped children will develop better self-concepts if they are placed in special settings than if they are placed in regular classrooms … but will they?

As far back as 1962 we learned that, when mentally retarded children are given official recognition by segregation, they develop much clearer and more negative self-concepts than similar children not placed in special classes (Meyerowitz, 1962). It seems clear that segregation means different and that being different, when attached to a label like mentally retarded or learning disabled, is not highly desirable. Perhaps the safe harbors are not so safe after all.

## ADMINISTRATIVE CONCERNS: COMMITMENT TO THE REGULAR CLASS

The third factor that has contributed to the popularity of the notion of classroom integration is the role played by special education in traditional school programs. To quote Milofsky (1974), "unavoidably, the first commitment of the public schools is to the vast majority of students attending regular classes. Special education is a marginal enterprise" (p. 439). He might have qualified his statement to read: "special education *as a segregated and administratively isolated entity* is a marginal enterprise." Public schools are committed to educating all youngsters. But, as in most markets, attention is paid to the largest consumer group. Regular classrooms significantly outnumber special classrooms. As a result, more administrative attention is directed to regular classroom teachers and pupils than is directed to special classrooms. However, concern for the quality of educational programming should be equal for all students—handicapped as well as nonhandicapped. Where quality education takes place is an administrative concern.

Providing high-quality programs for special students and providing for the administrative concerns of regular classrooms can be complementary functions. By improving the educational flexibility of regular classrooms, public schools can ensure that many special students receive an appropriate education in regular classrooms. Flexibility can be increased by strengthening those factors that help reduce the size or number of special classrooms. Support for inservice education for the regular class teacher, purchase of appropriate materials, and provision of support services to the regular teacher (e.g., a specially trained consultant or master teacher) each contribute to improving instruction in the regular classroom. Improved instruction leads to fewer special classrooms. Reducing the number of special classrooms can lead to reallocating instructional funds to support strengthening the factors that contribute to a flexible regular classroom setting. This cycle is depicted in Figure 2.1 as an endless loop. No single point represents the beginning of the cycle. All parts are related, so a change in one component will produce a related change in another. The more flexible the regular setting, the less will be the need for more special classes. The more funds allocated to the regular classroom, the more support received by the regular teacher. The loop continues endlessly.

# LABELING PRACTICES

## HOMOGENEOUS GROUPING

The practice of labeling special populations grew out of the belief that certain characteristics identify homogeneous groups of exceptional children for instructional purposes. According to this belief, if we educate children whose

**Figure 2.1** Administrative Support Cycle
The complementary nature of administration for regular education classes and
providing high quality programs to special populations.

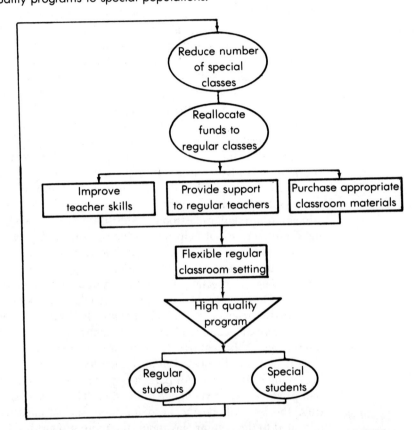

needs are similar, we can be more effective in our instruction. If children are
the same, then texts can be the same, assignments can be the same, and rate
of learning may be the same. However, review of the education literature
undermines the premise that ability grouping in education benefits the students. Research (Kirp, 1974) examining effects of ability grouping and special education revealed that classification, as typically used, does not promote
individualized learning, permit more effective teaching to groups of students
of similar ability, *or* accomplish any other goals classification is meant to
achieve.

   As classroom instruction becomes more skill-oriented, the need to label
handicapped children diminishes. Classroom demands become more focused
on a child's particular skill needs and less on identification for the purpose of
classification. Since the emphasis in mainstream classes is on skills of individ-

ual children, mainstream classrooms are multilevel; all students are not expected to progress at the same rate or to need the same instruction.

## TRADITIONAL SPECIAL EDUCATION CATEGORIES

The major purpose of labels and categorization of children is to provide information that can be used in education. Basically, the immediate practical purpose of diagnosis is to identify an educational problem in order to correct it (Adelman, 1979). To diagnose Bobbi as physically impaired has no practical value unless educational needs related to Bobbi's physical impairment are made explicit. If Bobbi's physical impairment causes her to tire easily, a modification in her educational program is warranted. She may need to take a short rest midmorning, midafternoon, or both. If Bobbi's physical impairment has no educational ramifications, then her diagnosis as physically impaired is about as useful as knowledge that she has blue eyes and blond hair.

Traditionally, special education labels or categories have been used to "describe." The basic categories are mentally retarded (MR), emotionally disturbed (ED), learning disabled (LD), visually impaired (VI), hearing impaired (HI), crippled and other health impaired (COHI), speech and language disordered, severely-multiply handicapped (SMH), and gifted. These categories are defined in Table 2.1.

As in all classification schemes, the conceptual process of classifying exceptional students involves establishing categories to which children can be assigned. The number of categories changes constantly, expanding or shrinking as various experts or advocacy groups abstract or consolidate identified or assumed characteristics of children. Consider, for example, the "Do-It-Yourself Terminology Generator" developed by Edward Fry (see Figure 2.2). It is a facetious approach to labeling and classifying learning disabled children. According to Fry, an LD child can be "defined" by simply appending a qualifier, as in "minimal brain disfunction," "mild brain disfunction," or "minor brain disfunction." Since the development of this generator by Fry, many new terms have been coined that could be added to columns 1, 2, or 3.

This method will generate 1,000 terms. While this estimate seems ridiculous, the process of term generation it represents is a fairly accurate representation of what really happens. In classifying children, we typically attempt to identify a problem, an area of involvement, and any relevant qualifier.

## PROBLEMS OF LABELING

The power of language to shape our behavior and attitudes is well established (Sapon-Shevin, 1979). Therefore, the language we use in describing children is important. When labels with negative connotations are applied to a child,

**Table 2.1**
Major Categories of Handicapping Conditions

| Label | Acronym | Definition | Estimated Prevalence in Childhood | Educational Expectation |
|---|---|---|---|---|
| Mentally Retarded/ Mentally Handicapped | MR/MH | A significantly subaverage general intellectual functioning existing concurrently with defects in adaptive behavior and manifested during developmental period. General term. IQ range 75–below 20 (Grossman, 1977, p. 11) | 3% of the total population | |
| Educable Mentally Retarded/Educable Mentally Handicapped | EMR/ EMH | IQ range 75–50 | 2.5% of the total population | • 2nd to 5th grade achievement in academic areas<br>• Social adjustment permitting partial or total self-support |
| Trainable Mentally Retarded/Trainable Mentally Handicapped | TMR/ TMH | IQ range 49–20 | 0.3% of the total population | • Learning primarily in areas of self-help; very limited academic achievement<br>• Social adjustment generally limited to home and surrounding area |
| Custodial/Profoundly Retarded | PMR/ PMH | IQ range below 20 | 0.2% of the total population | • Usually unable to achieve even sufficient skills to care for basic needs<br>• Usually requires total care for duration of life (Chinn, Drew, & Logan, 1979) |
| Emotionally Disturbed/Behavior Disordered | ED/BD | Extreme and chronic behavior that deviates from social or cultural norms. Average IQ of 90 (Heward & Orlansky, 1980) | 2% (OSE) Range 0.1 %–30% | • Underachievement in reading and math<br>• Social adjustment relative to demands of environment |

| Category | Abbr. | Definition | Prevalence | Characteristics |
|---|---|---|---|---|
| Learning Disabled | LD | A disorder in one or more of the basic psychological processes involved in understanding or using language, spoken or written, which may manifest itself in imperfect ability to listen, think, speak, read, write, spell, or do math calculations. Includes perceptual handicaps, brain injury, minimal brain dysfunction, dyslexia, and developmental aphasia. Does not include learning problems resulting from visual, hearing, or motor handicaps; mental retardation; or environmental, cultural, or economic disadvantage (Sec. 5(b)(4) of P.L. 94-142) | 1.8% (OSE) Range 3%–28% | • Underachievement in reading and math • Social adjustment relative to demands of environment |
| Visually Impaired/ Visually Handicapped Blind | VI/VH | Correct visual acuity of 20/200 or less in the better eye, or a visual field of no more than 20° in the better eye (Glass, Christiansen, & Christiansen, 1982) | Less than 0.1% VI 1 in 3,000 Blind (academic range normally distributed; social behavior normal range) | Educationally advantaged children aligned in developmental areas with children having sight and usually functioning at normal level by or soon after school age (Fraiberg, 1977) |
| Partially Sighted/ Low Vision | | Correct visual acuity of 20/70 or less in the better eye or the visual field subtends an angle no greater than 140° (Glass et al., 1982) | 1 in 500 partially sighted | • Academic range similar to normal population • Social behavior similar to normal population |
| Hearing Impaired/ Hearing Handicapped Deaf | HI/HH | Hearing loss so severe or begins at birth or before 2 to 3 years of age so it precludes the normal spontaneous development of spoken language (Dunn, 1973) | 0.1% HI 0.08% Deaf | • Educational retardation of 3 to 4 years • Social maturity expected to be below normal |

**Table 2.1**
Continued

| Label | Acronym | Definition | Estimated Prevalence in Childhood | Educational Expectation |
|-------|---------|-----------|-----------------------------------|-------------------------|
| Partially Hearing/ Hard of Hearing | | Hearing loss not severe enough to preclude the development of some spoken language, or begins after age 3 (Dunn, 1977) | 0.05% PH | • Educational retardation of ½ to 2 years<br>• Social maturity will be influenced by degree of hearing loss |
| Crippled and Other Health Impaired/ Physically Impaired | COHI/ PI | Broad category of individuals who are alike in not being average in physical ability (Telford & Sawrey, 1981) | 0.5%–1% PI | • Educational achievement as varied as normal population.<br>• Social adjustment as varied as normal population |
| Speech and Language Disordered/ Communication Disordered | | Communication disorders occur whenever speech interferes with communication, calls undue attention to itself, or causes the speaker to take remedial measures. In addition, problems can exist in language processing and production, and social perception (Wiig & Semel, 1976) | 10% | • Educational achievement will vary with the nature and degree of severity.<br>• Social adjustment will vary with the nature and degree of severity. |

**Figure 2.2**
Do-It-Yourself Terminology Generator

Directions: Select any word from Column 1. Add any word from Column 2. Then add any word from Column 3. If you don't like the result, try again. It will mean about the same thing.

| 1<br>Qualifier | 2<br>Area of Involvement | 3<br>Problem |
| --- | --- | --- |
| Minimal | Brain | Disfunction |
| Mild | Cerebral | Damage |
| Minor | Neurological | Disorder |
| Chronic | Neurologic | Dis-Synchronization |
| Diffuse | C.N.S. (Central Nervous System) | Handicap |
| Specific | Language | Disability |
| Primary | Reading | Retardation |
| Disorganized | Perceptual | Impairment |
| Organic | Impulse | Pathology |
| Clumsy | Behavior | Syndrome |

The above system will yield 1,000 terms but if that is not enough you could use specific dyslexia, aphasoid, neurophrenia, or developmental lag.

Source: From Edward Fry, "Do-It-Yourself Terminology Generator." Used with permission of Edward Fry.

prejudice toward and rejection of the child are likely to result (Thurman & Lewis, 1979). To label Bonnie Sue mentally retarded conjures a more vivid set of expectations than does labeling her as lagging 2 to 3 years behind in reading. Bonnie Sue's reading performance remains 2 to 3 years behind whether she is called *mentally retarded, emotionally disturbed, gifted,* or *normal.* The power of the label is to attribute a whole set of behaviors to Bonnie Sue. If she were called *emotionally disturbed,* characteristics stereotypic of emotionally disturbed children might be ascribed to her. If she were labeled *normal,* a different set of expectations would occur. In each case, her reading behavior might be explained as a function of the label. Bonnie Sue can't read because she's mentally retarded. Bonnie Sue can't read because she's emotionally disturbed. Bonnie Sue can't read because she's lazy. (We can't say "Bonnie Sue can't read because she's normal," so we have to substitute a behavior often exhibited by normal children—in this case, laziness.)

Another illustration of the power of language seems appropriate. On a school playground, a group of children are heatedly debating the coach's decision to call a penalty on one of the soccer players. Eric, whose team has the dubious honor of receiving the penalty, is thoroughly convinced the coach's decision is wrong. As Eric moves back on to the playing field, he can be heard muttering under his breath, "That coach! Oh, brother, what a retard!" Whether or not little Eric is aware of his behavior, he is demonstrating the use of trait theory. In trait theory, behavior is explained in terms of traits thought to be relatively consistent across situations. Eric explained the coach's behavior in terms of traits often ascribed to persons who are mentally retarded.

According to Polyson (1979), objections to the use of trait theory as an explanation of an individual's behavior center on four major arguments. He states:

> First, traits are not explanatory constructs and their use involves circular logic. Second, the way people define traits in others is influenced by stereotypic expectations related to sex, age, appearance, etc. Third, attitude and perception of the receivers prevent trait inference from being unbiased. And fourth, the assumption that people do in fact have stable and identifiable response dispositions across situations is challenged or in effect a skepticism that traits exist at all. (p. 34)

The influence of trait theory can be diluted by replacing labels that have negative connotations with descriptions of observable social or academic performance.

Problems in the use of disability labels as the basis for grouping children have been described by Meyer (1966). The first problem is that there is considerable overlap in characteristics of different types of exceptional children. The second problem concerns the temporal status of characteristics of exceptional children. Performance and characteristics of exceptional children change with maturation, effectiveness of instruction, and general environmental factors. Unfortunately, the labels tend to remain even after the characteristics change.

One further problem with labeling children as handicapped warrants discussion. The official process of labeling children handicapped frequently leads to assigning different labels to children who exhibit the same behaviors (Mehan, Meihls, Hertweck, & Crowdes, 1983; Shepard & Smith, 1983; Ysseldyke, Algozzine, Richey, & Graden, 1982; Ysseldyke, Thurlow, Graden, Wesson, Algozzine, & Deno, 1983); that is, Jose and Susie exhibit similar behaviors but are assigned different labels. This discrepancy is often the result of factors other than the child's school performance. The time of year of the diagnosis (early versus late in the school year), availability of a place in a special program, teacher preferences for working with specific types of children, and related factors determine whether a child is labeled mentally retarded, learning disabled, emotionally disturbed, or normal. If factors other than child performance determine the label assigned to a child, the wisdom of continuing to label children is seriously suspect.

## IMPLICATIONS OF LABELING

Overlap in characteristics has had funding ramifications as well as eduational implications. In the past, funds for special programs were typically allocated on the basis of officially described categorical groups of children. However, some states now recognize the overlap in characteristics between learning disabled and emotionally disturbed children and the vagaries in the evaluation process. In these states, state law does not demand that a child be labeled exclusively as ED or LD to receive services. For example, in Minnesota the critical criteria for providing state funds for program support are (a) whether a child requires a special service and (b) what kind of service the child needs to prevent failure and to increase skills (Boucher & Deno, 1979).

In 1968 Dunn suggested that we abandon many disability labels and the practice of grouping children into special classes on the basis of our labels. His position on the use of labels and his rejection of homogeneous grouping kindled a major controversy in education. Many educators contend that the learning and behavioral characteristics of mildly retarded children necessitate special class placement. However, in the years since Dunn's initial suggestion, special learning difficulties that characterize mildly retarded children have not been found and the advantages of special curricula or teaching strategies have not been documented adequately (Madden & Slavin, 1983; Smart et al., 1980).

On a daily basis, more and more handicapped children are returning to mainstream classrooms. Homogeneous grouping, if used at all, is no longer centered on traits and categories. Grouping is centered on the types of skills that a child needs for a successful school experience. When the goal of educating all children in the least restrictive environment is met, classroom teachers can use special services to provide consultation about skill needs rather than an explanation of outmoded and invalid diagnostic categories.

## SUMMARY

General information relating to integration of handicapped youth into regular classes has been the focus of this chapter. With the passage of the Education for All Handicapped Children Act (PL 94-142), Congress declared that all hand-icapped children have the right to education in the most appropriate educa-tional setting, that is, the "least restrictive environment." Attempts to comply with this mandate of PL 94-142 are referred to as the **mainstream** movement. Factors contributing to the mainstream movement include the normalization principle, failure of special class placement, administrative concerns, and dis-satisfaction with the identification and labeling process for handicapped chil-dren.

The normalization principle emphasizes experiences for retarded persons that approximate, as closely as possible, experiences of nonhandicapped people. This principle suggests that, whenever possible, social, vocational and life goals of handicapped people should approximate goals of mainstream populations. Further, choice of placement is related to the nature and degree of the handicapping condition.

Another factor contributing to the mainstream movement is the inability to document effectiveness of special class placement. The degree to which special class placements have positively affected both social and academic growth of handicapped children is not clear. Administrators concerned with the quality of educational programming for handicapped and nonhandicapped students have sought to improve the educational flexibility of regular class-rooms. Such flexibility has allowed for participation of many more handi-capped children within regular classroom settings.

As classroom instruction becomes more skill-oriented, the need to label handicapped children diminishes. Classroom demands become more clearly focused on children's particular skill needs and less on identification for classi-fication purposes.

# 3

# Learning Disabled, Mentally Retarded, and Behavior Disordered Children

Six people crowded around the conference table. Last week there were four; the week before, five. The team's tune was no different from those of other weeks or months of weeks—dancing pencils, periods of paper shuffling, and stilted sighs that sounded more like thunderous grumbles. At each of the meetings, faculty members had been lulled by their own medley of garbled sounds. Today, as before, the principal ended most of the restlessness with the pronouncement, "It's time to vote."

Beyond the privacy of arched fingers pressing against the table, a few letters of the alphabet were affixed on six slips of paper. Within moments the paper collection moved into the principal's palms, where it sat limply like a wounded dove until each slip was opened, smoothed, and carefully placed into its new home on the table: two slips in one stack, two slips in another, and two slips in the last stack.

Two and a half hours of deliberation had produced three small stacks of paper. And George's destiny had yet to be resolved. Two members of the IEP (Individual Education Plan) staffing team had voted for learning disabled, two for behavior disordered, and two for educable mentally handicapped. Somewhere in the distance the plaintive cry of a child could be heard. This story is real—only the names have been changed to protect the innocent. The "innocent" party in the case of a staffing for a mildly handicapped child is everyone.

While there are some characteristic differences between learning disabled (LD), behavior disordered (BD), and educable mentally handicapped (EMH) students, many characteristics overlap. In fact, so many of them overlap that in most educational circles the three categories have been abandoned in favor of a broad-based category called either mildly handicapped or learning and behavior disordered. Movement toward the broader classification system has focused attention on the individual's specific behavior and abilities—that is, individual differences (Hallahan & Kaufman, 1976). The result of this movement has been a shift away from categorical programming (e.g., methods and materials for retarded students) to an examination of each child's needs relative to the regular classroom curriculum.

In this chapter we will briefly discuss the evolution of cross-categorical programming for mildly handicapped students, and in our discussion of the evaluation of cross-categorical instruction we will differentiate between severity of disability levels. In our presentation of cognitive and social learning, we will focus on three sets of variables that influence performance.

# EVOLUTION OF CROSS-CATEGORICAL PROGRAMMING

## BEGINNINGS

Historically, the first children with intellectual and emotional disabilities to be treated had extremely severe impairments. Treatment was based on medical, rather than educational, findings, so it was not unreasonable to find physicians initiating educational programs for disabled children, nor was it farfetched since many of the more severely handicapped children have problems in physical development along with their intellectual or emotional problems.

Children who exhibited extremely low intellectual functioning were fairly easy to distinguish from those children who displayed highly abnormal emotional responses—or so it seemed. But even with some children who showed extremes of intellectual or emotional behavior, "the chicken-or-the-egg" problem arose. Were certain children severely disturbed because they were severely retarded or were they severely retarded because they were severely disturbed? Was the child exhibiting a severe intellectual deficit or a severe emotional problem or both?

During the late 1800s, awareness of severely disabled persons in the community led to the development of institutional programs for the "feeble-minded" or "mentally defective." For adults and children to qualify for such a program, a judgment was made to determine if the person was sufficiently subnormal to warrant specialized care and training.

### Intelligence Tests

With the development of the intelligence test in the early 1900s, an "objective" means for determining degree of subnormality became available. Traditionally, the intelligence test was given by a psychologist. It was given only once to each potential defective. After the testing, the psychologists assumed a more clinical role. As clinicians, they were free to examine "left-over" behavior that could not be measured on an intelligence test. Often this left-over behavior was identified as pathological (Balthazar & Stevens, 1975). Based on the assumption that different "conditions," such as mental retardation and emotional disturbance, required different treatments, segregated institutions sprang forth. Institutions for the severely mentally handicapped coexisted with institutions for the "insane." A certain uneasy inertia set in for a short time.

### "Traumatic Dements"

During this period, a psychologist, Goldstein, decided to investigate a group of people he labeled "traumatic dements." His subjects were brain-injured soldiers from World War I. Through careful clinical observation, Goldstein identified five behavioral characteristics in his patients: forced responsiveness to stimuli, figure-background confusion, hyperactivity, meticulosity, and catastrophic reaction (Goldstein, 1939). In other words, Goldstein found traumatic dements to be easily distracted with problems focusing their attention. They also exhibited extreme motor activity and had such bizarre perceptions that they frequently lost contact with reality, which ultimately led to a total emotional breakdown (Hallahan & Kaufman, 1976). The institutional walls of the asylums for the mentally retarded and insane began to quiver in the breeze. Goldstein's patients were demonstrating behavioral overlaps with the severely retarded and the emotionally disturbed.

Perhaps not much more would have happened if Adolph Hitler hadn't risen to power. Ironically, Hitler's own behavior set up the situation that led to the collaboration of Alfred Strauss, a neuropsychiatrist and associate professor at the University of Heidleberg, and Heinz Werner, a developmental psychologist and associate professor at the University of Hamburg. Strauss and Werner each fled Germany to emigrate to the United States.

## Brain-Injured Children

Building on Goldstein's research, Strauss and Werner turned their attention to children who were mentally retarded and were presumed to be brain injured. Through a series of investigations, Strauss and Werner concluded that brain-injured, mentally retarded children were behaviorally similar to Goldstein's brain-injured adults. They also found that non-brain-injured mentally retarded children were unlike either Goldstein's adults or brain-injured mentally retarded children. Strauss and Werner's research methods were criticized. Yet the fact remained all retardates did not behave identically. Individual differences did exist. As a consequence, within a relatively short time, the dawn of individual educational or psychological programming began to peak over the institutional horizon. As the first rays of individualization struck, asylum walls began to crumble. The era of learning disabilities had begun.

The learning disabilities movement produced two major results. First was the acknowledgment of subgroups within the categories of mental retardation and emotional disturbance. Second was recognition of the fact that not all learning and emotional problems are medically based.

The acknowledgment of subgroups resulted in new and more specific classification schemes. While it is not comprehensive, Table 3.1 lists characteristics related to classification of mental retardation, emotional disturbance, and learning disabilities.

## Continuum of Involvement

As can be seen from the table, an easier way to discuss children who are classified as mentally retarded, learning disabled, or emotionally disturbed is to

## Table 3.1
Characteristics of Educable Mental Retardation, Learning Disabilities, and Emotional Disturbance

| | Severe | Moderate | Mild |
|---|---|---|---|
| **Educable Mental Retardation** | | | |
| Time of Identification | • Birth or an early age | • Birth or an early age | • Often not until school entrance |
| Social and Emotional | • Dependent on others for social direction<br>• Minimal speech | • Outer directed<br>• Failure expectancy<br>• Delayed social and emotional growth<br>• Delayed speech | • May withdraw from •peers<br>• May seek attention in inappropriate ways<br>• Delayed speech development |
| Intellectual and Cognitive | • Self-help skills, e.g., toileting and feeding<br>• Do not appear to profit from academic programs | • Self-help skills with emphasis on daily living, e.g., simple food preparation or making change<br>• Heavy emphasis on vocational training | • Problems appear to be specific to one subject or generalized to all subjects<br>• Profit from academic programming |
| Physical and Health | • Poor motor coordination<br>• Dependent on others for physical care<br>• Often multiple handicaps | • Distinct physical characteristics<br>• May have more than one handicap | • May show slower development than normal<br>• No general statement |
| Educational Experience | • Institution or sheltered group home | • Self-contained public school programs (usually referred to as EMH) | • Public school in special classes, resource room, or regular classroom |
| **Learning Disabilities** | | | |
| Time of Identification | • Birth or an early age<br>• After a stroke or tumor | • Early childhood | • Often not until school entrance |
| Social and Emotional | • May be compulsive<br>• Tend to be ego-centric<br>• May show inappropriate or excessive emotional response | • Reduced social perception<br>• Confusion in interpreting nonverbal language, e.g., facial expressions | • Social immature behaviors more frequent than conduct disorders |
| Intellectual and Cognitive | • Impairment in expressive and receptive language<br>• Abnormal perceptual experiences<br>• Perceptual distortion of time and space | • Attention deficits<br>• Specific developmental disorders, e.g., reading or math disorder<br>• Language disorders<br>• Perceptual disorder, e.g., of time, space, vision | • Problems appear to be specific to one subject or generalized to all subjects<br>• Profit from academic programming |

**Table 3.1**
(Continued)

|  | Severe | Moderate | Mild |
|---|---|---|---|
| Physical and Health | • May be multiply handicapped, e.g., cerebral palsy and LD<br>• Same as severe for ED | • May be hyperactive or immovable<br>• Perseveration behavior<br>• Physical development appears normal | • May show slower development than normal<br>• No general statement<br>• May be clumsy or awkward |
| Educational Experience | • Institution<br>• Special schools | • Special schools<br>• Self-contained classes in public schools | • Public school in special class, resource room, or regular classroom |

**Emotional Disturbance**

|  | Severe | Moderate | Mild |
|---|---|---|---|
| Time of Identification | • Variable (though specific disorders can be age-linked, e.g., infantile autism | • Variable | • Often not noticed until school entrance |
| Social and Emotional | • May be peculiar speech patterns or elective mutism<br>• May be self-destructive<br>• May be lack of responsiveness to others or extremely dependent | • Intense anxiety<br>• Personal discomfort<br>• Inappropriate or ineffective copying<br>• Depression | • May be withdrawn from peers<br>• May seek attention in inappropriate ways<br>• Exhibit socially immature behaviors or conduct disorders |
| Intellectual and Cognitive | • Abnormal perceptual experiences<br>• Distorted space and time orientation | • Attention deficit disorders<br>• Specific developmental disorders, e.g., reading or arithmetic disorders<br>• Language disorders | • Problems appear to be specific to one subject or generalized to all subjects<br>• Profit from academic programming |
| Physical and Health | • May be hyperactive or immovable<br>• Perseveration behavior<br>• Physical development appears normal<br>• Severe problems in eating, sleeping, and elimination | • May be hyperactive or immovable<br>• Perseveration behavior Physical development appears normal<br>• Severe problems in eating, sleeping, and elimination | • May show slower development than normal<br>• No general statement |
| Educational Experience | • Institution<br>• Special schools | • Special schools<br>• Self-contained classes in in public schools | • Public school in special class, resource room, or regular classroom |

apply the terms mild, moderate, or severe to the categories. For each category, there is a continuum of characteristics. Depending on how you approach this continuum, the degree of handicap becomes either more severe and results in total care or less severe and results in relatively little special education.

## Distribution of the Population

The continuums of involvement for the three handicapping classifications are strikingly similar in distribution of numbers involved. In all three categories the vast majority of students fall into the "mildly handicapped" category, while very few of the students fall into the "severe" category. Take, for example, the prevalence estimate of 3% given to the group "mentally retarded children." When IQ scores are used as the sole basis of identification, about 3% of the population is defined as retarded. Given the additional measure of adaptive behavior, then only about 1% of the population can be considered mentally retarded. In fact, regardless of the diagnostic measure employed, the vast majority, that is, 75 to 80% of those classified as mentally retarded, are mildly retarded and may be placed in a regular class (Glass, Christiansen, & Christiansen, 1982). The number of mild to severe BD students is even more telling. The federal government suggests that only 2% of the population of children is behaviorally disordered; that is, seriously disturbed to the point that a highly restrictive placement, such as a self-contained special class, is most appropriate. When mildly to moderately emotionally disturbed students are added, the total percentage may actually be closer to 7% (Rubin & Balow, 1978). The most extreme and loaded on the mildly handicapped end of the continuum is the LD population. The percentages range from 1% to as much as 41% (Bryan & Bryan, 1978). The most severely handicapped LD students are those who are below grade level in one or more academic subjects in spite of the fact that they have at least average scores on intelligence tests.

It is interesting, but not too terribly surprising, that the development of these three specialty areas began with the identification of the severely or extremely handicapped. The severe or the extraordinary is always the most obvious and easily identified. The severely handicapped are also the most difficult to forget, and it is this image that is often left with an unsophisticated public. After all, a TV documentary or plea for financial aid which depicts an engaging but severely handicapped retardate or a chronically and dramatically depressed, disturbed individual is far more likely to arouse public interest and concern than is an image of the "boy next door" who looks and acts much like most of the other children in the neighborhood. While it may not be newsworthy in the commercial sense, the public must take care to recall that the vast majority of those persons labeled LD, EH, and EMH are much more like their own friends, neighbors, and colleagues than unlike them.

From the study of the extreme emerged the more subtle and less easily identifiable mildly handicapped, who comprise by far the largest number in the three categorical blocks. Identification began initially with the medically abnormal and then proceeded to refine diagnostic procedures to include social and intellectual areas as well. Given this orientation, it can quite clearly be seen why the first identified handicapped group in this country (aside from sensory impaired) and the longest studied was the severely mentally handicapped.

## Similarities among Groups

Children within the severe or moderate or mild level of the continuum are more like each other than they are different. Furthermore, children with the same degree of disability across categories are often more similar than children along the continuum within the same category.

For example, Marty and Ellen are mentally retarded. Margo and Maria are learning disabled. When placed along a continuum of degree of handicap, Marty is severely retarded, Ellen is mildly retarded, Margo is severely learning disabled, and Maria is mildly learning disabled. Both Marty and Margo exhibit poor motor control and minimal speech and are extremely dependent on others for social and emotional support. Ellen and Maria, in contrast, use appropriate speech and language, but both have difficulty learning to read. Ellen and Maria need some encouragement to perform academically, but overall they are both pleased with school and enjoy participation in a regular classroom. While it is true that Marty and Ellen have been classified as mentally retarded and Margo and Maria as learning disabled, Marty (a severely handicapped retardate) functions much more like Margo (a severely handicapped learning disabled child) than like Ellen (a mildly handicapped retardate). Ellen, classified as a mildly handicapped retardate, functions much like Maria, who was classifired as mildly learning disabled. The degree of handicap across the three categories, rather than the category itself, determines the educational and social program provided for the pupil.

During the early years of special education, specific categories of exceptionality were developed in the attempt to explain or clarify differences between populations of children. As more information about each of the categories was discovered and, over time, researchers became more sophisticated, differences between some of the populations (primarily the mentally retarded, emotionally handicapped, and learning disabled) began to decrease. Researchers pooled their knowledge and discovered that categories and labels overlapped. This was especially true for the majority of handicapped children: those exhibiting mild deviations in academic and social skills. Researchers also led practitioners to recognize that many learning and social problems had no medical base.

**Educational and social programming**—Educational and social programming turned to an examination of the degree of the condition. Particularly in the areas of mental retardation, learning disabilities, and emotional disturbance, the degree of handicap dramatically influenced educational programming.

Some educators would argue that the labels EMH, LD, and BD have simply been traded for a new set of labels: severe, moderate, and mild. That argument is, at best, both shallow and naive. The shift to programming for mild, moderate, and severe problems in cognitive and social development lessens the need for arbitrary labeling. All the energy and more spent on choosing categorical labels such as EMH, LD, or BD could better be directed toward identifying the child's current academic and social skill levels and developing a skill- or level-based curriculum.

A skill-based curriculum is, in fact, an extension of the curricula used in the public schools. To be most efficient, it feeds into the regular public school curriculum. Children enter the curriculum upon a given skill-based level rather than a level based on a categorical label.

**Similarities among regular and special classes**—While the odds are very low that the progress of severely handicapped students through the curriculum sequence will lead them to regular classroom placement, the odds for regular classroom integration (mainstreaming) increase as the severity of the handicapping condition decreases. Special classes look more and more like regular classes as the degree of disability decreases. By dropping the labels *retarded, learning disabled*, and *emotionally disturbed*, we are able to get on with the business of providing programs that match entry skills with a desired outcome. The great debate over whether a child is mentally retarded, learning disabled, or emotionally disturbed is greatly reduced when a skill-based curriculum is matched with a skill level of a child.

This new emphasis on basing programs on skills has led to the combining of separate classes for the mentally retarded, learning disabled, and emotionally disturbed. These classes are usually called *cross-categorical*. Some resistance to cross-categorical classes for the mildly handicapped has been expressed by a few specialists and parents. Their resistance seems to be related to a misunderstanding of basic educational practice. A fear, based on the old "it only takes one rotten apple" mentality, is in part a cause of their resistance. Fortunately for all concerned, children are not apples.

# WHO ARE THE MILDLY HANDICAPPED?

## CHARACTERISTICS OF MILDLY HANDICAPPED STUDENTS

The mildly handicapped are the children down the street, the next door neighbor, and the first prize winner in the school coupon drive contest. Most mildly handicapped children look, act, feel, and talk just like anybody else. In fact, if no one had labeled them, they would be indistinguishable from the children who were labeled normal. To be sure, some idiosyncrasies would pop up here and there, but who doesn't have an "Uncle Isaac" who is regarded affectionately as a "little spacey" or a cousin Harry who's great at math, but who can't spell his name without a dictionary? The mildly handicapped are accurately characterized as being *mildly* handicapped, i.e., just a little bit handicapped.

Not all mildly handicapped people are handicapped in the same way. Some mildly handicapped children have problems in a very selected area, e.g., fine motor skills that involve handwriting or cognitive skills that require matching shapes. Other mildly handicapped children can be multiply handicapped. Ayla, for example, can't read or write very well; she also has some minor problems expressing her thoughts clearly. When a child's primary mild handicap is focused around some academic or social behavior, the child then becomes noted for that behavior and as a consequence becomes the recipient of a special education label. The most popular labels for mildly handicapped children with academic and social problems are learning disabled, emotionally disturbed, and educable mentally handicapped. A quick inspection of Table 3.1 shows characteristics associated with these three categories within a continuum of severity. What is quite clear is that the mildly handicapped across the three categories are much more similar than dissimilar.

### Role of the School in Identification

Children in these three categories are almost never identified until school age. But school, with its ever-present and rigidly adhered-to curricula, does not allow for much deviation. All first grade children will learn to read the first grade basal; all second grade children will read the second grade basal; and third grade children ... ad nauseam.

Socialization in the schools also has its prescriptions: Hands must be raised before speaking; affectionate jabs are reserved for the playground; lines must be silent, straight, and orderly. A label of mildly handicapped awaits any child who violates the school norms with undue frequency.

**Quality of behavior**—Norm violators, i.e., mildly handicapped children, who remain in school may exhibit some minor social and emotional problems. They may have brought these problems with them or they may develop these problems as a result of their school attendance. Some mildly handicapped children will withdraw from their peers, preferring either solitude or the companionship of much younger children. Other, but by no means all, mildly handicapped children may need assistance in practicing the appropriate social skills that will enable them to be more acceptable to their peers (Greshman, 1982; McDowell, Adamson, & Wood, 1982). Some, in an attempt to make a statement of personal worth, may seek attention in clearly unacceptable ways. Talk outs and fights are time-tested techniques, used by both normal and mildly handicapped children, to draw recognition even if the recognition is somewhat questionable. In fact, the distinction between the quality and the number of talk outs and fights exhibited by the mildly handicapped may be more in the mind of the beholder than in the actual numerical count (Gottlieb, Semmel, & Veldman, 1978).

**Variability of behavior**—What is quite clear is that the academic and social behavior of mildly handicapped children as a group demonstrates more variability than does the behavior of normal children. Within the category of mildly handicapped, there are greater differences in academic performance than within the category of normal. Children classified as mildly handicapped will appear to be more of a "mixed bag" than children who are classified as normal. If, for example, 50 normal children take a spelling test for grade level, most of the children will spell from 45 to 50 words correctly, with a few of the children misspelling more than 5. If a group of mildly handicapped children were given the same spelling test, the range of scores is more likely to be between 40 and 50, with a few children misspelling more than 10. In other words, predicting the spelling score for a mildly handicapped child is harder than predicting the spelling score for a normal child. The normal child has a very small range of probable scores, i.e., 45 to 50, while the mildly handicapped has a range of scores twice as large, i.e., 40 to 50.

Another characteristic often associated with mild handicaps is inconsistency of behavior, especially academic behaviors. After three days of successful school work in addition of mixed fractions, the child may suddenly become confused by the process and revert to previous patterns of errors. Yet, on the following day, the entire process may return to the child as if computation of mixed fractions was the most natural event in the child's mathematical repertoire. No one really knows why this variability of behavior occurs, but with the mildly handicapped a good educational rule of thumb is to take each teaching day one day at a time. (This rule of thumb may be safely applied to nonhandicapped children as well.)

Experimental studies with mildly handicapped children have shown that, on the average, they will perform the same as normal children on some tasks and below normal on other tasks (Prehm, 1976). The same statement can be made with respect to academic and social behaviors. These observations, taken together with the notion of variability, strongly point to the unique nature of the individuals within the category of mild handicaps. Just like normal children, not all mildly handicapped children have specific problem areas unique to the individual that need special attention from the teacher. Just as with normal children, the assumption cannot be made that the mildly handicapped child will have problems learning academic or social behaviors. It is through instruction that problems may be uncovered, and it is through instruction that problems can be corrected.

## DEGREE OF THE PROBLEM

What sets the mildly handicapped child apart from the more moderately or severely handicapped child is the degree of the problem and the type of teacher who is able to help the child learn. With a minor adjustment of teaching strategy, an educational problem of a mildly handicapped child can easily be solved within the regular classroom. Not too surprisingly, the types of adjustments in teaching strategies that work well with mildly handicapped children work very well with learning problems that surface with normal children, too.

### Advantages of Cross-Categorical Classrooms

Just as in a regular classroom, a wide range of skills will be found in a special setting. The advantage of cross-categorical classes is that the skill range is a bit more refined than the typical regular class. This slightly more restricted skill range allows for intensive remedial work that the children need but are not likely to receive in the regular classroom. By providing intensive programming, the special setting can give some "catch-up" time to the mildly handicapped child. The child may catch up to the regular class curriculum or at least attain the level where only minor modifications in regular class methods are necessary.

Academic and social achievement is the major thrust of special programs for the mildly handicapped. Therefore, you will find fewer and fewer "special" materials in classrooms for the mildly handicapped and more and more regular materials. You will not find "exotic" teaching techniques in use in the special program either. The same subtraction concept taught in regular classes will be taught in special classrooms. The difference between regular and special instruction is the rate of presentation, number of concepts introduced at one time, and the amount of practice time available to the student.

In most classrooms for the mildly handicapped, instruction is focused on observable academic or social behaviors, e.g., the rate at which a child produces short vowel sounds or the number of times a child uses appropriate question-asking techniques. Primary instructional emphasis is on those areas that will lead the child to success in a regular classroom setting, regardless of the child's classification as LD, BD, or EMH. The tremendous similarity in methods, materials, and curriculum between classes for the mildly handicapped is, then not so surprising, nor is the reported practice of placing a child into whichever class has room—be the class for LD, BD, or EMH students.

Theoretically, the "room for one more" practice is pedagogically sound. More than likely, the greatest difference between LD, BD, and EMH mildly handicapped children is in the mind of the labeler. Teachers treat the labels or constructs as mutually exclusive, especially when eligibility for special services is to be determined. When program planning decisions are made, labels—especially LD and BD—become mutually inclusive (Boucher & Deno, 1979). Classroom goals and the extent of regular class participation seem to be about the same across traditional categories of mildly handicapped students.

## INSTRUCTIONAL METHODS TEACHERS CAN USE

Ways to increase learning that teachers can use include (a) setting expectancies, (b) providing instructional feedback, (c) assisting the child to organize information, (d) furnishing practice, and (e) delivering systematic incentives or consequation. You should use these methods as a kind of mental checklist when considering the mental operations for the learning task.

These five methods are by no means all the variables that teachers can use to encourage learning. They do, however, contain the major areas of teacher influence. If you effectively use these five methods, many of the cognitive and social learning problems within our schools could be eliminated or greatly reduced. The degree to which you involve yourself with these factors is relative to the needs of the child.

The teacher of the severely handicapped child will, no doubt, attend to all methods in great depth. The teacher of the moderately handicapped child will continue to be concerned with all five, but will emphasize only two or three. For the mildly handicapped child (and to a slightly lesser degree for the normal child), the teacher will attend to all factors.

## SETTING EXPECTANCIES

### Role of Reinforcement

Setting expectancies basically means that the chance for a behavior to occur in any situation is a function of the belief that the behavior will result in a particular reinforcement in that situation (Rotter, 1975). If Margaret believes that paying attention in health class will result in a good grade, she is likely to pay attention to her health instructor. If Joel believes that he is going to receive a poor grade in health no matter how much he pays attention, then he is not likely to pay attention and is very likely to receive a poor grade. Both Margaret and Joel base their expectancies for success and failure not only on their experience in health class, but also on their other classes. While Margaret is used to experiencing success in academic work, Joel knows only failure. Because of Margaret's previous successes, she sharpens her attending skills while Joel's lack of success has decreased his attending to the teacher. On those rare occasions when he actually attempts to attend, his knowledge base is so incomplete that he is lost. Saddled with unpracticed attending skills and a shaky knowledge base, Joel is well prepared to fail again. If the teacher doesn't watch out, Joel can even be a triple loser. If he uses Margaret as the standard by which to judge his own worth, his self-concept is liable to take a meteoric plunge.

### A Failure Mentality

Teachers used to be concerned with student failure, particularly the teachers of children with cognitive and social learning problems, for they appear to have a high generalized expectancy for failure. A "failure mentality" leads to an excessive use of energy directed at avoiding academic and social school behaviors. With continued failure on school tasks, the child can resort to noninvolvement, token observance of tasks, or reduction of the sense of failure by not competing (MacMillan, 1977).

Take the case of Emmett. Emmett was being devoured by fears of academic and social failure. Some days he seemed like a squirrel frantically running in an exercise wheel with lots of motion but getting nowhere; other days he seemed like a puppet with all its strings removed. Emmett finally stopped doing his classwork and reduced his interactions with peers and teacher. Life was not too sweet for Emmett.

The classroom teacher realized that she had a very scared and lonely child in her room. She had to reduce his fear of failure, so she removed possible sources of failure. Out went formal written tests. In their place came informal teacher conferences and small group discussion. Grades were the next to go. Many written and verbal praises made Emmett feel that his work was valued. Through encouragement and reduced pressure (internally and externally produced), Emmett began to develop a more positive view of himself. Through the continued use of teacher-assisted self-evaluation, Emmett began to assess both his strengths and his weaknesses more realistically. As the layers of academic and social learning problems eased, a very bright and happy child emerged—so bright, in fact, that he exchanged one set of labels for another. By the end of the school year Emmett was accepted into a class for the gifted in math and reading.

Not all stories may end quite as dramatically as Emmett's, but you can establish a classroom in which an expectancy of success is fostered for all children. Because most mainstream students have experienced academic and social failure, every teacher must be sensitive to expectancies of failure while simultaneously providing occasions for success.

## PROVIDING INSTRUCTIONAL FEEDBACK

After a child has given an answer, the teacher provides feedback on the answer's correctness. Based on teacher feedback, the child can continue answering or adapt the response. If, for example, Kevin's teacher tells him his penmanship is very good, Kevin knows to continue using that style of penmanship. If, on the other hand, Kevin's teacher tells him his handwriting bears a remarkable resemblance to chicken scratches, Kevin may choose to alter his penmanship style.

The way in which feedback is provided to students can also influence learning. Let's return to Kevin. Kevin's teacher can provide feedback in a number of ways. The technique that his teacher uses will determine the effect of the feedback on Kevin's future penmanship performance.

## Nonfunctional Feedback

A partial list of rather useless but commonplace feedback techniques is as follows:

1. Appeal to the child's "thinking habits"
2. Appeal to the child's "work habits"
3. Appeal to the child's "sense of history"
4. Appeal to the child's "sense of fair play"

**Appeal to the child's "thinking habits"**—"Now Kevin, just think about how those letters should look!" Kevin may have been thinking about those letters and he may have produced them the way he thought they should look. The teacher has given him two feedback messages. Feedback message number 1: Your penmanship is awful. Feedback message number 2: Your thinking skills aren't too sharp either! What Kevin's teacher has *not* provided is instructional information. Kevin could sit and think about penmanship all day. But unless he is given some focus, he may not know what to think about—though bike riding is a rather pleasant alternative.

**Appeal to the child's "work habits"**—"Kevin, don't be so lazy. Try harder!" Assuming Kevin is willing to "try harder," he is still left with a rather vague notion of what to try harder about in penmanship. Should he press his pencil harder or should he hold his paper tighter?

**Appeal to the child's "sense of history"**—"Kevin, I've taught both your older brother and your older sister. They were excellent handwriters, and I expect the same from you!" Poor Kevin, not only must he improve his handwriting without being given any instructional information, he must also follow in the penmanship steps of his brother and sister.

**Appeal to the child's "sense of fair play"**—"Kevin, I've worked very hard to teach you to write. Now please show me that you can do better." Not only does Kevin have a penmanship problem, but he's also being drenched in guilt. Guilty or not, Kevin still doesn't have a clue about how to improve his handwriting.

## Functional Feedback Techniques

The key to providing functional feedback is to give the child useful instructional information. Techniques that provide useful information to the child include:

1. Provide rules.
2. Provide immediate feedback.
3. Provide for correction of responses.

**Provide rules**—Not all instructional information is actually very useful. Take the example of Kevin one more time. His handwriting is still not the model of perfection. Kevin's teacher has avoided all the "appeals" feedback techniques. She says, "Kevin, your handwriting is too large; you need to write a little smaller." At last Kevin has been given some instructional information, but, alas, not quite enough. The next time Kevin shows his work, his teacher exclaims, "Kevin, now your handwriting is too small! You need to write a little larger." What's the poor child to do? The poor child needs to demand a rule. In Kevin's case the sought-after rule is "the upper-case letters are a whole space high and lowercase letters are a half space high."

**Provide immediate feedback**—For all children, but especially for children with social and cognitive learning problems, the more quickly feedback is given, the more willing the child is to proceed with the task. If the fear-of-failure syndrome is to be avoided, the child must be given some sort of feedback signal that all is well. If all is not well, then the teacher needs to provide feedback even more immediately to prevent the child from practicing incorrect work. In a class of 30 to 50 students you may not be willing or physically able to bound from desk to desk providing feedback. Personal delivery of feedback is neither necessary nor recommended. If you remember that feedback provides a rule, then any technique for presenting the rule should be acceptable. Several alternatives for providing rules are used with a group response, self-correction, and peer or cross-age tutors.

Group responses can be delivered orally or in writing. In a typical classroom, an example of a written group activity might be centered on a lesson in addition facts. The teacher calls out a fact: "3 + 7"; the students write their answer on a small chalkboard (a piece of scrap paper, a 3 × 5 index card, etc.) and hold up the answer for their teacher to see. The teacher is the only one who can see the answers (thus eliminating a potentially embarrassing situation) and with one quick scanning motion she can immediately see who has the correct (or incorrect) response. The teacher can then provide the rule "3 + 7 = 10" and proceed to the next number fact.

Oral group responses can be a little more tricky. While the teacher can usually pinpoint the child in the group who is saying the short *u* sound for the long *u* sound, so can everybody else. Most of the children will not be attending to anyone but themselves, but that in itself can become a problem for the child who expects failure. In a situation where a child is likely to become embarrassed, judicious use of group response is recommended. The teacher may want to set the child up to answer correctly, especially if the child has just erred. Consider the following example.

Mr. Alexander has just introduced the basic rule for adding *-ing* to words. He has written the following list on the chalkboard:

hum_____        humming

stop_____       stopping

set_____        setting

pet_____        petting

As he points to each word, he says, "Hum becomes _____" and waits for the children's response. All goes well until the word *set*. From Cleo's tiny little voice comes the response "setter." Mr. Alexander now needs to set Cleo up to answer correctly. He repeats the correct answer, "*set* becomes *setting*. Everyone, what does *set* become?" We hope the word from Cleo is *setting*. To single Cleo out could have become a source of embarassment to her. Mr. Alexander provided Cleo, along with the rest of the class, with the rule, feedback on her response, and a chance to try again, all within the context of a large group setting.

Self-correction allows children to monitor themselves. If you have provided correct responses, children can check their work against the responses. Checking can be immediate and not create a demand on the teacher. Self-monitoring also allows children to actively engage in their own learning.

Answer keys can come in various shapes and formats. How a teacher chooses to use an answer key will depend on the lesson's purpose. The rule for getting the correct answer should be available on the key. If the children are working on equations, the rule on the answer key should clearly state that if you change one side of the equation, you have to change the other side. An example of the rule is always helpful; if the answer lends itself to a step-by-step solution, the steps can also be shown.

"But what if the child simply copies down the work from the response key?" is a cry raised by the ever-present cynic. What if the child does? At least the child is copying the correct response rather than copying a potentially incorrect response from a neighbor. Granted, no teacher wants the child copying every response every time, but occasional copying to complete assignments is certainly preferred to no attempt or repeated incorrect attempts.

To decrease the chance that the children will feel they've fooled the teacher or gotten something for nothing, the teacher can simply state that it is all right for students to copy answers they can't solve and that they should indicate in some way when they have copied. Teachers can also control copying by providing answers and models for every other problem.

The use of peer or cross-age tutors is a third method of providing immediate feedback. When students from upper grades work as classroom aides or assistants, no one child is isolated for tutorial assistance. The cross-age tutor's primary function would be to answer questions and check seat work.

Another technique for peer tutoring is to use the children in your own classroom. Instead of working in isolation, children can work together on special projects. Most children are quite capable of completing their work if they get some help from one of their peers. Some authorities have suggested that children learn more from their peers than from adults. The point is not whether children will copy, but rather to provide them with immediate and regular feedback.

**Provide for correction of responses**—Corrections are necessary and vital to the teaching/learning process. Children need to be told when their responses are incorrect as well as when their responses are correct. Unfortunately, some teachers fall into the "Oh-dear-I'm-afraid-I'll-hurt-their-feelings" syndrome. This is a sure guarantee that students feel they will be in much greater danger of being hurt if they build their knowledge base on faulty information.

## The Child's Self-Image

Preserving the child's self-image is a critical part of the correction procedure. Engelmann (1969) has provided an excellent correction technique: (a) repeat the child's correct answers, perhaps adding "good," and (b) do not repeat the child's incorrect answers, but say "no," and then give the correct answer. Suppose the teacher was trying to teach Clara how to identify parallel lines for a geometry lesson. Clara indicates that she thinks parallel lines mean perpendicular lines by pointing to a set of perpendicular lines and saying, "These lines are parallel." If Clara's teacher responds positively or doesn't respond at all, Clara will accept perpendicular lines for parallel ones. Clara's teacher must let her know immediately. She could say, "No, Clara, these lines are not parallel," and then demonstrate the concept of parallel and perpendicular lines with two sets of pencils, pointing out how parallel lines can never touch.

In a very concrete manner, Clara's teacher has provided a corrected response, a rule for the correct response, and a model for getting the correct answer. The teacher's tone of voice and body language will reassure Clara that she is valued even though her response was incorrect. Corrections frequently comprise as much as 60 to 70% of teacher responses. When this is the case, the task should be restructured. Not only are the children not learning the task, they may also be feeling like failures. Restructure the task, not the goal, so that the children will succeed. As Engelmann (1969) would suggest,

> Simplify the task, or distribute it over a number of teaching sessions, so that he will see your (the teacher's) yes and no responses in proper perspective—as sources of information and not as punishment or as proof that he is stupid. (p. 54)

## ASSISTING THE CHILD TO ORGANIZE INFORMATION

Young children or developmentally young children (Belmont, Butterfield, & Borkowski, 1978) such as those with academic and social learning problems often do not have an active organizational plan for selecting strategies for remembering information. A child's ability to organize information appears to develop with age.

### Learning Strategies

**Mnemonic devices**—You can help children to use learning strategies. Coding or categorizing techniques are often taught in the regular classroom. Some commonly used mnemonic devices are attaching labels to pictures to be recalled, grouping long series of numbers or words, or forming associations to isolated or meaningless words (Ross, 1976). An example of attaching a label to a picture to be recalled would be to take a picture of a dog and label the picture "d-o-g." The next time the child saw a real dog, the letters d-o-g and picture would come to mind. Grouping long series of numbers or words is most often seen in the primary grades, but is also an appropriate strategy at any grade level. When children are learning numbers, they are taught to group by even numbers or odd numbers. Math problems that teach sets, such as sets of shapes, also teach children the basics of how to categorize. Most children eventually categorize new information seemingly automatically. Children with social and academic learning problems may need direct assistance from their teachers. Techniques for teaching children to form associations are well within the scope of the regular classroom. Memory hints like "Your principal is your pal" help to teach the difference between *principle* and *principal*. Or "Your basic nine number fact quotients add up to nine." For example, $9 \times 4 = 36$; 36 is the quotient. In the quotient, $3 + 6 = 9$. Another trick of mnemonic teaching is to use the first letters of a list of answers. Perhaps a child has been asked to memorize the five Great Lakes. A student might remember them as "HOMES"—*H*uron, *O*ntario, *M*ichigan, *E*rie, and *S*uperior.

**Grouping**—Grouping or clustering material prior to presentation is more beneficial to children with learning problems than presenting material in random order (Spitz, 1973). Grouping is probably the easiest method of organizing information. Information may be grouped spatially, by presenting different visual arrangements; temporally, by presenting the material with a pause or time lapse between items; perceptually, by enclosing certain items in a shape or configuration; or categorically, by content or commonality of items (Payne & Patton, 1981). Examples of spatial grouping are phone numbers, 965-6198, or addresses, 46 51 S. 29th Avenue. Visual arrangements can also assist children to group information, e.g., in teaching the components of good nutrition or a well-balanced meal all the pictures or labels of dairy products, proteins, produce, and grains could be grouped separately. The components of good nutrition are presented simultaneously but in four distinct visual clusters. Temporal grouping usually means that information is grouped by time spacing; for example, $3 + 5$ is—pause—8. Another variation of temporal spacing is relating information to rhythms or melodies, such as "The Alphabet Song." Perceptual grouping usually refers to enclosing information is specific shapes or highlighting it somehow. An example in reading might be to indicate the first letter of each printed word by drawing a circle around the letter, e.g., a ⓡed ⓑall ⓕell ⓓown. The last grouping or organizational variable, categorical grouping, refers to some inherent grouping of the information. As an example of category clustering, take the words *diamond*, *pearl*, and *emerald*. While these words might appear at widely separated times in various contexts, they may be typically recalled together when the teacher asks questions or discusses content relevant to the general category "precious stones." "Precious stones" would serve as a cue for the child to recall these words as a group.

## Other Operations

Other operations that can assist a child to learn are referred to in psychological jargon as *stimulus selection*, *mediation*, and *coding*. Ability to use these processes develops as a result of the child's experience with language. As language experience develops, so does the ability to organize information for recall (Hall, 1971).

**Stimulus selection**—If the concept to be learned (*concept* will be used instead of *stimulus*) has a number of distinctive or different parts, you can help the child focus on important components or features. Focusing or choosing the feature on which to concentrate can be related to the position of that feature. In reading, for example, many poor readers will focus on the beginning of a word but not on the middle or end. Hillary would always get the first letter of words correct, but beyond that, her response to new words was unpredictable. She might say *bed* for *beautiful* or *relief* for *rat*. Hillary's teacher helped her to look beyond the first letter when identifying words. She showed Hillary how to focus beyond the first letter and how to see other important features of the word, such as length of word, middle sounds, and endings.

**Relevance**—Meaning of material can also help a child to organize information. If you use the child's past experiences or current interests to build new experiences, the child is more likely to cluster or categorize the new information. Jed is absolutely enamored with mini-bikes. His teacher has capitalized on that interest by relating mini-bikes to the transporation systems of Indo-China. As a result, Jed can explain why mini-bikes can and cannot be used in Indo-China. Jed can also explain the economic and social impact of mini-bikes versus alternate forms of transporation used in Indo-China. Jed's educational history suggested that his memory capacity was barely greater than a water bucket riddled by a shotgun blast. Thanks to Jed's creative teacher, that "water bucket" image is a quickly fading relic of the past.

**Distinctiveness**—Distinctiveness of the material can also help the child organize and remember information. A well known phenomenon is the confusion of *b* and *d*. While some people view this confusion as a potential harbinger of brain damage, many others view it as a developmental problem. Very young children (up to around the age of 7) commonly confuse *b* and *d*. By the time most children are 8 years old, this "problem" disappears. In part, the problem has been created by the arbitrariness of our Arabic alphabet. If *b* looked like @, then very few children would confuse @ for *d*. Unfortunately for our school children, *b* and *d* look identical except that one faces left and one faces right. To further complicate matters, *b* and *d* are very close in the alphabet and are often taught consecutively. Problems in teaching *b* and *d* could be eliminated if *b* and *d* were distinctive from one another.

Distinctiveness with the letters *b* and *d* could extend beyond their shape. Changing the color of either *b* or *d* to red or underlining only the *b* or *d* (e.g., b) can also add to the distinctiveness of the two symbols.


## FURNISHING PRACTICE

### Drill and Practice

The delivery of drill and practice as an instructional procedure is another critical factor you can use to influence student learning/Drill is a technique in which the child repeats a series of tasks that all have the same components. An example of drill is to have children redo the addition of double-digit numbers with regrouping. Practice is an activity in which a child uses a skill to solve problems that may have other components. An example of practice is to regroup double-digit numbers for addition in balancing a checkbook. Validation of both drill and practice, when carefully arranged and designed, should come as no surprise to competent teachers (Haring, Lovitt, Eaton, &- Hansen, 1978).

Appropriateness of the activity is the key to using drill and practice. Drill and practice activities have recently come under heavy attack from some theorists (Hresko & Reid, 1981). This attack has been directed at behaviorists (behaviorists, by the extreme definition, are those folks who are often associated with B.F. Skinner and others). In highly behaviorally oriented teaching, instruction begins with small amounts of information. Then it is sequenced with the easiest material presented first. As material is mastered, new information is introduced. Until the child produces the desired response or the correct answer, practice and drill are presented. The behavioral approach to instruction has proven to be highly successful when working with children with social and academic problems. So why the attack on behaviorism and the notion of drill and practice?

Behaviorism has been attacked primarily because of the theory that it doesn't represent rather than the theory that it does represent. Confused? Extreme behaviorism suggests that all learning is a kind of additive event and that all learning is observable. First a child learns one "thing." That "thing" then allows the child to build to the next level of information. When dealing with basic discrete or concrete skills (e.g., sound/symbol relationships), the behavioral viewpoint has been very effective. When dealing with more abstract notions like reading or language comprehension, behavioral techniques have not been so favorably reviewed (Chomsky, 1959). Because behavioral theory cannot adequately explain the acquisition of a process like language or thinking, some extremists have suggested eradicating behavioral theory and all associated techniques from the face of the teaching world. Extreme notions like that are just that—extreme. Drill and practice, only part of the behavioral bag of teaching techniques, are probably among the most effective and powerful teaching techniques articulated. As with any technique, behavioral techniques are highly appropriate for some types of lessons while rather questionable for others. Drill and practice activities are appropriate for some activities while rather questionable for others. If Norris is having creative writing problems, his teacher would probably use a combination of drill and practice and cognitive or child-centered techniques. Cognitive theories heavily emphasize building the teaching instruction upon the information the child already knows (Ausubel, Novak, & Hanesian, 1978).

To use Norris' previous knowledge and his immediate interests, the teacher might have him dictate or write a story from his own experience. His teacher might then choose sight vocabulary or spelling terms from Norris' own story. She might even examine his grammar and punctuation and initiate a language arts program. The teacher's techniques for teaching sight words and the mechanics of grammar and spelling words will probably involve a lot of drill and eventually practice. Cognitive theorists would view this practice favorably.

Another and, probably, more serious reason for attacking drill and practice techniques has arisen from their inappropriate use. In some classrooms, teachers have mistakenly misunderstood the purpose of drill and practice. Drill and practice are techniques used to strengthen or to help the child retain newly acquired information. By drilling and practicing with new information, the child's ability to use the information becomes less labored and more automatic. Consider how difficult manuscript writing is for a child just learning to write. Even printing the first and last name becomes a major event. But after having written the name roughly 100 times, i.e., practiced at least one time on every worksheet for the first 2 or 3 months of school with proper feedback, most children can write their names without so much as a second thought.

## Problems with Drill and Practice

The major problems with drill and practice activities lie in two mistakes: (a) failure to provide appropriate feedback and (b) providing inappropriate work levels. Appropriate feedback techniques apply to drill and practice exercises as well as to any other area. (For a refresher on feedback, see the section earlier in this chapter.)

Providing appropriate work levels has special meaning for drill and practice activities. First to be considered is whether the child will be working independently or with someone else. If you, the teacher, are drilling sounds with a child, you are in a position to provide immediate instruction. This means that the child's skills may still be in the acquisition stage and you are there to provide instructional assistance. When the child is acquiring new knowledge, practice and drill must never be done independently. Without instructional guidance during a new learning task, a child, no matter how hard he or she tries, will not have a knowledge base for completing the exercises. Asking a child to complete a drill exercise without the necessary prerequisite knowledge is setting the child up to be classified as having a social or academic learning problem.

Once the child has acquired knowledge, drill and practice exercises can be given as independent work. In other words, children must already know a basic concept before they can be given independent drill and practice activities.

"Busy work?" Did someone say "busy work?" Why drill and practice material the child already knows? The answer is: Practice makes perfect. Drill and practice provide the child with additional opportunities to use previously gained knowledge. The activities only become busy work when they are no longer increasing efficiency. Children, just as adults, need to judge when a drill or practice exercise has reached a point of diminishing return. That judgment is based on intuition and experience for the teacher and on written recordkeeping.

## Retention

Three additional aspects of drill and practice that can enhance learning and retention are (a) prompts and cues, (b) spaced reviews, and (c) overlearning. Prompts and cues are aids such as saying the first sound of a word that a child is having difficulty remembering. Spaced reviews involve the amount of time that passes between instruction and recall of instructional material. Overlearning is the repetition of the learning task past the point of criterion.

**Prompts and cues**—Prompts and cues are instructional techniques designed to help the students give the correct response. They can be physical, verbal, written, and imitative. They are generally used with specific drill and practice exercises in which the child is acquiring or has just acquired a skill. Physical prompts consist of physically assisting a child to perform fine or gross motor acts. A fairly routine prompting technique is helping children learn to use a pencil. The teacher actually moves and holds the pencil, but gradually reduces the hand pressure so the child can write independently.

Verbal prompts also help the child to produce the correct answer. Voice inflections and verbalization (modeling) of the correct answer with a child are two commonly used verbal prompts. For example, the teacher could be leading a discussion about World War I and Wilson's beliefs about peace. He could be explaining Wilson's belief that the only way to prevent another war was for all countries to join an organization in which worldwide discussion could be held. The teacher could write the term "League of Nations" on the board and say, "Wilson believed that the League of Nations could help prevent future wars. What organization did Wilson believe could help prevent future wars?" Before the class could answer (correctly or incorrectly), the response "League of Nations" is given by the teacher. The teacher can also give verbal prompts like "What organization did Wilson believe could help prevent future wars?" Before the child can respond, the teacher can produce the sound of the letter *l* (for "League") or mouth the phrase.

Written prompts or cues are most likely to occur during drill and practice exercises where the child is strengthening previously learned behaviors. The prompts or cues are used as reminders. Let's look at Albert and his spelling words. His teacher has provided him with a model of each word on his spelling worksheet. Albert's practice is cued by having him look at the model, trace the first letter and fill in the spaces, and then write the word. Another example of a written prompt can be seen by putting an arrow over math problems to show children where to start the problems.

Building cues or prompts into instructional material is called *accenting* or *highlighting*. Some common ways to highlight are to make important features bigger, underline them, or present them in a contrasting color or type. By the manner in which they are organized, many texts prompt or cue students. For example, the phrase "I wish to make three points" contains no factual content, but it does signal the three important facts that will follow. Cues and prompts, like signals, appear to increase recall of children with comprehension problems (Meyer, Brandt, & Bluth, 1980).

Children themselves are perhaps the greatest users of imitative prompts and cues. For proof, just picture their imitations of teachers and peers. Children model the tone, body movements, and personal idiosyncrasies of their teachers with a precision that could win each of them an Oscar. Many social behaviors are learned through observing and imitating the teacher. Children often "practice" their learned social behaviors on other classmates. If the classroom climate is tense and structured, children will tend to be tense. If the teacher is zestful and curious about life, the students are likely to show interest in the world around them.

Social behaviors and attitudes are not the only behaviors learned through imitation. Teachers will often demonstrate work on the chalkboard and overhead projecter. Students can then use this work to model their own. Teachers routinely use modeling techniques when they take their students through a step-by-step process, such as diagramming a sentence, and have the students copy each step throughout the demonstration.

Phrases like "Watch me" or "Do this with me" alert children to be ready to imitate the teacher and are handy openers for a drill or practice exercise. For example, a teacher trying to teach a child natural pauses in reading material may read a passage out loud. She may then ask the child to read the same passage using the same expression. Generally, imitation is used during guidance rather than independent instructional drill and practice.

**Spaced reviews**—Practice and drill exercises can also help children with academic and social learning problems by being spaced. Spacing exercises require recall at reasonable intervals after initial learning. Teachers often provide practice of a newly learned concept immediately after instruction (and learning) has been completed. If the practice is done immediately after the presentation, a somewhat limited amount of value is gained, but recall or memory of the new concept is greatly enhanced when additional practice is spaced in time over days or weeks (Gagné, 1975).

For some children, spacing practice may occur within a day. Consider Joey. Joey's teacher has given him flashcard practice every day for 5 minutes. Joey looked at the flashcards and checked his answers on the back of the card. After 5 minutes, Joey's teacher, Mr. Hassett, gave Joey a 1-minute timing. At the end of 2 weeks, Mr. Hassett noted Joey's multiplication facts were unchanged from when he started. So he initiated another plan. Five times throughout the day, Joey pulled out his flashcards. Using a timer, Joey practiced for 1 minute only. Mr. Hasset continued recording Joey's 1-minute timings. By the end of the first week of Joey's new five-times-a-day practice schedule, correct multiplication facts were flying left and right. By spacing out the 5 minutes of practice each day, Joey was able to assimilate his multiplication facts.

Spacing practice for two or three children like Joey is possible in a regular classroom. The teacher would need to be highly selective about the tasks to be spaced in terms of the type and length of the task to be spaced. In Joey's case, 2 weeks on an intensive schedule worked. If Joey had required an intensive schedule like this for much more than 2 or 3 weeks, his instructional needs would be too great for the regular setting. The demands of such an intense schedule or spaced review would need to be shared by both the regular and special teacher. Again, depending on the degree and extent of the spaced review, some children with social and academic learning problems may not find the regular setting the most appropriate one.

Mike is a child who found that a regular setting was not for him. So he was removed from the room where he was not only unable to complete any assignments, but where he was rapidly developing some very inappropriate classroom behaviors. After all, what's a child to do when he can't do anything? Mike's special teacher initially provided him with tasks that lasted 5 minutes. The same task or concept occurred a minimum of 15 times each day and was presented in a variety of formats. The special teacher gradually reduced Mike's spaced review from 15 times to once a day. When Mike had reached grade level and, more importantly, could recall and learn material with a spaced review of once a day, he was sent back to the regular setting. Mike had much less time to develop inappropriate social behaviors because now he had a lot he could do in the regular classroom.

Spaced reviews that seem most reasonable in a regular classroom are those that center around basic or foundation skills. These skills are necessary for continued or advanced work. Three examples of foundation skills are reading, writing, and math. Regular classroom teachers must be selective about the degree to which skills will be presented in a spaced review. Reading, for example, might be spaced twice a day, once in the morning and once in the afternoon. New vocabulary could be introduced during the early reading period and reviewed once later in the day. No one ever said you must have one reading period a day and that it must last for 60 minutes. If a teacher is tied to a number, then that number could be split to 45 minutes in the morning with a 15-minute afternoon review. Whatever works for you should work for you and your students and vice versa.

**Overlearning**—Overlearning is repeated drill beyond the point where acceptable learning has been achieved. Take, for example, a situation where you had set a goal of having a child read 10 new vocabulary terms at the end of 3 days. The child achieves this goal, i.e., she accurately reads the 10 new words at the end of 3 days. To insure that she maintains those vocabulary terms, you schedule at least two more practice or drill activities with these learned words. These two "extra" activities are examples of overlearning. Overlearning is the most commonly suggested technique for maintaining a skill (Travers, 1967).

Overlearning suggests that a child has learned a skill to some prespecified standard. Standards could be stated in terms of accuracy, e.g., Ted can define 18 out of 19 world history terms. Standards can also be set in terms of fluency, i.e., how quickly a task can be done: Mary Jo will accurately diagram 19 sentences in 15 minutes. Naturally, a fluency criterion would not be set until accuracy had been met.

In addition to fluency and accuracy, standards can have another component. Tied in with spaced review, this component has to do with length of time for which criterion must be met. For example, Aaron completes an independent practice exercise with 100% accuracy for 3 consecutive days. The "3 consecutive days" is a length of time standard.

Setting a length of time standard is strongly recommended for children with learning problems in either academic or social areas. Length of time provides for overlearning or more opportunities to practice a desired skill or behavior. A common problem, linked to insufficient practice, is the seemingly inconsistent behavior of children with academic and social learning problems. Very often we hear teachers say, "I just taught Harold how to write his name. Yesterday he could write his name perfectly. Today he acts like he's never even seen a pencil and a piece of paper!" Harold, bless his little inconsistent fingers, may have given the appearance of being capable of writing his name, but he obviously still needed more guided practice before he was ready to write on his own. Before Harold's teacher can decide that he has forgotten to write his name, she needs to establish that he has, in fact, learned to write his name. Setting a length of time standard can help you to determine whether a child has actually learned a task.

The question now becomes how long the length of time standard should be. The answer is that it must be determined by the needs of the individual student. For some students only 2 or 3 days of overlearning may be required to establish learning. For other students the practice of overlearning is unnecessary. The basis for the answer lies within your own class structure. You must realistically assess your own organizational plan to determine how it can accommodate overlearning. If no scheduling time is set aside for overlearning to a specific length of time, then you need some guidance in how to reorganize your instructional time. If, on the other hand, time for overlearning has been incorporated into the teaching schedule, you must examine the depth of the children's needs. If only one or two children need the length of practice to be a week or more per concept, it may not be possible to meet their needs in the regular setting. If, however, more than four to five children need the length of practice per concept to be about a week, then the needs of these children might be met easily in the regular classroom.

A cry of dismay has just been uttered from the harried classroom teacher. "Why should one or two children be sent from my room when at the same time I may be expected to work with five or six who have similar practice needs? Why can't I keep the one or two and send out the five or six?" Of course, you can always keep the one or two, but the demands of a class of 30 or more may actually make teaching more difficult if you have only one or two children with special practice needs than if you have a small group. A small group with similar practice needs allows you to provide the same practice materials for several children. With one child you may have to spend the same amount of time developing materials as you would for five or six.

Another consideration in setting the length of time for overlearning is that a child's practice needs will vary from one task to another as well as within a task. Most children will rarely need the same degree of overlearning for all areas. Fred is a whiz in science. He can learn science concepts almost before the teacher has had a chance to decide what he wants to teach. The same cannot be said for his ability to spell scientific terms. While Fred needs no teacher-directed drill or practice for science concepts, he most definitely requires drill and practice to the point of overlearning in order to spell his science terms.

Bradley provides an example of a student whose length of time standards changed within a task. When Bradley was first introduced to letter sounds, he needed at least 3 days of overlearning before he could proceed to the next sound. Without those 3 days of overlearning he would either forget previously learned sounds within a week or confuse learned sounds with each other. After having learned the first eight letter sounds, Bradley's teacher noticed how he was more involved with the task. She had the feeling that Bradley's learning had accelerated since the beginning of the year. To test her hunch, she reduced his overlearning practice to 1 day. Her hunch was correct. Bradley proceeded to learn the rest of his sounds with only 1 day's worth of overlearning. He had learned how to learn his letter sounds.

The technique of overlearning lends itself well to the regular classroom for both social and academic tasks. Prentice may need overlearning in asking questions and hand raising. Georgie may need to overlearn how to clear off her desk. Any behavior, social or academic, that lends itself to drill and practice is suitable for overlearning.

## DELIVERING SYSTEMATIC INCENTIVES OR CONSEQUATION

In popular jargon, "systematic incentives" have been given a status somewhat lower than a snake's belly. Visions of bribery, corruption, and imminent moral decay have been attributed to providing incentives (consequation). If incentives happened to be the proverbial M & M's, then decay (of teeth, at least) might be an appropriate attribute; bribery and corruption are somewhat far-fetched.

### Types of Incentives

Incentives come in many shapes and sizes. Three types of incentives appropriate to the regular classroom are social reinforcement, tangibles, and activities that would be valued by the child (Payne, Polloway, Smith, & Payne, 1977). Incentives and consequation can be applied to both academic and social behavior, and, as is true with most learning principles, their use applies equally to nonhandicapped and handicapped students.

**Social reinforcement**—Social reinforcement requires that we have a reinforcer. A reinforcer is something provided after a behavior that causes it to reoccur more frequently. A social reinforcer is generally some nontangible occurrence or event that the child likes and would like more of. For many children, attention from the teacher is a powerful reinforcer. Social reinforcers in the classroom can include many different kinds of teacher behaviors, e.g., smiling at a child, touching, or giving verbal praise. For most mildly handicapped learning problem children, teacher-directed attention is sufficiently motivating. For some moderately or mildly handicapped learning problem children, however, attention from the teacher appears to be intolerable. These children actually resist positive attention, but will actively seek negative attention. These children beg to be told they are not worthy or that they have no value. James was such a child.

For an 11-year-old, James had amassed a very long history of inappropriate behaviors. His teachers said that James was bright, curious, and a basic pain in the neck. He could best be described as the colossal mouth. If his teacher explained that $2 + 2 = 4$, James would find some way to argue his case for $2 + 2 = 5$. He would argue, confront, and argue some more. James managed to use a lot of class time and his teacher's energy through these confrontations. When his teachers tried to ignore him, he only protested, "You don't like me" with renewed vigor, or "Why do you hate me?" Putting teachers on the defensive side of guilt had become a perfected art for our friend James.

When James' teachers smiled at him or gave him praise (occurrences that had become few and far between), he seemed to double his efforts to torment them. James was a paradox. He acted as though he wanted teacher attention (monopolizing class time through one-sided diatribes), but when it was given to him he set himself up for reprimands or avoidance.

After 11 years of practice, James ran up against a rather formidable force: a teacher who knew how to play the operant conditioning game by the rules—one, in fact, who had spent 35 years perfecting the operant game plan (kids like James do grow up and to no one's surprise often head straight for the operant gameland vocational fields of psychology, social work, and education).

James' teacher, Ms. Rinehart, knew a lot about him and his desperate need for attention. She also knew that he felt very badly about himself. She realized that, when he was given praise, James had no choice but to reject that praise. To James, the praise was a lie. In his reality he was "no good," and anyone who praised a "no good" had to be a liar. James was not to be done in by a liar.

Ms. Rinehart set her goal. She had to improve James' self-esteem before she could provide him with the more commonplace reinforcers like a gentle touch or a kind word.

Her plan was simple. She would begin by assigning James menial classroom tasks. His jobs were to dust off desks, sharpen pencils, and erase the board. Amidst screams of loud protestations, James dutifully completed the jobs he claimed to hate. (He also claimed to hate Ms. Rinehart for making him do such "dumb stuff.") James was receiving attention from his teacher, and some limited feedback which clearly spelled out that he was okay, at least at sharpening pencils, etc. Slowly and systematically, "old stoneface" Rinehart began to thank James for completing his tasks. Carefully, she added a smile to a thank you. Eventually, she even told him that the board looked good or that she'd never had such dustless desks. Note that Ms. Rinehart did not tell James he was good, but rather implied his "goodness" by complimenting the tasks. On the day that James casually remarked that he'd stay after school to help Ms. Rinehart straighten out the art supplies, the game was over. They were both winners.

A couple of lessons can be learned from the James/Rinehart game plan. The lessons are:

1. Reinforcers vary from child to child—not all children will value the same social reinforcer.
2. A child's sense of self will strongly influence the manner in which a social reinforcer can be delivered.
3. Never underestimate the power of a good teacher.

**Tangibles**—Tangible reinforcers usually fall into the categories of food, money, and tokens. Tangibles are just as the name implies—something that can be touched or tasted.

Food, a primary source of delight to most living beings, is occasionally used as a tangible reinforcer in regular classrooms. One popular technique has been to hold the Friday afternoon popcorn payoff. If the class has met the teacher's prescribed rules for the week, the reward is to make, eat, and from time to time surreptitiously throw popcorn on Friday afternoon. Of course while the children are making and eating the popcorn, not much other classroom learning is taking place. Popcorn payoffs can be fun and certainly successful in maintaining classroom standards.

Other than using food as an incentive for the entire class, food as a tangible reinforcer is not usually used in the regular classroom. If a child in the regular classroom needs food to be motivated to learn, the odds are fairly high that the child does not belong there. The regular classroom is not the place to be dispensing food incentives on an individual basis.

The same logic that is reflected in presenting food as a tangible reinforcer also applies to money. Money earned in class can go to the class, but not to individuals in the classroom. Using money to encourage ecological practices (e.g., picking up papers on the playground) or to help children control noise pollution (e.g., keeping the conversational level down in the hallways) has value other than monetary. If Mom and Dad want to pay Kay a dollar for each *A* she earns, that is their business, not yours. If money is the only incentive for which the child will work, you may need to consult with a special educator. Together you can develop a plan that will not include distribution of funds in your regular setting.

Distribution of play money to buy desired items from a play store should be restricted to teaching economics and should not be used to consequate behavior. Money and play store rewards can be more appropriately used with children who have moderate and severe learning problems.

The infamous classroom stars are a primary example of a tangible reinforcer. If Harry finishes his English composition correctly, he gets a gold gummed star on his paper. If Juanita does all 10 math problems, she gets a happy face. For every library book read, Hector gets to move his cut-out rocket ship one space closer to the cardboard moon and ... everyone gets to see the rocket move in the classroom bulletin board universe.

Stars, happy faces, and rocket ships are forms of token reinforcers. In the typical classroom everyone gets to participate and generally an earned token is there for all to see. Most often the token is given for a task, e.g., number of math problems completed or library books read. For some children, a "perfect" task may not be a reasonable goal. Besides fostering the inevitable "I guess I'm not as good as the other children" mentality, the inability to earn token reinforcers can affect the child's willingness to learn new tasks. Attention and all related learning activities can be restricted.

So, should the regular classroom teacher eliminate the happy face from the tops of children's papers? NO. As a regular classroom teacher you can set up conditions for earning the happy face. For Marsha, who has problems with her spelling words, you can reduce the number of words required for her to learn to earn a happy face. Instead of the class norm of 10 words a week, Marsha's weekly goal might be 6 words.

The rule for earning a happy face for all children is the same: Correctly spelled words earn a happy face. The variable factor is the number of words for each child. Very few children in class will either notice or care that the length of the spelling list is geared to the individual. For those who do notice, a simple explanation will usually be accepted. "Spelling is easy for you and that's why you can do 10 words." Or, "Spelling is harder for Martha, so I want her to concentrate on her special words."

As children progress through the elementary grades, the value of gummed stars decreases with meteoric speed. High scores written at the top of a paper or written phrases like "good work" or "nice job" still retain the gummed star flavor of success. Just as with social reinforcers, tangibles must have some value to the students. If tangibles don't maintain or increase desired behavior, then the tangible needs to be reassessed.

**Activities**—Activities are by far the most appropriate reinforcers in the regular classroom. Activities refer to events or occurrences that appeal to a particular child or group of children. Common group activities used as reinforcers are class parties, games, and extended recesses. The right to an activity is earned. An exchange (or a pact) is established between some teacher-desired behavior and the class or vice versa, depending on class structure. Though the time and subject may differ, we have all heard, "If you [the class] work quietly and carefully in geography, at the end of the session I'll give you 10 minutes of free time."

Group activity payoffs can be an excellent means of directing a group to learn. Some considerations must be given when presenting group activities. Directions for expected behavior need to be so clear that no one has any difficulty whatsoever with procedures. Sometimes mildly handicapped children are confused about expectations or directions. "Working quietly" and "carefully" may not be explicit enough for some children. A better way to state "working quietly" might be to detail your expectations. For one teacher, working quietly may mean that the students work silently—looking neither to the left nor to the right. For another teacher, "working quietly" may allow children to talk in a low voice with their immediate neighbors. For some children, "working quietly" may allow for any behavior short of outright howling! To lower everyone's stress level, expectations must be clearly stated. Assumptions about expectations can very quickly lead to confrontations— confrontations between the teacher and student, or worse yet, confrontations between the student and the class. Remember, everyone in the class must meet your expectations.

Group activities sometimes invite the problem of the child who actively seeks confrontations. Some mildly handicapped children with academic and social learning problems may choose to interfere with the ability of the class to earn an activity. You need to prevent such a child from incurring the wrath of classmates and thereby confirming the "nobody likes me" or "I'm no good" mentality. One way to sidestep this problem is to make a rule for violators. For example, suppose the plan is to sit quietly and not talk to neighbors to earn a 10-minute free time. Alex deliberately turns to Joe and they proceed to hold a 5-minute football chat. The whole class should not forfeit their free time—only Joe and Alex should.

Class activities can also be earned for academic tasks. Respecting your students' individual differences, you can arrange for group incentives for learning. If, for example, the students "look at you" as you present information or they "participate" in class discussions, you can allow for some class reward.

Activities can also be planned for individual students. In a regular classroom setting all students should be given the chance to be reinforced for appropriate behavior. Students can have tailored tasks, e.g., Suzanne may be given the privilege of leading the flag salute each day she correctly completes her phonics workbook exercise. Barbara may be allowed to read any story book of her choice after she has completed her penmanship assignment.

For delivering both class incentives and individual class member incentives, the rule to keep in mind is that the child or class already has the skill or ability to do the required task. The incentive should not be offered until the teacher has seen the child correctly perform or complete the desired task on at least one occasion. No matter how much the incentive is desired, if a child does not have the skills to complete a task, the end result is frustration.

## Consequences for Undesirable Behavior

At times, children with or without learning problems display classroom behaviors that you would rather not encourage. Some behaviors are physical (e.g., hitting, punching, and spitting), others are verbal (e.g., swearing, sassing, and incessant talking), while still others are academic (e.g., failure to complete assignments, refusal to do classwork, and excessive daydreaming). The frequency with which these behaviors are exhibited by any one child determines a child's educational placement.

For children who are physically violent to the point of injuring themselves or others, a special placement is likely to be appropriate. For children who are easily managed through incentives and whose behavior is more irritating than harmful, the regular classroom is likely to be the appropriate educational setting.

Techniques commonly used to decrease undesirable behaviors are also based on the notion of incentives or consequation of activities. The most frequently used incentive techniques are negative reinforcement and punishment.

**Negative reinforcement**—Like any kind of reinforcement, negative reinforcement causes a behavior to increase. With negative reinforcement, the desired behavior increases when the negative reinforcer is removed.

Steven had a tendency to break his pencil tips, especially during spelling or math classes. He learned he could use a great deal of class time by wandering over to the pencil sharpener and returning to his seat. Steven's teacher decided to decrease Steven's wanderings and, more importantly, increase his time in spelling and math.

On Monday, before Steven had an opportunity to break even his first pencil tip, the teacher initiated his plan for increasing Steven's time on-task. Mr. Ross presented Steven with a primary pencil designed to be tip-unbreakable. He explained that Steven was to use this pencil during all spelling and math exercises. Steven could substitute his regular pencil on Wednesday, provided he would be able to use it without breaking the tip. Wednesday's pencil tips somehow became much stronger. In fact, they no longer broke, and Steven spent more time on his spelling and math activities.

Steven did not like the primary pencil. He associated it with "little kids," which interfered with his "macho" self-image. To be assigned a more acceptable writing tool, Steven willingly increased his time on-task. Appropriate behavior resulted in the removal of the aversive stimulus (the primary pencil).

In the incentives game plan, two kinds of negative reinforcers exist: primary negative reinforcers and secondary negative reinforcers. Primary negative reinforcers, such as loud noises and electric shock, affect the senses of the child. Their use is inappropriate in all classroom settings. Secondary negative reinforcers become aversive by being associated or paired with events that are already aversive. Disapproving facial expressions or saying the word "no" are examples of behaviors than can serve as aversive events after being paired with spanking or yelling (Lovaas, Schaeffer, & Simmons, 1975).

Negative reinforcement is often, but should not be, confused with punishment. Negative reinforcement involves the removal of an aversive consequence. The main purpose of negative reinforcement is to increase the occurrence of a designated response.

**Punishment**—Punishment is, basically, a penalty approach to behavior control. It can be either punishment by application of an aversive or punishment by removal of a reinforcer (Craighead, Kazdin, & Mahoney, 1976). Examples of punishment by application are spankings and reprimands. A spanking or reprimand must decrease the undesired behavior to be considered punishment. For some children, a reprimand will increase the undesired behavior because attention is more highly valued than the reprimand is punishing. Punishment by removal refers to removing a positive reinforcer. For example, if George continues to be naughty, he will not get to play with his sailboat. If he values his sailboat, he will decrease his naughty behaviors.

A punishment-by-removal technique that has slipped into regular education by way of special programs is called *time-out*. Time-out has been construed to mean the removal of a child from the environment. In an extreme form of time-out, the offending child is placed in literal isolation (e.g., a small room or behind a screen). However, unless isolation reduces the offending behavior, it may not serve as a punishment. If it provides the child with opportunity to engage in desired behaviors, isolation is not punishment.

A form less extreme than physical isolation is to have children lay their heads on the desk for a few minutes. By keeping children in the room, you can supervise their activities while keeping a low-key perspective on the use of time-out. This procedure establishes your own role in relation to the child, as opposed to the much too familiar trip to the principal's office or the vigil outside the classroom where the child is outside your control and your authority.

If a child's behavior requires an extreme form of time-out, the regular class is probably the wrong placement. If you find that you have such a child in your room, you may wish to develop a plan with the special teacher. The plan could include the use of the regular classroom as a positive reinforcer. That is, attendance in the regular classroom becomes a privilege.

Whether or not you decide to use punishment, certain guidelines should be followed.

1. Punishment should be immediate.
2. Punishment should be consistent for each occurrence.
3. The reason for the punishment should be clearly understood by the child.

You should need to employ punishment only infrequently. Punishment teaches a child only what *not* to do, not what to *do*. "Being punished for undesirable behavior couldn't possibly (in a million years) teach the desired behavior" (Carter, 1977, p. 46).

You do have other options. You can let the child know that you prefer other behaviors. You can say, "Dwayne, your vampires would look much better if they weren't drawn all over your math pages. So, after you finish your math assignment, why don't you put them on a separate piece of paper?" Another option is to praise a behavior incompatible with the undesirable behavior. Suppose that Melanie has terminal talkitis. The first time she stops talking for a few minutes you can say, "Melanie, I'm proud of you. You've been working so quietly. Thanks for the nice, quiet work." You've hit two birds with one behavioral stone. You have reinforced a desired behavior without having to punish an undesired behavior. This technique is sometimes called "catch the child being good."

A final note on alternatives to punishment is ignoring. Ignoring gets to be a tricky technique. Ignoring treads the thin-ice line of decreasing behaviors on one side and, on the other, falling head first into cold waters by increasing undesirable behavior. For some children, ignoring is very effective. For other children, it merely increases the undesired behavior to the point that you will have to respond. When that occurs, you run the risk of reinforcing the undesired behavior.

## FIVE TEACHING METHODS REVISITED

The degree to which the teachers must attend to the five teaching methods described in this chapter is directly proportional to the needs of the mildly handicapped child. Whether an LD, EMH, BD, or regular classroom teacher, you need to decide how to balance your instructional program so that you can use each of the methods: setting expectancies, providing instructional feedback, assisting the child to organize information, furnishing practice, and delivering systematic incentives. Your use of these methods will vary with needs of your individual students. While all children benefit and need instruction influenced by each method, some children will need more or less emphasis on any one.

## SUMMARY

So, whatever happened to LD, BD, and EMH? The labels changed, but the behaviors remained the same. In this chapter, we presented the degree of the handicapping condition as a more educationally valuable categorization system than the labels LD, BD, and EMH. Severely handicapped children with these labels have educational needs beyond the range of the regular classroom. A few of these children have behaviors so extreme that they require medical as well as educational treatment. For the moderately handicapped LD, BD, or EMH child, behavioral and educational needs are often served in a special setting with some involvement in the regular education program. Mildly handicapped children are most often found in the regular classroom because their educational needs are most similar to those of the typical child.

You can assist mildly handicapped and normal children to increase desirable behaviors and decrease undesirable behaviors. You can provide an environment for instruction that directs learning through the selective use of the five teaching methods important for instruction.

# 4

## Physically, Visually, and Hearing Impaired Children

*Mirror, mirror on the wall, who's the fairest of them all?*
*Is it Hari big and tall or Daphne limping down the hall?*
*Is it Mabel in the chair or is it Mildred tapping there?*
*Is it Susan with aid in ear or is it Teddie with freckles so clear?*
*Is it Fenny playing in the sand or is it Sarah with cane in hand?*
*Mirror, mirror, we can't tell because we love them all so well!*

Without regarding the entire child as a whole, no one can choose "the fairest of them all." Physically, visually, and hearing impaired children like Daphne, Mildred, and Susan are as caring, trusting, and special as Hari and the rest of his nonhandicapped friends.

Most regular classroom teachers have had limited, if any, first-hand experience interacting with children with physical or sensory impairments. Watching some heart-rending made-for-TV movie about a physically or sensory impaired child no doubt has often left you with a strong sense of commitment to these children and a deep resolve to assist them in any possible way. But the strength of this commitment can be sorely tested when such a child crosses your classroom threshold and actually does become one of your students. Initially, you may feel a great deal of anxiety and have serious doubts about your ability to provide appropriate educational experiences for such a child. Relax, your feelings are normal; so please don't change professions or pay an analyst large sums to help you through a potential teaching crisis. Dealing with your feelings might be easier than you think, especially if you have some insight into the nature of the physical or sensory problem and how you can use your current teaching skills to provide the child with a positive educational experience.

The major classifications of sensory and physical impairments typically include children with crippling or other health impairments (COHI), visual impairment (VI), and hearing impairment (HI). These children may be multiply handicapped, e.g., both visually impaired and suffering from a persistent health problem or both visually impaired and hearing impaired. Although educational provisions take into account all conditions relating to academic and social growth, children are classified by their most severe handicaps. Thus, 7-year-old Tommy may be classified as deaf even if he also has chronic heart problems. Educationally, both Tommy's deafness and his heart condition must be considered in the normal routine of his school day.

# CHILDREN WITH CRIPPLING
# OR OTHER HEALTH IMPAIRMENTS

As Telford and Sawrey (1981) have noted, the category "children with crippling and other health impairments" (COHI) represents a diverse group of people who are lumped together because they are not average in physical ability. This category includes children with disorders of the nervous system, musculoskeletal problems, and congenital malformations. (Oddly, it also includes pregnant school-age girls.) Examples of disorders of the nervous system include cerebral palsy, epilepsy, other convulsive disorders, and multiple sclerosis. Musculoskeletal problems include conditions such as clubfoot, rheumatoid arthritis, and muscular dystrophy. Examples of congenital malformations are dislocation of the hips, spina bifida, and malformations of the heart. Many other disorders, such as cancer, diabetes, and limb malformations, could be included. Our list will grow and shrink as new health disorders are discovered and old ones conquered.

## COHI CHILDREN IN REGULAR CLASSROOMS

### Academic Provisions

As a teacher, your best bet in understanding the educational and social needs of a child classified as COHI is to question parents, medical specialists, and special educators who have worked with the child. You can gain the most useful information by asking questions that are educationally relevant; i.e., asking questions the answers to which can assist you in developing an educational program for the student. Table 4.1 presents a format for sorting information about selected motor impairments. Eight basic questions can be asked. These questions are:

- What is the expected intelligence range?
- What kind of speech communication should be expected?
- How does the condition affect hearing?
- How does the condition affect vision?
- Where is the site of the condition, or how does the condition manifest itself?
- What is the prognosis, while the student is in an educational setting?
- What kind of mobility will the child have?
- What general classroom considerations should be anticipated?

Given background information of this type, you are more informed about designing or modifying your classroom to fit the academic and social needs of your COHI students, other class members, and yourself.

Suppose you have just been informed that Lorraine, a child diagnosed as having osteogenesis imperfecta, is earmarked to enter your classroom. Before you enroll in medical school or take a crash course in Latin, you might want to ask the eight basic questions. From answers to these eight questions,

**Table 4.1**
Selected Motor Impairments

| | Intelligence | Speech | Hearing | Site | Vision | Prognosis | Mobility | General Classroom Considerations |
|---|---|---|---|---|---|---|---|---|
| **Cerebral Palsy** | | | | | | | | |
| Spastic diplegia | Normal range | Normal | Normal | Major involvement of lower limbs; minor involvement of upper limbs | Crossed eyes | Static, non-progressive malfunction of the brain | Restricted | Walk unaided but can fall backward easily |
| Spastic hemiplegia | Some mental retardation | | | Involves one arm and one leg on the same side | | Static, non-progressive malfunction of the brain | Restricted | Involved hand lacks sensation; should not force use |
| Total body involved | Normal or above normal | Non-existent or non-intelligible | | Involuntary motions of all limbs, trunk, and often the head | | Static, non-progressive malfunction of the brain | Restricted | Most cannot walk and many lack sitting balance; compensating devices such as wheelchair and special typewriters will be necessary |
| Muscular Dystrophy | Normal | Soft but normal | Normal | Progressively weakened muscles | Normal | Irreversible, progressive weakness of all muscles; death in early 20's | Restricted | Wheelchair and occasional use of an electric typewriter |

| Condition | | | | | | | |
|---|---|---|---|---|---|---|---|
| Spina Bifida (Meningomyecele) | Normal range | Normal | Normal | Lower limbs paralyzed according to line of spinal cord disruption | Normal | Static, non-progressive | Restricted | Braces or wheelchairs; toileting will involve use of a catheter or bag fixed to an abdominal wall opening |
| Juvenile Rheumatoid Arthritis | Normal | Normal | Normal | Involvement of joints | Normal | Progressive | Restricted to site | Adaptive equipment for writing |
| Osteogenesis Imperfecta | Normal | Normal | Normal | Bones | Normal | Progressive | Normal | Limited playground participation; may use wheelchair or braces |

you learn that Lorraine has normal intelligence, speech, hearing, and vision but that her bones break easily and her condition will deteriorate over time. A major implication for your classroom is to ensure that Lorraine does not participate in activities that may cause damage to her bones. In other words, you may need to restrict physical activities like running and hanging from monkey bars. Equipped with this basic information, you may proceed to prepare the other children in your class for Lorraine's special physical needs. No other special modifications are needed in your classroom materials or teaching techniques. Having obtained answers to the eight questions, you have no need for further assistance in developing your program. Proceed as you would for any other child.

But what about a COHI child whose disabilities have more serious educational implications than Lorraine's? Suppose Hugh, a child with cerebral palsy (specifically, spastic diplegia), is enrolled in your class. In obtaining answers to the eight questions about Hugh, you learn that Hugh's intelligence, speech, and hearing are normal, but that he may have vision problems. Hugh's mobility is restricted; his legs are affected seriously by the cerebral palsy, and his arms are affected slightly. Hugh can walk, but he has trouble maintaining his balance. His condition is stable, so no major changes are expected to occur during the time he is in your classroom.

If you have not had much experience with children who have problems like Hugh's, you will need assistance. At this point, you can ask very specific questions. Questions like, "Can he hold a pencil or should he be taught to use a typewriter to complete his classwork?" are specific to your classroom needs. Figure 4.1 provides a set of checkpoints that can help you ask specific classroom questions. This set of checkpoints is divided into four basic categories: (a) physical condition, (b) visual systems, (c) auditory systems, and (d) other communication. Information concerning these categories has immediate and direct consequences for educational planning. A list of checkpoints completed for Hugh is presented in Figure 4.2. Using Hugh as an example, we will consider implications of knowledge about each category.

First, Hugh's physical condition, while serious, merely requires a desk that does not open from the top; his weakened arms would not be strong enough to lift a heavy desk top. You can solve this problem by providing Hugh with a desk that opens from the front or a table with drawers. Second, the condition of his visual system (slightly crossed eyes) is corrected with glasses, but still drains his energy. You may want to decrease the amount of reading or close work that you require of Hugh. Third, no special modification or adaptations are needed for Hugh in work that requires use of his auditory system. Finally, Hugh's communication skills, both in speech and writing, require no special materials or teaching methods. However, you may need to judge the amount and quality of Hugh's handwriting with less writing, require no special materials or teaching methods. However, you may need to judge the amount and quality of Hugh's handwriting with more

**Figure 4.1**
Checkpoints for Regular Classroom Participation

Name of Student _____ Date _____

| Physical Condition | Visual Systems | Auditory Systems | Other Communication |
|---|---|---|---|
| _____ No special considerations | _____ No special considerations | _____ No special considerations | _____ No special considerations |
| _____ Special desk | _____ Cannot use any visual materials | _____ Cannot use any auditory materials | _____ Cannot produce intelligible speech |
| _____ Rest area | _____ Problems with chalkboard | _____ Special equipment, e.g., hearing aid | _____ Cannot use writing tools |
| _____ Mobility assistance | _____ Special reading materials | _____ Sign language | _____ Modified writing tools, e.g., typewriter |
| _____ Special toileting | _____ Talking books | _____ Lip reading | _____ Other |
| _____ Special equipment to use in manipulating text | _____ Large print books | _____ Special adaptations by speaker, e.g., speaks more slowly or loudly | |
| _____ Medication | _____ Glasses | _____ Other | |
| _____ Cannot manipulate texbooks | _____ Visual aids, e.g., magnifying glass | | |
| _____ Other | _____ Other | | |

| Remarks: | Remarks: | Remarks: | Remarks |
|---|---|---|---|

| Contact Person(s) | Contact Person(s) | Contact Person(s) | Contact Person(s) |
|---|---|---|---|
| _____ | _____ | _____ | _____ |
| Phone _____ | Phone _____ | Phone _____ | Phone _____ |
| Times Available | Times Available | Times Available | Times Available |
| _____ | _____ | _____ | _____ |
| Agency _____ | Agency _____ | Agency _____ | Agency _____ |

**Figure 4.2**
Checkpoints for Regular Classroom Participation

Name of Student ___Hugh_____        Date ___September_____

| Physical Condition | Visual Systems | Auditory Systems | Other Communication |
|---|---|---|---|
| ____ No special considerations | ____ No special considerations | _x_ No special considerations | _x_ No special considerations |
| _x_ Special desk | ____ Cannot use any visual materials | ____ Cannot use any auditory materials | ____ Cannot produce intelligible speech |
| ____ Rest area | ____ Problems with chalkboard | ____ Special equip- ment, e.g., hearing aid | ____ Cannot use writing tools |
| ____ Mobility assistance | ____ Special reading materials | ____ Sign language | ____ Modified writing tools, e.g., typewriter |
| ____ Special toileting | ____ Talking books | ____ Lip reading | ____ Other |
| ____ Special equip- ment to use in manipu- lating text | ____ Large print books | ____ Special adapta- tions by speaker, e.g., speaks more slowly or loudly | |
| ____ Medication | ____ Glasses | ____ Other | |
| ____ Cannot manip- ulate texbooks | ____ Visual aids, e.g., magnifying glass | | |
| ____ Other | _x_ Other | | |

| Remarks: | Remarks: | Remarks: | Remarks |
|---|---|---|---|
| Can't lift heavy desk top | Fatigues easily— decrease dose of sight work | | |

| Contact Person(s) | Contact Person(s) | Contact Person(s) | Contact Person(s) |
|---|---|---|---|
| Janitor | | | |
| Phone _____ | Phone _____ | Phone _____ | Phone _____ |
| Times Available | Times Available | Times Available | Times Available |
| Agency _____ | Agency _____ | Agency _____ | Agency _____ |

stringent standards than those applied to the writing of children who have no muscular problems. You must determine standards of handwriting for Hugh. Once established, these standards should be adhered to, just as the other children must adhere to their standards.

Even after you have gone through the checkpoints with an expert, you may not be sure your program is appropriate. Don't hesitate to continue working with the experts. Their job is to assist you in providing the most appropriate setting for each child.

Sometimes keeping a record of interaction with the expert or contact person can be useful. Especially important is a list of times when the contact person is available; nothing is more frustrating than making phone calls repeatedly and receiving no response. You may also want to give the contact person a list of times when you can be reached.

## Social Adjustment

Just as no single physical characteristic applies to all individuals classified as COHI, no gross generalization applies to psychosocial interactions and development. Personalities of some COHI children are not affected by their disability, while personalities of other COHI children are affected in some way. Some experts have suggested that the greater the disability, the more involved will be related psychological problems. To date, however, no specific set of psychological characteristics has been associated with the nature or extent of disability (Bigge, Sirvis, & Carpignano, 1976).

## Self-Care

For COHI children, self-care can be divided roughly into the areas of moving or mobility, eating, toileting, and medicating. These four areas go beyond academic growth. Careful planning in these areas allows a COHI child to experience a more simplified and efficient work routine.

**Mobility**—This term refers to a child's ability to move. In the classroom, space for wheelchairs or other equipment may be needed. Modification of doorways and walkways may be necessary. Building structures that cause a physically handicapped person to be dependent on other individuals are called *architectural barriers*. A checklist of architectural barriers is provided in Figure 4.3.

Ideally, no architectural barriers should exist. Recent legislation has required that all new buildings constructed with federal funds must provide for the needs of physically handicapped people. But suppose Penny, a child with muscular dystrophy, shows up at your school—a school which fully intends to comply with the legislation, but has not quite gotten around to making some of the necessary modifications. What are you to do? In a word, "impro-

**Figure 4.3**
Checking Your School for Accessibility

Use this brief checklist to find out if your school is free from architectural barriers and accessible to students with physical and health handicaps.

**Sidewalks**
Are there curb cuts which provide access?
Is there a width of at least 48"?
Are they level, without irregular surfaces?
Is there a level area of 5' by 5' if the door swings in?

**Ramps**
Are handrails present (32" high)?
Is the grade of the ramp more than a 1" rise in every 12' length?
Does it have a non-slip surface in all types of weather?

**Doors (including elevator)**
Is there an opening of at least 32" when door is open?
Are floors level for 5' in both directions of the door?
Are the thresholds navigable (½")?

**Floor**
Do hallways, stairs, and class areas have carpeting or some other non-slip surface?

**Toilets**
Is one stall 3' wide by 4'8" deep with handrails 33" high?
Is the toilet seat 20" high and urinals 19" from floor?
Are sinks, towel dispensers, mirrors, etc., 36"–40" from floor?

**Water fountains**
Are the controls hand operated?
Is the spout in the front of the unit?
Are they mounted 26"–30" from the floor?

From B.B. Greer, J. Allsop, & J.G. Greer, "Environmental Alternatives for the Physically Handicapped." In J.W. Schifani, R.M. Anderson, & S.J. Odle (Eds.), *Implementing Learning in the Least Restrictive Environment*. Baltimore: University Park Press, 1980, pp. 128-129. Copyright © 1980 by University Park Press. Reprinted with permission.

vise." If a light switch is too high, give Penny an extension of her arm, e.g., a a bent coat hanger, to pull and push the switch. If your classroom desks are too low, put them on cement blocks for extra height. If the floors are too slick, put self-adhering bathtub grips on the floor. Your janitor may not appreciate sweeping over little frogs and fish, but you'll keep your student upright. In fact, if you elicit help from your school custodian, you may find a wealth of ideas and a veritable warehouse of materials to be used. You are limited in modifying your classroom only to the extent that your imagination and principal are limited.

**Eating**—Eating may be difficult for a child who has coordination problems, head and trunk control problems, or problems directly related to the shoulder, arm, hand, or mouth. Adaptations may be useful in helping COHI children eat independently. Many adaptations will involve silverware, e.g., changes in the size and type of handle. Contoured handles are often made of clay or sponge rubber. As a classroom teacher, you are expected to be sure that any special modifications and equipment for a child are available to the child during eating periods. Your responsibility may simply entail a quick inspection of the child's lunchbox to see if it contains the necessary equipment. You may also need to provide enough cafeteria space to enable the child to eat comfortably. You may need to consider the height of serving lines.

Specific eating or drinking problems are unique to each person. As a classroom teacher, your best bet in finding specific information about a child is to ask one of the child's parents or a specialist, preferably one who has worked with the child. Occasionally, dietary restrictions are necessary. While you are not expected to determine the child's diet, you may be expected to monitor the food eaten (or not eaten). Again, consult with a parent or specialist.

Any modification of eating utensils or equipment will tend to draw attention to itself. Prepare your other students for these modifications. Use a preparation you feel comfortable with, perhaps a discussion or examination of utensils. Whatever preparation you use, be sure you don't overkill and cause embarrassment to the child. Role playing a COHI child eating with modified utensils is an example of overkill. Use your own judgment concerning the extent and degree of classroom preparation.

**Toileting**—Bowel and bladder care are an integral part of toileting, another major component of physical independence. Some COHI children require special consideration. Before a child is mainstreamed, most basic instructions in toileting self-care have been learned. As a classroom teacher, you are not likely to need to teach a toileting program, but you may need to monitor or assist in a program already developed.

Consider Richard, a child with spina bifida. Because of the location of damage to Richard's spinal column, he is unable to control his bladder. To allow Richard normal freedom of motion and to reduce embarrassment associated with a bladder accident, Richard wears an external device that collects urine. At appropriate times, the device is emptied. You may need to help Richard establish a routine to avoid accidents and to be maximally comfortable. You may also need to help him in case of an emergency leakage. Help in determining your role in toileting can be found by consulting with parents, school therapist, and perhaps an interastomal therapist.

Special fixtures may be needed for some COHI children. Handrails can help a child maintain balance. The size and shape of a toilet stall also determine usefulness for a COHI child. Some young children may need help transferring from a wheelchair to a toilet seat; most older children either transfer themselves or use their home facilites.

**Medicating**—Some handicapped children, COHI children included, need to take medication. As a classroom teacher, you may be asked to monitor a child's behavior on or off medication. The importance of monitoring a child's behavior cannot be overstressed. Thanks to the alertness of Eleanor's classroom teacher, Ms. Smith, Eleanor was given prompt and necessary medical attention. Ms. Smith had noticed Eleanor was dropping her pencil more frequently than usual. Some days it seemed Eleanor dropped her pencil eight or nine times. For 2 weeks, Ms. Smith counted the number of times Eleanor dropped her pencil each day. Ms. Smith discovered she had underestimated the frequency; Eleanor was actually dropping her pencil an average of 25 times a day. Ms. Smith conferred with Eleanor's parents and, as a consequence of a thorough medical examination, Eleanor was discovered to be epileptic. Given proper medication, she was able to lead a normal and full school life in the regular classroom.

When a teacher is given monitoring responsibility, teachers or parents may be misled into thinking the teacher is a doctor. As a classroom teacher, your job is to teach. You are not a doctor, and your job is not to prescribe medication. Whether or not you administer medication is determined by local policy; in most states only authorized medical personnel can administer medication. If your district has no policy concerning medication, be sure to obtain written parental and medical permission if you are asked to administer medication. Many children medicate themselves and require only a reminder from you. The ideal arrangement is one in which the child is able to self-medicate.

## COMMUNICATION OF THE COHI CHILD

Communication is a two-way street between sender and receiver. Without a sender, no one gives information; without a receiver, no one gets information. The receiving function in communication is referred to as receptive language. COHI children in the regular classroom rarely have extreme difficulties with receptive language. Most language problems for COHI children in a regular classroom are difficulties of expressive language.

Among COHI children with expressive or sender communication problems, the type of problem depends on the physical area of the child that has been affected by the COHI condition. Involvement of the throat, mouth, or vocal cords will affect a child's ability to produce sounds. Speech may be garbled or difficult to understand. Some physical disabilities affect the fine motor muscles in the hands, the gross motor muscles of the arms and shoulders, or both; children affected in these areas may have difficulty writing.

## Working with a COHI Child Who Has Difficulty Speaking

When working with a COHI child whose disability results in an expressive language problem manifested in difficult speech, the following tips may be helpful.

1. Use signals, especially for common words or phrases like "yes," "no," "I don't know," and "maybe."
2. Allow time for the child to produce a response.
3. Recognize frustration or deadlocks.
4. Teach the other children what works.

Each of these tips will be discussed separately.

**Use signals**—Signals are nonverbal signs used to communicate. The key to effective use of signals is to be sure that the sender and receiver share a common understanding of the signals. If a lowered head means yes to the sender and not to the receiver, confusion and misinterpretation will result.

The simplest way to determine the need for signals is to work with the child. If you honestly cannot communicate with each other orally, set up a signal system. The simpler the system, the more likely you will find it useful. Many signal systems exist; some use pictures, some use printed words, and others use bodily movement. Use whatever system works for the two of you.

**Allow time for sound production**—Some children need more time to express their ideas than do other children. Motor movements may be difficult, or a child may need time to recall which motor movements to use. Some children with cerebral palsy have major problems producing intelligible sounds. Be careful not to assume that a slow response means no response. Similarly, do not equate slowness of response with slowness of thought. After you have worked with a child for a while, you will be able to judge the appropriate response time. Each child will have a unique response time—just like children without motor problems.

**Recognize frustrations or deadlocks**—Sometimes communication is blocked. As a teacher, you have learned to identify frustration cues in normal children. The process of identifying frustration in COHI children with oral communication problems is the same process used with normal children. Think about what you do to alleviate frustrations of normal children, and do the same for COHI children with communication problems.

Deadlocked conversations can impede communication. Bigge (1976) presented an excellent example of reaching a premature conclusion in a deadlocked conversation:

> A cerebral palsied boy told about a party at school, the refreshments, activities, and people invited. The teacher checked all the details and said, "You must have enjoyed that."
>
>      C: No.
>      T: You didn't?
>      C: No.
>      T: But you told me all about it. Did something bad happen?
>      C: No.
>      T: But you didn't enjoy it.
>      C: No.
>      T: Well, you did go, didn't you?
>      C: No.
>      T: You didn't! Were you somewhere else?
>      C: No.
>      T: Were you ill?
>      C: No.
>      T: I don't get it then.
>
> The problem was the child was attempting to tell about a party that his class had planned, but which hadn't yet taken place. The assumption by the teacher was that the party was a past event. (pp. 116-117)

When you reach a deadlocked conversation (clue: you are getting only one response from the child), try another means of communication. Children have a way of communicating with each other that adults are not privileged to know. Sometimes having one of your other students "translate" will break the deadlock.

**Teach the other children what works**—More than likely, other children in your classroom will pick up ways to communicate with the COHI child. You can shorten the learning time by teaching the other children any signals or codes that have been established. You should also inform the other children about waiting time. Depending upon the age of your students, a quick lesson in empathy might be appropriate.

### Working with the COHI Child Who Has Difficulty Writing

Writing is difficult for some COHI children, especially children who have difficulty controlling their shoulders, arms, hands, or fingers. Some children with gross-motor coordination problems can use pencils and pens, but may need more time to write or copy information. Writing may be labored and cause the child to tire easily.

Special equipment to accommodate motor problems is available. The equipment can range from a piece of clay wrapped around a pencil to a miniature typewriter complete with a telephone receiver and a visual display of what is typed. Each child's need for equipment relates to the child's physical problem. A quick consultation with the child's physical therapist or occupational therapist should clarify classroom considerations.

As the child's teacher, you monitor the child's writing progress. If progress seems too slow, you may want to see what other equipment is available for your student. In the case of Richard, a child with minimal brain dysfunction resulting in poor gross motor and fine motor control, his classroom teacher was the first to notice problems in writing. Richard had been using a typewriter for his classwork. During the first part of the school year, the typewriter seemed quite appropriate. However, as the school year progressed, the teacher observed that Richard was becoming reluctant to use the machine. She also noticed him carrying pencils and pens in his pockets. After a short talk with Richard, his teacher discovered he was embarrassed to use his typewriter. Richard wanted to be more like the other kids.

Consulting with Richard's physical therapist, the teacher discovered he had more fine motor control than previously thought. While his fine motor control was minimal, he could grasp a specifically modified pencil. Richard's teacher constructed a 1/8-inch grooved template of Richard's name (see Figure 4.4) and taught him how to use it. Richard and his teacher reached a compromise. Richard would be allowed to write his name on the top of every written paper. The teacher was pleased because Richard was completing his assignments. Richard was pleased because he could write his name just like everybody else.

## CHILDREN WITH VISUAL IMPAIRMENTS

The number of visually impaired (VI) children in the public schools began increasing rapidly around 1953. During the late 1940s and early 1950s, many

**Figure 4.4**
1/8" grooved template

premature babies were placed in oxygen-rich incubators; a belief at this time was that if a little oxygen was good, a lot of oxygen must be better. Unfortunately, this was not the case. The oxygen-enriched environments caused the capillaries in the retina to burst. A burst capillary results in a scar-like condition in the retina. Fibrous tissues replace the retina, often resulting in total blindness in both eyes. The condition is known as *retrolental fibroplasia*. By 1954, the relationship of excessive oxygen to retrolental fibroplasia was recognized, and the practice of administering excessive oxygen was limited to only those premature babies who could not otherwise survive. For practical purposes, retrolental fibroplasia is a relic of the past.

The welcome demise of retrolental fibroplasia, however, did not signal the end of the educational practice of integrating blind and partially sighted children in the public schools. The increase in visual problems led to a need to educate large numbers of school-aged blind children. Since 1960, over half of the legally blind children in this country have been attending public schools (Jones, 1969), and almost all partially sighted children have been enrolled in regular classrooms in the public schools (Misbach & Sweeny, 1970).

## UTILITY OF CATEGORICAL DEFINITIONS

Categorical definitions of visually impaired children offer no clues to successful classroom programming. Visually impaired individuals form a highly heterogeneous group whose one common characteristic is some degree of visual loss (Jan, Freeman, & Scott, 1977). Some visually impaired children, like Sarah, are totally blind, while others, like Jim, are able to distinguish between light and dark. William can even see several feet away. Margaret, with tunnel vision, has good sight for distance, but is handicapped by a very narrow visual field. Some children, such as Harry, have such a high degree of light sensitivity (photophobia) that, even with minor visual impairment, they are restricted in many activities. Although all these children have some kind of visual impairment, they function differently from one another in both their school and home environments.

Clinical information such as age of onset and visual acuity have varied levels of utility for educational planning. According to VanderVolk (1981), a multidimensional approach to assessment is best since it provides useful information for educational planning and programming. In making decisions about teaching a child print or braille reading skills, an educational setting can play a more significant role than rated acuity. Functional ability and need plus capability of benefitting from a service form a practical basis for describing children with visual impairment.

Two additional factors that can have major impact on abilities and needs of a visually impaired child are age of onset of the impairment and manner of occurrence (Ashcroft & Zambone-Ashley, 1980). A child who has been blind from birth will have a set of visual experiences very different from those of a child who became blind at a later age. Joey, who was born without true eyeballs (anophthalmos), has never seen anything. Wes, who inherited degeneration and atrophy of the retina (retinitis pigmentosa), gradually lost his sight at the age of 10. Both children are considered blind, but Wes has a set of visual experiences that Joey can never have. Thus, their abilities and needs are quite different. To teach Joey about "the soft, fluffy white clouds" will require a set of techniques different from those required for teaching Wes. For Wes, the terms "white" and "clouds" are already within his repertoire of experiences. For Joey, the terms "white" and "clouds" will need to be related to something for which he has meaning.

Manner of occurrence of visual impairment has profound psychological implications. A child who gradually loses sight due to a degenerative condition may be psychologically prepared over time. However, major personality shifts may occur for a child who has lost sight due to trauma such as an automobile accident. Interpersonal relations, self-concept, body image, and other aspects of personality may be altered temporarily or permanently (Hanninen, 1975). Counseling for the child, parents, and teachers is strongly encouraged.

Whatever the cause, visual impairment is unique to each child; characteristics, consequences, and implications are child-specific. Visual impairment is just one characteristic of the child.

## VISUALLY IMPAIRED CHILDREN IN THE REGULAR CLASSROOM

### Academic Provisions

Generally speaking, the most appropriate curriculum for a visually impaired child enrolled in a regular classroom is the curriculum used for all the other children. Adaptations in the curriculum usually do not involve content, but involve the use of special equipment or textbooks. Adapting educational materials is not the responsibility of the regular classroom teacher. If a child needs large print materials or braille materials, a special vision teacher will make the modifications.

**Itinerant teachers**—Usually, special teachers for the visually impaired are referred to as *itinerant* or *resource* vision teachers. The itinerant teacher often plays an active role in the education of a visually impaired child by providing supplementary instruction. As a specialist trained in meeting the instructional needs of visually impaired children, the itinerant teacher may also show the child how to use the special visual aids, such as the loupe (a hand reading glass), spectacle magnifiers (ordinary glasses fitted to give a closer focus), and litescopic aids (appliances that can clip over the lenses of ordinary glasses).

The itinerant teacher supports regular classroom instruction. For this reason, you and the itinerant teacher must have open, clear lines of communication. If you let the itinerant teacher know what content you are going to teach, he or she can provide appropriate materials for the visually impaired child. In addition, the itinerant teacher can provide tutorial time for the child.

If you are teaching a visually impaired child, you will probably want to encourage the itinerant teacher to be in your classroom. By being in your room, the itinerant teacher can ensure that the VI child is completing work appropriately and using special materials or equipment efficiently. Furthermore, if the itinerant teacher works in your room, the two of you may save a tree by reduction of note exchanges. Consider the situation where you put weekly spelling words on the chalkboard. Instead of you handing a list of words to the itinerant teacher, he or she can simply copy the words in braille (if necessary) or modify them on the spot for the child. In any event, the content of classroom instruction will be determined by you, the classroom teacher. The itinerant teacher will assist you to the degree that special services are required.

**Key questions for the regular class teacher**—Even though an itinerant teacher will help you, you will spend most of the school day with the child, and the primary responsibility for teaching the child will belong to you. You may want to ask some educationally relevant questions. Since approximately

80% of all blind and partially sighted children have some remaining sight, your questions might address issues related to the use of vision in the classroom. The following are four questions the answers to which can help you make decisions concerning a child's education:

- How does the child use the remaining vision?
- For the child who is partially sighted, what should the viewing distance be?
- How much illumination should the child have?
- What medium for reading should the child use?

Several VI children may have the same acuity rating or classification, but need very different educational provisions. Consider Santina and Conrad; they both have low vision and cannot see without some sort of optical aid. Santina has a condition known as albinism. One result of albinism is a reduction in visual acuity to 20/200, compared with normal acuity of 20/20. In addition, albinism is often associated with nystagmus, an involuntary, rapid movement of the eyeball. Finally, albinism often causes acute light sensitivity, photophobia. Conrad has a condition known as open-angle glaucoma. He has lost all of his peripheral vision and is left with a very narrow visual field.

Educational provisions for Santina and Conrad will be quite different. Santina cannot tolerate light, but Conrad needs high intensity lighting. Santina needs books with large print, while Conrad can read regular type as long as he uses a hand magnifying glass. As a classroom teacher, you cannot be expected to diagnose Santina's or Conrad's educational needs, but you are expected to accommodate needs that have been diagnosed. No special training is required to seat Santina away from direct sunlight. Similarly, no special training is necessary to remind Conrad to use his hand magnifier.

By analyzing the needs of Santina and Conrad, you may realize that no single answer prescribes the way all VI children should be taught. All VI children cannot be limited to a single medium or piece of equipment.

**Adjustment factors**—Whatever the medium or equipment selected, helping the child learn with the greatest efficiency and effectiveness is a primary objective of the educational program. Consideration of the following areas may increase the rate at which a VI child adjusts to your educational program.

1. *Introduction to the setting.* Since a visually impaired child will be limited in the visual environment of your room, you need to provide

the child with orientation. The child will need to know the location of your work spaces, i.e., desks, teacher desk, tables, learning centers, etc. In addition, the child will need to be shown where to find common classroom materials like the pencil sharpener and waste baskets. Orientation will occur more smoothly if you introduce places sequentially, perhaps adding one or two new locations a day. Another means for assisting a VI child to learn locations is by applying the "All Roads Lead to Rome" technique, i.e., by providing a focal point or pivotal spot from which all locations can be found once the child has a permanent reference point. More than likely, the child's own desk will be the most appropriate pivotal point. Remember to tell the VI child whenever you rearrange furniture or add new equipment.

2. *Presentation of learning material.* For a child who sees poorly or not at all, the clarity of your verbal directions can be crucial. Other than your tone of voice, the child may be unable to read your nonverbal communication. For the child to know what is expected, you may need to give a verbal signal. The start of a lesson, for example, can be signalled with the word "listen" or the phrase "get ready." In addition, your instructional purpose should be stated clearly at the beginning of the new lesson and repeated at the end of the lesson. The beginning or ending of a lesson should be vocalized in such a way that the child has time to gather or put away any required materials.

3. *Quality of voice.* You may need to listen to a recording of your own voice to analyze what you hear. If you find that your voice is putting you to sleep, you can guess how interesting the VI child finds your presentations. A grating or unpleasant voice may cause the VI child to stop listening to you. The loudness of your voice and competing sounds must also be considered in relation to the child's auditory needs.

4. *Accommodation for special equipment.* Many VI children use braille-writers, typewriters, or tape recorders in the classroom. You may need to create a space to house these materials. If the child's desk is not an appropriate place for storing materials, a small table or stand next to the child's desk may be helpful. To save your eardrums and to diminish the noise created by these devices, the child can use a rubber pad to soften the sound of a braille-writer or typewriter. Earphones can be used with a tape recorder.

5. *Providing opportunities for reinforcement.* Sighted children are presented with multiple incidental learning experiences that assist them in the classroom. A sighted child may learn the word *street* in school.

On the way home, the child may see the word *street* again on a street sign or billboard. In contrast, a child who is visually impaired has limited chances to have formal learning reinforced by incidental learning. A partial solution to this problem is for you to provide multiple experiences in a variety of situations for *street* or whatever concept you are presenting.

6. *Encouraging independence.* For the VI child, like all other children, self-sufficiency is a major goal. Helping the child to be aware of his or her own responsibilities is one step on the road to independence. Other steps include the development of orderly work habits with regard to storage and retrieval of equipment and working materials. As much as possible, a VI child should be increasingly responsible for getting out books and work. To help the child function actively in the classroom, desks, shelves, and other work areas can be labeled in clear print or braille.

Overall, working with a VI child in your classroom should be a positive experience for both you and the child. Educationally advantaged blind children usually function at a normal level by school age or shortly after (Fraiberg, 1959). When low-vision children are given special training in visual development in kindergarten, they are able to perform as competently in the regular classroom as their sighted peers (Hull, 1973).

## Social Adjustment

VI children exhibit a wide range of personality characteristics and social adjustment. Because they are initially quite dependent upon the people in their primary social environment, personality and social adjustment are shaped intensely by those people. If a child is raised in the natural home, primary influence will come from the family. If a child is raised in an institution, primary influence will come from the institutional environment and personnel. Variables like education, intelligence, residual vision, and social class also influence a VI individual's feeling of worth and independence.

**Realistic dependency**—Like most disabled persons, VI children risk being dependent and passive. There is a delicate balance between realistic dependency and overdependency. As a classroom teacher, encourage the child to do as much as possible independently. Your most serious problem may not be a VI child's unwillingness to cooperate, but rather the oversolicitousness you and your other students feel. While empathy is to be encouraged, sympathy is to be discouraged. An empathetic teacher understands the need for independence; a sympathetic teacher is likely to create dependency. If you are not sure how independent a child is, ask the vision teacher how the child works in other school or home environments. You may even need to observe the child in other environments.

Ana, a child with low vision, presents the classic "shrinking violet" pose in the classroom. She sits quietly waiting for the world, i.e., her teacher, to come to her doorstep. Ana makes no attempt to finish assignments or even to begin them. On the playground, a miracle occurs. The violet transforms into a wonderfully interesting bouquet. She laughs, tells stories, and finds friends at every turn of a corner. Ana is not socially maladjusted. If anything, Ana has learned the system too well. If Ana can be a trailblazer on the playground, she is capable of showing the same initiative in the classroom.

**Stereotypic behaviors**—One problem that may cause you concern is the management of stereotypic behavior. Stereotypic behaviors, or "blindisms," are repetitive behaviors that are age-inappropriate and excessive. Common stereotypic behaviors are body rocking, light gazing, and hand flapping. Not all VI children exhibit stereotypic behaviors, and no one is sure why these behaviors develop. However, it is clear the behaviors are distracting and draw attention to the person emitting them. Should a VI child exhibit blindisms, you need not panic. You can probably arrest the behavior by providing the child with an activity that is incompatible with the blindism. If Josh is flapping his hands, give him an activity that requires use of his hands. If Kevin is light gazing, direct him to his media for reading. In general, frequency of stereotypic behaviors can be reduced by keeping a VI child interested in classroom activities.

Any attempt to shame or punish the child is likely to increase the undesirable behaviors. If the behaviors interfere with normal classroom routine, consult a vision specialist. The two of you can develop an appropriate management program.

## Self-Care

**Mobility**—For VI children, the aspect of self-care most often discussed is mobility. Mobility refers to both locomotion and independent travel. Common mobility aids for VI persons are the seeing-eye dog and the white cane. In many states, use of a white cane has been restricted to persons who are legally blind. In addition to providing information to the blind person who is using a cane, the cane is also a signal for traffic to yield the right of way. Various electronic devices have been developed to assist in mobility, but only a few are available commercially.

Mobility training is the responsibility of the vision teacher. One of the first things taught in mobility training is body image. An awareness of body parts helps VI children in conceptualizing themselves and their relationship to the environment. This conceptualization of self in relation to the environment is vital to successful travel and movement.

In the early grades, the regular curriculum includes activities centered around left–right discrimination and naming body parts. As a classroom teacher, you can reinforce the vision teacher's instruction through the regular curriculum. In addition to learning body parts and "what is connected to what," VI children (like most children) need to learn position terms like *up*, *down*, *forward*, and *backward*. Most VI children are given instruction in position terms relative to their bodies, e.g., "shoulder level" or "feet together"; this instruction can be beneficial to normal children, too. Working on these activities as a total classroom allows the VI child to share experiences with everyone in the classroom. However, teaching body parts and left–right discrimination may not be grade-appropriate activities. If these activities are not grade-appropriate, don't teach them. Support activities in the regular classroom are intended to integrate the VI children, not segregate them from other children or make them stand out as different.

Physical education is another excellent area for integration of VI children, whether the physical education is formal, as in regularly scheduled gym classes, or informal, as on the playgound. For a VI child to participate fully in physical education, some modifications may be required. Physical exercises in noncompetitive activities like rope climbing, dancing, and swimming are quite appropriate for VI children. Participation in competitive activities will vary with the skills of each student. At a minimum, each student should have a chance to learn the rules of games, the lay-out of the playing areas, and the basic skills involved, such as how to throw a baseball or dribble a basketball (Martin & Hoben, 1977).

Perhaps the greatest handicap a VI child experiences in mobility is the overconcern of others. As a classroom teacher, you must be sure to encourage other children in your room to allow the VI child to experience movements for himself or herself. A normal reaction on the part of sighted children is excessive assistance in guiding the VI child. To help your sighted students understand the mobility needs of your VI student, you may want to arrange some form of presentation by the vision teacher and the VI student. This presentation can be used as an information exchange session where preconceptions are dispelled and new information conveyed.

**Eating, toileting, and medicating**—Eating, toileting, and possibly medicating are also everyday occurrences for VI children. As a regular classroom teacher, your primary responsibility is to expect the VI child to participate in these activities just like your other children. You may again need to discourage your other students from "killing with kindness." Blind and low-vision students are capable of preparing their own food trays and walking through a serving line. The vision teacher will teach the child the physical arrangement of the cafeteria. You may want to reinforce cafeteria procedures and be certain that the child is made aware of any changes—either physical, such as rearrangement of lunch tables, or procedural.

To assist a VI child in achieving independence in toileting, you need to teach the child the location and room lay-out of the bathrooms. Beyond this, little instruction is necessary.

As with any student, you should not administer medication unless you have been certified by an appropriate medical authority. You can be alert to problem signs and report any peculiarities to the vision teacher. If an emergency occurs, do the best you can to protect the child from injury, just as you would with any other child.

## Communication

VI children in the regular classroom rarely have problems of expressive language per se. However, for the VI child, some receptive language problems can influence expressive language. For example, if Jonathan has never seen a volcanic mountain, he will probably have conceptual difficulties when you discuss the eruption of Mt. St. Helens. Unless Jonathan is given specific instruction compensating for his visual impairment, the next time he speaks about mountains or eruptions, he is likely to misuse the terms. The misuse of terms may or may not be noticed by the receiver; a major language problem experienced by VI children is that receivers or listeners often do not share the same conceptual basis as the VI child. Several tips that may be helpful when working with a VI child who has receptive language problems are discussed below.

**Verbal references**—First, when using verbal references to objects or actions, relate them to references that are known or experienced by the child. Clarification of references may mean presenting information tactilely as well as verbally. Consider the term *mountain*. You can verbally describe a mountain and also present an embossed referent sheet that depicts in scale a mountain, a hill, and flat ground. Given sufficient notification, a vision teacher can usually provide materials you need. If you need an immediate referent, some glue, a ball of string, and a tiny bit ingenuity can create raised surfaces on ordinary paper for tactile discrimination.

**Anticipatory sets**—Second, establish an anticipatory set. Establishing an anticipatory set goes beyond providing a child with a signal for attending. An anticipatory set focuses a child's auditory attention by setting up anticipation for what is going to be heard and then comparing what was expected with what is actually heard. Normally, VI children and other children must be taught to establish an anticipatory set. Teaching children to use a verbal anticipatory set can occur any time during the school day when you want the children to attend to auditory information. If, for example, you are teaching a lesson on frogs, you might use the following format:

Signal: "Okay everyone, I've got something to tell you."
Anticipation: "I've got something in this box that's green and hops and swims in a pond."
Expectation: "What do you think is in this box?"
(Allow time for children's responses.)
Comparison: Open the box and show the children a frog. "Look, I've got a frog. What made you think I had something else?"

By establishing some kind of format, you will train the children to develop the habit of using an anticipatory set.

**Visual and auditory presentations**—Third, combine visual and auditory presentations. Research comparing auditory and visual presentation of information suggests strongly that a combined auditory and visual presentation leads to more efficient comprehension than does the presentation of auditory or visual material alone (Day & Beach, 1971). For children with visual impairment, presentation in braille or large print can approximate the visual presentation experienced by children with normal sight. This "visual" presentation allows a VI child to review or to refer to material presented previously. The vision teacher will supply modified materials for your instructional units.

Notes are an important source of visual information for children with normal vision. Blind or low sighted children are often capable of taking their own class notes. However, transferring information from auditory to visual media is time consuming. Visually impaired children often use cassette tape recorders to record verbal information that is transferred later into another form. Some VI children use a slate and stylus to take notes, and others take handwritten notes; in either case, note taking is slower for visually impaired children than for children with normal vision. You may need to repeat key points several times or allow for longer pauses between critical ideas. Note taking for a VI child may also require more energy than note taking for a sighted child. If you can't reduce the amount of content over which you expect notes to be made, perhaps you can have your notes transcribed by the vision teacher. You may want to provide the vision teacher with carbon copies of notes taken by one of your other students.

# CHILDREN WITH HEARING HANDICAPS

## IMPACT OF HEARING LOSS

Children who have hearing handicaps are usually referred to as deaf or hard of hearing. In both conditions, something has altered normal auditory reception, interfering with the ability to hear and understand speech sounds. The age at which the auditory system is impaired is a critical variable. Children who are born deaf or become deaf before 2 or 3 years of age do not have a chance to acquire normal speech and language. Children who have relatively normal hearing up to about 2 or 3 years of age can build upon their language with more facility. Generally, the ease with which children acquire language varies inversely with the severity of the hearing loss. However, as with all generalizations, exceptions occur. Hearing impairment is a highly individualized problem. Helen may be able to perceive some sounds well, but she may still be considered deaf if, even with a hearing aid, she cannot hear and

**Figure 4.5**
The ear

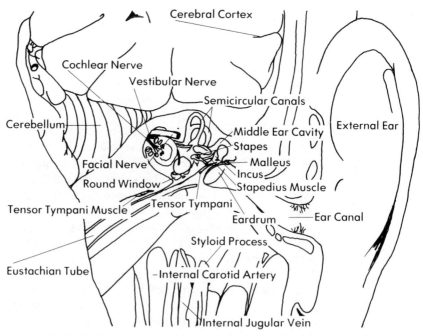

From P. Whitfield and D.M. Stoddart, *Hearing, Taste and Smell: Pathways of Perception.* New York: Torstar Books, 1984, pp. 17-18. Used with permission.

understand connected speech (Katz & Mathis, 1978). Other factors that contribute to the individual nature of a hearing impairment are the cause and type of hearing impairment.

As shown in Figure 4.5, the ear has three major parts: (a) outer, (b) middle, and (c) inner. Hearing loss has been classified into two major types, conductive and sensorineural, according to which part of the ear is affected.

### Conductive Hearing Losses

A conductive hearing loss is caused by some problem in the outer or middle ear. If, for example, a bean has been lodged in the ear canal, a conductive loss will occur. Wax build-up also leads to conductive loss. Another common problem leading to conductive loss is interference with movement of the bones in the middle ear. Up to about the age of 5 or 6, many children frequently experience a middle ear infection called *otitis media*. Frequent repetitions of otitis media can impair the movement of the middle ear bones and produce a conductive loss.

For children with a conductive hearing loss, lower and middle frequency

**Figure 4.5**
(Continued)

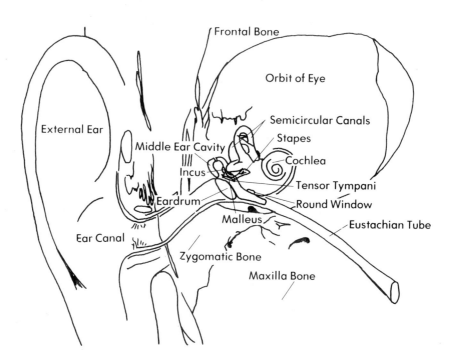

tones (*m*, *n*, *ng*, and vowels) are usually heard as muffled or faint. Children with conductive loss may show severe articulation errors of substitution or omission (Van Riper, 1963). The overall speech signal is depressed. A child with a conductive hearing loss must expend a great deal of effort in order to hear. Some children may appear lazy or inattentive when actually they simply cannot expend the energy necessary to make sense of an auditory kaleidoscope of muffled sounds.

A child with a conductive hearing loss may speak in very soft or quiet tones. The speech of a child with a conductive disorder may also seem to reflect a syntax problem, but the problem often turns out to be an articulation error of omission rather than a syntax error. Nickie often leaves out plurals and the word *is*. An example of a typical Nickie sentence is "The six boy went home." Nickie understands the plural concept of six boys, but she has difficulty hearing and thus producing the appropriate plural ending.

## Sensorineural Hearing Losses

The other type of hearing loss, sensorineural, results from a problem in the inner ear, the acoustic nerves, or both. Sensorineural losses vary in severity but are usually more serious than conductive losses. In a sensorineural loss, sounds may be both muffled and distorted. High pitched sounds like *th*, *f*, *ch*, and *t* present problems for many children with sensorineural losses. If any sounds are heard at all, they are so distorted the child has a difficult, if not impossible, time matching his or her speech sounds with the sounds of others. Communication can be quite frustrating.

For many children with a sensorineural loss, lip-reading is a viable communication tool. In order to read lips, however, a child must be able to see the lips of the communicator. As a classroom teacher, you may need to be sensitive to the position of your face in relation to the child's line of vision. Windows that expand the visual world of most childen in a classroom may close the world of a lip reader. If a window is behind you, the glare or light from the outside will make your lips almost impossible to see.

Another problem in the regular classroom is background noise. Typical background noise in a classroom can interfere with whatever residual hearing a deaf or hard-of-hearing child has. Distance from the communicator, usually the teacher, is a critical factor. A child with a hearing impairment should probably be not more than 4 feet away from the speaker. Maintaining such a distance is not difficult when a teacher is standing still. However, most classroom teachers tend to walk around the room as they lecture. If you have a child with a hearing handicap, you may want to spend less time traveling during group instruction and circulate more during individual or practice instruction.

Since sensorineural disabilities affect sound processing to a great degree, care must be taken to ensure that a child truly understands the concepts you are attempting to communicate. Jane represents a classic example of a deaf child who seems to understand classroom concepts, but actually has no idea what she is supposed to be learning. Jane is very agreeable; whenever her teacher asks if she understands, Jane smiles and nods her head in agreement. She completes all her assignments on time, ususally with accuracy. Jane has learned an excellent survival tactic; she can imitate. She looks around the classroom and gets cues as to what she's to do from the other kids or from directions in the text. The trap is that Jane is doing busy work rather than the conceptualization that the material is supposed to engender. On the surface, Jane seems to be developing her vocabulary and participating in class activities like her classmates who hear normally. Digging a little deeper, one discovers Jane is sadly lacking in basic information. As a classroom teacher, you will be in an excellent position to guard against the "imitation syndrome." You and a hearing specialist can devise a classroom strategy that is most comfortable and likely to help children like Jane truly conceptualize information.

## THE HEARING IMPAIRED CHILD IN THE REGULAR CLASS

### Academic Provisions

**Other professionals**—Educating hearing impaired children in a regular classroom is a team responsibility. The regular classroom teacher and other professionals must develop open lines of communication to ensure that appropriate help for the child is available. Two professionals with whom you might work closely are the teacher of the hearing impaired and the speech–language clinician.

The teacher of the hearing impaired can work directly with the child and can be a resource person for you. If you share your class curriculum with the teacher of hearing impaired children, he or she can develop strategies for teaching concepts from your curriculum. These strategies will revolve around the child's level of language development. The teacher of the hearing impaired will also be able to use various special communication modes such as signing or total communication. Keeping a list of new vocabulary words or key concepts in your weekly lesson book and providing access to your lesson book can greatly facilitate communication of classroom materials.

A speech–language clinician works primarily on remediation of speech and language problems, working directly with the child, but not necessarily instructing on curriculum subject matter. The clinician can provide suggestions for use in your classroom, and you may be able to describe areas in which the child needs help from the speech–language clinician. A common practice is to keep a daily notebook of the kinds of errors you hear a hearing impaired child commit. The notebook need not be exhaustive, nor do you need to be compulsive about your observations. All you need to do is provide

**Figure 4.6**
A Weekly Speech and Language Notebook

Teacher _____ Ms. Jones _____
Student _____ Russell C. _____
Date      _____ 9/18–9/22 _____

| | Speech | Language |
|---|---|---|
| Monday | Dropped "-s" off words Left out verb "is" | |
| Tuesday | Problems with "-s" | Confused about "beside" and "around" |
| Wednesday | | |
| Thursday | Final "-s" problem Leaving out words like "the" and "a" | |
| Friday | Still final "s" and omission of "the" and "a" | Confused about science vocabulary |

a rough picture of typical classroom performance of the hearing impaired child. An example of entries into a weekly notebook for Russell is presented in Figure 4.6.

Armed with notes from the regular classroom, the speech clinician can institute remedial work with the final -s sound, science vocabulary, or whatever else is an apparent problem for the child. Russell's progress in speech and language can be evaluated in the regular classroom. The evaluation not only allows the speech clinician to determine areas for remedial work, but also to determine how effective Russell's instruction has been.

**General guidelines**—While responsibility for educating a hearing impaired child will be shared, you will spend most of the school day with the child. You may want to follow some general guidelines related to the use of hearing in the classroom. The following guidelines have been developed to help you:

- Use whatever hearing capacity the child has.
- Provide visual access to classroom information.
- Provide classroom work on the basis of subject matter performance.
- Establish opportunities for incidental learning.
- Establish opportunities for regular feedback.

We will discuss each guideline individually.

*Use whatever hearing capacity the child has.* Many hearing impaired children have some residual hearing; the amount and utility of this residual hearing vary with each individual. Try to capitalize on residual hearing by having the child use hearing whenever possible. Encourage the child to listen as well as look when information is presented. Consider the following classroom activity. You have been putting reading material on tape and your students are to listen to the tape and follow the words in a book. The hearing impaired child should also "listen" to the tape and follow along in the book.

Encouraging a child to use residual hearing is called *auditory training*. Auditory training for hearing impaired children is very much like auditory training given to children with normal hearing. Training may begin with identification of selected environmental sounds (such as a lunch bell), localization of sound sources, and distance listening. Training may gradually lead to word discrimination on the basis of vowel or consonant differences (Northcott, 1980). With a hearing impaired child, you can capitalize on auditory events throughout the day to provide reinforcement for specific auditory training content. A quick check with a hearing or language teacher can be useful in determining the level of expectation you can demand from the hearing impaired child in your classroom.

Residual hearing can also be enhanced through amplification provided by a hearing aid. The trick with hearing aids is to first and foremost be sure that the aid is working. More than likely, the child will not be able to recognize a malfunction of the hearing aid. As the power of the battery diminishes, so does the effectiveness of the aid. Be sure to set up some kind of periodic check system. Who does the checking is of little consequence; of prime importance is that the aid is checked often and thoroughly.

There are four important points to remember if you have a child using amplification in your classroom. First, amplification raises the level of sound, but does not decrease distortion in sound. Distortions, like all other sounds, will be louder. Second, most children using amplification use a monaural or one-receiver system. Place the child so that the "good" ear is toward the most important source of sound. Third, your voice may become lost in other sound signals. Fourth, a child with amplification hears whatever sound source is closest.

*Provide visual access to classroom information.* One of the most obvious ways to convey information to a hearing impaired child is through the visual system. A deaf or hard-of-hearing child learns a lot by seeing things. As a classroom teacher, you must take special care to provide visual aids with your teaching. Fortunately, visual media that are appropriate for use with a hearing impaired child can also be used with students who hear normally. Transparencies, films, filmstrips, and pictures can be valuable teaching aids. Providing printed words to accompany these visual aids will enhance their teaching value. By furnishing outlines of lectures or films prior to delivery, you can maximize input for a hearing impaired child. Finally, displaying classroom directions and directions for assignments is an additional technique for clarifying classroom expectancies.

Jeremiah was a very lucky child. When he first entered the regular classroom he seemed inattentive. He appeared disoriented and rarely completed assignments. His teacher, Ms. Jones, sensed an impending crisis and began to analyze the problem. She noticed that Jeremiah, rather than being obstinate, seemed not to know what he was supposed to do. Because Ms. Jones didn't want to embarrass Jeremiah or single him out from the rest of the class, she began to write directions for assignments on the chalkboard. Jeremiah's problem disappeared. By eliminating a major source of frustration for Jeremiah, Ms. Jones also eliminated the possibility that Jeremiah might be placed incorrectly in a class for emotionally disturbed children.

*Provide classroom work on the basis of subject matter performance.* The critical determiner of subject matter placement for a hearing impaired child, as with all children, is the entry level skill brought to the learning program. Consultation with the speech and language clinician or the teacher of the hearing impaired should provide you with a sound estimate of a child's skills. Based on the child's skills, you will be able to design a program that fits the child's needs.

Degree and severity of a hearing disability will relate to the degree of successful classroom performance. A natural consequence would seem to be to determine placement within a classroom or within content matter according to the severity of the disability. On face value this logic seems fine, but closer inspection reveals glaring fallacies. Morgan, who suffered a sensorineural loss at the age of 9, presents a far different level of skill than Tommy, whose hearing loss occurred during infancy. Tommy did not have many of the auditory experiences Morgan has had. Both children share the label of sensorineural loss, and both are now enrolled in the fifth grade. For Morgan, whose loss of hearing was relatively recent, grasp of subject matter is normal for his age and grade. For Tommy, many problems in language comprehension persist. While Tommy is certainly capable of critical and analytical thought, the written style of fifth grade subject matter will need to be altered so that information is presented using less complex syntax. Sentences must be simplified, and Tommy will need many concrete examples of the fifth grade vocabulary terms. Tommy and Morgan are not likely to learn at the same rate; Tommy's progress will probably be slower than normal. As a result, subject matter placement should be different for Tommy and Morgan.

Expectancies for hearing impaired children are the same as expectancies for children with normal hearing. For a hearing impaired child with normal entry skills, you can expect basically normal performance. While modification of materials may be necessary, content need not be diluted or altered from content taught to your other students. For a hearing impaired child who enters your classroom with slightly lower than normal entry skills, modification of content may be necessary. Modifications for a low-achieving child who is hearing impaired are basically the same as modifications for a low-achieving child with normal hearing. The key to succesful programming in subject matter for hearing impaired children is to find a good match between entry level skills and expected classroom curriculum.

*Establish opportunities for incidental learning.* Incidental learning is learning that occurs without planning or formal instruction. In a classroom, incidental learning usually occurs as a result of some related learning experience that *is* planned. For example, if you are talking about fire engines, you may play a tape of a fire engine siren or you may simply ask the children to tell what a fire engine siren sounds like. Thus far, your lesson has been planned. Your discussion of fire engine sirens may lead to a general discussion of other warning systems, e.g., other sirens, chimes, bells, buzzers, and so forth. The discussion of other warning systems was not planned, but your students are able to relate or generalize from past experience. Your students may even identify additional warning systems as they walk home from school that afternoon. When children "pick up" information without formal instruction, incidental learning has occurred.

For hearing impaired children, a major source of incidental learning is curtailed seriously. Knowledge gained by a child with normal hearing through common, everyday auditory activities is often unavailable to a hearing impaired child. A hearing impaired child walking home from school may not experience the sound of a passing siren; thus, this chance for reinforcement of school information is not available to the hearing impaired child. Similarly, much incidental learning occurs from watching television, listening to a radio, and participating in everyday conversation. Hearing impaired children may not be able to participate fully in these activities.

As a classroom teacher, you can provide opportunities for incidental learning. Materials you have around the room can informally teach children new concepts or reinforce concepts presented formally. Materials suitable for a hearing impaired child can be used with all your students. Care must be taken that the materials are visual or audiovisual in nature. Special captioned films and television programs can usually be obtained through your school district. The major problem, if a problem exists, will be providing time for hearing impaired children and other children to use the materials.

*Establish opportunities for regular feedback.* Feedback lets children know whether their behavior matches expected behavior, enabling them to measure their performance against a chosen standard. A child with normal hearing has many opportunities for auditory feedback. These opportunities, much like opportunities for incidental learning, are part of the normal everyday environment. A student may overhear a classroom conversation about an assignment or may hear the teacher explain a task to another student. A hearing impaired child may be unable to use this kind of feedback. As a classroom teacher, you must be sure to provide systematic and regular feedback to the hearing impaired child. You cannot depend on environmental feedback.

When providing feedback to hearing impaired children, you must be more thorough than when providing feedback to students who hear normally. A smiling face on a paper may not be enough to let a child know what aspect of the performance was appropriate. You may need to be more specific. William's teacher usually takes a few minutes to write out feedback; feedback for William might include a smiling face accompanied by phrases like "Your penmanship was very neat" or "You solved these math problems just right." By writing out phrases, the teacher not only informs William that he has done good work, but also helps him understand what the good work was about. William may or may not be imitating the work of others around him, but at least he is aware of the purpose of the activity.

When chosen carefully, self-instructional materials provide an opportunity for immediate feedback. When using these self-instructional materials, you must make sure the hearing impaired child understands the vocabulary and concepts presented in the programmed self-instructional materials. A tendency to fill in the blank without really grasping the concepts is always a danger in programmed texts. This danger exists for children with normal hearing as well as for children with hearing impairments.

*Immediate* and *frequent* are two key terms to keep in mind when providing feedback to a hearing impaired child. The newer the concept, the more critical your immediate feedback becomes. When a hearing impaired child is struggling to acquire new knowledge, frequent feedback is necessary. As the child practices or rehearses prior learning, the need for immediate and frequent feedback is reduced.

## Social Adjustment

**Informed classmates**—To help a hearing impaired child become integrated socially into your regular class, you and your other students should be well informed about implications of a hearing loss. Jack wanted to be treated just like everyone else, so he kept his hearing problem a secret. He used his ability to read speech to understand others. Soon he was accused of being a snob. When other kids in the room talked to Jack, they didn't understand that he needed to see their lips in order for him to understand that he was being addressed. When he didn't respond to a normal hallway greeting or a passing remark, the other kids thought he was ignoring them. A vicious cycle developed. The other kids began to ignore Jack, and Jack became upset and withdrawn. Finally, Jack actually did begin to ignore the others.

A somewhat belated but quick classroom solution was instituted. Jack's teacher initiated a science program over the five senses, beginning with a unit on hearing. Through the course of this unit, Jack related some of his personal needs and explained that he was a speech reader. A classroom discussion ensued; feelings were aired and misunderstandings corrected. Children in Jack's class are now more sensitive to his hearing needs. Jack learned that he need not hide his condition and that people are much more accepting than he had thought previously.

**Age-appropriate behavior**—One adjective frequently attached to hearing impaired children is *immature.* Many hearing impaired children function at a developmentally younger stage than their normal hearing peers. Some of this behavior may be attributed to a reduced sensitivity to subtle social nuances. Tone of voice conveys much social information; a phrase like "the teacher is gone" can elicit fear or excitement depending on tonal quality. Frequently hearing impaired children are unable to discriminate tonal differences. Although tonal differences are usually accompanied by body language, which would seem to compensate for an inability to hear, hearing impaired children take longer than other children to learn to read body language because a critical cue in reading body language comes from hearing an accompanying vocal tone.

As a classroom teacher, you can help hearing impaired children act in ways appropriate for their age. You can work within the context of your classroom, just as you would for any immature child. For a hearing impaired child who is immature, use your standard teaching techniques, but be sure to accommodate hearing needs.

**Other social skills**—Other personal or social competencies that have been identified as of greatest concern for hearing impaired children are:

- Accepting responsibility for one's own actions
- Being aware of one's own value, strengths, weaknesses, and goals
- Making sound decisions
- Developing self-confidence
- Demonstrating initiative (Ayrault, 1977).

Social goals for a hearing impaired child are the same as goals for normal children and other exceptional children. As a classroom teacher, you already possess the skills to help children reach these social goals. If a lack of knowledge about the hearing impairment causes you to be uncertain about your teaching methods, discuss the problem with the teacher of the hearing impaired. You will provide each other with a good sounding board; this communication will certainly be beneficial for the child.

## Self-Care

**Classroom rules**—By the time a hearing impaired child enters the public school system, self-care skills in mobility, eating, and toileting are usually well developed. Generally, the most severe problem in self-care of hearing impaired children is an unclear or vague understanding or classroom or school rules.

When 6-year-old Lee Ann first entered a regular classroom, all seemed well; she appeared to be happy, adjusted, and enthusiastic about her new school environment. However, about 2 weeks later, after she was mainstreamed, a terrible event occurred. Lee Ann had an "accident"; she wet her pants. The child hid her accident from everyone. Five days later another one took place. This time it wasn't easy to conceal. Lee Ann's teacher helped downplay the incident, and life continued. Unfortunately, so did the accidents. Lee Ann's teacher became concerned, but rather than panic, she decided to see what she could do for Lee Ann. With gentle questioning, the teacher discovered Lee Ann didn't know how to ask to be excused. Lee Ann's teacher had explained the rules to her the first day of school, but in all the excitement, Lee Ann had simply forgotten. Because of her hearing impairment, she couldn't hear the other children ask to be excused, so she had no way of knowing what to do. What could have been thought to be some severe psychological problem was simply a small but significant communication problem.

As a classroom teacher, you can help your hearing impaired students avoid embarrassing situations by making sure you never leave knowledge of rules to chance. If a child can read, give the child the self-help rules in writing. For any hearing impaired child, consciously note the child's behavior at least three times after the rule or direction is first given.

**Eating**—Eating is a consistent daily occurrence, but lunchroom rules vary considerably. Hector's teacher made a list of nine steps for lunchroom behavior.

Step 1. Stand in line.

Step 2. Give your ticket to the cashier.

Step 3. Pick up a tray.

Step 4. Get your silverware.

Step 5. Go through the lunch line.

Step 6. Sit with your class.

Step 7. Wait at the table until your class is dismissed.

Step 8. Discard your trash.

Step 9. Play on the playground.

Hector's teacher watched him at lunch for three days in a row. On day 1, some confusion occurred on steps 5, 7, and 8. On day 2, there was a minor problem with step 8. Hector's teacher explained step 8 again. On day 3, Hector's behavior at lunch was free of problems and worthy of use as a model. From then on, Hector had no problems at lunch time. Thanks to the thoroughness of his classroom teacher, Hector was integrated successfully into the lunchroom scene.

## Communication

If you could choose only one area for helping a hearing impaired child integrate successfully into a regular classroom, communication should be your choice. Communication forms the basis for all classroom activities. A great deal of our communication is transmitted through speech and language, but for a hearing impaired child, avenues of speech and language are restricted. To receive and understand the communication of others, or senders, a hearing impaired child must use a less-than-perfect hearing, or receiving, system. To send a communication, a sender must have a set of speech sounds that can be understood by the receiver. Most people learn speech sounds through modeling and practicing the sounds emitted by others. A hearing impaired child is again at a disadvantage because he or she has less exposure to speech sounds in the environment than does a child who hears normally. Because modeling and practice are limited, hearing impaired children often have problems in speech and language. Thus, hearing impaired children often bear a double communication problem, being limited in both ability to receive and ability to send information.

**Expressive language**—Expressive language problems of hearing impaired children are most noticeable in speech production. A hearing impaired child may distort sounds, as in the phrase "wed wabbit" for "red rabbit." Some of the sound distortions are acceptable (and are even normal for certain parts of the country), and don't really interfere with communication. You can probably relax about sound distortions unless the distortions cause embarrassment to the child or interfere with classroom communication. In cases where distortions are cause for concern, work with a speech clinician. You will probably not design your own program for remediating a child's speech problems, but you may be able to reinforce the speech clinician's program. The speech clinician may be able to provide you with the child's personal speech code; e.g., "Mac substitutes *l*'s for *r*'s and leaves off *-ed* endings."

Expressive communication problems may also affect a hearing impaired child's ability to participate in group discussions. For some children, producing speech is a slow and laborious process. Not only can the speech activity be emotionally draining for the hearing impaired child, but the activity can also be draining for persons who are receiving the message. Care must be taken not to finish or anticipate the finish of a hearing impaired child's word or phrase. Care must also be taken not to rush the child to complete the communication; rushing the child will lead to more frustration. A critical point to remember is that a child with a hearing impairment may become extremely isolated if not given chances to participate actively in social groups (Gonzales, 1980).

As a regular classroom teacher you will need to deal with your own feelings and encourage empathy in your other students. At times, hearing impaired children with speech problems are treated cruelly simply because ignoring difficult or slowly produced speech is much easier than allowing for breaks in the conversation or irregularly paced conversation.

A hearing impaired child with communication problems may also have difficulty producing appropriate words. Because of limited interactions involving language, vocabularies of some hearing impaired children are not as great as vocabularies of their peers who hear normally. Restricted ability to hear language may also affect the order in which words are put together. Problems in expressive word order, or syntax, need not be a major cause for concern. As in problems with speech sounds, if a syntax disorder does not interfere significantly with communication, you may opt to reinforce the language clinician's program rather than develop one yourself.

**Receptive language**—Problems in receptive language, or problems in the ability to receive information through sounds, often beset the hearing impaired child. Because the child may not always clearly hear all the sounds, communication may be strained. What the child hears (aside from disorder) depends in part upon the child's position in relation to the sound source. When Carrie Ann sits away from her teacher, she just sits. She's not being obstinate; she just doesn't know what is going on. Resolving Carrie Ann's problem is simple—seat her close to the teacher.

Some hearing impaired children face a more formidable challenge. For some children, hearing is intermittent. On one day Matthew can sit close to his teacher and follow communication very well. On the next day, Matthew can have the identical physical relationship to his teacher's voice and not understand a word said.

Conferring with the hearing teacher may give you insight concerning receptive skills of a hearing impaired child. However, hearing ability may change frequently. Don't assume that a written report on a child reflects anything more than the child's ability on the date of the report.

As a trained teacher, you can easily determine if a child is not completing assignments, is not correctly following oral directions, or is not attending to you as you speak. If you bring the child closer to you and any of these problems continues, consistently or intermittently, then you may need to alter your communication format.

All oral information can be paired with visual information. If a child can read, you're home free. Putting information on paper is simple and effective. If the child cannot read, substitute symbols for words or model instructions directly.

To ensure that a hearing impaired child is receiving information, be sure to repeat, paraphrase, or both. Sometimes a hearing impaired child may not have a visual or experiential referent for a particular word or phrase. By altering wording slightly, you may present more complete information that is better understood. Your body language and the pace at which you deliver information are also factors to consider when delivering instructional content.

A hearing impaired child may require a little more time to process auditory information than a child with normal hearing. Patience on your part will produce the best results. Slowness in processing does not necessarily mean slowness in intellectual functioning. For some hearing impaired children, sorting out distorted sounds is difficult, especially when the child is trying to learn or recall a new concept. As a classroom teacher, you can reduce receptive language problems by controlling the length and complexity of your oral delivery or instructions. By using short, succinct instructions, you reduce both the memory load and the number of distortions experienced.

# SUMMARY

Physical and sensory impairments experienced by children impact on classroom instruction. Compensation must be made for limited or restricted sensory input. While instructional content or curriculum may be the same for the physically and sensory impaired children and normal children, media, style of presentation, and format are adjusted to fit individual needs. In making these adjustments for an individual child, classroom teachers are often assisted by specialists appropriate to the child's special needs.

# 5

## Did You Say IEP?

Feeling somewhat like a small child caught snitching cookies from the cookie jar, Ms. Smith waits nervously in the school conference room. She had referred Doré for special services, and now she must face her peers and Doré's parents. Had she done the right thing? Were Doré's problems really so severe that she needed special help? Ms. Smith almost regretted sending Doré's name to the principal. If she had just kept quiet she wouldn't be sitting here now. Instead she could be getting ready for her students in the safety of her own classroom. This was the first time Ms. Smith had referred a child, the first time she had determined that the child could be served better with more help than she alone could give. Now her judgment would be held up for scrutiny by the school psychologist, the special education teacher, the principal, and Doré's parents. What if she had made a terrible mistake and Doré really belonged in her class after all? Would Doré be misplaced because of a classroom teacher's error in judgment? What exactly was this meeting anyway? What was her role as a classroom teacher? As Dr. Gadzia, the school principal, came into the conference room, Ms. Smith looked up and tentatively asked, "Did you say IEP?"

## AN EDUCATIONAL REVOLUTION

Regular classroom teachers are experiencing a role change unlike any change they have seen before. Social and political forces are operating to produce a revolution in the way we think about the duties and responsibilities of regular classroom personnel. At issue is the basic question of human dignity. In more specific terms, the focus of the revolution is the right of handicapped children to receive an education as close as possible to education in a normal classroom.

### NORMALIZATION FOR HANDICAPPED CHILDREN

The cornerstone of this normalization process is the Individualized Education Plan (IEP). An IEP is a written plan that describes the educational program most appropriate for a handicapped child, whether the child is in a regular classroom for all, some, or none of the day.

The format of an IEP can vary from state to state and from district to district. The content of an IEP is, however, constant and must include a:

1. Description of the child's present level of educational performance;
2. Description of educational goals and the short-term instructional objectives related to each goal;
3. Statement of (a) the specific special education and related services to be provided to the child and (b) the extent to which the child will be able to participate in a regular eduational program;
4. Projected initiation date and an estimate of the anticipated duration of special education services;
5. Service evaluation plan including a description of appropriate objective criteria, evaluation procedures, and a schedule for determining the child's attainment of short-term instructional objectives annually.

## IEP TEAMS

Given an evaluation of a child's performance, a team develops, reviews, and revises an IEP. Members of an IEP team include a representative of the school district, the child's teacher, one or both parents, and a person who is knowledgeable about the evaluation procedures used and how to interpret the results of the evaluation. This person is usually a school psychologist or special education teacher. When feasible, the student is also included in the team.

The concept of team planning is not new, but including the regular classroom teacher in the educational programming of a handicapped child borders on radicalism. Although your level of team involvement varies, you must be involved. When serving as part of an IEP team, your observations carry the same weight and responsibility as the observations made by any other team member. If you are referring a child from your room to special services, you will have valuable insight into the child's day-to-day performance. If an IEP in which you have not been involved prescribes the return of a child to your classroom, you should participate in the review and *revision* of the child's IEP (Smith, 1978). No one is more knowledgeable than you about the performance requirements of your classroom.

Initially, being a member of an IEP team may be intimidating. The psychologist and the special education teacher may use terms that were not included in your academic preparation for teaching. Since no one likes to appear uninformed, discretion may seem to be the better part of valor. You may not ask questions that you need to have answered. Sometimes the psychologist or special educator will be unable to answer your questions. Communication problems may reflect gaps in your background. However, in truth these communication problems are more likely a reflection of the psychologist's or special educator's inexperience in translating terms for people who do not share their educational and experiential background. In any event, whenever a concept, term, or decision is unclear, ask for an explanation! Much more than your pride is on the line. As a member of an IEP team, you are making plans that affect the educational program and life of a handicapped child. Silence may be interpreted as tacit approval rather than a reluctance to question and discuss.

Advance preparation is one of the most effective techniques for avoiding the "sounds of silence" in an IEP preconference, staffing, or review. Being prepared implies that you have examined the child's file, can discuss the file's contents, and have prepared a short list of topics related to the child for discussion. Your list is essentially a set of notes or ideas that will help you to make a more informed contribution to the IEP. For example, if a child is referred from your room for special services in math, your notes might include one or two phrases describing modifications you have instituted, daily performance patterns, and what responsibilities, if any, you and the special teacher can share in teaching math to this student.

## COMPONENTS OF IEPS

Being prepared also means you have a thorough understanding of each component of the IEP. This chapter describes an IEP and examines what you, the regular classroom teacher, may need to know about each IEP component.

### PRESENT EDUCATIONAL PERFORMANCE LEVEL

A description of the "present educational level" of a child is simply a description of the child's current behavioral or academic performance. A child's present educational performance can be examined in two ways. First, norm-referenced tests may be used to compare a child's performance to performance of other children the same age or grade level. Second, criterion-referenced tests may be used to compare a child's performance to specified objectives. Both kinds of testing provide useful information if the skill tested has relevance to the classroom performance in question. However, if the skill tested is not relevant to the classroom performance in question, test results may have little value.

For example, suppose that one of your students has problems with math and also has cerebral palsy, complicated by defective speech. Results of various tests have been included in the child's file, including results of the *Templin-Darley Tests of Articulation* (Templin & Darley, 1960). The *Templin-Darley* tests are used to compare a child's production of speech sounds and general speech intelligibility with those of other children. *Templin-Darley* test results are useful to a speech therapist in designing and implementing a corrective speech program. Results of these tests may be indirectly useful to you by confirming what you already know: "The student doesn't talk too well." However, the test will not assist you in working with the child in math. Articulation tests do not measure math skills.

## Norm-Referenced Tests

As stated earlier, norm-referenced tests are used to compare performance of an individual with the performance of other individuals of similar age and background. Two types of norm-referenced tests are commonly used to describe a child's present level of functioning. One type measures academic achievement and the second type measures intelligence.

Results of both types of tests are usually indicated on an IEP as scores. These scores are designed to help you interpret standardized test scores found on IEP forms. Before moving on to the second component of the IEP—Annual Goals and Restated Short-Term Objectives—information that will tell you about the child's present level of intellectual and academic performance will be presented.

**Achievement tests**—Achievement tests provide you with "standard scores." A standard score is one in which the raw score, the actual number of items a student answered correctly, is transformed so that the set of scores always has the same mean and the same standard deviation. Two commonly reported standard scores are grade equivalents and percentiles.

Grade equivalents are always stated in years and months. Thus, a grade equivalency of 2.3 is read as "second grade, third month," and a grade equivalency of 7.9 is read as "seventh grade, ninth month." Grade equivalents are easy to interpret and comfortable to use because they are so straightforward.

Of course, just being straightforward doesn't make results useful for specific instructional programming. Identical grade equivalents of 4.5 for two children may actually represent differences in specific knowledge. Tests that are scored by simply counting the number of questions a child answers correctly can give two children identical scores when the children have correctly answered totally different questions. Consider the following. Gary and Bonnie have each scored 1.7 on the spelling section of a norm-referenced test. Gary has correctly spelled the words *dog, run, sheep,* and *salad,* but has misspelled all the words Bonnie spelled correctly. Bonnie has correctly spelled the words *noise, go, yellow,* and *pineapple,* but she has misspelled all the words Gary spelled correctly. Because both Bonnie and Gary have spelled four words correctly they received identical grade equivalency scores even though they haven't spelled any of the same words correctly.

The spelling test taken by Bonnie and Gary in this example is a screening test that has provided some general information about the spelling skills of the two students. As a classroom teacher, you know that the advantage of a survey or screening test is that it can tell you, within 10 or 15 minutes, who is going to need help in what. The more quickly general problem areas are identified, the more quickly performance on specific areas within a subject can be evaluated. Before administering the spelling test to Bonnie and Gary, you knew nothing specific about their level of spelling performance. If these two children are fifth graders, their test scores suggest they both need special instruction in spelling.

Percentile scores are another commonly reported standard score. Percentiles are based on a scale ranging from 0 to 100. A student's percentile score indicates the percentage of students who had scores equal to or lower than that student. Thus, if Nancy had a raw score of 72 and a percentile score of 55, this would mean 55% of the students who took the same test had scores of 72 or lower. However, the students who took the same test Nancy took are not the students in her class. Rather, the group of students against which Nancy is compared is the standardization group or normative group. Children in this standardization group should be of the same socioeconomic background, culture, age, and sex as Nancy. If the aim of a test is to compare Nancy's performance with performance of other children, it makes sense to compare her score with scores of a normative group of children who have experiential backgrounds similar to hers.

Both grade equivalency scores and percentile scores are obtained by comparing performance of an individual with performance of a normative group on the same test. In fact, all tests that provide a comparison between a score earned by an individual and scores of a normative group are called norm-referenced or normative tests.

**General characteristics**—Normative tests are used to compare a student's score to the distribution of scores earned by a child in a norm group. The norm group is supposed to represent all children of a given age and back-

**Figure 5.1**
Normal Curve

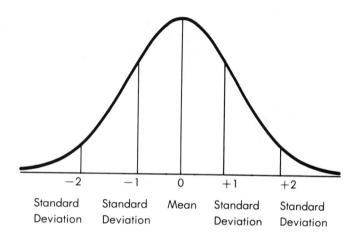

| −2 | −1 | 0 | +1 | +2 |
|---|---|---|---|---|
| Standard Deviation | Standard Deviation | Mean | Standard Deviation | Standard Deviation |

ground, hence the term *norm* or *normal*. For all norm-referenced tests, the distribution of scores obtained by the norm group is assumed to be a bell-shaped normal curve, as shown in Figure 5.1. This curve represents the frequency with which each possible score was earned by the children in the norm group. In constructing a norm-referenced test, test questions are given to a sample of children representing the norm group. Based on scores of children in the sample, test items are manipulated to create a test such that the frequency of scores obtained matches the normal distribution, i.e., so that a certain percentage of children score within prescribed intervals.

A basic understanding of means and standard deviations is necessary to understand the meaning of norm-referenced test scores. In Figure 5.1, the mean and standard deviation of the normal curve have been labeled. The 0 represents the mean score (the arithmetic average of all the scores), and the mean is obtained by adding all the scores obtained by people in the norm group and then dividing this sum by the number of people in the norm group. A score other than the mean score represents variability. Some people in the norm group earn scores that are higher than the mean and other people earn scores that are lower than the mean. The difference between individual scores and the mean is calculated and is called the *standard deviation*. Thus, the standard deviation is a measure of the variability of scores.

If a score does not differ from the mean, the score is 0 distance from the mean. Thus, if Jimmy's score is 50 and 50 is the mean score for the norm group, then Jimmy's score is 0 distance from the mean. Usually, when the mean and standard deviation for a test have been calculated, three reference points are considered on each side of the mean. There are reference points at +1 and −1 standard deviations, at +2 and −2 standard deviations, and at +3 and −3 standard deviations. Since the zero or mean score is at the middle of the normal curve and the curve is symmetrical, the distance (or number of points if you are looking at a test) between 0 and +1 standard deviation is the same as the difference between 0 and −1 standard deviation. However, the score earned is different.

Returning to Jimmy, recall that he received a score of 50, which is 0 distance from the mean. If the value of the standard deviation is 15 points and Jimmy's friend, George, obtained a score that was one standard deviation above the mean, then George would have a score of the mean (50) plus one standard deviation (15). As shown in Figure 5.2, George's score would be 65. Mary Lou, whose score was one standard deviation below the mean, would have a score of 50 minus 15, which is 35.

In constructing a norm-referenced test so that the distribution of scores can be represented by a normal curve, a test constructor manipulates items to

**Figure 5.2**
Scores of Children Representing −1 Standard Deviation, the Mean, and +1 Standard Deviation on a Normal Distribution Curve

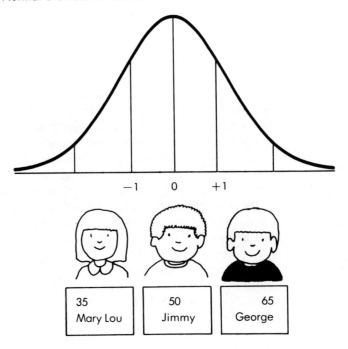

create a test on which 68% of the normative group earn scores in the interval between +1 and −1 standard deviations from the mean. That is, about 34% of the normative group earn scores between 0 and +1. Thus, the majority (68%) of the scores of the normative group are between −1 and +1 standard deviation. Moving away from the mean, about 14% of the scores earned by the normative group must fall between −2 and −1 standard deviations. Finally, only about 2% of the people in the normative group score between −3 and −2 standard deviations, and about 2% score between +2 and +3 standard deviations. The relationship of percentages and standard deviations is shown in Figure 5.3.

Besides determining where a student's test score falls under the normal curve, you must also consider test error. Tests and their respective scores always have some margin of error. This margin of error is called *test error, standard error,* or *error of measurement.* You can compute the standard error for a test using a statistical formula. For most published tests, however, the standard error of measurement has been calculated for you by the test constructor and is reported in the test manual.

Basically, the standard error of measurement accounts for chance variations in a student's earned score. Sometimes conditions like fatigue, improper lighting, or classroom distractions contribute to the variability of a test score. Thus, a student may receive a score slightly higher or slightly lower than the "true" score due to circumstances unrelated to the test. Although it is impossible to know precisely what the student's true score would be if chance variations were eliminated, a test constructor can use statistical analysis to calculate an interval within which the true score is likely to fall. For example, if

**Figure 5.3**
Relationship between Percentages and Standard Deviations as Seen in a
Normal Distribution

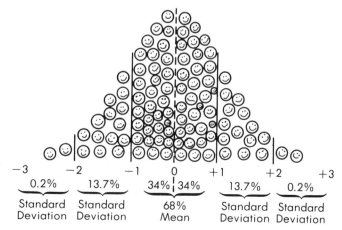

| −3 | −2 | −1 | 0 | +1 | +2 | +3 |
|----|----|----|----|----|----|----|
| | 0.2% | 13.7% | 34% | 34% | 13.7% | 0.2% |
| | Standard Deviation | Standard Deviation | 68% Mean | | Standard Deviation | Standard Deviation |

the standard error of measurement for a particular test has been calculated to be 6 and a student earns a score of 85, the true score (if chance variation did not exist) is likely to fall in the interval from 79 to 91. This range was determined by subtracting 6 from 85 (85 − 6 = 79) and adding 6 to 85 (85 + 6 = 91). You can be more confident in predicting that the student's true score falls within this interval than in predicting that the true score is exactly 85. Every normative test has a calculated standard error of measurement. The error of measurement is different for each test. For some tests, the error may be as small as ± .01; for other tests, the error may be as great as ± 30. In general, the smaller the error, the more confidence you can place in the test score.

Now that you have been fortified with information about the normal distribution and about percentile scores, compare the percentile equivalent scale with the standard deviation scale of the normal distribution. As can be seen in Figure 5.4, a percentile equivalent anywhere between 15 and 85 is within the range of scores which fall between one standard deviation below the mean and one standard deviation above the mean; that is, percentile equivalents of 16 to 84 represent a range including scores of 68% of a given standardization or norm group. Anyone whose percentile rank is 15 or lower or 85 or higher is not so typical. These atypical students must be watched carefully in case program modification is necessary.

Although the distribution of scores must follow a normal curve for all normative tests, the scale used to represent scores is arbitrary. For example, not all normative tests are based on a scale of 0 to 100 like the percentile equivalents. Some scales, like the College Entrance Examination Board scores, are based on a scale of 200 to 800. Others, like stanines, are scaled from 1 to 9; still others, like the WISC-R (an intelligence test) (Weschler, 1974), are scaled from 0 to 180. A test constructor may use any scale as long as the conventions prescribed by a normal distribution are followed.

## Intelligence Measures

Perhaps the most confusing of all norm-referenced tests is the intelligence test. As in any normed test, scores on an intelligence test represent the amount of information of a particular kind that a child has relative to other children of similar age, grade, sex, socioeconomic level, and cultural heritage. The score is a numerical score that often measures many of the tasks which a child must perform on a general achievement test (Smith & Neisworth, 1975).

**Group-administered tests**—Intelligence tests are designed for either group administration or for individual administration. Intelligence tests that are group administered are most often given by a classroom teacher. Group intel-

**Figure 5.4**

Comparison between Percentile Equivalents and the Normal Curve

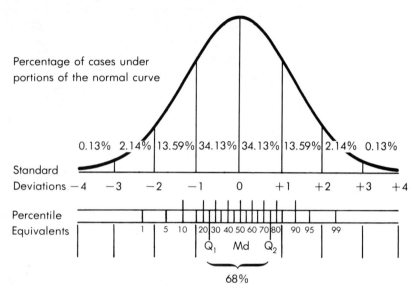

Reproduced from "Test Service Bulletin," THE PSYCHOLOGICAL CORPORATION, No. 43, January, 1955.

ligence tests have been developed to provide a quick estimate of scores for a large number of children. Often, group intelligence tests consist of a series of multiple-choice questions divided into timed subsets.

Most group intelligence tests intended for use with children in the fourth grade and up require reading ability. Poor readers often demonstrate relatively low scores on these tests, and it is difficult to determine whether a low score reflects poor reading skills, lack of familiarity with the concepts tested, or both. Thus, scores on group intelligence tests can be misleading for children who are poor readers. A typical group intelligence test with high reading demands is the *Otis Quick-Scoring Mental Ability Tests*, New Edition (Otis & Lennon, 1979).

Results of a group intelligence test must be interpreted carefully. These group tests have been designed as *screening instruments*. Group intelligence tests are thought to be useful in identifying children who are at the extreme ends of a normal distribution of intelligence. Generally, children are considered average if their scores fall within the range of scores of 68% of the normative population, i.e., within the interval from one standard deviation below the mean to one standard deviation above the mean. Children whose scores fall outside this interval may need to be referred for more specific intelligence testing.

No definitive statement can be made about a person's performance on the basis of group IQ scores. If the standard error of measurement is large for a group measure, a student's score can vary considerably. For example, if Josh earns an IQ score of 100 on a test with a standard error of 15, his true IQ might be as low as 85 or as high as 115.

Results of group intelligence tests sometimes fail to identify children who need special services. Conversely, sometimes the results of group IQ tests identify children as needing special services when they really don't need them at all. In reality, you are a much better "screener" than is the group intelligence test. You must consider your knowledge about the child's daily class performance as well as test scores when deciding whether to refer the child for evaluation.

**Individually administered tests**—When it appears that additional evaluation is necessary for determining the most appropriate educational setting for a child, the additional evaluation will probably include an intelligence test administered individually. Generally, classroom teachers are not trained to administer and interpret individual intelligence tests. Rather, individual tests are usually administered by a person certified as a psychometrician or psychologist who is often a school psychologist or special education teacher.

The two most commonly administered individual intelligence tests are the *Wechsler Intelligence Test for Children–Revised* (WISC–R) (Wechsler, 1974) and the *Stanford-Binet Intelligence Scale* (Terman & Merrill, 1973). Each test is administered individually in a setting that is relatively free of distractions. Administration time varies from about 45 to 90 minutes, depending on the skills of the examiner and the skills of the child. Both the WISC–R and the Stanford-Binet require verbal responses. However, the WISC–R includes both a verbal section and a performance section. In the performance section, a child is required to do some manipulation tasks, such as putting puzzles together. Administration of the Stanford-Binet results in one general IQ score. Administration of the WISC–R results in three IQ scores: (a) a verbal IQ score, (b) a performance IQ score, and (c) a total IQ score representing both verbal and performance scores. Each WISC–R subtest is scored individually and may reflect different skill levels within a child's repertoire.

Discussion of results of IQ tests and individual subtests brings us back to utility of test results in the classroom. As a classroom teacher, your teaching is modified directly by a child's performance in class; IQ scores probably make little difference in how you teach. If Sally Ann is having problems adding 2 + 2, you are likely to find results of tests directly assessing her math performance more useful than tests that provide you with a IQ score of 100, 85, or 115. Depending on the intelligence test administered, the skill of the examiner, and Sally Ann's experiential background, she may exhibit any one of these IQ scores—but no matter what her IQ score, she will still need to learn how to add 2 + 2. Information concerning how to teach her this math skill will more likely be found in a math methods text than in a manual for an intelligence test.

For teaching, an IQ measure is functionally useless. However, for placement in special program, results of intelligence tests have been relied on heavily. Traditionally, a normal IQ, as measured by an individual intelligence test, was likely to influence a placement decision toward a regular class setting, an LD setting, or an EH setting. An IQ two standard deviations below the mean was likely to influence placement decisions toward an EMH setting. Finally, a child with a IQ two standard deviations above the mean was likely to be placed in a program for gifted students.

With the increasing movement toward normalization, reliance on intelligence tests for placement is diminishing. Children who have been labeled but can profit from experience in a regular classroom will be educated in a regular classroom without regard to IQ. Emphasis will be placed on direct educational programming, which begins after specific skills deficiencies of a child have been identified.

**Specialized normative tests**—Normative or group-referenced tests have been developed for special populations. One example of a specialized normative test is the *Arthur Adaptation of Leiter International Performance Scale* (AALIPS) (Arthur, 1950). This test was designed to assess the intelligence of children who have problems taking verbal tests, e.g., deaf, hard of hearing, or speech-impaired children. A second example of a specialized normative test is the *Blind Learning Aptitude Test* (BLAT) (Newland, 1969). The BLAT was designed to evaluate the learning aptitudes of blind children.

The primary reason for developing tests for special populations is to ensure fairness in testing. If a child can't see, to ask the child to respond to questions presented in a traditional print format would be absurd. Another major consideration in developing specialized normative tests is the standardization population. Jane, a deaf child, has had a different acculturation or set of life experiences than Jim, who hears normally. Comparing children with such vastly different life experiences defeats the purpose of group comparison.

Many special tests have been developed to assess intelligence of handicapped children. For a classroom teacher, results of a specially adapted IQ test serve the same purpose as results of a traditional IQ measure. That is, IQ measures do not provide much information that is directly useful in teaching, whether the IQ measures are modified or not.

Other types of normative tests that may appear in the files of special children may focus on development or sensory or motor deficit areas. The *Carrow Elicited Language Inventory* (CELI) is a test designed to provide information about a child's competence in expressive grammar (Carrow, 1974). The *Snellen Wall Chart* or the *Snellen E Test* is commonly used to screen problems in visual acuity. For a child with middle ear disorders, you may find results of an audiogram in the file.

Information from tests that describe developmental or physical and sensory deficits can often be used to help develop classroom objectives. While the tests are normative, classroom provisons for individual children can be influenced by test results. If Kurt has an audiogram in his file, as a classroom teacher you have a responsibility to find out what the results of the audiogram mean to your instructional program. The subsequent development of services demands that you have a clear understanding of the child's sensory skills.

Translating results of tests of sensory acuity into meaningful classroom information is fairly straightforward. Based on results of Lou Ann's *Snellen* you may suggest that she sit in the front of the classroom. Similarly, Joe's audiogram may make it clear that classroom noise must be kept at a minimum. Interpreting test scores based on the five senses is clean, quick, and direct.

Assessment of perceptual-motor performance is not quite so clear, quick, or direct. Typically, constructors of normative tests of perceptual-motor performance have attempted to combine one or more sensory areas with some kind of intangible construct. For example, in the *Developmental Test of Visual Perception* (DTVP) (Frostig, Lefever, & Whittlesey, 1966), the sensory area is vision and the construct is perception. Tests of perceptual-motor performance abound in the files of special education children, especially the files of children considered for classification as learning disabled. These tests usually have terms in their titles like "psycholinguistic abilities," "visual motor gestalt," "developmental visual perception," and "memory for designs." While perceptual-motor skills may (or may not) exist, our inability to measure them is clearly evident. While most intelligence and achievement tests are technically adequate, research has shown that tests used to assess perceptual-motor skills are technically inadequate and do not measure anything consistently (Salvia & Ysseldyke, 1978). Furthermore, claims that these tests have a direct relationship to reading, math, and language arts are unsubstantiated. Educational planning based solely or in part on tests of perceptual-motor skills is highly suspect at best and immoral at worst. As a regular classroom teacher, you must be sure that information from appropriate tests is stressed, while information from inappropriate tests is downplayed. When evaluating academic or behavioral performance of a student, the most appropriate tests are those which measure academic or behavioral skills directly. You can be on firm ground by insisting that information from such direct measures is emphasized in the staffing.

## Criterion-Referenced Testing

Criterion-referenced tests are commonly used to identify specific instructional needs. Strictly speaking, criterion-referenced testing involves analyzing a test, item by item, and describing a student's results in terms of some expected level of performance (Gronlund, 1973). A criterion-referenced test (CRT) shows how well a student has learned a skill or concept.

**Interpretation**—Suppose you have three students in your class, Larry, Wendy, and Maggie, and you want to see whether they can do basic arithmetic problems. You set your criterion at 100%, i.e., an answer to a problem is either correct or it is not, with no partial credit granted. More importantly, you arrange the test problems sequentially so that the problems start at the lowest or simplest level of basic addition like 2 + 2 and extend to a complex level like 37,890 + 20,359. Each child is given the same sequentially arranged test. Scores earned by Larry, Wendy, and Maggie will reflect the degree of learning each has in basic arithmetic. Also, analysis of the errors will enable you to identify a clearly defined area that is related directly to instructional objectives.

Suppose analysis of Larry's performance shows that the only concept he has mastered is the addition of two single-digit numbers. Wendy, on the other hand, has mastered all the basic concepts of addition. Maggie's performance is erratic. Each student's performance is analyzed relative to the problems on the test; no regard is given to a student's performance relative to performance of another student. Testing that is criterion-referenced is designed to guide instruction as directly as possible.

Scores on criterion-referenced tests are based on a scale of 0 to 100% correct; expected criteria can be described in terms of the percentage of test items a child must answer correctly. The prescribed level of acceptable performance is arbitrary and is determined by the chooser's values. However, criterion levels for acceptable performance vary with the content being evaluated. By their nature, fundamental skills like letter sounds or sight words demand a higher level of proficiency than do content or supplemental areas of instruction, e.g., use of alliteration and metaphors.

**Relationship to classroom objectives**—In criterion measures, each test item can be reworded as a specific behavioral objective. The criterion test that will provide you with the most useful evaluation information is a test that measures the material in your curriculum. Ideally, this test will also test skills in the sequence that you teach them and in the format of your classroom materials.

Results from a criterion-referenced test can provide information concerning where a child can succeed in your particular sequence of skills and whether a child can use your materials and format. If a child can succeed at step 16 of a 225-step sequence of skills, as the classroom teacher you must decide if and how you can accommodate that child in your room. If the child with the next lowest skills in your room is on step 75 of the 225-step sequence, you may need special assistance before you are able to work with the first child.

### Use in Developing the IEP

Results of an evaluation of the present level of a child's performance should be presented in an IEP staffing. This information can help you and the rest of the team decide what content will be taught, who will teach which content, and when or in what setting the content will be delivered. Information gathered from normative tests will help you screen the child. Criterion-referenced tests will help you plan a specific program. Information from both normative and criterion-referenced measures is instrumental in determining exit from or entrance into the regular classroom.

## ANNUAL GOALS AND RELATED SHORT-TERM OBJECTIVES

### Relationship to Evaluation

Data from the evaluation of a child's present level of performance will help you set long-term goals and objectives. Goals refer to general areas and are usually written for the course of a year's instruction. Goals may be written for social as well as academic behaviors. An example of a goal in reading is: "By May, Josie will be able to recognize 85% of the sight words that have been taught to her through the use of her language experience stories."

Information provided from each evaluation measure should be related directly to the goals and objectives chosen for a student. You and the team should not simply abandon test information because you can't decide how to meet the needs identified by the test any more than you should develop goals and objectives that are not based on evaluative data. For example, if you feel that spelling is an important curricular area, you must be able to provide information on the student's current level of functioning in spelling before you write a spelling goal.

**Establishing priorities**—Of course, establishing priorities is important. The team must decide which goals and objectives to stress first. Determining priorities involves a decision-making process that moves from general areas to specific goals (Hudson & Graham, 1978). A systematic approach to establishing priorities must be developed and shared by all members of an IEP team.

The following four guidelines can help the team find a common basis for decision making.

1. Examine the student's present level of performance.
2. Examine areas in which the student's performance is inadequate.
3. Determine which areas are thought to be of highest priority by each team member.
4. Determine the demands of prerequisite skills required for the instructional setting.

Hayes (1977) suggested thinking in terms of curricular areas when setting goals. A grid that combines curricular areas with the four guidelines for establishing priorities can provide the team with a basis for planning goals and sharing communication regarding perception of a student's needs. Such a grid is presented in Figure 5.5.

Use of a grid of this sort can reduce time spent shuffling papers and help the team to zero in on instructional areas critically related to goal development. By using a curriculum grid, team members can communicate with a shared vocabulary, i.e., defining the elements of curriculum areas is relatively straightforward. More importantly, the demands of each curricular task can be stated in behavioral terms that can then be translated directly into classroom demands. As a classroom teacher, you must clarify how your classroom demands can interact with the curricular skills of the mainstreamed student.

Consider the case of Doris. She is currently enrolled in an extended resource special education classroom. She is instructed in all academic subjects in the extended resource room, but has physical education, music, and art with children in the regular fifth grade class. Doris' special teacher believes Doris may be ready to mainstream in some academic areas. The first mainstream area to be considered is arithmetic. According to results of normative tests, Doris is operating at a fifth grade level in math. However, closer examination reveals discrepancies between Doris' current arithmetic skills and the type of arithmetic skills she will need in the mainstream fifth grade. Doris can do the computations required in the mainstream room, but is hampered by a slow rate of recall for the number facts required.

**Regular classroom development**—In developing goals and objectives for Doris, an IEP team must consider the environment of the regular classroom and how it can best fit Doris' needs. The person most likely to understand the demands of the regular classroom is its teacher. By defining classroom demands in behavioral terms, the regular classroom teacher and the rest of the IEP team can make realistic and functional comparisons between goals and

**Figure 5.5**
Planning Grid

| Curricular area | Present Level of Performance | Area(s) of Inadequacy | Priority Areas | Demands of Setting | Other |
|---|---|---|---|---|---|
| Reading skills | | | | | |
| Word recognition | | | | | |
| Word analysis | | | | | |
| Oral reading | | | | | |
| Comprehension | | | | | |
| Language Arts | | | | | |
| Spelling | | | | | |
| Grammar | | | | | |
| Expressive Writing | | | | | |
| Handwriting | | | | | |
| Arithmetic | | | | | |
| Facts | | | | | |
| Computation | | | | | |
| Application | | | | | |
| Social Interaction | | | | | |
| Peers | | | | | |
| Teacher | | | | | |
| Others | | | | | |

Code:  **Present level of performance:** Fill in grade equivalency
　　　**Area of inadequacy:** Fill in with check (✓)
　　　**Priority areas:** Rank by number for main heading and number and letter for subarea
　　　**Demands of setting:** List prerequisite skills
　　　**Other:** Pertinent comments

behavioral objectives of the mainstreamed student. Employing a curricular grid as described above, a team can directly analyze Doris' needs in arithmetic as they relate to the demands of the regular classroom. Figure 5.6 presents a grid that has been completed for Doris for the curricular area of arithmetic. Her present level of performance has been listed and placement of a checkmark indicates that she has inadequate skills in the area of number facts. However, the classroom teacher has not ranked number facts as the highest priority in her arithmetic curriculum. Rather, the ranking suggests that the classroom teacher places a higher value on basic computation processes. The only problem with Doris' computation performance is rate. She is too slow. Computation drill seems acceptable in the regular classroom. Doris' number fact work is not at the same level as the demands of the classroom. The classroom teacher has recommended that Doris be given drill in number facts.

Assuming that the other members of the team have also filled out their curricular grids similarly, decisions are ready to be made. One decision will pertain to a goal statement for Doris in the area of arithmetic. If the team decision is to work with Doris in number facts, then her goal statement might be: "By the end of six weeks, Doris will be able to write 60 correct responses in 60 seconds with two or fewer errors."

Most short-term objectives can be taken directly from district-level curriculum guides. Frequently, short-term objectives can also be found in the teacher's manual for classroom texts. Ideally, you can draw short-term objectives directly from a criterion-referenced test developed from the texts used in your classroom.

Whether or not short-term objectives are written at an IEP meeting depends on policies of the district and state. Some states require that a student's placement be made initially, and then allow the teacher to work with the child for a period of time (generally 30 days) before developing short-term objectives (Evans & Hall, 1978).

## Task Analysis

Short-term objectives are often written on an Individual Implementation Plan (IIP), which consists of weekly or daily lesson plans. In writing an IIP, a team examines each short-term objective relating to an original goal on the IEP and breaks the short-term objective into even smaller, more discrete objectives. The process of breaking goals and objectives into subobjectives or tasks is called *task analysis*. Task analysis is simply a way of breaking the essential parts of a larger task into subtasks and then sequencing these subtasks. As students learn each subtask, completion of the larger task becomes easier.

**Specificity**—One major difference between instruction in a regular class and instruction in a special class is the specificity (and therefore number) of

**Figure 5.6**
Planning Grid for Doris

Child: Doris          Team Member: Classroom Teacher          Date: 1/25/85

| Curricular area | Present Level of Performance | Area(s) of Inadequacy | Priority Areas | Demands of Setting | Other |
|---|---|---|---|---|---|
| Reading skills | | | | | |
| Word recognition | | | | | |
| Word analysis | | | | | |
| Oral reading | | | | | |
| Comprehension | | | | | |
| Language Arts | | | | | |
| Spelling | | | | | |
| Grammar | | | | | |
| Expressive Writing | | | | | |
| Handwriting | | | | | |
| Arithmetic | WRAT: 5.0 | | 1 | | |
| Facts | 10 facts/60 sec. | ✓ | 1.b | 55 facts/60 sec./2 errors | drill |
| Computation | knows process | | 1.a | | |
| Application | slow | | 1.c | | |
| Social Interaction | | | | | |
| Peers | | | | | |
| Teacher | | | | | |
| Others | | | | | |

Code: **Present level of performance:** Fill in grade equivalency
      **Area of inadequacy:** Fill in with check (✓)
      **Priority areas:** Rank by number for main heading and number and letter for subarea
      **Demands of setting:** List prerequisite skills
      **Other:** Pertinent comments

subtasks written in a task analysis. When a child is placed in a regular class, it is assumed that tasks will not be broken down as much as they are in a special setting.

**Essential subtasks**—In writing a task analysis for either a regular or special setting, it is important to include only essential subtasks. For example, when teaching reading, many texts have the following objectives: "The student will be able to name the letters of the alphabet." This objective has some merit for spelling tasks because you can't spell aloud unless you have names for the letters. However, this objective has no relevance to a reading task since children are not required to say the names of letters while reading. In fact, learning letter names is sometimes confusing in the early stages of learning to read. Children often confuse the name of a letter with its sound. How many times can you remember saying, "No, *a* is the name of the letter. Please give me the short sound of *a*"?

Determining essential subtasks is usually a matter of common sense. Essential subtasks are those that assist the child in learning a larger task. To use our previous reading example, if a child can learn to decode and recognize words without learning the names of letters, then learning the names of letters is not essential to the task of decoding or word recognition.

**Sequencing**—Another consideration in task analysis is sequencing. Once you've identified the essential subtasks, you need to teach them in some prescribed order. The first rule of thumb in sequencing tasks is to see if the tasks have a natural order. In math, for example, an obvious progression is that the sequence of instruction or tasks presented will first deal with regrouping into units, next into tens, then hundreds, thousands, and so on.

Not all subject areas are sequenced so obviously. Subtasks in a sequence are not always dependent upon acquisition of a preceding subtask. In many cases, several subtasks are at the same level of difficulty, but are interdependent because knowledge of all the subtasks is necessary before the child can successfully learn the objective. When you are faced with interdependent subtasks, you can arbitrarily choose a sequence. Generally, the most efficient sequence is one which parallels your classroom texts. However, there is no single correct order for interdependent objectives or subtasks.

## Final Comments on Goals and Short-Term Objectives

**"Good faith effort"**—Annual goals and objectives are documented in an IEP. Specific short-term objectives related to annual goals and objectives are usually described in an IIP. Goals and objectives as stated in the IEP and IIP are essentially educational plans for the mainstreamed child; they are not binding contracts. If a child does not attain all of the goals and objectives, neither the team nor the school district can be penalized. However, the IEP team should make every attempt to help the child achieve these goals and objectives. The child's educational and social development will be influenced directly by the degree to which a "good faith effort" is made by the team.

In establishing annual goals and objects for a mainstreamed child, task hierarchy becomes apparent. Broadly stated, goals are divided into more specific objectives. In turn, these objectives are divided into subobjectives or subtasks. Specificity of the subtasks will influence the degree of special education and the extent to which the handicapped child will be able to participate in the regular classroom.

**Types of service**—After identifying goals and objectives for a child, an IEP team next determines what types of service will best meet the child's needs. Every member of the team has a professional responsibility for assuring the child's success. This responsibility includes an obligation to determine an appropriate setting and to designate teachers with appropriate skills. Usually, members of the team assume the major responsibility of providing educational programming for the child. However, people not on the team may also work with the child. For example, it is possible that a team does not include a speech therapist, but that the child's needs are such that a speech therapist is an appropriate service provider. In this case, the child will be assigned to a speech therapist for special services.

**Reentry to the regular classroom**—There is another common situation where service is provided by a person who was not a member of the original IEP team. Often, provision for a child's reentry into the regular classroom is set at an IEP meeting. However, between the time of the original IEP and the child's reentry, the mainstreamed child may have changed regular classroom teachers, perhaps by being promoted. While the original classroom teacher had been actively involved in planning for the mainstreamed child, the new classroom teacher has not.

If you are in this position, you will need to assess the skills of the mainstreamed child relative to the demands of your classroom. At a minimum, you will need to review the IEP. You may also request an IEP staffing to review the needs of the child and possibly to write a new IEP appropriate to the demands of your classroom setting.

No teacher, regular or special, should be designated to provide services that are not already a part of his or her repertoire of skills (Cleek, Gieber, & Mair, 1978). For a regular classroom teacher, this means your primary focus will be on instruction in basic academic and social skills. Modification of your materials and methods may be necessary. Sometimes you will be solely responsible for accommodations that occur in your class; other times you may call upon other school personnel to assist you.

## PLACEMENT OF HANDICAPPED CHILDREN

The school district should provide a continuum of placement options to meet the needs of handicapped children; this continuum should include instruction in regular classes, special classes, special schools, the home, and hospitals and institutions. It should also include supplementary services, such as resource room or itinerant instruction, to be provided in conjuction with regular class placement.

### Three Regular Classroom Factors that Determine Placement

As a regular classroom teacher serving a mainstreamed child, you have an opportunity to use special education support. At the IEP meeting, you and the team can determine the type and degree of special services needed. Three factors concerning the regular classroom are important for determining placement of a particular mainstreamed child: (a) skills of the regular classroom teacher, (b) demands of the regular classroom environment, and (c) availability of special services.

**Skills of the regular classroom teacher**—You will need to make an honest appraisal of your ability to instruct in a mainstreamed child's areas of academic need. If, for example, a child needs special assistance with reading comprehension, you must assess whether your expertise is adequate to meet the child's needs in the area of reading comprehension. If not, you may need assistance at some level from special education personnel.

You must also consider your classroom management skills relative to the needs of a mainstreamed student. You may be very capable of working with a child who acts out, but not quite so sure how to deal with a shy or withdrawn student. As a regular teacher working with a mainstreamed child, you have the right to ask for and receive assistance in both classroom management and academic management.

**Demands of the regular classroom environment**—The demands of your classroom are also factors that influence placement options for a mainstreamed student. Your classroom format, materials, and curriculum may need minor modifications. Once again, you have the right to request assistance in making these modifications. Type and degree of modification needed will vary with the needs of each mainstreamed student.

**Availability of special services**—The third factor that can influence the extent of placement in the regular classroom is the availability of support within the school. Essentially, three levels of support can be identified: (a) full-time, (b) part-time, and (c) outside. Full-time support means that there is a designated person in your building whose primary responsibility is to assist classroom teachers. This full-time person is generally called a *consultant* and works directly with teachers and indirectly with students. Part-time support usually involves a resource teacher or an itinerant teacher. A resource or itinerant teacher divides his or her responsibilities between direct involvement with classroom teachers and direct involvement with students. He or she may share responsibilities with the regular classroom teacher for the education of many mainstreamed children. With outside support, the classroom teacher may draw upon the resources of district-level consultants. There are multiple variations of the three levels. Thorough knowledge of these variations can help a mainstream teacher choose an appropriate placement efficiently.

## Placement Options

Placement options for handicapped children exist on a continuum ranging from regular class placement with no assistance to residential or boarding school. Since you, the classroom teacher, are a part of the IEP team, a general knowledge of this service continuum is appropriate. Figure 5.7 presents the original special education cascade (Reynolds, 1978).

**Options involving regular class placement**—In this special education cascade, consideration was given to five placement options involving the regular classroom: (a) regular classroom, (b) regular classroom with consultative assistance, (c) regular classroom with assistance by itinerant specialist, (d) regular classroom with resource room help, and (e) regular classroom plus part-time special class. The regular classroom teacher is expected to have primary responsibility for the education of a mainstreamed child in these five settings (Gearheart & Weishahn, 1980). As a classroom teacher, your input regarding placement in a regular setting is likely to be the most critical. As you and other members of the IEP team work to determine the most appropriate regular education option for the mainstreamed child, your decisions should be based on the relationship between the three regular classroom factors described earlier and the type of placement option. Figure 5.8 presents such a grid.

This grid illustrates the needs of the classroom teacher in relation to a particular child. Assessment and objectives for the child have already been determined. The classroom teacher now must consider what, if any, needs she will have in order to meet the objectives. As shown in Figure 5.8, the teacher indicated she would like consultation assistance in the skill area of so-

**Figure 5.7**
The Original Special Education Cascade

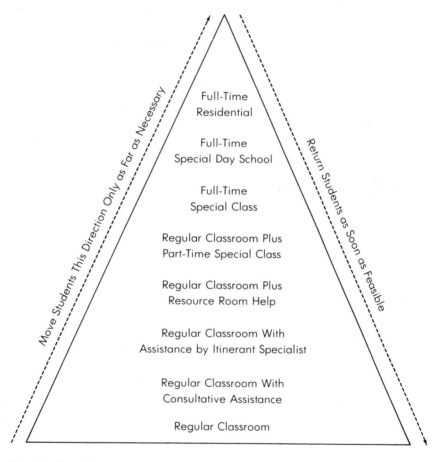

Full-Time
Residential

Full-Time
Special Day School

Full-Time
Special Class

Regular Classroom Plus
Part-Time Special Class

Regular Classroom Plus
Resource Room Help

Regular Classroom With
Assistance by Itinerant Specialist

Regular Classroom With
Consultative Assistance

Regular Classroom

Move Students This Direction Only as Far as Necessary

Return Students as Soon as Feasible

From M. Reynolds, *Teaching Exceptional Children in all America's Schools.* Reston, VA: The Council for Exceptional Children, 1978.

cial behaviors (2/A.2). She also feels that she will need consultation to assist in instructional formatting (2/B.1) relative to social behavior. The regular teacher is requesting materials (3/B.2), presumably related to social behavior and formatting. She further sees a need for part-time support (4/C.2).

By examining the classroom teacher's needs relative to the needs of the child, the team can focus more clearly on instructional placement and the amount of time the child will spend in the regular classroom.

**Figure 5.8**
Grid for Determining a Classroom Teacher's Needs for a Placement Option in the Regular Setting

Regular Teacher Needs
Continuum of Placement Options in the Regular Classroom

Name of M.S. _____
Teacher _____
Date _____

| Regular Class Factors | No Assistance Needed (1) | Consultative Assistance from Special Education (2) | Consultation plus Special Materials from Special Education (3) | Resource Room Teacher Service from Special Education (4) | Regular Class and Special Class (5) |
|---|---|---|---|---|---|
| A. Teacher Skills | | | | | |
| 1. Academic | | | | | |
| 2. Social | | need | | | |
| B. Demands of Classroom | | | | | |
| 1. Instructional Format | | need | | | |
| 2. Materials | | | | | |
| 3. Curriculum | | | | | |
| C. Level of Support | | | | | |
| 1. Full-Time | | | | | |
| 2. Part-Time | | | | need | |
| 3. Outside | | | | | |

**Dualistic placement philosophy**—Figure 5.7 shows that placement options vary with the needs of the mainstreamed student. Traditionally, placement options have been considered either regular or special, but this distinction is no longer clear. The either/or dualistic placement philosophy clouded processes of decision making. In the past, placement decisions involved choosing between distinct places. Now, however, placement options are no longer primarily places. Rather, placement decisions involve choosing between processes. These processes are not mutually exclusive, so a child can receive the benefit of several processes simultanously. The nature and degree of a child's needs determine the extent and type of processes most appropriate.

## INITIATION AND DURATION OF SPECIAL SERVICES

When planning an IEP for an individual child, an IEP team must indicate timelines for the anticipated beginning and duration of service. Typically, timelines are written in terms of years. The degree and nature of the required services will direct the estimated duration of the special service. For a child who is considered mildly handicapped in only one academic area, special services may be needed for only 5 or 6 months. On the other hand, a child severely handicapped in a sensory area, e.g., a blind child, may need special services for the entire school career.

### Annual Review

While the anticipated duration of services may exceed 1 year, an annual review of the IEP is necessary! The purpose of an annual review planning conference is to assess the degree to which the IEP is meeting the student's needs. The conference is held to adjust the IEP in light of the student's projected needs. If the student has been receiving special services, the planning conference is usually held at the end of the school year. If the student has recently begun receiving special services, the conference is typically held at the beginning of the school year. A projected timeline for meeting the student's objectives is outlined during the conference and compared with the student's actual performance. Discrepancies between real and anticipated performance result in an IEP change.

### Contribution of Regular Class Teacher

As a regular classroom teacher and member of an IEP team, you will recognize an obvious need for clarification of the special education related services to be delivered. In order to present classroom information, you need to help decide what services will be provided, when and for how long the services will be given, as well as who is responsible for providing service. Given the

**Figure 5.9**
General Schedule for Service Delivery

| Name | Lee Monday | Tuesday | Wednesday | Date Thursday | October 25 Friday |
|------|------------|---------|-----------|---------------|-------------------|
| 8:00– 9:00 | Opening<br>Reading<br>8:30– 9:00 | → | | | → |
| 9:00–10:00 | Reading<br>9:00– 9:30<br>1 | | 1 | | 1 |
| 10:00–11:00 | Math<br>10:00–10:30<br>Music<br>10:30–11:00 | P.E.<br>10:00–10:30<br>Language Arts<br>10:30–11:00 | Math<br>10:00–10:30<br>Music<br>10:30–11:00 | P.E.<br>10:00–10:30<br>Language Arts<br>10:30–11:00 | Math<br>10:00–10:30<br>Language Arts<br>10:00–11:00 |
| 11:00–12:00 | Language Arts<br>11:00–11:30 | | | | |
| 12:00– 1:00 | 2 | 1 | 2 | 2 | 1 |
| 1:00– 2:00 | | | | | Library<br>1:30– 2:00 |
| 2:00– 3:00 | | | | | |

Math 9:30–10:00

**Code**

| Services to be given | Hours per week | Duration |
|----------------------|----------------|----------|
| 1. Language Therapy | 5 | November–May |
| 2. Reading Resource | 3 | November–May |
| All other services in regular classroom | 22 | November–May |

constraints of your district, some service decisions may be automatic. You and the rest of the team will need to coordinate the service schedule. A form that can assist in planning a coordinated service delivery is presented in Figure 5.9.

While a child may spend most of the day in a regular class setting, the regular class teacher still must share school time with other specialists. In most schools, scheduling must account for time with music, art, and physical education teachers. Also, special library times are usually a part of the regular classroom experience. Careful analysis of a child's social and emotional needs can help shape decisions about service priorities. For a child who is having reading problems, decisions about scheduling must include consideration of where the child's reading needs are best met as well as the child's need for positive self-regard. One child may need to spend reading time in the regular classroom as well as in the resource setting. An intensified reading schedule may mean that this child misses art. If the child's primary source of positive self-esteem stems from artwork, it may be more important to keep him in art than to give him additional reading instruction. If, on the other hand, art has no major impact on the child's life, additional reading instruction during the art period is easily justifiable. Each decision must be based on the individual child in question.

No one ever said scheduling would be easy. Adjustments in both the child's and your program will need to be made. During this phase of IEP planning, you can save time and energy by bringing copies of your class schedule to the meeting. Once the child's schedule has been determined, teaching can begin.

## AN EVALUATION SCHEME

### Components

The final component of an IEP is a plan through which the instructional plan and progress of a child are assessed. As described earlier, an evaluation scheme describes appropriate objective criteria, i.e., a list of annual goals and objectives. An evaluation scheme must also describe evaluation procedures to be used for evaluating each goal and objective. Finally, the scheme must contain a schedule for reviewing the plan to determine, on at least an annual basis, the achievement of short-term instructional objectives. Designing the plan is fairly simple, but implementing it may require additional meetings outside the IEP staffing. An example of an annual evaluation plan is presented in Figure 5.10.

Additional time may be required to develop evaluation tools, record-keeping systems, and procedures for sharing reviews. As a regular classroom

**Figure 5.10**
An Annual Review Form

## Annual Review Form

| | |
|---|---|
| Student | Janie Jones |
| Date | 1/15 to 5/20 |
| Area | Math |

| Member of IEP Team | |
|---|---|
| Parent | Mr. & Mrs. Jones |
| Teacher | Mr. J. Ball |
| Resource | Ms. T. Flogel |
| Psychologist | Ms. J. Haggerty |

| | Type of Evaluation | Evaluation Procedure | | | Review Date |
|---|---|---|---|---|---|
| | | Instrument | Evaluator | | |
| 1. GOAL: By May, Janie will be able to do fifth grade math. | Computation | End of year | Entire team | | 5/15 |
| A. Short-Term Objective Janie will compute regrouping problems in addition with 3 or more digits. | Computation problems | Daily assignment In-class quizzes | Ms. Flogel Mr. Ball | | Daily Weekly |
| B. Janie will compute regrouping problems in subtraction with 3 or more digits. | Computation problems | Daily assignment In-class quizzes | Ms. Flogel Mr. Ball | | Daily Weekly |
| C. Janie will compute fractions involving mixed numbers, like and unlike denominators, and improper numbers. | Computation problems | Daily assignment In-class quizzes | Ms. Flogel Mr. Ball | | Daily Weekly |
| D. Janie will compute simple percentage problems. | Computation problems | Daily assignment In-class quizzes | Ms. Flogel Mr. Ball | | Daily Weekly |

Figure 5.11
An Example of Class Record Keeping

| Student Name | Skill 1 Criterion 100% 2 days in a row | | Skill 2 Criterion 100% 3 days in a row | | Review Skill 1 & 2 90% or 9/10 correct | | Skill 3 Criterion 100% 4 days in a row | | Skill 4 Criterion 100% 3 days in a row | | Review Skill 3 & 4 90% or 9/10 correct | Skill 5 Criterion 100% 2 days in a row |
|---|---|---|---|---|---|---|---|---|---|---|---|---|
| Jimmy | 9/15 | 9/20 | 9/20 | 10/1a | 10/3 | 10/3 | 10/6 | 10/15 | 10/15 | | | |
| Sally | 9/15 | 10/1b | 10/3 | 10/10 | 10/10 | 10/12 | 10/12 | | | | | |
| Ray | 9/15 | 9/20 | 9/20 | 10/1 | 10/3 | 10/3 | 10/6 | | | | | |
| Hank | 9/15 | 9/25c | 9/25 | 10/1 | 10/3 | 10/6 | 10/7 | 10/15 | 10/15 | | | |
| Louise | 9/15 | 10/1 | 10/1 | 10/14 | 10/15 | 10/15 | | | | | | |

Entry
date / Mastery
       date

Code
a. Modified materials
b. Modified method
c. Coordinated teaching

teacher involved in instructing the child, you need to insure that the evaluation tools and recording systems are compatible with your other classroom responsibilities. Any evaluation tool you use with a mainstreamed student should, with minor modifications, be similar to the tools you use with any other student in your class. Examples of minor differences might be the size of the print, number of items per page, or use of special aids, e.g., use of a calculator or number line in math.

### Record Keeping

Record keeping for the mainstreamed child should also be similar to record keeping for other children. The records need not be extensive, but should include (a) criteria for acceptable performance, (b) description of special methods or materials that helped achieve criteria, and (c) description of any coordination of teaching between you and another teacher. Examples of modified materials or methods can be dated and placed in the child's folder. Notes about conferences with other teachers involved with the child can also be dated and placed in the child's folder. An example of a possible record-keeping sheet is presented in Figure 5.11.

Be sure your record-keeping system is one that can be completed quickly. Long involved records are too cumbersome and time consuming to be useful. Develop a system that enables you to objectively evaluate the child's performance. Your records will help determine the extent to which the child has achieved the instructional objectives as specified on the IEP.

## SUMMARY

An individual educational plan (IEP) is a written document that provides information regarding a student's academic skills and needs; program goals, objectives, and timelines; the nature and direction of services to be provided the child; and a plan for evaluating IEP implementation. The IEP is at the heart of the process by which handicapped children are provided an appropriate education in the least restrictive environment. The plan guides both short- and long-term instructional decisions for the child. Conscientious implementation of the plan should guarantee that all handicapped children will receive the educational and related services they need and deserve.

# 6

# Classroom Organization

With glassy eyes, Ms. Smith looked at her class roster. For the twelfth time she added up the number of students in her charge. Yes, 25 plus 5 equals 30 on paper, but upon first count Ms. Smith found that 25 plus 5 equaled 32! One of the "plus 5," Courtney, was called *mildly learning disabled.* No big problem. Ms. Smith had worked with children like Courtney before. A little extra attention, somewhat like working with two children, was in order. Then Ms. Smith counted again; 25 plus 5 equaled 36! Nathaniel, another of the plus 5, was labeled emotionally disturbed and mildly retarded. Sinking slowly down into her chair, Ms. Smith counted again. This time 25 plus 5 equaled 40! Tom, another member of the "plus 5 gang," was legally blind. Beginning to chew her fingernails, Ms. Smith counted again; 25 plus 5 equaled 45. Sally, a "plus fiver," was hard-of-hearing and communicated in sign. In desperation Ms. Smith frantically counted one more time. The finale was Mimi. The last member of the "plus 5 gang," she would be rolling right into Ms. Smith's classroom this coming year. Ms. Smith didn't have to worry about finding a seat for Mimi. She would be arriving in her own wheelchair. A final count according to Ms. Smith was 25 plus 5 equals 50!

Clutching six rabbit feet, throwing a pinch of salt over her left shoulder, and whispering a silent prayer, Ms. Smith decided to forge ahead. After all, she could count at least one small blessing. Her classroom was strategically situated between the nurse's office and the teacher's lounge. On overly eventful days, Ms. Smith could rotate between her classroom, the lavatory facilities in the lounge, and the nurse's office. What more could a teacher of 50 want?

Ms. Smith might want a plan of action. If 25 plus 5 really does seem to equal 50, then Ms. Smith and other teachers like her need an organized plan of attack. Three parts of that plan are to reduce the extraneous, consolidate where possible, and manage time as efficiently as possible.

# REDUCING THE EXTRANEOUS

### TEACHER JUDGMENT

Reducing the extraneous means that you, the regular classroom teacher, have a clear and definite vision of what you want to teach. Guidance in what to teach is provided by the school district's adopted curriculum. Books and grade-level expectations are also predetermined by district policy. As all experienced classroom teachers know, there is a great deal of flexibility in how the curricula and materials are used. Your judgment determines the depth with which any aspect of the curriculum is covered. You also have the prerogative to use materials you see fit, and that "fit" needs to wear well on your students.

## Depth of Coverage

If the district curriculum in social studies includes an understanding of the need for cooperative effort in the family, you determine the extent and degree to which individual children within your classroom will learn that concept. You may decide that certain aspects of the cooperative family effort concept must be learned by all the children, i.e., minimum competency will be established for the entire class, while other concepts related to cooperative family effort may be extraneous and not necessary for learning the next major concept to be taught. Key vocabulary terms such as *family* and *cooperative* are essential in the understanding of the need for cooperative effort in the family. What may not be critical is for all children to be aware of *cooperative effort* in 40 different cultures or in 20 different families or in 13 different periods of history. While that sort of information is broadening and certainly can contribute to a greater understanding of cooperative family effort, not all children will be able to assimilate that much information in the same amount of time. The skilled classroom teacher knows the limits of her students, with limits being determined by the number of concepts to be learned and the amount of time given to learn those concepts. For some of the students, reducing the extraneous may mean to understand the concept of cooperative family effort in the context of one or two families from the student's own culture in the present historical period. By identifying the information that is critical to concept understanding, the classroom teacher may expand the knowledge base for those children whose experiences warrant more information by building from the minimum competency base.

## Individual Differences

"But wait!" cries the concerned educator. "Doesn't the principle of reducing the extraneous translate to the rich get richer and the poor get poorer?" The answer to this question is that the rich get richer and the poor get rich. In any regular classroom the goal is to encourage children to reach their highest intellectual potential. The more effective the classroom teacher, the greater the individual differences between children will be. Children who have difficulties learning, for whatever reason, are taught basic concepts. In most curricula the basic concepts are few, but scarcity of concepts doesn't imply that these few concepts are not rich in knowledge. Rather than attempting to rush all the children into learning essential and nonessential information, the wise classroom teacher teaches a few select concepts very well. All children leave with a strong basic understanding of key concepts; no one is impoverished.

## ESSENTIAL INFORMATION

The key to reducing the extraneous lies in decision making. You, perhaps in consultation with a curriculum specialist, must distinguish essential from nonessential information. Essential information is that information that must be acquired in order to learn new information. Essential information is the foundation upon which new knowledge can grow. In basic skill areas like reading or math, essential information is generally easy to identify. A child receiving reading instruction, for example, need not learn the names of the letters in order to sound out words. Naming the letters is not essential to sounding out in reading. Naming the letters is, however, essential to spelling tasks.

### Guidelines

Content areas such as science, health, or social studies provide you with more opportunity to make subjective choices. Three guidelines for choosing essential terms, concepts, or units in content areas are:

1. Is the term or concept one that will recur throughout the curriculum or is it isolated within a particular unit?
2. Is the term, concept, or unit one that will recur in other grade-level curricula?
3. Is the term, concept, or unit one that will recur in more advanced curricula?

If the term or concept is isolated to one particular unit, the chances are good that it is not essential. You must be careful, however, to become familiar with more advanced curricula to be sure that the isolated term or concept or unit does not become a major emphasis at a higher grade level. If it does, then you decide how much instructional time will be used for teaching the concept now. That decision will be based primarily on the individual make-up of your own classroom.

### Student Characteristics

If the majority of your students are motivated, have a positive learning history, and learn at a rate that allows for the introduction of nonessential information, you can probably teach an isolated term, concept, or unit. For the few children who may have some learning problem, you will be able to adapt or modify your instruction to meet their needs as well. If, on the other hand, your class has a low motivational level, a history of negative learning experiences, and tends to need a lot of time to learn new concepts, you probably cannot spend much instructional time in teaching nonessential information.

Establishing priorities for your curricular goals and objectives is essential to reducing the extraneous. Priority setting takes into account the characteristics of your students. Keep in mind that not all information warrants the same degree of emphasis. Don't be afraid to eliminate unneccessary information or to provide different amounts of information to the different children in your class.

# CONSOLIDATION

"Consolidate where possible" refers to consolidating the number of children you teach, the way you use your material, and the way you manage your time. Each form of consolidation is important to your success and effectiveness.

## CONSOLIDATING STUDENTS

### Basic Skills

By consolidating your students where possible and individualizing where necessary, your classroom plan will include large group, small group, and individualized instruction. As with reducing the extraneous, you are again called upon to be a decision maker. The decision this time is which subjects can best be taught under which conditions, i.e., lecture, small group, or one-to-one. Your decisions must take the needs of the individual students in your room into account.

Take the example of Augie and Raymond. Augie has been classified as mildly learning handicapped. Raymond has been characterized as being average to quick in completing his school work. Augie and Raymond are enrolled in the same classroom. Their teacher is expected to instruct them both in basically the same subject areas. When reading time begins, Augie is often found in a small group being instructed in basic reading concepts. Sometimes Augie will be found in a one-to-one story-writing session. During reading time, Raymond will also be found in a small group, but Raymond's group will be receiving more advanced instruction than Augie's group. Raymond, too, will be found in a one-to-one writing session. Both Augie and Raymond will be listening to their teacher during story-reading time.

Augie and Raymond's teacher has consolidated her basic skills instruction wherever possible. She chose one-to-one story writing as a means to meet individual needs; she chose small group instruction as a means to bring together children who shared similar skill levels. Finally, Augie and Raymond's teacher chose large group or total class participation when she read to the entire group. Each child could learn from the story reading at his or her own level in accordance with his or her own background experiences.

## Content Areas

Most teachers have more to teach than basic skills. Teachers also need to apply the consolidation principle to curricular content areas as well. Returning to Augie and Raymond, we find them in their respective science classes. Their teacher had shown them a film called "Insects Are Our Friends" the day before. The film was reviewed by the entire class. The teacher next solicited ideas that struck the students as being particularly interesting or relevant to the topic of insects. On the following day, the teacher suggested several projects related to the students' interests and asked them to pick a project on which they wanted to work. Children worked in small groups in the area of their choice. Augie and Raymond found themselves and three other classmates in a group that wished to study ants. As a group, Augie, Raymond, and the other three students (with a little guidance from their teacher) designed, developed, and presented the results of their project. Each child within the group participated, but at a slightly different level. Augie chose to collect or draw pictures of ants at work. Raymond and one other group member built an ant farm. Working within the framework of a small group, each child contributed at his or her own level.

**Whole-class presentation**—In consolidating students in a content area, the teacher chose to begin by presenting basic information to the entire class. A key to presenting information to the entire class group is to present only one major concept per lesson. Information is presented in such a way that all children understand the critical concept being conveyed. That critical concept is reviewed and class discussion is held. The need for class discussion is twofold. By listening to your students discuss a concept, you are given the chance to identify areas of weakness or misunderstanding. You can then reteach or review concepts as you conduct the discussion. The second value of the class discussion is that children are also given a chance to add new information related to the topic. Through guided class discussion, the teacher can work with the entire class at one time.

**Small groups**—As individual interests emerge from the discussion, you can form small groups composed of children whose interests are similar. The breadth, depth, and organization of the group can basically be determined by the students themselves. With a little trust on your part, you can teach them cooperative skills as well as subject matter content. Assuming the children are interested in their chosen topic, a minimum of direction may be necessary. You are then free to circulate between groups or spend time in any one group as necessary.

Within groups, children can divide tasks between themselves. Children, like adults, will usually choose to do those kinds of tasks in which they have previously been successful. While each child does his or her "own thing," the dynamics of a small group can also allow for a great deal of productive sharing and exchange of ideas. The group artist may be given a few points from the group bookworm; the group bookworm in turn might pick up a few fine points related to the artist's interpretation of the topic.

The consolidation principle takes into account both group and individual needs. By consolidating and allowing for flexibility of participation within large or small groups, the teacher can successfully accommodate the needs of all the students—handicapped as well as normal.

## CONSOLIDATING MATERIALS

Consolidation also applies to the ways in which instructional materials are used. As a regular classroom teacher, responsible for teaching both regular and special populations, you don't need the added aggravation and hassle of spending a lot of time developing materials to use with your students. While you may need to develop some materials to accommodate specific skill levels of certain students, in general, you will already have more than enough material at your disposal. Nine times out of ten, the problem with materials is not that you have too few, but rather that you have too many!

### A Materials Inventory

Performing an inventory is the first step in consolidating your materials. For years you have been gathering dittos, worksheets, and miscellaneous teaching tools. You have scavenged book fairs and acquired materials from the stockpiles of friends who have retired. Inventorying your materials allows you to throw materials away. Your files should be consolidated systematically, however. While there are many organizational systems, some are better than others. Filing alphabetically sells a lot of file dividers, and is also effective in burying material. Filing by course work taken in college classes is almost as effective as random filing, but not quite as useful. Since you are already operating under the consolidation principle, you may also want to reduce the extraneous as well. Recalling that the reducing-the-extraneous principle demands that you have identified and prioritized key curricular content, your throwing out and retaining file system can be shaped up fairly easily.

## Filing by Objectives

You can file by subject matter and, within the larger category, by objectives. Books may change, but objectives remain basically the same. Throughout time, intermediate grades have studied South America, North America, and Europe. Children still learn the basics about the geography, culture, and economics of these countries. While some of the teaching content varies over time (e.g., the royal wedding of the Prince of Wales and Lady Di), basic facts about the English monarchy remain stable.

Teaching aids such as worksheets and textbooks passages can be placed in a folder and filed by objective number. In general mathematics, for example, all material related to the student's ability to perform long division problems can be placed in a coded file. Material for each objective can be coded and filed sequentially according to your teaching priorities. Students who enter with different skills will, of course, be using materials commensurate with their skill levels.

## Special Needs

By having your files set up sequentially and prioritized by objectives, you will be able to match the skill level of the child with the material (coded by objective) that matches the child's level or special need. Take the case of Frances, who is hard of hearing. As with many hearing impaired students (Conley, 1976), Frances' understanding of idioms is poor. Suppose Frances was learning how to read maps. An expression like "follow the map" is sure to cause her some confusion. Special care must be taken to ensure that the material that she reads is either idiom-free or else has a source of an immediately available explanation for the idiom.

You could easily file a dictionary of idiomatic terms that are likely to occur with each objective. In addition, special materials, as idiom-free as possible, can also be filed along with other nonspecialized materials that cover the objective. An example of a file sequenced by prioritized objectives that accounts for special needs is presented in Figure 6.1.

Not all files would have these headings. If you were working with a hearing impaired child like Frances, you would probably gather a great deal of information that is useful to hearing impaired children rather than information that could be used with the visually impaired or physically disabled. Materials would be gathered as the need arose.

You don't necessarily have to be the one developing the special materials. You just need to have the material on file. Generally, very specialized

**Figure 6.1**
File Sequenced by Prioritized Objective for Special Needs

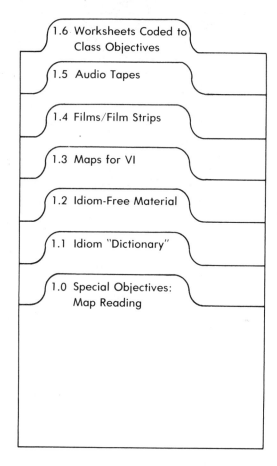

1.6 Worksheets Coded to
Class Objectives

1.5 Audio Tapes

1.4 Films/Film Strips

1.3 Maps for VI

1.2 Idiom-Free Material

1.1 Idiom "Dictionary"

1.0 Special Objectives:
Map Reading

material will be developed by a special education resource teacher or consultant. To help that specialist provide you with materials, you need to be specific about your content. By presenting the resource teacher with a list of your objectives and showing him or her your matched-to-objectives filing system, much time can be saved. Instead of having innumerable conferences, the resource teacher can simply go to your files to select materials you and your student will need.

## Saving Time

Initially, systematizing your files by objectives may seem time consuming. In the long run, however, such a system is very time saving. Once you've set up your major objective headings and file headings, the process is one that an aide, volunteer, or even a student could manage with minimal supervision. Further, you need not gather all material for every subject you teach before initiating your file-by-objectives system. During the initial "year-of-the-file," objective headings can be listed for your subjects. During the year, you can reorganize as you teach. Gather and file your materials as your students progress through the program. Be the end of the school year you may not have the total file, but you'll have a good start. Some subjects will be more complete than others, but at least you will have what you've collected organized and available.

One additional bonus to filing materials by objectives is that as you continue to collect materials, those materials can be used with future students. Once the materials covering a broad range of skills within an objective are collected and organized, you can spend more time with instruction. You have more time for working with your students and spend less time searching for teaching tools. If you choose to teach at each child's rate, organizing materials by objectives is also very practical. Because your material is sequenced, lower-level children will be able to use materials that have already been gathered for more advanced students. You really only collect one set of materials, but the rate at which the students move through the materials can be based on small group or individual needs.

By filing by objectives, you can manage the successful education of the mainstream student much more easily. In many ways, you become an educational manager or engineer, You identify the objective to teach; match the objective with the student's academic, social, and sensory needs; pull the materials from the file; and provide your students with a successful learning experience. Whoever would have thought that cleaning out a file could lead to such educational ecstasy?

# MANAGING YOUR TIME

## TEACHING TIME

Managing your time assumes that you know what you want to accomplish in the time you have available for teaching. At face value managing your time looks like a piece of cake, but looks can be deceiving. So before you dig in for a mouth-watering bite, put down your fork and inspect the ingredients a little more closely. *How much time do you have?* Surprisingly enough, a typical class day consists of approximately 8 hours. Roughly 6 of those hours are spent with students and 2 hours are used for planning and personal needs. In the time without students, planning implies organization in such areas as providing feedback through correcting papers, preparing the next day's lessons, and attending professional meetings. Personal needs entail eating lunch, drinking the eleventh cup of coffee, and solving world problems with your colleagues. In the time spent with students, each curriculum area has time management needs of its own.

Time as measured by clocks and calendars has a certain permanence that smacks of iron-clad limitations. Trying to fit all the activities you feel must be completed into the boundaries of measureable time might not be the most efficient or effective use of your day. Perhaps, then, the ingredient to look at is not time as constrained by clocks and calendars, but rather time as defined by values and goals (Lippit, 1969).

The school system has imposed some restrictions on physical time as well as educational goals. However, within the system, you have flexibility and can make choices. Instead of being overly concerned with covering all the material, you may need to reconsider and become more concerned with appropriate coverage of *some* material. Productivity is important, and your role is to teach children basic information. Counterproductive to your role is racing to reach the end of the book at the expense of leaving half the class behind. The way you parcel your teaching time must reflect your personality and past experiences. As you find your own time management system, you can assess your values and goals relative to your students' needs and your school's demands.

## VALUE SYSTEMS

The first step in assessing your value system relative to your students' needs and your school's demands is to learn to focus on the essential. Ask yourself the following set of questions:

* What academic and social skills do I believe are essential for my students' present situation?
* What academic and social skills do I believe are essential for my students' future situation?
* How do my beliefs correspond to my students' expectations?
* How do my beliefs correspond to my district's expectations?

## A PERSONAL TIME MANAGEMENT SYSTEM

Answers to these questions can help you define a personal time management plan for you classroom. By mixing clock time with value time, you have a basic framework from which to work. The initial considerations in managing your school time include:

*Teaching Purpose:* Achieving the greatest student benefits with the most effective use of teacher time.

*Goals:* All the realistic expectations.

*Clock and Calendar Time:* The actual countable minutes, days, weeks, and months of the school year.

*Plan:* How the teacher matches his or her current time management system from where he or she is to where he or she wants to be.

### Daily Activities

Accomplishing initial planning steps leads you very quickly to the everyday routine. The time in your school available for instruction is roughly the same for every teacher. Given that timeframe, some teachers are able to accomplish much more than others.

The first questions to ask yourself are: "What do I do with my time? Am I instructing or am I frantically running from one raised hand to the next? Do I find myself disciplining more than teaching?" In other words, find out what activities use your time.

The second set of questions is: "With whom am I working? Am I spending a lot of time with the student who always says 'please' and 'thank you'? Do I carefully avoid dealing with the children who need three or four explanations before even understanding the directions for the task? Do I interact more with some children than with others?" Find out who uses your time.

### A Daily Log

Your best bet for identifying the what and the who with activities is to keep some sort of daily log. Try to keep your log based on roughly 15- to 30-minute time increments and maintain that log for 1 to 2 weeks. A fairly quick analysis of that log should give you major insight into time use and abuse. The sample log presented in Figure 6.2 is just one of many ways that you might check your time use and abuse. Once you've figured out what activities you do and with whom you do those activities, you ought to have a fairly clear idea of where your classroom time is spent.

**Figure 6.2**
Sample Teaching Log

### Sample: Reading Period

| Time | Student | Activity |
|---|---|---|
| 9:15–9:30 | Johnny<br>Sally<br>Joe | Small group instruction: ă |
| 9:20 | Roger | Corrected for daydreaming |
| 9:20–9:30 | Rose<br>Larry<br>Elena<br>Will | Small group instruction: ā |
| 9:25 | Roger & Joe | Corrected for talking out |
| 9:30–9:50 | Jeff<br>Michael<br>Elizabeth<br>Ruth | Small group instruction: L.E. story |
| 9:35 | Roger | Corrected for talking out |
| 9:40 | Roger | Corrected for daydreaming |

## ORGANIZING TEACHING TIME

Having determined where you are spending your time, your next task is to examine how you organize your time.

1. Delegate all possible tasks.
2. Group work items that are similar.
3. Hold the number of starts and stops to a minimum.
4. Have an established schedule.

### DELEGATION

Delegation is the art of giving people things to do. It is an art because you must balance what is reasonable to expect from another person against what you can reasonably expect from yourself. In the classroom this means that the "I can do it better myself" fallacy will need to be overcome. A certain amount of trust, guided by your own judgment, will of necessity be bestowed on your colleagues and subordinates. Whether you are working with a peer or subordinate, delegation will be successful only if the task is explained thoroughly and expectations clearly stated. One other major consideration is the degree of task importance. Some tasks simply do not carry the same life-weight as others. Given your resources, you can delegate accomplishment of less critical objectives to other persons.

As you delegate, you should always remember that ultimate accountability still lies with you. Freedom from responsibility simply does not exist. Assigning duties to others does, however, help you complete your duties more efficiently. By delegating some authority, you can become more result-oriented and less activity-oriented.

### People Power

A vital question remains to be answered. Just whom does the regular classroom teacher call upon when he or she wishes to delegate? The regular classroom teacher has two major sources of people power: colleagues and kids!

**Collegial delegation**—Collegial delegation turns out to be more a trade-off than a straight request. The basic line is "If you do this for me, then here's what I can do for you ... ." With your special population, you and the special teacher can share teaching responsibilities and materials acquisition. The primary "here's-what-I-can-do-for-you" responsibility is for both of you to work cooperatively upon mutually chosen objectives and to determine where the primary instruction occurs and how to reinforce that instruction.

When working with other classroom teachers, you will also want to apply the same cooperative effort, but exchanges or tasks may be on a grander scale. You may wish to "exchange" three or four students in a grouping for particular skills. The exchange can cut down the number of groups you teach. You may wish to limit your exchange to materials but, again, even sharing materials can cut down considerably on your time demands. One teacher can choose to teach the science classes, while the other teacher helps develop materials for those units. How teachers decide to share teaching responsibilities is limited only by their imaginations, their fear of trying something that they've "never done before," and school policy.

**Student delegation**—Your other major source of people power is your students. As a teacher you can delegate certain tasks to your students. At most elementary grades, your students will feel flattered and, in some cases, even honored that they can do something to assist the teacher. Two major areas of "something" are tasks associated with class logistics and tasks associated with instruction.

Logistics tasks are those that must be completed in order to get on with the primary purpose of the school—instruction. Logistics are the strategies for handling the details of the day-to-day operation of the classroom. Common classroom logistical tasks are taking attendance, counting lunch money, and bringing the class together for the Pledge of Allegiance. All tasks take time to complete. The unwritten law of the educational community that all teachers must take time to complete these tasks does not specify *whose* time. Delegating responsibility for taking lunch count to a student is one possibility. By turning over some of the more automatic and less than thought-provoking daily tasks to your students, you can gather more time for yourself to spend in correcting papers, planning lessons, or just thinking about the needs of your students. Should you need a rationale for why you have abdicated some of your chores, you can always rely on the phrase, "I'm teaching them responsibility" and you know what? You really are teaching them responsibility, and in a smart way, too. It's smart for them because they are learning to be independent and self-directed. It's smart for you because you're not trying to be all things to all people.

The second area in which you can delegate tasks is instruction. Students can teach each other. Student-to-student teaching can occur on several levels. You can have formal one-to-one tutoring, usually referred to as *peer tutoring* or *cross-age tutoring*. Cross-age or peer tutoring can also include one student tutor to a small group of students. Another type of tutoring can be much less formal. For want of a better term, this type of tutoring can be called the *buddy* or the *love-thy-neighbor* system.

## CROSS-AGE OR PEER TUTORING

Cross-age tutoring refers to a system in which one child, usually the tutor, is older than the other child. In contrast, peer tutoring refers to a teaching system in which both the tutor and the tutee are approximately the same age. Typically, peer or cross-age tutoring refers to a fairly formal one-to-one relationship in which one child is assisting another in an academic area (Mercer & Mercer, 1985). Cross-age and peer tutoring have been found successful in the areas of written expression (Drass & Jones, 1971), spelling (Harris & Sherman, 1973; Jenkins, Mayhill, Peschka, & Jenkins, 1974), arithmetic (Johnson & Bailey, 1974; Kane & Alley, 1980), and reading (Howell & Kaplan, 1978; Trovato & Bucher, 1980). The most common academic tutoring can be in any area where the student needs either remedial help or extensive practice.

Many studies have shown that, across time, both the tutor and the tutored benefit from this kind of learning experience (Paolitto, 1976). Beneficial experiences are not just born by chance but are made by teacher design.

To arrange a successful peer or cross-age formal tutoring experience, you need to consider the following:

- Selection of tutors
- Selection of tutees
- Amount of tutor training
- Degree of supervision
- Spatial and material resources

## Selection of Tutors

In a formal cross-age or peer tutoring program, roles are firmly delineated. The tutor acts as a representative of the teacher and the tutee is expected to be the student. Because of this formal arrangement, tutors must be carefully selected. Tutors need to be proficient in the teaching subject as well as in teaching skills (Smith, 1981). Generally, children who are well behaved and who excel in their school work make good tutors. On the other hand, children who have experienced some academic weakness may be more empathetic and, thus, effective tutors. There is no formula for discriminating potentially good from poor tutors. A good idea is to select tutors who either volunteer or show some interest in the task.

## Selection of Tutees

The easiest (but fairly elusive) guideline to follow in selecting the tutee is to pick students who wish to be tutored. By capitalizing on a student's desire for a tutor, you may be saving yourself and your student from a potentially unpleasant teaching situation. Enthusiasm of the student aside, you also need to consider the personality of your student. Evaluate your student in terms of whether he or she has enough internal control to work in a one-to-one relationship. Some students can work well in a tutorial situation and others cannot. The match between the tutor's and the tutee's personality is critical. If your student is highly manipulative, you may need to match him or her with a tutor who is relatively sophisticated in social perception.

Selection of tutees can also be viewed from the teacher's perspective. Instead of asking students to volunteer for tutoring, you simply make tutoring a part of your normal class presentation. If tutoring sessions are a typical part of your class procedure, then almost everyone in your class should be provided with a tutor. In other words, almost everyone gets to be tutored in some area.

By providing tutors for all, you can avoid inadvertently segregating members of your class. If only the slow learners receive tutors, everyone soon figures out that the tutored children are in the "turkey" learning group while everyone else is an "eagle." Being tutored can easily become a stigma, and most children are not overly anxious to become stigmatized.

## Amount of Tutor Training

The amount of tutor training will vary with the type of task assigned. Essentially two types of teacher tasks are given to tutors. These tasks are ones which either help the child acquire a new skill (the acquisition stage) or practice an acquired skill (fluency building).

Since the acquisition stage is probably the first step in learning a skill, the tutor must be highly skilled in teaching. During the acquisition stage both normal and handicapped children usually make frequent mistakes (Haring et al., 1978). Tutors who are instructing in acquisition-level learning should be trained to learn how to use instruction, feedback, praise, and reinforcement effectively (Smith, 1981). Unless you have a lot of spare time to train tutors or unless someone in your building trains the tutors, you may want to seriously question the advantage of peer or cross-age tutoring at the acquisition stage.

A regular classroom teacher with 30 (25 plus 5) students and no aide can still develop and implement a highly effective peer or cross-age tutoring program without spending an extensive amount of time training tutors. Rather than have tutors work with acquisition level learning, direct them to activities focused on fluency building or practice.

In fluency building or practice activities, the child already can respond correctly to a task, but still needs assistance in using the task (Haring et al., 1978). Examples of fluency-building activities may be responding more quickly to math facts, reading instructional level materials out loud, or report writing. Most activities at the fluency-building stage are drill and practice.

Practice activities lend themselves easily to a tutorial situation. The tutor essentially provides feedback to the tutee. The major task of the tutor is to validate or correct the tutee's response. If you want a written record of the tutoring event, you should design a very simple form that requires almost no training to use. Whatever you want from the tutor should be simple, direct, and easily accomplished with a minimum of effort on your part. Access to materials should also be easy and self-directed.

## Degree of Supervision

Degree of supervision will vary as a function of the type of task assigned the tutor. Acquisition-level tutorial instruction must be closely supervised and controlled. There is more latitude for fluency building or practice activities.

How you schedule your own teaching time will also dictate the amount of time you can spend in supervising activities. In content area activities related to small group work, you may prefer to engage cross-age tutors as group facilitators rather than directly facilitating all the groups yourself. In other content areas, your instruction time may not allow you to directly supervise the tutorial event, e.g., when working directly with a small group on a particular skill, you cannot also directly supervise the children engaged in one-to-one tutorial sessions. Assuming that there is a good match and appropriate training has been given, you really shouldn't need to spend much time in direct supervision at all.

## Spatial and Material Resources

In a tutorial situation, teaching requires spare teaching tools. The way in which you arrange your classroom usually suggests the degree to which your tutorial program is successful. Room size, number of children, furnishings, materials and equipment, and the amount of closet, cabinet, and shelf space are all variables that determine your classroom arrangement (Stowitschek, Gable, & Hendrickson, 1980).

**Physical space**—While not too much can be done about the actual physical size of your room, your arrangement of furnishings can increase your workspace. First, eliminate unnecessary aisles. Push desks and children's work tables together to form small groups. By pushing the desks together, you will still have walking spaces, but you will probably free up some corner space for work tables. Should you have a wheelchair-bound child, you will need to be sure that the child's work space allows for ease of movement. Rather than seating that child in the center of a group of desks, seat the child on an outside aisle.

By freeing corner space, you have a private tutorial space. For those tutoring situations that require concentration, corner space isolation is a good option. If space for tables is limited, you can use the floor for seating or working.

Remember, too, that not all of your students will need isolated tutorial space. Most of your students can work at their desks with a tutor. To avoid extra crowding, schedule your tutors to come into your classroom at different times. In this way you can keep the number of students in your room reasonable and avoid overcrowding.

Station your work area so that you are in a position to see all the students and tutorial teams. As you work with a small group or an individual, constantly scan your class. By scanning, you can provide supervisory feedback to tutors and work groups as well as monitor progress, work flow, and other classroom events.

Physical space needs may also be influenced by various problems associated with certain types of handicaps. Miscellaneous considerations for various handicapping problems will appear as you work with your tutorial teams. Children with visual problems need to be able to see both your face and the tutor's face. Children with behavior problems may need to have their tutorial sessions close to you. Children who tend to be easily distracted may need to sit in a screened off area or facing a wall. While they may not be in visual line with you, you will still need to have direct visual contact with their backs. Body posture and amount of movement can tell you a lot about what's happening with the tutorial team.

**Material management**—Management of your tutorial materials is very much like managing your own instructional materials. You need to store materials in a predictable place and to know what information they contain. The elaborateness of your materials management system will again be relative to your available resources. Tutorial teams will need to know where to find materials and where to put materials after the session. The tutorial teams do not have time to play "hide-and-seek" with instructional materials. If the tutorial team is to work on reading skills, then materials for those skills should either be listed or already gathered. If the materials are listed, e.g., "page 5 in the classroom phonics workbook," then the tutorial team should know where to find the material.

To help teams find materials, you can organize your classroom into various areas. For example, you might have the three shelves on the far west wall contain reading books sequenced by level of difficulty and the two bottom shelves on the left wall might contain science books. If materials are already gathered, then the tutorial team should be able to find these materials without seeking help from you.

The key to materials management is predictability. Having established that predictability is important, the next issue is to decide where to store materials so their location is predictable. In most regular classrooms, a variety of locations are available. These include your filing cabinet, shelf and closet space, and the pupil's own desk.

With some handicapping conditions, special materials may be needed during tutorial sessions. A child who has difficulty grasping may need to use a special grip on the pencil. Visually impaired children may need to use large-print books. Other children may need specially constructed worksheets developed by the special teacher. In situations where keeping materials at the desk is not always feasible, specially designated space should be provided for storage. This special space should be easily accessible and relatively permanent.

The tutorial team will also need to be given directions as to where to put completed work. In a formal tutorial situation, you may have designated files for each student. In a less formal tutorial situation, completed work may simply consist of a finished workbook page. That page stays in the workbook and the workbook stays at the student's desk.

# SCHEDULING

## GROUP WORK ITEMS THAT ARE SIMILAR

### Combining Basic Skills with Content Matter

Grouping work items that are similar is a technique that allows you to stretch your teaching dollar further by killing the proverbial two birds with one stone. Consider the area of reading instruction. In reading instruction you usually teach children how to recognize words, sound out words, or gain meaning from a word or group of words. In eduational jargon we refer to these areas as word analysis, word recognition, oral reading, and reading comprehension. Normally teachers use a basal reader and an occasional phonics workbook to teach reading skills. Basal readers are convenient and the teaching steps usually well laid out. These same teaching steps can also be used with subject matter books, too. Instead of introducing the controlled vocabulary list from the sixth grade basal reader during the reading time, you can introduce the critical vocabulary terms from the social studies text. You can also practice oral reading and comprehension from the same social studies book. Free reading time can be taken from a library book on some aspect of the social studies content, and language experience stories in social studies can be a technique to build from the students' own vocabulary. Thus social studies and reading are intertwined. You save or rather gain time by (a) reducing preparation time, i.e., preparing only one combined reading and social studies class rather than two classes, one in reading and one in social studies; (b) reducing the number of class periods by one; and (c) providing more opportunities to work with those children who are having reading probems.

The child with reading problems will not be penalized for being unable to read the social studies material because you will be directly teaching those materials along with reading skills. By combining content and reading instruction you will also be able to reduce some of the behavior disturbances that occur when children are asked to complete work with materials they cannot fully understand.

## Combining Related Skills

In some cases, either due to a school board dictum or your personal belief system, you may not feel comfortable combining content material with basic skill areas in reading or math. You may feel more at ease in working with more obviously related areas such as the skills in language arts. Language arts skills center around aspects of reading, spelling, writing, and handwriting. Instead of having a separately scheduled instructional period for each language arts area, they can be combined. Table 6.1 shows various combinations of activities.

Let's look at the example presented in column one. In this column activities in oral reading, word recognition, spelling sight words, and handwriting have been combined. Using Sadie's work as an example, her teacher first identifies key words for Sadie to learn. These key words were taken in part from the basal series and in part from past words Sadie has used in her experience stories. Sadie's teacher has her practice the words through a flashcard exercise. Sadie is part of a small group working on the key vocabulary terms from the basal as well as six special or personal terms. The children in Sadie's group use the basal and special terms for spelling. Their teacher has them practice spelling and reading the words with each other. Naturally, when handwriting activities are needed, Sadie's teacher has a ready-made list of practice words. Finally, after Sadie's teacher is convinced that the time is right, i.e., the children in the group have learned all the words at the acquisition level, she is ready to hear them read from the basal reader. Proficiency is acquired. Success insured, the children complete their oral reading activity with a high degree of proficiency.

The way that Sadie's teacher, or any other teacher, chooses to present information is strictly a matter of personal style. Some teachers may choose to present four short lessons during an hour's time, i.e., a mini-lesson in oral reading, word recognition, spelling, and handwriting. Other teachers may opt for one or two longer lessons each day in only one or two areas.

The advantage of presenting work in combinations is that the children are shown the new concepts or ideas in a variety of ways. Children may do an oral drill and practice activity with a set of words, spell those words in a worksheet activity, and write those same words out for manuscript practice. Thus, children are continually reviewing and, as a result, spending more repeated time with concepts. For children with learning problems, the review

**Table 6.1**
Instructional Relationships between Language Arts Subjects

| Activities | 1 | 2 | 3 | 4 | 5 | 6 | 7 | 8 | 9 | 10 | 11 | 12 | 13 | 14 | 15 | 16 | 17 | 18 | 19 | 20 |
|---|---|---|---|---|---|---|---|---|---|---|---|---|---|---|---|---|---|---|---|---|
| **Reading** | | | | | | | | | | | | | | | | | | | | |
| Oral reading | x | x | x | | x | x | x | x | | | | | | | | | | | | |
| Word recognition | x | | x | | | x | x | x | | | | | | | | | | | | |
| Word analysis | | | x | x | | | | | x | x | | | | | | | | | | |
| Comprehension | | x | x | | | | | | x | | x | x | x | | | | | | | |
| **Spelling** | | | | | | | | | | | | | | | | | | | | |
| Sight words | x | | x | | x | | x | x | x | x | x | x | x | x | x | | | | | |
| Phonetically regular words | | | | x | | | | | x | x | x | | | x | x | x | x | | | |
| **Writing** | | | | | | | | | | | | | | | | | | | | |
| Creative | | | x | | | | | | x | x | | x | | | | | | | | |
| Guided/Topical | | | | x | x | | | x | | | | | | x | x | x | x | x | | |
| Handwriting | | | | | | | | | | | | | | | | | | | x | x |
| Isolated letters | | | | x | | | | | x | | | | | | | x | x | | x | |
| Words | x | | x | | x | | | x | | x | | | x | x | x | x | x | | x | x |

and reinforcement will aid them to perform successfully in a regular classroom environment (Smith, 1981).

## TRANSITION TIME

### Hold the Number of Starts and Stops to a Minimum

In the regular classroom there are stops and then there are STOPS. Stops are when the class completes an activity or class period and starts are when the class initiates an activity. The time in-between is called *transition time*. Transition time can be controlled on a number of levels by either the teacher or the student. Teacher-controlled transition time occurs when the teacher provides direct input into the transition. The teacher provides indirect input or control when students control transitions. The most obvious transition times occur between subjects, e.g., between reading and math periods. In transitions between subjects, children generally put away one set of materials and bring out another set or wait until further instructions are given. What occurs during that "wait" time can make the difference between a pleasant, well-run day and a potentially unpleasant environment bordering on chaos.

Starts and stops between subjects do take time. Whenever large group behavior is synchronized, time is spent in repeating directions, waiting for everyone to find the proper materials, and bringing the entire group to attention. The more between-subject transitions you have, the less time you will have for teaching. Reduction of large scale or whole class transitions, in most cases, can result in increased teaching time. To guide transition times, you can institute a few ground rules, including use of a clearly perceived message of intent and a predictable routine.

### A Clearly Perceived Message of Intent

Intent means that you have a definite idea of why you're stopping and what you plan to do next. Once you've established your intentions for yourself, make sure that your students understand you.

Take the example of Ms. Esch. Ms. Esch has decided to finish the spelling lesson and move into the natural science lesson. She closes her spelling book and pulls out her science materials. Meanwhile the students are hard at work with their spelling exercise. She gives them a signal that the spelling lesson is over. Her signal is a combination of verbal and nonverbal communication. Ms. Esch goes to the front of the room, stands very tall, and says in a calm but authoritative voice, "Please put away your spelling books and clear off your desks." The children do so. After the desks are cleared, she proceeds to say, "Today in science, we are going to learn about the plants that grow in our state."

Ms. Esch has provided a clear set of directions for conveying her intention. She has: (1) provided a stopping time, "Please put away your spelling books"; (2) allowed for a settling down period, "Clean off your desks"; and (3) set the stage for the next subject, "Today in science we ... ." For most children Ms. Esch has done a more than adequate job of controlling the transition between two subject areas. For a few, especially the sensory impaired children, Ms. Esch may need to go a little further. The hearing impaired child may need a more obvious clue to realize that a transition is occurring. The hearing impaired, or any child who may be inattentive, may need a slight tap on the shoulder or some similar physical signal to realize that a transition is taking place. If, for example, the child is looking down at his desk during the spelling period, he literally may not be able to hear his teacher's verbal signal. If a visually impaired child is listening to audio-tapes or working with a braille writer during the spelling time, she may not see the teacher move to the center of the room or hear the verbal signal. Some children with mild behavior problems may also find that transition times between subjects give them a chance to get attention, i.e., they may refuse to comply through either active or passive means. Another type of child that may need special consideration during transition time is one whose language skills are somewhat low. That child may need repetition of directions or may need to have the directions accompanied by some sort of visual aid. Rather than putting away materials before the transition is made, the classroom teacher can put her materials away as the children are putting theirs away. To return to Ms. Esch, she could come to the center of the room and hold up her spelling text, point to the text, and say, "Please put away your spelling workbooks." After she has made that statement, she could put her own spelling text on her desk. In this way, Ms. Esch is modeling the desired behavior for her students.

## Transitions during Independent Activities

Transition times, including stops and starts, can also be child-directed. Cases where the children determine when to begin and end a task usually occur during independent work time. During independent work time the child is also given directions on what to do if he or she has problems or needs help during the work time. The child is also provided with directions on what to do when the task is completed.

For children who have learning problems in social or academic tasks, many small tasks during an independent work time may be appropriate. Working for 30 to 45 minutes on one task may be too demanding. Concentrated effort may also be difficult for some sensory impaired or health impaired children. A child who is using less than normal physical equipment, e.g., an impaired visual system, may tire more easily from doing an extended independent activity.

**Stops and starts**—Stops and starts for the mini-lessons can allow a child to take acceptable and disguised breaks from assigned tasks. One caution is to be very sure that you, the classroom teacher, have structured the start and stop times very carefully. For example, suppose you have given the child three mini-assignments to complete during a 30-minute period. Some children will have no problems, but others may have a difficult time deciding the order in which to do the work. For some children you may need to number the top of the pages and have them complete the work in numerical order. For other children, use of time may become a problem. These children may spend the full 30 minutes on one task and not even begin with the others. For children with time judgment problems, you may want to indicate the amount of time to spend on the assignment at the top of the worksheet, e.g., 10 minutes. For those children who cannot tell time, you can either give them a kitchen timer and teach them to use it or draw a picture of a clock face on each assignment.

**Help signals**—Children also need to know appropriate means for getting help. Let's suppose that a child has a problem understanding how to complete an independent assignment. The child has begun the work, but bogged down toward the middle of the task. You have a couple of options open to you. You can:

1. Allow the child to interrupt you while you are working with other students.
2. Ignore your teaching group and rush to the child's side.
3. Set up a signalling system.
4. Provide sources of explanation other than yourself.

Allowing the child to interrupt you as you work with others is probably not a good choice. Not only do you have less time to give an appropriate response to the child, but you are also teaching the child to seek immediate self-gratification regardless of the needs of others.

Some children may have difficulty should you disregard option one. While most mainstreamed children were not allowed option one in special settings either, they also had less need to interrupt. In the smaller special classes, the teacher or aide could respond very quickly, and some of the children will have learned to expect immediate feedback. As a result you may need to teach some mainstreamed children that the class expectancies in a group of 30 are somewhat different than group expectancies in a class of 15.

Option two, like option one, is not such a good choice. You may have taught one child not to rush up to you, but you have set the child up to expect that you will rush over to him or her. Option two has the same drawbacks as option one.

A signalling system is one in which you and the student communicate the need for assistance. Appropriate signalling systems typically include visual signs, activities to be engaged in while waiting for help, and an understanding of delay time between the appearance of a signal and teacher attention. Visual signals can be a raised hand, a help sign on the student's desk, or the student's name written on the chalkboard. Signals for use with handicappped children are not much different than signals used by your nonhandicapped students. Common sense will guide you in your choice of class signals. If, for example, you have several highly distractible or overly active students, you wouldn't want a signalling system that requires a lot of movement. Getting up and writing a name on the board may add to the child's activity level as well as provide an opportunity for additional peer interaction—a chat with a neighbor, a friendly punch on a good pal's arm. Likewise, if your signal is some sort of desk object, e.g., a small flag or a picture of an unhappy face, you would want to ensure that all the children were physically able to manipulate the device. The blind child with physical involvement in the arms or shoulders may need some modifications. Likewise, children with language difficulties may need to be instructed through a modeling technique, i.e., you actually demonstrate to that child how to set up a signal and when to set up the signal.

**Appropriate waiting behavior**—Children also need to know what behaviors are appropriate while waiting for help. Just sitting and waiting begs for engagement in highly questionable activities, like daydreaming. If the child has more than one assignment, you may also direct the child to take out a reading book or to practice on some related task. In any event, the child needs to be kept occupied.

Choices will confuse some children. For those children or for those who find decision making difficult, allow only one prespecified waiting time activity. This activity should, of course, be one which the child understands independently.

An expectation of the length of the delay time should also be given. Children need to know approximately how long they will have to wait until they receive help. Knowledge of delay time may influence the type of request made. If the child knows that the delay is likely to be about 5 to 10 minutes, he or she is more likely to settle into the alternative activity fairly quickly. If, on the other hand, the child anticipates a delay of less than a minute or so, then the likelihood of initiating an alternative activity is lessened, and the child is more likely to wait patiently. Knowledge of delay time allows for clarification of expected student behavior and reduction of uncertainty— which brings us to another point. Children must also be able to have some consistency in the "getting back" time. Signals must be consistently honored if they are to be used effectively. Children need to be able to trust the system or the system will not work.

Response to signals, like all other forms of reinforcement, has a profound effect on how many times the child will continue to use the system. The way the child uses the system depends almost entirely upon how you, the teacher, respond to the signals. If, in the past, you appeared immediately each time the child signaled (continuous reinforcement), the child will expect you to continue to appear immediately. If you fail to appear immediately, then the child will rapidly quit using the signal to elicit your attention. If, in contrast, you set up a system of varying the amount of time (intermittent reinforcement) between the child's signal and your response, the child would learn to be much more persistent in waiting for your attention (Ferster & Perrott, 1968).

Option four assumes that you can trust others to convey the same information that you would. As a regular classroom teacher, your best source of "others" will be your own students. The odds are high that out of 30 children at least 22 or 23 will have a fairly clear idea of how to complete independent assignments. All you need to do is to decide how you want the children to assist each other. You have two basic systems available. In one system, a particular child functions as a designated teacher helper. In the other system, children simply work together as they deem necessary.

**Teacher helpers**—If you choose a teacher helper system, you may want to institute a signalling system. In effect, the teacher helper follows the signalling system just like you would. If you have several children who need assistance throughout an independent activity time, you may wish to have two or three children simultaneously functioning as teacher's helpers. Weekly or monthly rotation of teacher's helpers is also advisable, or fairly rapidly your teacher's helpers will be labeled teacher's pets. All of your students should get a chance to be helpers, even those children who are functioning at a lower level than most. The assistance these children may provide would be less instructional and more logistic than that provided by other helpers. Children who know content or directions can actually provide instruction, whereas a child with limited academic skills could distribute or collect assignments—in some cases even correct assignments.

In a system where no formal teacher's helper is designated, children simply help each other. You can have children form more or less permanent work groups, or the children can group as needed. As in all the systems mentioned so far, the students must have a clear understanding of your expectations. In a classroom setting, these expectations will probably center on the degree of assistance and the noise level tolerated. In some classrooms assistance may be two or three explanatory sentences. In other classrooms, children may be encouraged to complete joint assignments. Noise level will vary as a function of teacher tolerance and the needs of the classroom. With children who are highly distractible or who are hearing impaired, their needs are a critical determinant of a noise-level ceiling. In most settings a library-level whisper is more likely to result in an appropriate feedback setting than a noise level that can be likened to an air traffic flight pattern.

# MAINTAINING A SCHEDULE

## PREDICTABLE ROUTINES

Developing a predictable routine for teaching events is a technique that can reduce loss of teaching time during transitions as well as enhance the understanding of class logistics. Children, handicapped or otherwise, gain a sense of stability when events in their lives are fairly predictable. Some children, especially those with mild behavior or learning problems, need routine even more than normal children. Evidence has shown that children with learning problems are often viewed as impulsive (Epstein, Hallahan, & Kauffman, 1975). Generally, impulsive behavior reflected in the tendency to respond with a high rate of error in uncertain situations (Kagan, 1966) is restricted to academic tasks. If, however, all learning is basically founded on the same principles, then the finding can also extend to other situations as well. If the impulsive child is uncertain about the organization of the day's events, you should expect that child to have an incomplete notion of class requirements or at least to feel very uncertain of expected behaviors.

### Varying Activities Within a Schedule

All routine and no variety can make Jack a dull boy and his classroom a dull experience. The overall schedule can remain the same, but activities within the schedule can vary. For example, health can occur everyday at 11:30 a.m., but on Monday the health activity may be a movie and on Tuesday the health activity may be a small group activity.

A daily schedule can be provided for those children who have difficulty remembering even the overall structure. The format of the schedule will depend on the child's level of understanding or sensory need. A child who cannot read print will obviously need a different format than a child who does. A common schedule design uses a subject or time block format (Gallagher, 1979). In a regular classroom, you would most likely provide a schedule for the morning or basic skill activities. Morning activities usually require the most independent work.

Scheduling time either across activities, such as the reading time, the math time, or the science time, or within activities, such as independent and teacher-directed instruction during the spelling period, becomes fairly easy once you've decided what you want to teach. The trick, of course, is in deciding what you want taught, to whom, and how. What you want taught should flow from a list of observable (and some not quite so observable) objectives. What you want taught to whom should be based on the needs of your students. With children identified as handicapped the decision of what to teach will be made jointly between you and the special teacher.

## Complementary Scheduling

Choosing the manner in which the "what" is taught to the "whom" becomes a little tricky when dealing with handicapped children. While many of these children are in your classroom for part or most of the day, they also spend time with the special teacher. The special teacher time must also be considered when you set up your classroom routine. Your schedule and the special teacher's schedule will influence how the student is taught the "what."

Basically, you have two teaching options. You schedule either teacher-directed or student-initiated activities. If the handicapped child needs a concentrated amount of work that is teacher directed, then you may wish to schedule some of that student's teacher-directed time with the special teacher. You also need to spend some teacher-directed time with the student, but the advantage of working with the special teacher is that you will still have time to work with your other 29 children without feeling guilty about your special one. Time spent in teacher-directed activities can also be decreased through the use of peer or cross-age tutors. The introduction of tutors assumes that they too are on a predictable schedule and that their schedule is compatible with yours. With so many schedules weaving about, you may want to develop a master chart. Using a step-by-step procedure you can begin to fit the puzzle of schedules together in a fairly simple fashion.

## A Master Schedule Grid

Step one is to draw a grid for your weekly schedule, as shown in Figure 6.3. This grid blocks out time by day. Fill in the grid with general headings, such as math and reading. Step two is to fill out a similar grid for the special teacher and tutors, as shown in Figure 6.4. In the other teachers' schedule, the names of the children who leave the room are listed next to the special teacher's name. The time and number of tutors is also shown. Figure 6.5 shows a sample Other Teachers' Schedule.

Having established your general teaching schedule, your third step is to proceed to your more specific or daily schedule. Your daily schedule should be consistent for the day, e.g., every Monday, geography is presented be-

**Figure 6.3**
Grid for Weekly Schedule

Week _____

| | Monday | Tuesday | Wednesday | Thursday | Friday |
|---|---|---|---|---|---|
| 8:30– 9:00 | Opening | Opening | Opening | Opening | Opening |
| 9:00–10:00 | Reading | Reading | Reading | Reading | Reading |
| 10:00–10:15 | Recess | Recess | Recess | Recess | Recess |
| 10:15–11:00 | Math | Math | Math | Math | Math |
| 11:00–11:30 | Language Arts | Language Arts | Language Arts | Language Arts | Language Arts |
| 11:30–12:30 | Lunch | Lunch | Lunch | Lunch | Lunch |
| 12:30–12:45 | Story | Story | Story | Story | Story |
| 12:45– 1:30 | Science | Science | Science | Science | Science |
| 1:30– 2:30 | P.E. | Library | P.E. | P.E. | Art |
| 2:30– 3:00 | Geography | Music | Geography | Music | Geography |
| 3:00– 3:10 | Dismissal | Dismissal | Dismissal | Dismissal | Dismissal |

**Figure 6.4**
Grid for Special Teachers and Tutors

Week _____

| | Monday | Tuesday | Wednesday | Thursday | Friday |
|---|---|---|---|---|---|
| 8:30– 9:00 | | | | | |
| 9:00–10:00 9:00– 9:15 | LD-R | LD-R | LD-R | LD-R | LD-R |
| 9:15– 9:30 9:30–10:00 | 15 Cross-Age Tutors | | 5 Cross-Age Tutors | | 5 Cross-Age Tutors |
| 10:00–10:15 | | | | | |
| 10:15–11:00 | LD-R 13 Cross-Age Tutors | LD-R 3 Cross-Age Tutors | LD-R 3 Cross-Age Tutors | LD-R 3 Cross-Age Tutors | LD-R 3 Cross-Age Tutors |
| 11:00–11:30 | | Speech Therapist | | Speech Therapist | |
| 11:30–12:30 | Lunch | Lunch | Lunch | Lunch | Lunch |
| 12:30–12:45 | | | | | |
| 12:45– 1:30 | | | | | |
| 1:30– 2:30 | P.E. Teacher | Librarian | P.E. Teacher | P.E. Teacher | |
| 2:30– 3:00 | | Music Teacher | | Music Teacher | |
| 3:00– 3:10 | Dismissal | Dismissal | Dismissal | Dismissal | Dismissal |

**Figure 6.5**
"Other Teachers" Schedule

| Teacher | Student | Time | Subject |
|---|---|---|---|
| **9:00–10:00** | | | |
| LD-R (Mrs. C.) | George | 9:00– 9:30 | Reading |
| | CeCe | | |
| | Trudie | | |
| | Jim | | |
| | Ray | | |
| Cross-Age Tutors | | 9:00– 9:30 | Reading |
| Vera | Thomas | | |
| Tang | Robert | | |
| Phillip | Alice | | |
| Erich | Frank | | |
| Mikhail | Eliza | | |
| | | 9:30–10:00 | Reading |
| Vera | Thomas | | |
| Tang | Charles | | |
| Phillip | Harriet | | |
| Erich | George | | |
| Mikhail | Florence | | |
| **10:15–11:00** | | | |
| LD-R (Mrs. C.) | Jeff | 10:15–11:00 | Math |
| | George | | |
| | Jim | | |
| Cross-Age Tutors | | 10:15–11:00 | |
| Daisy—Small group working on 2 X's tables | | | |
| Frank—Floater | | | |
| Ken—1-minute timings with individuals according to schedule | | | |
| **11:00–11:30** | | | |
| Speech (Mr. B.) | Meiko | | Language development |
| **1:30– 2:30** | | | |
| P.E. (M/W/Th) | Whole class | | |
| Library (T) | Whole class | | |
| **2:30– 3:00** | | | |
| Music (T/Th) | Whole class | | |

tween 2:30 and 3:00. The schedule need not be the same every day, e.g., 2:30 to 3:00 can be geography on Mondays, Wednesdays, and Fridays and music on Tuesdays and Thursdays. Schedules can repeat once a week, once every other week, or any way you find that is convenient to meet your teaching needs and the needs of the students in your room (Sloane, Buckholdt, Jenson, & Crandall, 1979).

The fourth step requires that you mesh your schedule for other teachers with your specific schedule. Let's take Monday for an example. Figure 6.5 clearly shows that George, CeCe, Trudie, Jim, and Ray will be out of the reading period for a half hour. Ideally Ms. C. could work with these children on reading tasks. Of course, sometimes the ideal does not work out; Ms. C. may be working on math or some other area. In this case, the classroom teacher will need to be sure to work with the small group of children from 9:30 to 10:00. Direct teacher instruction, whether from the classroom teacher or the tutors, can occur from 9:30 to 10:00. The teacher will be able to schedule the tutors in reading activities. This sort of schedule now brings us to step five.

In step five, the teacher refines his or her own schedule once more, taking each subject and breaking down the activities for that time. Figure 6.6 shows this more detailed schedule.

Student schedules can vary as class periods do. You need not work with the same children or groups every day, e.g., you can hear Suzanna's oral reading three times a week and Morgan's only once. Suzanna needs more oral reading instruction than Morgan, and Suzanna needs your direct input much more than Morgan. Morgan's skills are such that he's merely refining or prac-

**Figure 6.6**
Student Schedules

| Time | Monday |
|---|---|
| 9:00– 9:15 | Group A (10 kids) works in small group with teacher on decoding<br>Group B (15 kids) works on an independent reading activity<br>Group C (5 kids) goes to Ms. C's room |
| 9:15–9:30 | Group A (10 kids) works independently<br>Group B (15 kids) works with teacher on word recognition<br>Group C (5 kids) still in Ms. C's room |
| 9:30–10:00 | Group A works independently<br>Group B works independently<br>Group C works with tutors on a one-to-one<br>Members of A, B, C work on a one-to-one with teacher in oral reading |

ticing a learned skill. How often you schedule direct instruction time with your students will be a direct function of student need.

While the steps in scheduling may initially seem superfluous, when working with 30 children you need a master chart. The chart can keep track of who's doing what to whom and when. With so many curious minds at stake, your planning schedule can prevent the loss of the shrinking violets and the development of the out-of-control thistles.

## FLEXIBILITY IN SCHEDULING

Don't be surprised if your initial schedule is rapidly in need of repair. A little schedule bending, poking, and shaping is the rule and not the exception. Your schedule will change as your needs, your team needs (special education and cross-age tutors), and your children's needs demand. Teaching is a vital process and as such, instruction, events, and plans are directed toward growth. Flexibility in scheduling is not only to be desired, but rather to be expected.

### Entry/Exit Tips

Many of your mildly handicapped children will be in and out of your classroom. Special classes in reading or language or whatever often require the child to go to the special teacher's room for one or two periods and then return to the regular setting. Each time that child enters or leaves the regular setting, two kinds of disruptions occur. The first disruption affects the child. When the child reenters the classroom, he or she must reorient to the ongoing classroom activity—an activity for which the child has not been formally prepared. Take the example of Viola. Viola leaves the classroom Mondays, Wednesdays, and Fridays to go to a special reading class. She knows that the rest of her class is working on language arts while she is out of the room. After Viola finishes her reading, she knows that she is expected to work on a language arts activity, too. The problem is that Viola is not quite sure what the language arts activity is supposed to be. She has a general idea, but because she was out of the room when the directions were given, she isn't quite sure what she's expected to complete.

Meanwhile, Viola's teacher is in the middle of the teaching activity. Enter disruption two. Viola's teacher, no matter how patient or understanding, is also disrupted. The teacher must stop her group activity to help Viola. She runs the risk of being exasperated to mildly annoyed. Viola runs the risk of feeling guilty for some unknown crime or feeling rather bewildered by the whole reentry experience.

## Possible Solutions

The most desirable solution to this problem is to set up your classroom in such a way that the special teacher can work with Viola in your room. In other words, Viola doesn't ever leave. Her special teacher comes to Viola's room and helps her reorient to classroom activities. In cases where the special teacher cannot work in the regular setting, the next best bet is to have a peer orient the reentering child.

Most importantly, the teacher needs to try to remember that the reentering child is often confused—granted in some cases only momentarily. The point of reentry, depending on the ease with which the child readjusts, can be a very delicate time for both of you, the classroom teacher, and all the Violas in your charge.

## SUMMARY

Chapter 6 has dealt with classroom organization strategies. Three major topics of discussion centered on identification of teaching objectives, consolidation of teaching activities, and time management. The identification of teaching objectives focused on the need for reducing extraneous objectives and pinpointing critical ones. The use of the regular elementary curriculum was presented in relationship to handicapped children and their needs. The relationship of objectives to materials was also discussed. Consolidation where possible emphasized grouping techniques for instructional purposes. Ways to efficiently organize children and the instructional materials were considered. Management of time isolates and contrasts clock time with value time. In this section, the teacher was also shown a way to track or record what he or she actually does with school time.

In addition, this chapter investigated specific variables involved in organizing teacher time. Delegation of tasks grouping work items and establishment of a predictable schedule were emphasized. Another useful device is peer or cross-age tutoring. Techniques for scheduling in a regular classroom were also presented.

# 7
# Pinpointing Reading Skills

"Open your books to page 15." All 28 students must have heard the familiar request, chanted in its usual soft tone. Instantly, the basal readers' pages were hurried along on their flight in the direction of one page. Except for eight outstretched arms, reaching for the ceiling, subdued calm was almost restored to the second grade classroom. Five more arms suddenly joined the force, only to withdraw from the race when all arms lowered once Mrs. Price had called on Suzie to read.

Reading instruction had begun. Excitement to read had started the day, and Mrs. Price was pleased. And why shouldn't she be pleased, even delighted? After all, teachers' manuals have been promoting the ever-popular theme "children love to read" since time began. Even our reading instructors in all our universities and colleges have agreed with them.

So why then is Al kicking his table partner Dougie? Why is Bruce hiding a comic book behind his reader and Robbie falling asleep? Are the notes Kay and Homer exchanging about the main idea of the story? At least Fred seems busy—he's recording every time his teacher yawns.

## HISTORICAL PERSPECTIVE

### READING INSTRUCTION: GOOD NEWS, BAD NEWS

Research on the effects of reading instruction in the schools has resulted in sales of innumerable books and popular magazines. Ever since Rudolf Flesch produced his best-selling *Why Johnny Can't Read* (1955), the area of reading instruction in the public schools has been the target of intense and continuing public debate. What is a teacher to do! Not only have teachers been accused of allowing normal, inquisitive children to slip into a "rapidly sinking morass of ignorance" (Flesch, 1979), but now they are asked to teach reading, however best they can, to handicapped children—children who, for the most part, were removed from the regular classroom in the first place because they couldn't read! Estimates (Carnine & Silbert, 1979) have placed the rate of referrals to special education programs because of reading problems three times higher than any other reason.

We do know that successful reading practices occur and that not all slow readers become "special education" representatives. Literate environments in which reading and writing are stressed and lessons are stimulating meet the needs of many of our students (Anderson, Hiebert, Scott, & Wilkinson, 1985).

Data suggest that most children are learning to read. However, until *all* children attain their potential, we have a long way to go (Micklas, 1980).

Handicapped children are included. As a regular classroom teacher, you are an important "cultivator" in the "garden" of reading success. The instructional thorn in the side of many teachers can be found in a multitude of places, but perhaps the real root of the problem stems from a rather incomplete picture of a very complex process.

## WHOLE-WORD VS. PHONICS CONTROVERSY

### Look-Say Method

For years, the great debate in the area of reading instruction has centered on whether to teach the whole-word method (often referred to as the *look-say* method) or to teach phonics. The whole-world method advocates that initial reading instruction should focus on meaning. Enter the medium of instruction of the basal reading series. To teach children to read for meaning (whole words instead of isolated sounds), only a very limited sight vocabulary would be taught. With the basal reader the child was able to recognize a limited set of words as wholes. These words were arranged into sentences and stories about topics of interest. Perhaps you can recall your own level of involvement with such passages—"Spot, Spot. See Spot go. Go, Spot. Go, go."

Vocabulary was not all that was restricted. Reading instruction with the basal series was firmly based in the folkways of school reading practices. Then along came Chall.

### Phonics Approach

In 1967 Chall researched phonics teaching versus the whole-word approach and found that initial intensive and systematic phonics teaching was superior not only in developing word recognition, but also in developing reading comprehension. Chall was not alone. Research demonstrating the need for phonics instruction as a base for teaching nonreaders to recognize words continued to deluge the educational community. Intensive phonics instruction develops and maintains superior word recogntion at least through the third grade reading level (Dykstra, 1974).

With this plethora of evidence, you might wonder if the basals should be rewritten, and in place of "Go. Spot. Go, go, go," read, "Go, Spot. Go, went, gone." As fate would have it, a new wave of antiphonics persuasion has swept across the reading instruction debate. Some theorists are suggesting that the development of reading skills or literacy is innate. They contend that children begin to read only where the written symbol is meaningful, contextualized, and social (Halliday, 1969). Many 3- and 4-year-olds score 100% with such words as "McDonald's," "Coke," and "ice cream." More sophisticated toddlers are even able to read foreign print, e.g., "Haagen-Daaz." Beginning reading is viewed as a communication system, and the way that children find significance of written language may even be cultural (Clay, 1976). To this point the phonics versus meaning debate pot has been kept on simmer.

With a little help from Goodman and Burke (1973), the pot began to boil. A key conclusion they reached was that nonproficient readers tend to get bogged down in their preoccupation with letters and, as a result, words lose meaning. In fact, Goodman and Goodman (1979) have even gone so far as to say that creating curricula based on artificial skill sequences and hierarchies is a serious mistake. The "watched" pot boiled with statements such as phonics is "a very trivial skill in learning to read" or "a peripheral concern" for the child learning to read. While basals were not entirely ruled out, the emphasis on meaning became stronger than ever.

## Bridging the Phonics vs. Whole-Word Chasm

Next, linguists attempted to bridge the phonics versus whole-word chasm. In the linguistic approach, a restricted vocabulary based on phonetically regular words was to be the chain that reunited the phonics and whole-words methods camps. Early passage attempts, such as "Fan the tan man," proved to be a weak link at best. The linguists moved on and appeared to melt into one or the other of the two reading camps. Some of the linguists and many of the classroom reading teachers continued to wonder "whether the difficulties in reading are to be found at a visual stage (sound-symbol association, i.e., phonics), or a subsequent linguistic stage (meaning) of the process" (Shankweiler & Liberman, 1972). While the linguist continued to ponder, classroom teachers continued to teach. Some classroom teachers dealt with basals only, some with phonics only, but many more teachers felt a little guilty and began to deal with both.

While many classroom teachers were incorporating both whole-word and phonics instruction into the reading program, researchers began to make some distinctions between practiced and beginning readers. New jargon began to evolve. Skilled readers use a "top-down" reading process while developing readers use a "bottom-up" reading process (Weaver & Resnick, 1979). But top-down by any other name is still a meaning-based approach (Fredericksen, 1979; Smith, 1971), and a bottom-up process quite clearly refers to phonics (Perfetti & Lesgold, 1979). If you are gearing reading instruction to primary-level children, emphasis in reading skills might focus on phonics. If, on the other hand, reading instruction was geared to intermediate or more advanced readers, the classroom method may tend to draw heavily upon experience or meaning.

Fortunately for some reading theorists, recent reading research has discovered what guilty and effective classroom teachers have known for a long time. Top-down and bottom-up processing should be occurring at all levels of reading at the same time (Adams & Collins, 1977; Rummelhart, 1977). Instruction in reading will need to take both phonics skills (or decoding) and meaning into account. The only cloudy issue in this silver-lining view of reading instruction is the extent to which emphasis is placed on teaching phonics skills and meaning-based instruction.

### Using Skill Level in Instruction

At this point, common sense should assume center stage. Add a little bit of verifiable research data, and the knotty problem begins to untangle fairly easily. First and foremost, we know that skilled readers and novice readers perform differently. New readers as well as readers who have reading problems tend to read slowly. They may even attend to isolated letters or words instead of phrases or clause units. New readers sometimes get lost on the page and skip whole lines or ignore punctuation. Skilled readers, in contrast, tend to read smoothly and in phrases. Expression for skilled readers is typically appropriate, and the reading act is generally performed relatively comfortably. While the terms used to describe skilled and novice readers are not measurable, differences in their oral reading performance are certainly distinguishable.

The passage from novice to skilled reader is a mysterious one. Even though research has shown a number of the processes involved in skilled reading, we are still not sure when or in what manner reading behavior evolves from novice to skilled proficiency (Gibson & Levin, 1975). As teachers of reading, this information could guide the format of our reading program. For the new or unskilled reader, emphasis on meaning and instruction in phonics should go hand-in-hand. Since both types of instruction have obvious merit, both methods can be used simultaneously and accorded equal instructional time.

## COMPONENTS OF READING

Because reading is a complex act, we can't just talk about teaching "reading." Reading, as we've seen, a la the top-down/bottom-up people, can consist of many related components. Perhaps the easiest way to teach the Big R, total reading, is to examine some parts, the little r's. While the Big R pie can be divided many ways, one suggested way is to consider *word analysis, word recognition, oral reading,* and *comprehension.* Word analysis refers to decoding, word attack, phonics, or any other activity that requires a reader to analyze sounds or combinations of sounds. Word recognition refers to the ability to read or recognize whole words instantly. Oral reading typically combines word recognition skills and word analysis skills with oral language expression. Comprehension implies the ability to grasp the meaning behind the sound of a word or a group of words. To instruct in the components of reading, you need to identify in which of the four areas the child needs instruction. You also need to determine the depth of instruction.

## IDENTIFICATION OF SKILL LEVEL

### Screening Tests

Identification of what to teach the child begins with screening tests. If the child has not been in special education, the scores from an achievement test will help you arrive at an approximate grade level. If the child has been in special education, you can work directly with the special education teacher to establish reading entry into your class.

### Placement in Class Materials

Whatever the situation, you need to determine where the child is reading relative to your class materials. David, Becky, and Jack are students in a fifth grade class. All have been screened and the results of their general achievement test indicate that they are at grade level. While the results of the screening test were negative, their teacher was not satisfied. When David tried to read from his text, he couldn't finish his assignments. The difficulty seemed to be that he was unable to find the main idea of the stories. Becky showed the same kind of problem. She, too, seemed unable to complete her work. Their teacher realized that these possible comprehension problems could stem from many sources. To begin the process of identifying David's problem, his teacher asked him to read a passage out loud. David could barely read 50% of the words. His teacher had him read in two more texts from the series until she found one where he could read with 95% accuracy. Once she had established a reading level at which David could read accurately, she found that his comprehension problems disappeared. David needed some assistance in word analysis. Further testing clarified his problem.

Becky's story was somewhat different. She was being mainstreamed. The teacher conferred with the special education teacher and learned that Becky had a language problem that interfered with her comprehension of written material. Instead of further testing, Becky only needed some special assistance in learning how to use the fifth grade text.

While the screening test was used for David, Becky, and Jack, three different evaluation decisions became apparent through daily class participation. David needed additional evaluation in a specific area of reading. Jack didn't need more evaluation or special instruction. Most children in the regular classroom are like Jack, but for the students like David and Becky (if no special teacher can provide insight), additional testing is necessary before teaching can begin. David needed additional evaluation in a specific area of learning. Becky needed no more evaluation, but she did need special instruction.

## SKILL CATEGORIES IN READING

Many reading tests have been designed to measure one specific skill. Many other reading tests have interspersed questions over the four component skill areas. With most tests you can usually use a question under one of the following four categories: word analysis, word recognition, oral reading, and comprehension.

### Word Analysis

Following are several examples of word analysis tests.

Example 1: What sounds do these letters make?
a    c    e    t

Example 2: How do you break these words into syllables?
hungry
communion
Tuesday

Example 3: Read the following nonsense words to me.
nad    blop    nit    sup

Nonsense words are used to determine if a child understands the principles of how sounds work together. Questions that focus on sounds or sound combinations almost always relate to a child's skills in word analysis.

### Word Recognition

Tasks for oral reading and word recognition are very similar. The major difference is that in some kinds of word recognition tasks the child reads the word in isolation, usually in the form of a word list. In oral reading, the child generally reads a cluster of words. The cluster might be a phrase, sentence, or even a short passage. Reading the words in isolation is much more difficult than reading a word or words in clusters. When you are testing a child's ability to read words in isolation, you are simultaneously testing the ability to remember whole words. When testing for words in isolation, time limits are often given, i.e., the child must read a word in 5 seconds or less. The primary reason for the time constraint is to impose a control factor to discourage the use of phonic or word analysis skills for determining words. The ability to read a word without hesitation (to draw upon memory automatically) is the basic focus of word recognition skills. Here are some examples of word recognition tests.

> Example 1:  Read the following list of words:
>> go   sit   hop   now   play   house   dog   help
>
> Example 2:  Read the following list of words:
>> harass
>> yesterday
>> involve
>> participate
>> enjoy

## Oral Reading

Oral reading is often thought of as an extension of word recognition, but it is more likely the first step in word recognition. When children read aloud, they use their skills to predict appropriate words. If I ask Paco to read the word "you," he has no clues or helping word to give hints. But if he gets the sentence, "We do it all for you!" the odds are higher he will read the word correctly. Paco can use his TV-watching experience plus his knowledge of how language usually works to arrive with more ease at the correct word. Examples of oral reading are:

> Example 1:  New Deal reforms
>> rights of people
>> civil rights movement
>> protection of resources
>
> Example 2:  Most mountains are very old. Mountains have been here longer than people. Mountains seem to last forever. But some mountains will not last. Some mountains are volcanoes.

## Comprehension

Comprehension questions may also focus on isolated sounds, words, or passages. Typically, comprehension items focus on main ideas and detail questions. But defining terms is also related to meaning. The ability to understand the difference in the meaning of words that change endings is also a comprehension task. Adding the -s at the end of most words has meaning, e.g., *the duck* vs. *the ducks*. As can easily be seen, reading comprehension and language comprehension are related. When analyzing a child's reading comprehension skills, you need to deal with the written words in some discernible fashion. Unless the child can read the words, at least in a short passage, reading comprehension cannot be tested. (Language comprehension for written material can be tested for the nonreader, i.e., nonword analyzer or nonword recognizer, as will be discussed later in this chapter.) Here are some examples of comprehension test items.

Example 1: Define the following words:

constitution  _____

_____

independence  _____

_____

authority  _____

_____

taxation _____

Example 2: Read the following:

Margaret has two dogs. One dog is black and the other dog is black and white. The black dog's name is Pepper. The other dog's name is Max. Margaret likes her dogs.

What is this story about? _____

_____

What color is Max?  _____

_____

## IDENTIFICATION OF READING PROBLEMS

Having identified four basic areas of reading skills, the next step is to identify the level and, possibly, the rate at which the child is reading. Identification of level and rate will easily lead into selection of appropriate material. The catch-all is how the rate and level may vary for each reading component for a particular child. Children having problems in reading may not have problems in each of the four components; i.e., whenever Cliff reads orally, he stumbles over words. He often confuses the middle of a word and also substitutes one word for another. Cliff was asked to read the following passage.

An Indian put his ear to the ground. He heard many horses. They were coming his way. He ran to tell his people. Then he ran to tell the people of the next village. He was a runner. Using runners was one way Indians sent messages. (Liddle, 1970, p. 74 )

Cliff's version sounded more like this:

> The Indians put their ears on the grass. He heard many horses. They are
> coming to him. He ran to talk to some people. He ran to let the people of
> the next town know. He was running. Running was the way Indians sent
> messages.

Cliff received a little help now and again from his teacher. Very few
top-down or bottom-up reading teachers would argue that Cliff has a reading problem. At best, his oral reading skills seem a bit shaky. The surprise is
that he comprehends exceedingly well. When given main idea and specific
detail questions, Cliff could rank alongside Albert Einstein. How Cliff can
comprehend with such restricted word recognition and word analysis skills
ranks among the seven wonders of the world. Although the goal of all reading instruction is comprehension, Cliff could still use some reading instruction in word recognition and word analysis.

## SELECTED READING TESTS

### Normative Measures

Information provided by most achievement tests will only give you a very
general notion of areas of difficulty for each child. If a child's overall reading
score is quite low, you may want to give an additional reading test. Many
standardized diagnostic reading tests are available. Some of the more commonly used standardized diagnostic reading tests are the *Diagnostic Reading
Scales* (Spache, 1972), the *Durrell Analysis of Reading Difficulty* (Durrell,
1955), and *Stanford Diagnostic Reading Test* (Karlsen, Madden, & Gardner,
1976). These tests, and others like them, are usually administered individually.
The tests have been designed for use with primary or intermediate grade children or with disabled readers.

### Diagnostic Measures

Diagnostic reading tests are divided into more than just the four areas of
word recognition, word analysis, oral reading, and comprehension. They
may also examine specific areas within a general reading area. The
*Diagnostic Reading Scales* (Spache, 1972), for example, examine the area of
word analysis through eight subtests:

Test 1: Consonant Sounds

Test 2: Vowel Sounds

Test 3: Consonant Blends and Digraphs

Test 4:  Common Syllables of Phonograms

Test 5:  Blending

Test 6:  Letter Sounds

Test 7:  Initial Consonant Substitution

Test 8:  Auditory Discrimination

Obviously, diagnostic tests may require a great deal of time to administer. As a teacher of 30 children, you may find the thought of giving seven or
eight of these tests to your low readers a little less welcome than facing an on-
coming locomotive.

## Alternatives to Diagnostic Measures

As usual, options need to be considered. One option for obtaining diagnostic
information is to get that information from others. If some of your low readers are also considered handicapped, you could ask the school's special education teacher to provide you with additional test information from a standardized diagnostic test. Other low-functioning readers can be referred to the
remedial reading specialist or the school psychologist for reading evaluation.

A second option is that you could administer the tests yourself. Little in-
depth training is necessary to properly administer, score, and interpret test
results. Parents may give assistance, but more than likely you should be the
examiner. If you have results from the previous year's general achievement
test, you could examine the results for problems.

Let's explore third grader Kevin's test results. His total score for reading
was low on the *Metropolitan Achievement Test* (a standardized survey reading measure) (Prescott, Balow, Hogan, & Farr, 1978). On closer inspection,
Kevin's subtest scores varied considerably. Word knowledge was at the second grade, second month (2.2), comprehension at 3.3, and word analysis at
2.1.

Both word knowledge and word analysis are low, but comprehension is
about grade level. Roughly translating word knowledge to mean word recognition, we can see how word knowledge and word analysis need to be evaluated further.

**Error patterns**—If there is test information in the child's folder, you can begin to look for error patterns. But you can only get a rough idea of what a
child can do from a score. In trying to identify error patterns, you not only
observe what a child can or cannot do, but you also may identify the procedures the child is using. In analyzing the child's response, you may be able to
determine specific areas for further testing. For example, the problem may
be one of substitution in word endings, so you wouldn't need to test all areas

of word analysis, but only for additional information on the child's reading technique as related to word endings.

## INFORMAL TESTING

You are now at a juncture in the crossroads of evaluation decision making. One choice is to ignore the results of the test, place the child in the lowest reading group in the class, and hope to see progress by the winter break. A second choice is to forge ahead and continue testing with more specific standardized diagnostic tests in the areas of word recognition and word analysis.

A third choice is to initiate informal testing, based on class materials, in the areas of word recognition and word analysis. Choice one is obviously undesirable. The second and third choices will provide you with information on which to base your instruction.

Choice two directs you to formal diagnostic tests. Based on an analysis of errors, you can choose a specific subtest that focuses on the suspected problem. Returning to Kevin and his apparent difficulty with word endings, you might choose to administer the Consonant Blends and Digraphs subtest on the *Diagnostic Reading Scales* (Spache, 1972). Having done so, you have a formal score that can be translated into a grade equivalency. The only problem is that sometimes the grade equivalency, as measured by the test, does not always match the grade level of your class materials. A formal diagnostic measure may support your teaching decision, but may not help you choose among the available classroom materials.

### Informal Reading Inventories

The third choice—use of informal assessment—may be your best choice. Informal assessment makes use of the informal reading inventory (IRI). Typically, IRI's are created in the following steps (Betts, 1957; Haring et al., 1978; Otto, McMenemy, & Smith, 1973).

### Conducting an Informal Reading Inventory

Step 1:  Select a reading series for instruction.

Step 2:  Select a 100-word passage from each level. Some systems recommend three 100-word samples from each level.

Step 3:  Develop about six comprehension questions for each passage. Questions should focus on literal meaning, inferential meaning, and meaning of vocabulary. Questions can also be reduced to two recall, two sequence, and two interpretation.

Step 4: Have the child read one of the passages. A good place to begin is to have the child read a passage that is one grade level below his or her standardized score. So if Bill's score on the *Metropolitan* is 4.5, then you would have him begin reading a sample passage from the third grade reader. Reasons for choosing one grade level below the standardized score are:

1) Standardized scores usually represent the frustration or most difficult level of reading.

2) Sampling on a level slightly below grade provides the child with a chance of immediate success in an evaluation session. Children with a history of reading failure may need to feel successful during an evaluation situation if you are to get an accurate picture of their skills.

Step 5: Once the initial passage has been selected, the child reads to you orally. As the child reads, you note errors. The simplest way to record errors is to use a follow-along sheet. A follow-along sheet is a duplicated sheet identical to the child's reading page that can be as personalized as you want. As the child reads, you can record the errors on the follow-along sheet. By recording what the child actually reads, you will be able to determine error patterns. If you are not interested in identifying patterns, you can simply note errors by crossing out words or by tallying the errors (e.g., ////). If the decision is to determine error patterns, the child's problem will likely fall under five major headings: omissions, substitutions, mispronunciations, insertions, or repetitions.

## Interpreting Results

*Omissions* are words that are left out or words to which the child responds with "I don't know." Four or more seconds hesitation is usually considered an omission. Upon careful analysis of omissions, you may wish to adhere to the spirit of the rule rather than the letter (or in this case the word) of the rule. Inadvertently skipped words are probably not the same kind of error as "I don't know" words. Sometimes children omit words in a passage; the occasion and number of times this problem occurs should influence your judgment as to whether the omission is a significant problem.

If Eddie, for example, omits 1 or 2 words in a 100-word passage, it is more than likely that he does not have a major problem. Nor would Eddie have a serious problem had he omitted 11 words out of 100, if 6 of the 11 words were "the" and 5 were "a."

*Substitutions* occur when a child reads (or misreads) one word for another. There are two major types of substitution. Some substitutions are obvious guesses, referred to as *confabulations* (Otto et al., 1973). Others are the type that make sense contextually. An example is when Sandra reads the sentence "The flower is pretty" as "The flower is beautiful." Substitutions in context are not always a cause for alarm. The occasions for and frequency of substitutions should influence your judgment.

Substitution error patterns are found in the beginning, middle, or ending of a word. Children will often read the first letter of the word correctly, but then substitute the second consonant sound. Examples of words with initial letter substitutions errors are *bleak* for *break*, *plow* for *prow*, and *slop* for *step*.

Medial substitutions usually involve vowel sounds. Examples of medial substitution errors include *dasy* for *daisy*, *cat* for *cot*, and *trap* for *trip*.

The short *a* sound is a popular substitution choice, but sometimes the only discernible pattern is random substitution of vowels. This type of error is referred to as a *hit-and-miss* error. Another fairly common substitution error occurs when the child employs the "heads it's one vowel; tails it's another" strategy. The child has usually confused one or two vowels and is lucky or unlucky with a guess. If the child is consistently unlucky, you need to teach one or both vowels. Kelly always read short *a* words correctly, but when doubting another vowel, he continued to substitute the short *a*. Kelly needed not only help with the vowels *e*, *i*, *o*, and *u*, but also to discriminate when not to use short *a*.

Substitution of word endings is another common error pattern. Dropping -*s*'s or -*ing* or -*ed* can reflect a reading problem. Caution must be taken when working with children whose native language is not English. For these children, errors in word endings may be a reflection of spoken language rather than a misreading.

*Mispronunciations* refer to errors where no apparent rule has been applied. Miscalls or mispronunciations suggest that the child is simply unable to attack new words.

Tienna's pattern (with the correct words in brackets) provides a good example of mispronunciations:

> Once out [upon] a time, a beautiful red saw [rose] grew in the house [garden]. The rose had some [many] water [friends]. Birds after [landed] on its vase [branches] and sang going [sweetly]. Bees buzzed now [happily] on the lovely red water [petals].

For the sake of illustration, Tienna's errors have been kept only to mispronunciations. More than likely, in a real sample of Tienna's work, she would also make omissions, substitutions, insertions, and repetitions. A child like Tienna who mispronounces words may have no concept of the relationship between sounds and symbols. This problem may be easily resolved in the regular classroom or, depending on the cause, may need extensive remedial assistance in a special setting. If Tienna has actually learned sounds in isolation she may just need the teacher to help her realize that these same sounds apply to words. Some children, especially those with mild learning problems, need assistance in making generalizations. Simply calling attention to the sound can often end the problem with mispronunciations. For other children, the remediation required may need to be more extensive. If the remediation activity is beyond the scope of the classroom, then either the reading specialist or the special education teacher can work with the child. Once again, degree and kind of mispronunciation become the teacher's guideline for instruction.

*Insertions*, unlike omissions, occur when a child adds an additional word or words. Larry, for example, tends to make frequent insertion errors. He may read the sentence, "The man called the dog" like this: "The great big man called the little white dog." Similar to the situation with mispronunciations, Larry's problem may be resolved quite easily by calling attention to his errors.

In general, an insertion error pattern is probably not too serious. If the child is adding words, then at least you know that he or she is actively involved in reading. Active involvement is definitely a plus in the grade book of reading. The only serious problem that insertions can create falls in the area of comprehension. The child may be reading much more than the author's intent. As such, the child may not really understand the information communicated by the reading material.

*Repetition* errors occur when a word is read correctly but then reread. Repetition errors, like spontaneous self-corrections, are not always regarded as errors. Self-correction occurs when the child misreads a word and, without teacher intervention, rereads the word correctly. However, for some children, repetition becomes a style of reading. If the repetition errors occur infrequently, there may be no real concern. Manuel, for example, repeats each new vocabulary term before he proceeds to the next word in a passage. This technique helps him remember the new words, and since it doesn't interfere with his comprehension, there is no major problem.

Blanche, in contrast, will repeat both old and new words. She seems to use repetitions to avoid reading further in the passage. Not only are Blanche's repetitions tedious to hear, but they also slow down her reading rate. In turn, Blanche's slow rate may be responsible for her poor comprehension performance.

## Relationship of IRI to all Areas of Reading

By implementing an IRI in conjunction with the five major error types, you will quickly determine the child's appropriate classroom reading text as well as areas for specific teaching. If you are a primary grade teacher, you may find that some of your students cannot read any text at either the instructional or independent level. Some upper and intermediate grade children with learning problems, uneven experiential backgrounds, or a past history of failure may be similar to the primary grade children. They too may not be able to use their classroom texts for oral reading practice or comprehension activities. Even if the child cannot use the text for oral reading practice, you can still use the text to test for word recognition, word analysis, and comprehension.

**IRI and word recognition**—To test for word recognition, begin with the textbook which the child can read best. Identify the text's key words. Key words are often listed in the teacher's manual prior to each chapter. If key words are not listed in the teacher's manual, they can often be found listed in the back of the text or in accompanying workbooks. In the rare event that your district has adopted a text that does not identify key words, you can identify them yourself. With little effort, you can compare a list of the most commonly used words in the English language with the words in the text.

When a certain word is important for a student to learn, then include that word as part of the child's key words. The decision will be based on your own experience with the English language, the particular frequency with which a word is used, and the word's relevance to the textbook.

For each unit or story in the text, develop a word list. The list can be presented to the child as another measure of word recognition. How you format this list is really a matter of personal taste. Most primary teachers prefer flashcards; others like flip charts. Upper elementary teachers usually like to present the words in vertical or horizontal columns or rows.

The purpose of using word lists is to determine a starting point for instruction. Word lists, in whatever format, need an accompanying follow-along sheet. This guide sheet will provide you with a record of errors, day of testing, and level or source of words. Once a child misses approximately 8 to 10 words, you have identified words that need to be taught. Testing can continue once the initial set of words has been learned.

Two very useful sources of information can be obtained from this type of testing. The first relates to the rate of student progress. The second relates to the type of student progress.

Presented in Figure 7.1 are samples of Lynn's follow-along sheets. Even before any formal instruction had begun, Lynn got more words correct per unit, as noted on the follow-along sheet between November 3 to November 21. Lynn's errors also began to change in character. In her first sample, she refused to try some words by responding with "don't know" (dk). In five of the new words, word endings were either omitted or substituted. Nearly 2

**Figure 7.1**
Samples of Lynn's Follow-Along Sheets

Sample 1　　　　　　　　　　　　　　　　　　　　Date: _November 3_

| | (dk) | | (vegⱸ) | | (dk) | (exch) |
|---|---|---|---|---|---|---|
| age | cage | wage | vegetable | huge | change | exchange |
| (dk) | | (dang) | (dang) | | | (bag) |
| strange | danger | dangerous | large | orange | baggage |

Sample 2　　　　　　　　　　　　　　　　　　　Date: _November 14_

| (cab) | | | (vill) | | | |
|---|---|---|---|---|---|---|
| cabbage | cottage | village | package | sausage | voyage |
| | | (gent) | | | |
| carriage | college | gentle | gentleman | general | giant |

Sample 3　　　　　　　　　　　　　　　　　　　Date: _November 25_

| gingerbread | giraffe | magic | magical | engine | engineer |
|---|---|---|---|---|---|
| (pigⱸ) | | | | | |
| pigeon | ache | toothache | school | schoolroom | character |

weeks later, on November 14, Lynn had mastered the first set of words and was ready to be tested on the words for Unit 2. The new test results indicated that Lynn attempted every word; "don't know's" were absent. She still showed evidence of some difficulty with word endings, but not quite as much as on the first test. By the time Lynn had been tested over Unit 3 material, there was even more evidence of her reading growth. She read the majority of words correctly and had word ending problems on only one word.

By inspecting Lynn's three tests we can see that she was not only learning unit words at a rate of about 1 to 2 weeks, but that she was also mastering learning skills (i.e., word endings). Lynn's progress demonstrated how quickly she learned new unit words and her progress in the regular class.

We find the opposite result with Brian. Samples of his sheets are presented in Figure 7.2. A quick glance at Brian's testing dates show that he is taking longer and longer to master word lists. His learning rate is a signal that success in the regular classroom may be difficult for Brian to achieve. A closer inspection of Brian's errors adds to his teacher's concerns. Unlike Lynn, after 3 months of instruction, Brian continues to make the same type of errors. He either says "I don't know" to a word or uses the first two letters of the word to form the basis of a substitution.

Apparently Brian is not learning from past experience. For whatever reason, he is not making much progress in the regular classroom. Brian may need special help or some other form of instruction. From information on Brian's follow-along sheets, the teacher can easily request assistance from a

**Figure 7.2**
Samples of Brian's Follow-Along Sheets

Sample 1                                           Date: _November 3_

| | | | (dk) | | (chair) | (dk) |
|---|---|---|---|---|---|---|
| age | cage | wage | vegetable | huge | change | exchange |
| (dk) | (dark) | | (dk) | | | (dk) |
| strange | danger | | dangerous | large | orange | baggage |

Sample 2                                           Date: _November 30_

| (dk) | (color) | (dk) | | (sam) | (dk) |
|---|---|---|---|---|---|
| cabbage | cottage | village | package | sausage | voyage |
| (dk) | | | (dk) | (gentle) | |
| carriage | college | gentle | gentleman | general | giant |

Sample 3                                           Date: _January 12_

| (dk) | | | (dk) | (enter) | (dk) |
|---|---|---|---|---|---|
| gingerbread | giraffe | magic | magical | engine | engineer |
| (pick) | (dk) | (dk) | | | (chair) |
| pigeon | ache | toothache | school | schoolroom | character |

reading or learning specialist. There is certainly a basis for questioning Brian's placement. Whether he remains in a regular classroom may depend on the type and degree of instruction that best fit his needs.

**IRI and word analysis**—To test for word analysis, begin with the passage from your reading text. To be most efficient, use the same passage that was used when you tried to establish the child's independent or instructional reading level. Since you've already noted errors, you are ready to begin looking for error patterns. Once you've found them, the patterns can be compared with the types of errors that emerged from the word list.

**IRI and comprehension**—Use the passage of the IRI at the child's independent reading level to test comprehension as you would any other passage. Ask questions that demonstrate how well the child can read for information and for understanding. Informational types of questions are those that are literal or factual in nature. Questions that begin with the "who," "what," "where," "when," and "why" will help establish the child's ability to recall factual information. With a little probing, main idea questions like "What is the passage about?" can lead you into asking questions that reflect understanding.

Three additional questions you might wish to use are:

1. What is the author trying to tell you?
2. How is the passage possible, in part or in whole?
3. What is important to you about this passage?

Answers to these questions will provide some insight into how active your student is in reading. If your student responds with the animation of a piece of petrified wood, then the odds are high that his or her involvement is somewhat fossilized. That piece of information will alert you to the need for creating active involvement for the child.

## Other Class Evaluation Tools

**Word lists**—Other ways to use class materials for evaluations center around your text or a method of teaching. Word lists, for example, can be used to examine both word recognition and word analysis skills. The list itself can come from sources other than reading texts. Word lists can be generated from a child's own vocabulary or taken from content materials such as health, social studies, or English literature. Identification of error patterns from word lists is the same as identification of error patterns in the IRI. The words the child miscalls will become your whole vocabulary list. The types of errors the child makes provide you with word analysis problem areas.

Take Nguyen's work, for example. Nguyen, with a little help from his teacher, wrote a story about the Chinese New Year. He dictated the story, and his teacher printed it for him. The day after the story had been printed, Nguyen "read" his story to the teacher. She helped him "read" the words he couldn't remember. Nguyen's story, complete with errors (and correct words in brackets), is as follows:

The Chinese New Year is a good [great] day in Vietnam. The New Year is called [named] after animal [animals]. The animal for this year is the rat. Persons [people] give presents on New Year's Day. I got a real [red] packet of money.

Based on Nguyen's errors the teacher developed the following word list: *great, named, animals, people, red.* The words were all part of Nguyen's vocabulary. The teacher also analyzed the kinds of errors Nguyen made.

| Correct Word | Student Response | Teacher Hypothesis |
|---|---|---|
| good | great | using correct initial response |
| named | called | similar semantics |
| animals | animal | left off ending |
| people | persons | same semantically/same initial consonant |
| red | real | same initial consonant |

The teacher concluded that Nguyen was using initial consonant sounds and that medial sounds should be emphasized.

**Content textbooks**—Reading evaluations taken from content textbooks are just as simple to use. Instead of using a basal series for reading evaluation and instruction, you could use the social studies text as the basis of your reading program. Again the basic techniques used in an informal sampling can be used with the text. Identification of frustration, instruction, and independent reading level can be based on a 100-word passage from the text. Using a reading sample will help you to decide how the text can be used with the student.

**Timed samples**—A typical technique for assessing a student's performance is the 2-minute timed reading sample. The major differences between the timed reading sample for a content text and an IRI are that you have only one book from which to sample reading and that the reading sample is timed. Instruction for taking the sample and techniques for recording errors are the same.

To score, you need to establish a reading rate and an error percentage. To determine the reading rate (correct words read per minute), count all the words the student read correctly in the 2 minutes and divide by 2. Harold read 350 words correctly in 2 minutes. Therefore 350 divided by 2 equals 175 words per minute. Next we need to determine Harold's error percentage. Harold missed 70 words. To find his error percentage you'll need to divide the number of errors by the number of words in the sample. With lightning fast speed we can quickly determine that the passage read by Harold contained 420 words: 350 words read correctly plus 70 words read incorrectly results in a total of 420 words. And now for the finale.

$$420 \overline{) 70.00}^{\,.17}$$

.17 converts to a 17% error rate, which tells us that the text is too difficult for Harold to read. With 17% errors, we have 83% reading accuracy, and frustration begins to set in at around 90% correct (10% error rate).

So shall you throw out the text as useful classroom material? The answer is yes and no. Yes, the book is far too difficult for oral reading practice, so throw it out. No, don't throw it out; you can still use the text to establish word lists and provide direction for word analysis instruction.

The words chosen for the lists reflect the material's content and your professional judgment. Usually important words are isolated in the text in some fashion. Words may be listed in the teacher's manual, at the at the front of the chapter or unit, or at the end of a chapter, unit, or text. Key words may also be found within the chapters of the text, perhaps italicized or printed in bold type. As a reading evaluator, you would present these selected words just as you would present any other word list. Errors are noted, patterns identified, and you have clear direction for word analysis instruction.

About now you may be questioning the value of teaching sight words contained in a book that your student is unable to read. The fact that the student can't read the text actually provides you with the strongest argument for using the content words. By teaching the student key words, at least you can cover basic information from the text. The student's vocabulary—sight and comprehension—will grow and, through discussion, he or she may be able to keep pace with the knowledge gained by other students in the class.

## Establishing Evaluation Sequences

**Purpose**—The purpose of reading evaluation is to determine areas of instruction. Skill sequences that are used for reading instruction can come from a variety of sources. To be most efficient, the skill sequences found in currently existing classroom materials would be a logical first choice to use in evaluation/instruction. Evaluation procedures involve establishing or identifying existing hierarchies or skills sequences as presented in classroom materials. For reading, the skill sequences that are most often selected for evaluation and subsequent instruction are word analysis, word recognition, oral reading, and comprehension. The child's reading performance is then compared against the standards set for mastery of a particular skill in the sequence.

**Pretests based on class sequences**—If a student is having problems in all areas of reading or is just beginning reading instruction, the evaluation should be based on a sequence of skills by unit. The actual order of the skills is unimportant in most cases. The systematic evaluation and subsequent instruction of the sequence is critical.

One of the most practical techniques for pretesting word analysis skills is to sequence the pretest to materials available in the classroom. Several sources of skill sequences are commonly found in the classroom. For example, phonics workbooks present sounds in a sequence. Simply start with the first sound on the first page and continue with the sounds that follow on the succeeding pages.

Basal readers also provide a sequence of sounds. The sequence may need to be culled from the teacher's manual or reader. Generally sounds will be introduced in some segment of a meaningful word. By careful analysis of word order presentation, a sequence of sounds directly corresponding to the reader can be compiled. For example, students may be presented with the following sight words: *mother, mouse, come, summer*. The lesson in the basal has two objectives: to teach the four sight words and to teach the sound of the consonant *m*. The focus of the basal reader's next lesson could be on the sight words *saw, lesson, sit, kiss*. The intent of this lesson is to teach four sight words and the sound of *s*. With this approach, we can see the emergence of a sequence of sounds. The first letter sound is *m* and the second is *s*. A glance at ensuing lessons will reveal the remainder of the word analysis sequence for that particular basal reader. Ideally the sequence of sounds for word analysis can be coordinated with the sequence of words presented in the text.

# READING EVALUATION FOR SPECIAL POPULATIONS

## THE MILDLY HANDICAPPING CONDITIONS: LD, EH, AND EMH

Mildly handicapped children, be they learning disabled, emotionally handicapped, educable mentally handicapped, or a combination thereof, will need only minor modifications in the testing techniques described thus far. The areas to be evaluated remain the same regardless of the disability, i.e., word analysis, word recognition, oral reading, and comprehension.

### Positive Testing Environment

As with any child who has experienced failure in testing or other school situations, the teacher will need to promote a positive testing environment. Smiling and maintaining a friendly posture are good first steps. During initial testing the teacher may also wish to provide the child with sure-fire success activities. If, for example, the teacher knows that Maude is terrified of taking formal tests, he or she may wish to adapt or disguise the test form. Instead of presenting Maude with a 20-word typed list, the teacher could print the words with colored pens and put them on individual cards.

Two variables in the environment can help lessen test-taking anxiety—classroom routine and the evaluator. First, you could adjust the environment from a formal to a less formal one by including the evaluation activity as a routine part of daily classwork. Second, probes can be routinely given and valuable information gathered through whole class activities. You do not have to serve as the evaluator. With a little training, children can time each other and record errors in many reading areas. Older students can also be used as cross-age evaluators. As long as you've identified a sequence of skills and a standard of acceptable performance, you can be flexible about who is directed to collect evaluation information.

## Specific Suggestions

The following suggestions could help you adapt your evaluation materials.

- Put isolated words or sounds on individual 3 × 5 cards.
- Print words on regular tablet paper or on a magic slate.
- Print words in colors other than the standard black.
- Use a flip chart.
- Put words on a word wheel.
- Play games like *word bingo* or *Boggle*.
- Duplicate passages from books instead of using an entire manual.

One word at a time is a lot less threatening than a whole page of typed words. Giving words on a regular tablet or a magic slate lessens the formality of the testing event. Children are used to teachers writing on tablet paper so the activity itself might reduce a certain amount of test-taking anxiety. After all, who could really equate reading words printed on a Mickey Mouse or Snoopy magic slate with the Dolch word list, or the presentation of words in different colors? Since you would only be using the colored words for inital screening or posttesting, the risk of having the child "read the color" is totally eliminated if you don't provide the child with corrective feedback, i.e., tell the correct response to a miscalled word or sound.

The informality of flip charts and word wheels can also lessen test-taking anxiety. They are especially useful for word analysis evaluations. Both flip charts and word wheels are easy to make and can be directly coded to classroom material. To make a flip chart, all you need is a three-ring binder, a marking pen, and some 3 × 5 index cards. Consonant cards, i.e., one consonant per card, go on the first and third rings of the binder. Vowels, or vowel cards, are placed on the middle ring. The word wheel is made from heavy construction paper that can be laminated to preserve it. Playing games with test items is a little more elaborate and time consuming. Word games like Bingo, card games, and even Tic Tac Toe can be adapted to test sounds and words found in predesignated sequences. Of course, it takes time to construct these games, so this form of evaluation modification in your classroom may not be practical. Nevertheless, you could adapt any game by just using a correct reading response to earn the right to move a player or take a turn.

Billy, who's terrified of formal tests, loves to play checkers. So he and his teacher have a weekly checker game. The teacher has a stack of 3 × 5 cards with a word from Billy's word list on each card. When it's Billy's turn to play, he picks up a card, identifies the word, and moves his checker. It's not necessary for Billy to get the word correct in order to move. Billy's teacher has a follow-along sheet. She records Billy's response and notes deviations. Since this is an "evaluation-by-checkers" approach, Billy's responses are not corrected, but simply noted. Based on Billy's answers, his teacher knows whether or not to proceed to the next set of words. This same kind of technique can also be used to evaluate sounds or sound combinations.

Finally, you can test oral reading outside of a standardized test and even outside of a textbook. Instead of just handing a child a book to read, you can duplicate pages from the various texts in your room. Duplicated pages mask the source of the pages and are advantageous because most children know which books are for the "smart" kids and which are for the "not-so-smart." Passages taken from each level of a particular series can be used for informal reading inventories. Rather than thumbing through an entire set of basals, you can have your selected passages in one handy, unmarked spot.

## SENSORY HANDICAPPING CONDITIONS AND
## READING EVALUATION: SPECIAL CONSIDERATIONS

As must all children, children with sensory impairments need to learn to read. The areas of evaluation are the same, i.e., word analysis, word recognition, oral reading, and comprehension. Reading evaluation of children with sensory impairments must, of course, consider the special nature of the particular deficit. A blind child, for example, should not be tested on word recognition presented from a typed word list. Nor should a deaf child be tested for letter sounds—at least not in a way that is appropriate for the regular classroom.

Two critical areas of consideration for the evaluation of reading with the sensory impaired are format and mode of response. Format refers to the way that evaluation is administered. Mode of response refers to the way in which the child is expected to demonstrate knowledge.

### Format

There are many formal tests that have been developed for use with sensory impaired children. Unfortunately, informal tests or test coded to classroom materials are generally most useful in a regular classroom. If you are not certain how to adapt your testing to the sensory needs of a handicapped child, you should run, not walk, to the nearest specialist and request immediate assistance.

It is worth noting that most teacher-made and standardized tests can be transcribed for the visually impaired student by vision specialists. The transcribed tests can be made available in large print or braille.

**Format changes**—You may wish to consider various ways to modify the format. Modifications can range from extending time limits to major changes in format. For example, you might allow a multiple-choice response rather than require verbal explanation (Bigge & O'Donnell, 1976). Modification in format may also include altering the material in some fashion, e.g., producing words in larger print for visually impaired children or presenting sounds to a hearing impaired child through a headset to eliminate competing noises. Testing materials for the visually impaired usually have large clear type, nonglossy finish, and maximum contrast between background and printing. Testing materials for the hearing impaired should be presented in a noise-free environment, on glare-free paper, and with a good overall lighting system. Testing materials used with physically handicapped children also need to take into account the child's particular disability. Materials that require the arthritic child to spend a great deal of time in one physical position may actually interfere with the child's ability to complete the task.

**Modification of materials: Test characteristics**—Modification of testing materials usually takes into account the properties of the materials. Some properties to consider are:

*Visual*, including
- Size of print
- Clarity of print
- Contrast between print and background
- Number of items presented on the page
- Distracting factors, e.g., pictures or designs that detract from the evaluation material

*Auditory*, including
- Loudness (amplitude) of presentation
- Clarity or crispness of oral directions or items
- Contrast between item and competing background noise
- Speed at which items are presented
- Visual access to evaluator's lip movements

*Mechanical*, including
- Length of time required to complete the evaluation task
- Type of response required to complete the evaluation, e.g., vocal as in speech or fine motor as in writing
- Language requirements, i.e., type of syntax and grammar used when delivering directions

## Handicapping Condition and Test Materials

With a little imagination, most teachers can alter their testing materials by considering their properties and the disabilities exhibited by the sensory or physically handicapped child.

**Child disabilities**—Suppose that you are teaching Leon, Steve, Edward, and Charles. You wish to evaluate their ability to identify a certain sequence of sounds. The sequence happens to be *m, a, i, n, s, t, r, e.* The evaluation question is: When presented with a letter (visual symbol) can the child identify the corresponding sound? Two questions immediately leap into your mind.

1. Is there any particular physical, sensory, or psychological characteristic which I must consider for each child?

2. Is there any particular physical property of the test that could interfere with the results in determining if the children know the sounds?

A mental checklist that will help you evaluate the children is presented in Figure 7.3. A check appears in the grid wherever a problem needs to be addressed.

**Figure 7.3**
Checklist Matching Child's Needs to Test Properties

| Properties of Test | Leon | Steve | Edward | Charles |
|---|---|---|---|---|
| Visual | | | | |
| Size of print | | ✔ | ✔ | |
| Clarity of print | | ✔ | ✔ | |
| Contrast between print and background | | | | |
| Number of items per page | | ✔ | ✔ | |
| Distracting characteristics | | ✔ | ✔ | |
| Auditory | | | | |
| Loudness of presentation | ✔ | | | |
| Clarity of oral presentation | ✔ | | | |
| Background noise | | | | |
| Speed of presentation | ✔ | | | |
| Visual access to examiner's lips | ✔ | ✔ | | |
| Mechanical | | | | |
| Time requirement | | | | |
| Response requirement | | | | ✔ |

Your mental grid shows you that Leon needs assistance primarily in auditory areas. Yet Leon is not immune to a potential psychological problem either. If you had guessed that Leon was hearing impaired you would have been close. Leon does not actually have a sensory handicap. He has a mild learning/behavior problem. Leon's attention is best while performing tasks that present some sort of auditory demand.

So how about Steve? Is he visually impaired or isn't he? There's no guess work. He is visually impaired; therefore, the quality of his visual materials must be very good. Edward's problems seem a lot like Steve's, but he has no known visual impairment. Edward has cerebral palsy, which accounts for some difficulty in the controlling of his neck muscles. Frequently, though just momentarily, he loses sight of a page. Visually clear and clutter-free evaluation materials are easier for Edward because he can find his place more quickly on them than on visually disorganized or distracting materials.

Finally we come to Charles. His only major problem involves the response required to complete the task. Charles does not have enough fine motor control to use a pen or a pencil.

**Properties of the test materials**—Now back to our original evaluation question: When presented with a letter (visual symbol) can Leon, Steve, Edward or Charles identify *m*, *a*, *i*, *n*, *s*, *t*, *r*, *e*? The evaluation question remains the same, but the means of answering the question has been changed. The answer is obtained by using your basic classroom evaluation materials, especially the ever-popular 3 × 5 flashcards.

No particular change in evaluation material is necessary for Leon. You simply need to determine whether or not he needs to hear the directions each time you present a card. To check on his needs you present the first card with oral directions and then show the next two or three without oral directions. If he miscalls the sounds you know that (a) he doesn't know the sounds, (b) he's not attending, or (c) he doesn't know the sounds *and* he is not attending. Since your objective is to evaluate Leon's knowledge of sounds, you need to rule out the "attending or not attending" question. To rule it out, you just present the miscalled sounds individually and provide oral directions each time the sound is shown. If Leon is still miscalling, the odds are high that he doesn't know the sounds. With no major adjustment you have answered your original question for Leon.

What about Steve and his visual impairment? If his disability does not permit him to use print, you may have a problem. Since your question has to do with actually looking at a letter and producing a sound, you would not be able to test him. Back to the original question, if Steve is a braille reader, his special teacher would need to evaluate him. But if Steve does have some vision, you would need to adjust the material to account for his vision level. A quick check with the special teacher should help with specific materials to be used to answer your question. In Steve's situation, a modification of print size was the only major adaptation required.

Edward needs no modification. His teacher alternates the 3 × 5 cards, which contain only one sound each. Even when Edward's lack of muscle control causes him to lose his place, he has no difficulty re-establishing visual focus.

Charles also needs no modification. His major problem involves the use of fine motor skills. The classroom evaluation question does not demand the use of fine motor skills. His teacher can find the answer to the question for sounds Charles knows through the use of 3 × 5 cards. If the task were to demand that Charles make a fine motor response, we would have to examine the mode of response.

## Response Mode

How a person is mechanically required to respond to a test item is the response mode. Reponse modes in most classrooms require fine motor skills, i.e., the ability to complete a paper-and-pencil test, or they demand the use of speech, i.e., the ability to respond orally to an item or test question. If a child cannot speak well enough for the teacher to understand or cannot write (print) legibly, the teacher may need to alter the response mode of the evaluation instrument.

**Communication problems**—If a child cannot use speech to communicate, the following guidelines may be helpful.

Word Analysis/Word Recognition
- Print, write, type the sound
- Circle or underline the correct sound/word
- Identify (match, circle, etc.) objects/pictures that contain the desired sound/word
- Discriminate (match, touch, underline) the desired sound/word from a list

If the child cannot use speech or fine motor responses to communicate, the teacher may also wish to consider the following responses:

- The child signals yes/no responses when asked to identify particular sounds or words
- The child signals yes/no responses to the examiner's verbal selection of specific sounds or words

**Level of response demand**—Response modes can be thought of in terms of a sequence hierarchy or level of response demand. A response that requires the student's head to nod in agreement or disagreement with the examiner's response requires much less effort than a response that requires legible writing on designated lines for answers. Ideally no single response mode is mandatory for a child to answer a question. If changes become necessary, then the teacher/evaluator should structure the modified response mode as close to the original mode as possible. The teacher wants the evaluation question answered rather than to gather information on whether a child can respond, i.e., speak, point, nod, gesture, etc., in a manner required by the evaluation tool. There are many simple ways you can modify the response mode for a handicapped child.

1. The child agrees or disagrees with the teacher's selection or answers. For example, the teacher prints three letters on the chalkboard and says "Tell me when I touch the letter that says *m*." Each time the teacher touches a letter, the child either agrees or disagrees with the *m* sound.

2. The child sorts pictures, objects, forms, and sounds according to categories corresponding to the teacher's models. Categories may be either sounds, words, phrases, or passages. For example, the teacher provides a word list for the child to underline all the words that contain the short *a* sound.

3. The child compares and selects or points to a picture, object, form, or letter to correspond to the teacher's model. For example, the teacher shows a picture of a farm scene. She asks the child to read a card with the word *cow* and points to the corresponding animal.

4. The child selects one of a series that is different from the rest of the series. For example, the child reads a story about the pet show before the teacher asks for the animal that was not in the story. The teacher can elicit the response by either presenting the material orally or in the form of a written multiple-choice question like the following:

Animals *not* in the pet show are:
    a. Dogs
    b. Kittens
    c. Frogs
    d. Rabbits

## Factors Influencing Skill Scores

Two other areas that could lead to false interpretation of a skill level include amount of time demanded and type of written response.

**Time demands**—The amount of time demanded to complete the evaluation has to be considered for all children, but especially for the mildly handicapped or slow learners. For speed tests, the extra time allowed for the visually handicapped will not influence the test's reliability or validity. A helpful rule allows two and one-half times the amount of testing time for braille students and one and one-half times for readers of large print.

With our educational question always in mind, a teacher may wish to explore to see whether that question can be answered in more than one way. If, for example, your question tries to determine story comprehension, you could either ask the child to write as much of the story as he or she remembers or to answer multiple-choice items about the story. For children who tire or frustrate easily, you'd probably have a more accurate answer to your question if you asked for a short multiple-choice response.

The time allowed between test items can also affect a child's performance. If change easily flusters the child, you may need to allow for more time between test items. For example, Willy can tell you isolated letter sounds, and he can blend CVC words accurately. Yet if you ask him to respond to a CVC item immediately after he has responded to a short vowel, he may have problems. It's almost as if Willy needs a little start-up time to reorganize his thinking before he's ready for the next task. So why not give him a few extra seconds before he processes the task?

Unlike Willy, Ryan does not need extra time to think the question through. In timed test situations, the clock will beat Ryan every time. It's almost as if the second hand on the clock has blocked his ability to respond (or respond correctly) at all. With his inbred fear, Ryan needs to know that he's totally in charge of the time. When we apply the educational question to children like Ryan, timed reading probes don't make a great deal of sense. Yet two questions remain. "Can Ryan accurately produce the correct sound or combination of sounds?" and "How can you determine Ryan's reading rate?" First of all, you don't time Ryan, and then you make an intelligent decision on when his rate should be increased.

**Type of written response**—As mentioned earlier, written responses require a certain proficiency with fine motor skills and expressive language. When evaluating reading, written response demands must also be kept in mind. If your evaluation response requires fine motor skills, be sure that your student has fine motor skills. If the response requires that your student have good expressive language, be sure that your student does have good expressive language. But if your student lacks fine motor skills or expressive language, alter the response demand.

Sanford can use a pencil, but his skill level can be likened to a cat barking. A concerted effort with the pencil will produce some spider-like, barely recognizable letters of the alphabet. A truer evaluation of Sanford's skills would involve questions which ask him to circle, underline, cross-out, or mark the correct answer. For other children, who may be more seriously handicapped in the fine motor skills, typewriters with special modifications have been developed. District specialists can assist teachers with evaluation materials.

## SUMMARY

Reading and reading evaluation for handicapped and nonhandicapped students must consider the components of the reading act. As discussed throughout this chapter, the components of reading are word recognition, word analysis, oral reading, and comprehension. Aside from isolating reading components, the demands of the evaluation task must be examined in relation to the skills of the children to be evaluated. Without confounding responses with task demands, a modification of format and student response can aid the teacher in assessing a child's reading skill level.

# 8
# Reading Methods

Ms. Smith had finally met her goal. She rolled her chair away from the reams of paper and flung her tired pencil on top of the desk. Our fourth grade teacher was pleased, to say the least. It was the end of the last day of the first week of school, and she had survived the process of evaluating all 30 of her students. And that was only in reading. Next week would be math.

Although her students were gone for the day, Ms. Smith was left with new data on specific sounds for specific students. Her IRI was also helpful. It not only conveniently placed all her students in various levels of the basal, but it had produced customized word lists for each child. So Ms. Smith steadied her gaze at some lightly crunched paper balls cornered under the phonics chart until she rested her head on her hand to peruse some of the questions from the evaluation instrument. Thanks to newly discovered error patterns, she was soon in complete command of every comprehension skill need of each of her students.

Just about the time that she noticed that the phonics chart was a little crooked, Alicia, Norton, and Winston invaded her thoughts. Her chair slowly slid closer to the paper stacks piled so neatly in front of her. The steady tapping of her pencil picked up the pace of her thoughts as she continued to ponder. Alicia's comprehension is good, so why is she reading one grade below level, especially since she knows all the letter sounds? But then again, she does need help with three-syllable words. And poor Norton. He's not quite sure how sounds relate to reading at all, but his comprehension is probably the best in class. Too bad he can't use any of the basals. But thank goodness for Winston. His oral reading is like listening to a Shakespearian actor performing Hamlet—a shame he can't remember a word he's read. And then, one by one, Ms. Smith turned the pages for a review of her prized evaluation scores. One by one, Ms. Smith felt confident that she could teach her students the necessary skills. One by one by one ... by one by 30.

But alas, Ms. Smith developed cold hands. She rubbed them together for warmth and clasped them for strength when she suddenly realized she had 30 Alicias, Nortons, and Winstons. Within seconds she opened the subject of her own ignorance and immediately related it to bliss. Perhaps she could have blissfully taught all 30 students the same skill at the same time. But Ms. Smith was not really ignorant. She had merely evaluated her students and, in so doing, had discovered the most dangerous culprit of all—a little bit of knowledge.

Now, what does one do with a little bit of knowledge? Ms. Smith wasn't sure, so she began to assess her role, her plight, her capabilities, her task, her students, her ..., and in her search she accepted several basic facts. *Fact:* She had 30 students who needed reading instruction. *Fact:* All the children had individual reading needs. *Fact:* Some of the children, and not necessarily special students, needed a great deal more assistance in reading than others.

*Fact:* Ms. Smith is an intelligent human being fairly well versed in the methods of teaching reading.

# MAJOR READING STRATEGIES

## RELATIONSHIP OF SOUNDS, WORDS, AND MEMORY

There are three broad approaches to teaching reading: decoding, meaning, and memory strategies. Decoding focuses on breaking words into small units of sound, e.g., matching sounds or groups of sounds to letters. Meaning, in contrast, emphasizes reading words or sentences in a familiar and meaningful context. With the memory strategy approach, the child learns to read by reciting words, sentences, and even stories from memory.

The history of reading instruction has seen hours of heated debate, with advocates lauding one approach over another. Proponents and antagonists have cited both anecdotal and empirical evidence to strengthen their positions. These arguments can be traced back at least 350 years. Yet actual observations of children who learn to read before they begin school show that all three methods are used. Children deserve the credit, for they were the ones who uncovered the answer to the debaters' questions. Children discover and coordinate all the approaches by themselves (Carter & Stokes, 1982). The educational implication is quite clear. With all due respect to the debaters of the last 3½ centuries, the classroom teacher needs to use an instructional method that combines all three approaches.

The combination of approaches can meet the varying needs that exist within an individual and across individuals. While good readers have been characterized as text-driven or bottom-up readers (decoding to read), new reading situations may also require them to extract meaning from context and memorize new words or phrases. Poor readers, in contrast, have been characterized as being concept-driven or top-down readers (meaning and memory more than decoding). As poor readers become more skilled, they begin to move to a text-drive style (Juel, 1980). Both good and poor readers often use context whenever they are reading low frequency words or decoding hard words.

In other words, Gershon, a good reader, and Arthur, a poor reader, both use decoding, meaning, and memory techniques to read. Their major difference is the degree of use of each technique. In new reading situations, Gershon probably relies heavily upon decoding to pronounce new or unfamiliar words. Arthur is more likely to rely on memory or the context of the story to read the unfamiliar words. Both boys will apply whatever skills they can to the new word situation.

## THE WHOLE READING ACTIVITY

Many reading experts have equated reading to a set of interrelated subskills. The separate subskills should be taught, practiced, and integrated with other skills being taught. Most important, though, is that these subskills, while initially taught in isolation, should always be practiced liberally in the context of the whole reading activity (Anderson, Hiebert, Scott, & Wilkinson, 1985).

### Practicing Subskills

To teach decoding for the sake of decoding is as senseless as teaching isolated words to increase sight vocabulary. Children learn decoding skills and sight words so that they can read material that has been written by themselves or by others. Reading is a communication act. The building blocks of this act (decoding skills, meanings, and memory strategies) must be presented in such a way that the reader can apply the skills for building the communication bridge between himself and the author. So while Sal is pronouncing the short sound of *a*, he is also going to practice reading the short sound of *a* in selected vocabulary words. The actual selection will be the words from the story that Sal and his classmates are reading for oral practice. In this mode, Sal gets to practice three subskills: identifying a sound in isolation (decoding), memorizing vocabulary (memory), and reading words in context (meaning).

### Using Context Materials

For the older, poor reading student, teaching the subskills in the context of another subject is even more important. Poor readers at the upper and middle grades aren't too thrilled with the prospect of reading for the sake of reading. For too many of them, reading texts have become reminders of their own reading failure. Reading instruction at upper levels should shift the emphasis to something other than reading, e.g., social studies, science, health. Almost any content area text that requires extensive reading will provide an excellent disguise for the basal reader. While using the three reading strategies of decoding, memory, and meaning, students will be applying their reading skills for a purpose other than reading for the pleasure of reading. They will be focusing their attention on the text material, learning reading by what they are doing in the content textbook (Anderson & Armbruster, 1984).

Hilary never liked to read. She said that reading was boring. Since Hilary, a fifth grader, read at about the second grade level, her performance may have had something to do with her feelings about reading. Her teacher, Ms. Green, realized that the child had a twofold problem. Hilary *could not* read very well and she *would not* even feign interest in trying to read from the basal. Ms. Green switched tactics.

During the reading period, Ms. Green worked with Hilary and a small group of students on social studies. The teacher chose not to use the class's social studies book for oral reading practice, but she did take key vocabulary words from the text and related topics. Ms. Green taught key vocabulary terms (memory) and used isolated sounds and sets of sounds (e.g., prefixes, suffixes, and roots) to teach sound/symbol relationships. She also had the children write stories using the vocabulary words. For oral reading practice, Ms. Green brought texts that were written at each of the children's reading levels. The levels in the group ranged from low second to high third grade. Hilary blossomed. She no longer had to do the dreaded reading, and she was delighted with her progress in social studies.

"Fine," you say, "that's all well and good for reading instruction. But what did Ms. Green do with these children during the social studies period?" The answer is elementary. She taught them social studies along with the rest of the class. Hilary's small group used the social studies text that was now filled with familiar and previously learned key vocabulary. Besides, Hilary's group had an experiential basis. Remember the low-level text that helped them to gain meaning from the context of the text?

The subject of "bored" never again arose from Hilary's group either. They read the social studies text just like everybody else. They even had correct answers and contributed to class discussions. Our formerly bored Hilary succinctly stated her group's findings when she said, "I'm sure glad I don't have to do that dumb reading anymore. It's nice to be smart!"

# TEACHING READING TO SLOW LEARNERS

## DIRECT INSTRUCTION

One of the ways the classroom teacher can help students "be smart" is to set the children up to succeed. The teacher can manipulate key instructional variables, i.e., direct instruction, time on-task, and overall classroom management.

Direct instruction (as used here) occurs when the teacher teaches the objective or task. In direct instruction the teacher sets and presents the reading goals and assesses the students' progress (Fry & Lagomarsino, 1982). The teacher leaves very little learning to chance when providing direct and explicit instructions to the students. The connection between what is being taught and how to read is highlighted, underscored, and never, never, never assumed.

Some reading specialists (Carnine & Silbert, 1979) have specified six aspects of direct instruction: specifying objectives, devising problem-solving strategies, developing teaching procedures, selecting examples, providing practice, and sequencing skills and examples. Any reading text can be adapted and modified to follow these six guidelines.

## Specifying Objectives

Reading texts generally supply an abundance of goals and objectives. You can consider yourself fortunate indeed if the text objectives are stated in specific observable behaviors. If the book presents vague or global goals, then isolate subobjectives of those goals. For example, the basal specifies that the children will be able to decode short vowels at the completion of the book. Without a doubt this is certainly a valuable goal, but you, as a direct implementer, and your students could certainly experience suceess a lot sooner. Break the goal into subskills, e.g., by the end of chapter 1, the students will be able to identify the short sound of *i* in isolation and in all the short *i* words in the chapter. This rewrite lets you clearly identify what you will be teaching (the short *i*) and provides the necessary conditions for the children to demonstrate their learning (in isolation and in all the short *i* words contained in the chapter).

## Devising Problem-Solving Strategies

"Devising problem-solving strategies," when translated, becomes "teaching the child how to generalize." Unfortunately, many educationally handicapped and slow-learning students do not often use efficient strategies for learning, let alone generalize to new situations (Martin, 1978). A prime contributor to confusion is the "never leave anything to chance" approach to reading. So what are teachers to do? They simply teach strategies and provide generalization for the children.

For example, when teaching the sound of the letter *m*, you might list several words that begin with *m*, such as *mother, mouse, man, mistletoe*. Together you and the students read the words. Before long, you ask the children for the sound that is the same in all the words. The odds are favorable that you'll get the correct response.

This technique is fine for most children; for others, a few extra steps are needed. One strategy step for focusing attention is to highlight the initial consonant sound of the words as they are being read. A typical scenario might be as follows:

The teacher underscores the initial letter with chalk or her finger and says, "*Mother. This* word is *mother. Mother* starts like this." (She makes the *m* sound and points again to the letter.) The children repeat the sound with her. They repeat it for each word. Then she asks for the sound that is the same in all the words. The teacher can now present the strategy that they all used for finding the letter that sounds the same. "All these words have the *m* sound. All these words begin with the letter *m*."

The number of times she needs to repeat this strategy for this particular group of words is influenced by the students' responses and by the teacher's judgment of her students' knowledge of the *m* sound and, at least for the moment, their understanding of why the *m* sound is the solution to the problem.

The more often the teacher uses and orally states a strategy, the better are the chances that the child will recall that strategy and use it when entering a new situation.

While not all aspects of reading lend themselves to decoding strategies, e.g., unfamiliar or nonphonetic words, many other strategies are available. The primary source, the quickest and most practical source for all strategies, is you, the teacher. All you need at first is to identify what you'd do in a new reading situation, and it is more than likely that you have a strategy that can be stated out loud. Ask yourself what you'd do if you came to a word you couldn't sound out. Besides skipping the word, chances are you would use context clues to figure it out. This strategy also works for students. Then, too, if the sentence itself doesn't help, the next two or three may offer a clue to the unknown. Remember, if you want the student to apply strategies to the reading act, you may need to teach the strategies.

## Developing Teaching Procedures

Developing teaching procedures is the other side of the same reading instruction coin. Teaching procedures are the methods used for instructing the child to decode sounds, use strategies, read for meaning, and perform all the other tasks involved in reading. These methods are often associated with some sort of format or presentation style. In a direct instruction approach to reading, the teacher usually provides the student with a structured format or curriculum. This approach is in line with research findings. Many children, especially low achieving or low socioeconomic status (SES), perform better with a structured curriculum than in a more open-ended one (Brophy, 1979; Resnick, 1979).

In a direct instructional approach, not only is the curriculum sequenced, but each lesson is also. The teacher follows a prescribed routine when presenting reading information during a lesson. This routine usually has five elements: (1) setting attention, (2) providing direct or explicit instruction, (3) completing group practice, (4) reviewing objectives, and (5) completing individual practice activities. These five elements can be used in any academic area, not just reading. Each element is accompanied by feedback.

Let's look into a typical reading lesson using the five elements for direct instruction. Mr. Cooper is teaching a lesson in word meaning. His *objective:* The children will pronounce the words *augment, deficit,* and *salary.* Mr. Cooper's *available technique* from the teacher's guide is to teach the new words in sentences that provide (a) examples of appropriate use and (b) a context of familiar points.

1. Setting attention. Mr. Cooper points to the three words on the board and says, "Today we are going to solve the meaning of these mysterious words." The children's participation in a short guessing game is encouraged. They can guess a meaning for each word and write it on their papers.

2. Providing direct or explicit instruction. Mr. Cooper next reads aloud a sentence with one of the new words. The sentence is "I'd like to augment my matchbox car collection by buying two new models." After giving some time for guessing at the new term, Mr. Cooper presents several more sentences until the students eventually arrive at a direct definition of the word *augment.* He then shows how the word *augment* makes sense in the example sentences.

3. Group practice. The group practices using the word *augment* through a group activity. Each student gets a chance to use the word in a sentence. The child reads the sentence to the other members of the group.

4. Individual practice. After the group practice, Mr. Cooper distributes practice activities to all his students. For his lower achieving students, he developed a very simple worksheet, designed for filling in the blanks with each of three new words. His most advanced students were to create a story using the three new words at least twice in the story, or to compose two sentences for each of the three new words.

5. Reviewing the objective. After the individual practice, Mr. Cooper defines the words and uses them again in the original sentences. He asks the children to check their first attempts at the word's meaning; for fun he has them apply those guesses to the newly stated meanings.

Every time Mr. Cooper teaches a lesson, he follows the same five-step routine. This is not to say that the activities within the routine cannot be as varied and creative as the teacher wishes. The important point to remember is that the teacher is systematic in the approach to teaching an objective.

## Selecting Examples

When selecting examples, the teacher needs to be certain that they are familiar to the child. An obvious, everyday example or a particularly bizarre one can help the child remember the concept much better than one which has no particular meaning for the child. No teacher in Micronesia should spend a great deal of time using examples of arctic animals to explain the principles of the food chain. Obviously, Micronesian animals would be more meaningful. The child's own experiential background, directly or indirectly, provides the richest source of familiar examples. For the visually impaired child, especially the blind, some common examples that most children know have not been experienced at all. The same is true of many other children who have been in segregated classrooms. The focus in most segregated classrooms, i.e., self-contained special education classes, is on basic academic skills. At the primary and intermediate levels, academic direction is especially directed at reading and math skills. While the children spend instructional time acquiring these skills, they are not experiencing activities related to other content areas, e.g., social studies, science, art. These children often miss the typical guest speakers and field trips that other classes have. This segregation practice has inadvertently widened the gap between the experience base of the handicapped child and the children enrolled in the regular classroom. To use our "never leave anything to chance" approach to instruction also means preparing the experiential background of the children to receive examples. An activity as simple as reading a short story or holding a group discussion can provide a common experience base for producing meaningful examples.

The more technical aspects of reading are another area for meaningful examples. To avoid confusion, children need to be presented with only one new concept at a time. This concept needs to be presented in the context of already known and related concepts. If, for example, the child knows the letter sound for *m*, *s*, *a*, *d*, *i*, and *t*, you would not present the word *sand* because *sand* contains an unknown letter (*n*) (Carnine & Silbert, 1979). You would teach the word *sand* only after you had taught the *n* sound.

## Providing Practice

Practice gives the child an event or situation in which to use a previously learned skill. It allows the learner a chance to gain proficiency with a newly acquired piece of information. Reading achievement improves when children are given the chance to practice individually (Anderson, Evertson, & Brophy, 1979). Teachers need to remember that children must be allowed to practice extensively if they are to go beyond accuracy to basic usage and from basic usage to automatic reading responses (Samuels, 1979). The practice scenario is similar to the notion "you have to crawl before you can walk, and you have to walk before you can run." The first practice stage permits the beginning reader to crawl. Stage 2 directs the reader to wobble around on two reading legs, and Stage 3 graduates the reader to stride effortlessly through the reading act.

There are two main kinds of practice activities: dependent and independent practice. Dependent practice is geared for children who are just beginning to acquire a particular reading skill. Dependent practice is always done with another person, a teacher or peer, who is already skilled in the activity.

Riko and her group completed several exercises with six vocabulary words from chapter 3 in the basal. All totaled, Riko had done about 15 exercises. After this instructional time, Riko could, with a little prompting, identify all six words correctly. Without any prompting or feedback as to the correctness of her responses, she needed to practice the words. Very soon, she progressed to the stage where dependent practice once again became most beneficial. If Riko tried to read chapter 3 by herself, she could easily practice new words incorrectly, only to "unlearn" what she had practiced. With a class size so large, Riko's teacher could not give her dependent practice every day. So she scheduled her reading session with Riko for twice a week and a cross-age tutor from the sixth grade for the other 3 days.

Independent practice is most effective when the student has mastered a concept but needs to get proficient with it. For Riko, independent practice would have been beneficial only after she had practiced the new words with her teacher or tutor. Independent practice with "new" words only makes sense if the new words are no longer new. It means the child no longer needs prompting or immediate feedback upon encountering the words because he or she always recognizes the words correctly.

Once you respect the distinction between dependent and independent practice in reading and its importance, you have the basis for sequencing your practice activities as well as the necessary skills. You also avoid the pitfall of offering numerous applications and practice exercises in lieu of explicit instruction. You'll be able to provide the link between what is being taught and how to read (Durkin, 1981).

## Sequencing Skills

The sequencing of skills refers to the order in which you plan to teach objectives. Objectives are sequentially organized by level of difficulty according to your best judgment. The logical order of teaching evolves from the simplest or least complex objective toward more difficult ones. Within each objective you also need to be cognizant of any subskills and the hierarchy of subskills that logically flow from that objective. Even though the actual order of letters, words, sounds, etc., is not particularly critical, the point to remember is that skills and objectives do have a logical and hierarchial sequence of instruction.

"The student will pronounce the word *sand*" was the objective that appeared earlier in this chapter. Recall that the student had learned the sounds *s*, *a*, and *d*, but not *n*. Therefore, the sound of *n* is a subskill. Another subskill is the student's ability to blend a four-letter word. Depending on the student, you may just need to use the sound of *n* in isolation, then as an initial consonant sound in a two-letter blend (as an initial sound in a CVC and as a final sound in a CVC). At the initial reading level, especially in the early primary grades, mastering many subskills is not beyond regular classroom instruction. An intermediate student who needs direct instruction in most of the subskills probably ought to pay a visit to the special education teacher or the remedial reading specialist.

## TIME ON-TASK

Time on-task refers to the actual amount of time the child works on a particular activity. The actual amount of time is not always easy to determine. It often involves calculations, subtracting specifically for malingering, daydreaming, stalling, etc. Examples of task activities in reading include the time spent with the teachers, as well as the time spent working on objectives, either independently or with another student.

Most children improve in reading in direct proportion to the amount of time spent actively engaged in reading activities at an appropriate level of difficulty (Guthrie, 1982). Two related key components to reading achievement logically follow: the task and working at an appropriate level of difficulty.

### Attending to the Task

Good readers have been shown to be on-task more than poor readers during reading instruction time (Samuels & Turnure, 1974). One study (Gambrell, Wilson, & Ganett, 1981) even analyzed how the on-task time of good and poor readers was spent. Good readers spent about 57% of their reading time in contextual reading and only about 36% of their time in nonreading activities like listening, speaking, and writing. Poor readers, in contrast, spent about 54% of their time in activities other than reading. These findings support the notion that poor readers spend very little time reading during reading time (Allington, 1978). Here the instructional need is to teach children to attend to the reading task. Fortunately for all of us, poor readers can be taught to attend to the reading task. In one task activity program, the entire process took only 8 weeks (Wyne & Stuck, 1979). In this program, poor readers (second to third grade level and fifth and sixth grade level) spent the school morning in a special classroom for 8 weeks. This room was similar to a typical classroom except that a row of red 25-watt lights, numbered 1 to 10 (coded to correspond to each child), was mounted in a visually prominent place in the front of the room. A panel switch, also numbered 1 to 10, was placed in an adjoining observation room. (Guess who got to press the switch? Want to bet it wasn't little Sally?)

Each child had a daily assignment sheet. It specified the daily tasks, the order in which the tasks were to be completed, and the minimum level of acceptable performance, e.g., the number correct or number of pages or items to be completed.

The students could earn points for each completed task. They had a signalling system to indicate assignment completion or need for help and were told not to sit and wait, but to move on to the next task. Students could also earn points for being on-task. Points were given according to a variable interval schedule. The checkpoint times varied between 5 and 20 minutes, and became less frequent as children moved toward the end of the 8 weeks. If a child was off-task when checked and did not return to task within 5 seconds the light would go on for 30 seconds. Students could lose points if they were off-task. Ultimately, when the child was off-task when checked, there was a loss of one point. If the child didn't return to the task within 5 seconds after the light came on, another point was deducted. If a child stayed off-task for more than 30 seconds (six 5-second intervals), he or she was removed from the classroom. This rather drastic measure occurred only twice during the entire school year. During the first 3 weeks of the 8-week program, students could trade points for tangible rewards, i.e., puzzles, games, pencils, etc. By the fourth week, points could be traded for the right to participate in a group activity, i.e., bowling or a movie.

Two months after the children returned to their regular classroom, they still continued to attend to task. Better yet, they kept their reading gains. When compared to a matched set of children who had not received the intervention program, their gains in reading achievement were more than twice as great. The gains were more dramatic for the second and third graders than for the fifth and sixth graders, who also demonstrated a steady increase in reading. By increasing the time on-task, reading performance improved. The red light study is indeed impressive. But is it practical for teachers who happen to have more than 10 children in their rooms and an outdated electrical engineering degree? The answer is yes.

## Regular Classes

Specifying behaviors and providing feedback in your program are both possible within the normal classroom domain. While this next section borders on classroom management, let's examine the implications of the bright electrical study in light of its academic and attention components.

1. Specifying behavior for the academic tasks
   a. Defining the assignment by using a daily assignment sheet
   b. Defining the sequence of daily work by putting the tasks in order of completion
   c. Defining acceptable work by listing the minimum
   d. Level of performance
2. Setting conditions for academic tasks
   a. Constantly working on an assignment by giving directions for not sitting and waiting for help
   b. Rewarding work activity by attaching points to completed tasks
3. Recognizing attending behaviors needed for the academic tasks
   a. Reminding the child to stay on-task by turning on the red light
   b. Rewarding the child to stay on-task by providing points for appropriate behavior

Attending behaviors can be trained without too much additional organization—and certainly without any nonverbal prompts such as red lights. One advantage of lights is that inappropriate behaviors do not lead to any noise. If you wanted to use a visual prompt you could modify the numbering system. Instead of a one-to-one correspondence of child to light, you could have a particular light match a row or table of children. This approach could impose group pressure on certain children who need to attend to task. If you're not particularly fond of electrical lighting systems, you could set up any number of on-task/off-task symbols. One example that would work just as well as lights to prompt behavior is a set of flip cards. The flip cards and you, the power behind the cards, could be positioned in a visually prominent place. If a child is off-task, you could flip the card to a prearranged signal, e.g., a particular color (red or green), a word (*good* or *oops!*), or even an image (happy or sad).

Points can also be earned in the regular classroom, where group privileges are omnipresent. Children can purchase games, free time, or even activities, like becoming line leaders or attendance monitors. You can include a bulletin board display depicting the progress of the children or the group. If displays are good enough for the United Way, they are good enough for your class, too! Whether you select individual visual prompts or group prompts would depend entirely upon your personal philosophy and the make-up of your class.

Recording points should be no problem either. Keeping track of the points should be even easier with a flip chart than with the red light system. Remember the variable schedule and the freedom it brings for scanning your class when you're able rather than having the restrictions of a set time. While you are working with a small group or an individual, you can flip cards as need be. Just as quickly, you will receive a guarantee that the nonattender will be attentive to your prompt. (That child would rather be watching your activity than working on the reading task. If this were not the case, then the child would be attending to the reading task to begin with.) The only minor fly in the visual prompt ointment is to be sure that you don't fall into a predictable scanning routine. Make sure that you vary your observation schedule; otherwise the 30 pairs of eyes will be oh-so-attentive to the task when you are predictably monitoring.

At the end of the class period, all you need to do is count the number of cards per child or group that have been flipped and record it in a convenient place. (Could counting and recording be yet another one of those privileges a child could earn?)

## WORKING AT AN APPROPRIATE LEVEL OF DIFFICULTY

Just what is the appropriate level of difficulty? In part, it depends upon the nature of the activity. If a child is working with the teacher or a student, the level of task may be somewhat, but not extremely, more difficult than if the child were working alone.

We will now focus on independent work time as it relates to time on-task. One of the surest ways to get a child off-task during reading time is to give material that is too difficult. To test this hypothesis, place yourself squarely in front of a graduate level quantum mechanics text. In an amazingly short time you may discover the wandering eye and squirming body syndrome. According to Gambrell et al. (1981), when reading from materials used for instruction, good readers usually meet an unknown word in 100 running words whereas poor readers don't know 1 out of every 10 words. While good and poor readers are reading the same text, they are obviously not getting an equal opportunity to learn. Poor readers are placed in difficult material for instruction while good readers are placed in easy materials (Clay, 1972). In anybody's book, that's discrimination—a violation of a person's guaranteed reading rights. On the other hand, if reading material is adjusted to the instructional level of poor readers, they are just as capable of the same reading behaviors as good readers (Gambrell et al., 1981). Referring to time on-task, the authors of this study strongly suggest that on-task behavior increases when students are given instructional materials that they can read with ease. So if you'd like little Roger to improve in reading, then you must set the stage for him. You need to give him the chance to spend time reading. To insure that Roger spends the time reading, you need to help him so he can continue to work on the reading task. Probably the biggest help of all comes from the reading materials. They should be selected with care, providing Roger an easy reading level.

# OVERALL CLASSROOM MANAGEMENT FOR READING

## CLASSROOM REALITIES

The wail of the bewildered, rather hostile teacher is beginning to be heard. "But I'm a fifth grade teacher. I teach reading in the fifth grade reading curriculum, and the Rogers in my fifth grade room range in reading level from middle second to high fourth!" To this teacher we must reply "good job" for recognizing the individual differences in the fifth grade class. And now to all good teachers on the job, "Attention to the next realization—the fifth grade label (as any grade label) is an excellent one for estimating the number of years of formal education a child has received, but the number, in and of itself, is rather misleading when used to indicate the degree of learning acquired by any child."

Once we get rid of the "fifth" grade myth, we are still left with several realities: teaching reading, reading materials, reading curriculum, and a fairly wide range of reading performance levels in your class. The inherent problems are vast in scope, yet the solution is simple. It can be found in your overall classroom management for reading instruction. (Not too surprisingly, most of these management techniques can be modified a little for the other basic skill areas—math, spelling, writing, etc.)

There is fairly strong evidence that the teacher's ability to manage the classroom is positively related to students' achievement (Brophy, 1979; Good, 1979). Classroom management for reading instruction has two major related aspects: time and attention.

## TIME

### Student Time

As already noted, time spent reading during the reading period enhances reading achievement. To increase that amount of reading during the reading period, the teacher must examine her classroom structure. For effective use of student time, there are two areas to analyze: (a) the possible use of teacher time across students and (b) providing special attention to children who are falling behind in direct reading activities (Lernhardt, Zigmond, & Cooley, 1981).

### Borrowing Time

Borrowing time can be as simple as reducing wait time for management chores. The time spend getting ready for a reading activity and concluding one is a management chore. Wait time becomes a chore for students as well, as they wait for "something," e.g., instructions, feedback, or someone like the teacher or another classmate. If these two time-consuming areas are reduced, the surplus time can be added to the instructional/productive reading time.

Time can also be borrowed from other areas like social studies, science, or even music. Instead of scheduling social studies 5 days a week, the teacher can have social studies 3 days a week and gain 2 extra days of additional reading. If the social studies text or content material is used in place of the basal, then there will be no "lost" social studies time at all. If you feel that social studies (or whatever) truly demands 5 days a week, then reduce the 45-minute class period by 15 or 20 minutes to gain reading instruction time. Ideally, reading instruction will include the vocabulary and concepts of the borrowed time area.

### Refocusing Teacher Time

Instead of providing lengthy general instructions, the teacher can provide the students with situations for hearing explanations or watching the teacher model the correct reading components of reading. To avoid listening to overall instructions, like what activities are planned for Groups A, B, C, and D, direct the students to a standard prearranged transitional reading, and let them listen to group directions. (See the section on Putting It All Together, pages 222-230, for an example of efficient refocusing of teacher time.)

### SPECIAL ATTENTION

Simply stated, children who are falling behind, i.e., failing to maintain previously learned knowledge, need to be retaught before going to additional concepts. They need time with the teacher on the new task or to practice previously mastered independent tasks. For a child to spend time reading in the reading period, he or she must have materials or activities that allow for on-task behaviors. Although children may be physically present, assigning material or conceptual work that exceeds their skill levels will more than likely lead them mentally out of the reading area.

**Teacher time**—During the reading period, the teacher should be spending the majority of time with the direct instruction of reading skills. How the teacher manages this time is a major factor in the achievement of the students. In some instances, a teacher may be able to increase student reading achievement by spending more time monitoring the class for on-task behavior. The red-light reading system lives on (Anderson et al., 1979). Time spent in reading group transitions or in initial reading instruction is a management factor that can either increase or decrease a student's performance. Teacher activities that create a minimum of disruption and a maximum of student involvement would be the keystone for organizing reading instruction (Fry & Lagomarsino, 1982).

## ORGANIZATIONAL STRUCTURES

In presenting instruction, teachers have three basic organizational approaches: large group (whole class), small group (leveled or mixed), and one-to-one. Self-contained classroom teachers are all too familiar with the practice on day one, minute one, of receiving students according to age and number of grades completed. Given the variety of skill levels and learning rates in a typical 30-student classroom, day one, minute two becomes the crucial, pivotal point in the reading careers of many students. Long before minute two on day one the teacher should have already established entry-level reading skills for each student and made an instructional decision, i.e., chosen each student's objectives based on entry behaviors. Just about now, there might be some protests and mild grumblings over the approach that resembles the dreaded term "individualization"!

Before you bend, tear, or mutilate this page, reflect on a quotation from Sloane, Buckholdt, Jeson, and Crandall (1979):

> Individualization is an important and necessary component of successful teaching; what should be reassuring to teachers is the fact that individualization can occur within practically any approach or model of instruction. (p. 289)

The passage reads smoothly enough, but how can individualization occur in a large group or whole class setting? You decide upon your reading content. You also have the basic reading areas: word analysis, word recognition, oral reading, and reading comprehension. Each area needs to be covered, especially in the primary grades.

## Large-Group Instruction

**Word analysis**—With each higher grade level, the range of students' decoding skills becomes wider. The "pass the buck" class increases over the years and through each grade level as we hear the ever-popular "Just what did they teach those children last year anyway!" Remember Sloane et al. (1979) and the phrase "within practically any approach or model"? Well, decoding and other related word analysis skills lie just outside of the "within practically any approach."

Decoding, if taught systematically and sequentially, builds on itself. One step basically leads to the next. With levels, you can teach isolated skills. The teaching of consonant sounds is an example. You can teach them in any order. If some students have not learned the first three sounds in the lesson, you can still teach the fourth sound to the entire group and have clarity with no confusion for those children who didn't learn the first three sounds. Tony, Judd, Jackie, and Steve didn't learn the *l*, *r*, and *t* sounds, but they had learned all the others. The teacher progresses to the next step, which, in this case, is consonant blends (except those containing *l*, *r*, and *t* sounds). Now these sounds are in a different and more complex context. Not only do Tony and his group have problems with the isolated sounds, but with certain blends. They had been taught vowels in isolation and then shown how to use these vowels with their archenemy blends *l*, *r*, and *t*. Because these blends have been associated with unpleasant memories (like failure and frustration), attaching them to newly acquired sounds can elicit the same unpleasant feelings.

Before the top-down teachers charge at us with "Ah, we told you not to teach sounds in isolation!" let's recall the eclectic approaches to reading.

**Word recognition**—Word recognition skills, unlike word analysis skills, are good for large group instruction, at least in initial lessons with specific words. If you choose to teach vocabulary words from a prespecified list for the first lesson, then the majority of your students could either benefit from the instruction, or for your slower readers, a short review. Class discussion about the meaning of the vocabulary can also be profitable. Lesson 2 is the danger zone where large group instruction begins to break down. Independent practice activities are best suited for those children who already know the words. For those who don't, you'll need to provide additional direct instruction or dependent practice activities. The major problems with this method for large group instruction are supply, demand, time, and selection. Select enough relevant and useful practice activities for the accelerated and average readers while they are waiting for the less skilled readers to learn the words.

Another potential inequity in using large group instruction for word recognition is finding the time to permit slower readers the same amount of independent practice as the advanced readers. Time management becomes a juggling problem, but it can be done. The more advanced readers could be working on other reading skills, e.g., dictionary work, while the less advanced group practices new vocabulary terms.

Perhaps a better use of large group instruction for teaching vocabulary is the language experience approach (LEA). The LEA uses the children's own experiences and vocabulary. Children compose their own stories while the teacher writes the story on either a chart or the board. Depending on the age and the reading skill level, children can copy the story from the chart or board or wait until the teacher distributes a copy of the story. After the teacher completes whatever activities seem appropriate to group instruction, e.g., choral reading or line by line reading, he or she can attend to specific vocabulary. At this point, even though the teacher has been working with the whole group, he or she can select different terms for different children. The simplest way to do this is to require particular lines of the story for particular children.

Assume you have a 20-line story. Sam, a very good reader, may be required to learn all the words. Joanne, a more typical reader, may be assigned the first 15 lines. Janet, who has more difficulty learning vocabulary, may be expected to know the words up to line 10. This method is the most expedient, but not necessarily the most reasonable, way to assign vocabulary.

A better way to assign vocabulary is to choose the critical terms after the story has been dictated. You can individualize by underlining or circling the words on each student's personalized copy of the story. Sam gets them all, Joanne gets all the words underlined on her copy (15 words), and Janet only gets 6 words.

The most efficient technique of all is to have each child read the story the next day. Based on the individual child's errors, you can assign the vocabulary. Restrictions on the number of words would depend on the child's reading skill. If Janet missed 25 words, you'd want to be especially careful in the selection of her words. A more reasonable goal for Janet might be to select 5 of the 25 words.

**Oral reading and comprehension**—Whether a blessing or not, we are somewhere into posterity with the basal or content textbooks from which all children are "reading" all the material at the same time. Some pros: poor readers get to see and hear the correct reading of a text that may be beyond their instructional level. Good readers get to practice reading and show off

their skills. Some cons: good readers and poor readers alike can get BORED
as they listen to each other read. The poor reader can get lost in the text. The
good reader can master the art of page flipping, and settle comfortably into
the book's last story while appearing to be wildly engrossed in the class story
that is getting ground out like pepper from a dulled pepper mill.

Comprehension activities have similar pros and cons. Class discussion of
comprehension may be useful to some class members, but overall, the large
skill range in a typical 30-pupil classroom is usually too wide to be highly
beneficial for all levels.

Oral reading practice demands not only different levels of reading materials but different amounts of practice at specific skill levels. Reading comprehension is directly related to the reading material and skill level of the individual. When children read from different texts with comparable
information, you could generate subject-related comprehension activities
and lessons. If children are required to read from the same text to complete
the comprehension lesson, you'd have similar problems to those you'd find
any time a wide range of skills exists. Poor readers will probably be unable to
identify the words in the text. Better readers will more likely reject repetitive,
nonchallenging discussions, lessons, and activities.

### Small-Group Instruction

There are least two major types of small group instruction in the classroom.
Small group instruction can be designed according to ability or special inter-
est, e.g., playing a reading game that focuses on sounds, words, or concepts.
In ability grouping, the focus is on *who* is in the group; in the special interest
group the focus is on the structure of *how* the participants will learn (Sharan
& Sharan, 1976).

**Ability grouping**—In ability grouping, the teacher tries to reduce the wide
range of skill levels by creating a more homogeneous skill group. The number
of groups formed relates directly to the teacher's management skills and the
range of reading abilities. Ability grouping maintains the traditional relationship between teacher and students in that the teacher is the primary di-
rector of the group.

**Special interest grouping**—In contrast, the special interest group alters the
teacher/student roles somewhat. The teacher becomes more of a facilitator;
the group usually acts upon the students' interest in studying a particular
problem. Sometimes the group is formed on the basis of friendship.

All aspects of reading fall easily into small group formats. Because one of
the primary goals of small group reading instruction is to maximize teaching
efficiency, children can be grouped according to particular needs if they can

be taught together without holding up or interfering with the reading progress of their classmates (Veatch, 1966). Teachers can provide direct reading instruction in small teaching groups. A teacher can also allow for the cooperative and student-centered small group teaching. While the teacher is working in direct instruction with an ability group, the other children can be in small groups working on a common goal or helping one another complete reading assignments.

Much research on interaction in groups has shown that giving and receiving help are positively related to achievement, whereas off-task and passive behavior tend to reduce achievement (Webb, 1982). The effectiveness of small group, traditional large group, and individual learning methods has been examined in relation to academic achievement. The relationship clearly shows that the cooperative small group method overall is the most effective (Swing & Peterson, 1982). Small group work seems especially valuable for low ability and high ability students. Each group works very well when paired with one another (Amaria, Brian, & Leith, 1969; Peterson, Janicki, & Swing, 1981). A final recommendation for small group learning where students work cooperatively is found in the reading of subject material, in this case, social studies, as well. Superior thinking, i.e., ability to comprehend, analyze, and synthesize material, is associated with small group learning. In addition, lower-level thinking skills, e.g., finding facts, are also promoted in small group settings (Sharan, Ackerman, & Hertz-Lazarowitz, 1979).

**Word analysis**—Specific examples of both types of small group settings are very easily found in the area of word analysis. The more structured small group setting focuses on a narrower skill range than that of a large group setting. The teacher may form several groups for different aspects of word analysis, e.g., group 1, consonant digraphs (*sh*, *wh*, *th*, *ch*); group 2, short vowel sounds; and group 3, contractions.

Ms. Smith's students demonstrated a wide range of phonics skills. She has not grouped her students according to high, low, and average, but by the skill needs found in the previous paragraph. Tommy is in two of the three groups, consonant digraphs and short vowels. Valerie needs help in all three areas and has had a difficult time learning to read. Even though Valerie could benefit from placement in all the groups, to reduce stress, Ms. Smith has placed her only in the short vowels group. Later in the school year, Valerie will join the other two skill areas. Jonah has mastered all these skills and needs no specific instruction in word analysis. Allison has also mastered the three skills, but she needs dictionary review, so Ms. Smith paired her with Jonah on a dictionary assignment.

Ms. Smith works directly with each skill-level group. She also provides class time for group members to work on projects related to specific skills.

The digraph group is making a digraph cut-and-paste picture book. The short vowel group is working on a vowel-coded coloring puzzle, and the contractions group is playing "contractions bingo" (instead of numbers, the caller reads words for children to match their contractions).

**Word recognition and oral reading**—In ability grouping for small group instruction we create the ever-popular and embarrassing "red birds," "blue birds," and "black birds" reading groups. Somewhat less popular is the word list grouping, which can be disguised when a content textbook vocabulary is used in place of a basal reader vocabulary. Oral reading groups with associated word list groups can also be less obvious when using a language experience approach. Every group member becomes associated with every other rather than with a particular reader. Members within a language experience group can also be rotated for a different combination of students. A language experience approach is also quite useful as a cooperative learning venture. Children can work together to create a story. The teacher can then choose the vocabulary from within the story and assign the appropriate vocabulary to each group member. Let's return to Ms. Smith, who has assigned Tommy, Valerie, Jonah, Allison, and three other children to a language experience group. The children choose their own topic and write their own story. In the directed group setting, Ms. Smith assigns word lists taken from the story to each child. Tommy received four short vowel words, two with consonant digraphs (reflecting his word analysis needs), and three other commonly used words. Valerie was assigned the same four short vowel words as Tommy, plus two other commonly used words. Jonah was given the eight words and Allison the six words that they were unable to read in isolation. All the children, however, read the story in a group supervised by Ms. Smith.

**Comprehension**—Aside from the rather informal but useful "who, what, why, where, when, and how" (wwwww & h) questioning approach to reading comprehension, formal grouping for particular comprehension skills can also occur. The wwwww & h usually occurs after a particular passage or story has been read. If children have been grouped according to reading levels, the wwwww & h approach is an automatic part of the group's activity. In contrast, if grouping is based on specific comprehension skills, mixed ability groups can be formed. As mentioned earlier, small mixed ability groups are quite functional for all levels of readers.

Another visit to Tommy and his classmates will show us how easily they can be grouped according to the specific comprehension skills identifying main ideas and determining sequence. The reading material could come from their own language experience stories or from any text written at the instructional level of the lowest skilled reader in the group. Obviously, this practice has just one flaw. If the lowest skilled reader is functioning at a pre-reading level, the latter activity would not be advisable. The teacher could, however, read to the students to provide a common basis for the group activity. Because the group size is much smaller than 30, the teacher can provide more immediate feedback and individual attention. Opportunities for boredom are considerably fewer since children in small groups can more easily get involved with both the task and the teacher.

## Individualization

Individualized instruction means that the content and process are provided either by student choice or teacher prescription at the appropriate times. Individualized instruction does not necessarily mean that the teacher works with only one student at a time or that students work alone all the time (Blackburn & Powell, 1976). In fact, "the exclusive use of one-to-one instruction is usually very inefficient, especially if the teacher is responsible for more than one or two students during any instructional period" (Sloane et al., 1979, p. 293). One-to-one reading instruction works well in the classroom where the teacher checks students' skill mastery of materials or during individual conference time.

If teachers have provided different word lists for each child (like Ms. Smith and Tommy), they will need to test individually. Conference times allow teachers the opportunity to hear children read from a text, a library book of their own choice, or a language experience story. During this special time students receive corrective feedback or continued direct instruction on a concept to be mastered.

Perhaps the most important point about individualization is that the one-to-one instruction is only one aspect of this system. Recall that individualization basically places a child in materials and instructional techniques that match his or her entry level skills. The critical factor is the match between the entry skills and the concepts to be taught. Individualization as such can be done in a large group setting. In most regular classrooms individualization will need to occur in all size groups. The large group will be the most difficult to implement in the classroom, but activities such as listening to stories read by the teacher certainly can qualify as appropriate to the whole group's entry skill level.

Probably the most useful and efficient form of individualization found in the classroom is instruction through small groups formed on the basis of mutual specific skill need. A one-to-one individualized reading approach would also be found in a regular classroom, but primarily for specific types of instruction, e.g., a mastery checkout.

## PUTTING IT ALL TOGETHER: A MODEL OF READING INSTRUCTION

Let's take all that's been said about general reading behaviors to see how this information can actually be used in the real world of the classroom. We will visit a typical third grade classroom of 30 children, whose reading levels range from 1.5 to 5.0. The teacher, Ms. Bartel, needs to assess reading entry levels in word analysis, oral reading, word recognition, and reading comprehension. Once the entry levels in each area for each student have been identified, Ms. Bartel faces an organizational task. She has to determine just how she will meet the needs of her students as effectively and efficiently as possible and still keep her sanity. She begins the process by delineating what has to be taught, to whom it should be taught, and during what time period it should be taught.

**Time Periods**

Ms. Bartel started with the major reading instructional topics by sketching out in global terms what needs to be taught and the approximate teaching time. She decided on 95 minutes a day for reading instead of the prescribed 45 minutes. She took time from two sources: the normally scheduled allotment for reading and borrowed time.

**Normally scheduled time**—Approximately 45 minutes was allotted for the reading period. During this time, she wanted children to participate in silent reading, word analysis, and word recognition/comprehension. This was not enough time for reading activities, so Ms. Bartel explored borrowed time. She needed about 45 more minutes for group work in phonics and comprehension activities. To find this time, Ms. Bartel needed to establish a weekly time schedule for other subjects, so she devised the following schedule:

| | |
|---|---|
| 8:30– 8:45 | Attendance and Opening |
| 8:45– 9:30 | Math |
| 9:30– 9:45 | Recess |
| 9:45–10:45 | Reading |
| 10:45–11:15 | Music (M/W); PE (T/Th/F) |
| 11:15–11:30 | Handwriting (M/W); Math Facts (T/Th/F) |
| 11:30–12:30 | Lunch and Recess |
| 12:30– 1:00 | Word Analysis Groups (M-Th); Library (F) |
| 1:00– 1:35 | Science (M/W/F); Health (T/Th) |
| 1:35– 1:50 | Recess |
| 1:50– 2:45 | Social Studies (M-Th); Art (F) |
| 2:45– 3:00 | Story Time |

Ms. Bartel "borrowed" time by choosing to teach subjects such as health, science, and social studies less than 5 days a week. She recognized these areas as important; and because the material overlaps with reading skills, she can use these topics to teach reading skills during the reading time.

**Students' schedules**—Ms. Bartel first relocated the normally scheduled time as follows:

   a.  15 minutes for silent reading

   b.  15 minutes for word analysis

   c.  15 minutes for word recognition/comprehension

She didn't want to highlight skill differences, so she organized the class into three small groups. The organization by topic and membership was arbitrary, with 10 children each in groups A, B, and C. Now Ms. Bartel had a new schedule:

| Time | Silent Reading | Word Analysis | Writing (Word Recognition) |
|---|---|---|---|
| 9:45–10:05 | A | B | C |
| 10:05–10:25 | C | A | B |
| 10:25–10:45 | B | C | A |

There is a discrepancy between the 15 minutes allowed to the tasks and the actual schedule, which suggests 20 minutes per task. Transition times, however smooth, do take some time. To account for possible time lag and yet to insure a minimum of 15 minutes per child in each area, schedule additional time by 2 to 3 minutes for each activity. If children don't need this extra time, you have gained instruction minutes.

"What" has to be taught and "to whom" it gets taught fall together. For word analysis, Ms. Bartel found two relatively homogeneous skill levels. Approximately half of her class was in the 1.5 to 3.0 decoding level, while the other half was above grade level. This translated to the 1.5 to 3.0 group being badly in need of work in consonant letter-sound relationships and vowel letter sounds. The other half of the class was firmly scattered along a structural analysis skills continuum, i.e., inflectional endings, doubling final consonants, working with plurals, and so forth, up through dictionary work. Oral reading level and word recognition levels were so widespread that only at the very lowest reading levels did grouping even begin to make sense. Even at that level, grouping of text seemed questionable. Comprehension skills, however, presented a chance for grouping.

Once Ms. Bartel had determined that some skill areas could be taught in groups while others could not, her next consideration was to decide on how much instructional time she could afford with each child. The time spent would include large group, small group, and one-to-one teaching. Time with each child also depended on the instructional need. For children who learned more slowly than most, she would need to spend more time monitoring progress.

## Scheduling Activities

While beginning to look and feel like a circus performer, spinning a plate on a stick with her right hand and juggling three oranges with her left, Ms. Bartel devised two schedules. Both were for the reading period. One represented her activities and the other her students' activities.

**Children's tasks**—Once the children were busily working, we could take a look at just what they were doing. Some were working independently, some in small groups, and some with Ms. Bartel. They knew what they were supposed to be doing through verbal and nonverbal cue signalling. The verbal signalling system was used when Ms. Bartel announced that the group members were to change activities. The main verbal cue came from Ms. Bartel every time she designated a group for silent reading. The nonverbal prompt consisted of a "Time Wheel." The Time Wheel, as shown in Figure 8.1, was nothing more elaborate than a circular piece of construction paper joined to another piece at the center by a brad. Either Ms. Bartel or a student rotated the wheel at 20-minute intervals. As long as students could remember what group they were in, all was well. To avoid anyone's memory loss, perhaps Ms. Bartel's the most, she used a class bulletin board to post monthly group membership. This and a schedule of activities allowed the students to be aware of what they were supposed to be doing and also granted Ms. Bartel the same privilege. (Whoever said remembering the activities of 30 children had to be committed to memory?) Refer to Table 8.1 for the schedule.

**Table 8.1**
Group Membership Schedules

| Group A | Group B | Group C |
|---|---|---|
| Larry | Alfonso | Kevin |
| Doug | Robbie | Billy |
| Willie | Kenny | Dennis |
| Lavonda | Stanley | Cathy |
| John | Randy | Clark |
| Brian | Ellie | Herb |
| Ana | Joanna | Marilyn |
| Bruno | Alva | Peggy |
| Anne | George | Shelly |
| Jimmy | Francie | Johnnie |

**Figure 8.1**
Time Wheel for Reading Activities

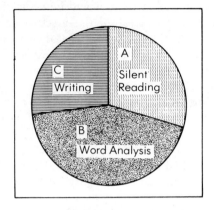

A. Silent Reading
B. Word Analysis
C. Writing

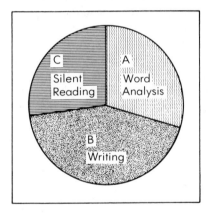

A. Word Analysis
B. Writing
C. Silent Reading

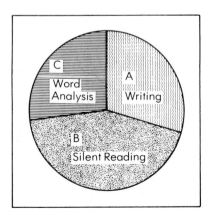

A. Writing
B. Silent Reading
C. Word Analysis

A quick inspection of each activity would immediately clarify the students' tasks and subsequently demonstrate the effectiveness of the small heterogeneous group setting. Children read books at their independent reading levels during silent reading. Some teachers feel more comfortable assigning various basals during this time, while others prefer the children's selection of library books. Ms. Bartel combined the two approaches. She allowed all the children to choose library books, but for some of her slower students she restricted the topics and sometimes directed their reading to science, social studies, or health materials. If the students had problems with a word, they were encouraged to ask their neighbor for help and then write the word on a $3 \times 5$ card. Thus in the silent reading group each student read at the appropriate entry level and yet had the opportunity for cooperative small group learning.

The word analysis group was a little more complex, but not much. Because Ms. Bartel matched her phonics teaching sequence to the one in the textbook, she assigned children to specific pages in the text. She also supplemented text pages with worksheets coded to the objective. (Did someone screech out, "But I don't have any class phonics books!" Remember the $50.00 you get to use for ordering materials? Ms. Bartel's room may be short on red and green crêpe paper, but it's long on phonics books.) Students could help one another again, with the material matched carefully to the child's entry-level skills. For those children whose skills were beyond the phonics book, Ms. Bartel provided alternate activities commensurate with their needs. Spencer, for example, really had no major need for phonics instruction so he was allowed to extend his silent reading time to work on his choice of reading projects in either science, health, or social studies.

Word recognition activities were individualized. Each child, or pair of children, wrote a language experience story every day. On most days the students selected the themes, but occasionally Ms. Bartel broadened the budding authors' literary scope. Kevin and Billy were fascinated with monsters, dragons, and weird nocturnal events. Each horrifying day invited the next, even more bizarre story, with their cranked-out tales that could set even Dracula's heart aflutter. Ms. Bartel complimented them on their imagination, then restricted monster stories to 1 day a week. With due respect to any who fear possible damage to the creative psyches of two third-grade boys, educators take heed. The remaining days of the week brought reptiles, volcanoes, cannibals, and other daytime horrors into vivid, sometimes livid, graphic color.

During the writing time, children also corrected the punctuation and spelling errors that Ms. Bartel had noted on their previously written stories. She circled misspelled words and attached $3 \times 5$ cards with each correctly spelled word onto the top of every page of the story. The attached words became the child's spelling list and were used for practice with other members of the group.

**Teacher's schedule**—Ms. Bartel had more work to do. Aside from providing one-on-one checkpoints during the reading period, she had to accommodate differences in her students' learning rates. She also had to determine the amount of direct intervention versus the level of independent work for each child since some students needed minimal guidance while others demanded a lot. She carefully monitored student progress to insure that no one got lost in the 30-member reading shuffle.

Checkpoints and one-to-one instruction are the two major activities for Ms. Bartel during the reading period. During the silent reading group time, Ms. Bartel called students for individual conferences, and for about 2 minutes she sampled their reading. Errors were noted and corrective instruction given. Her primary goal was to check the students' fluency, their independent reading levels, and their spelling. She also reviewed the students' language experience stories by listening to the child read the story, but especially to the vocabulary words selected for spelling and handwriting activities. Spelling was checked through a short recall test. If the word was spelled correctly, the child filed the word alphabetically in a personal $3 \times 5$ word file box. Incorrect words marked with an $x$ became the property of the teacher. They were kept in the front of the student's file box and could gain their alphabetical status only through the next conference with correct spelling.

"But how could Ms. Bartel work with 30 students every day in these activities?" The answer is, she couldn't. She carefully assessed her students and identified which children needed daily monitoring and which ones did not. Ms. Bartel's schedule appears in Table 8.2.

The Table 8.2 conference schedule outlines the reading period for Groups A, B, and C. Ms. Bartel held one-to-one conferences throughout each of the silent reading groups. The asterisk beside a child's name means that he or she would be in conference with Ms. Bartel during that time and on that day. Not all children met with Ms. Bartel every day. In fact, she met with eight to ten students each day on a rotational basis, about every third day. In Group B, for example, Alfonso met with Ms. Bartel on Monday and with three other Group B students on Wednesday. Her Group B conference list began again on Thursday. Alfonso's next conference was scheduled on the following Thursday.

Students in need of more individual checkpoints met with Ms. Bartel every day. (See Larry, Group A.) Some groups rotated more quickly than others. From Group C, Kevin met with Ms. Bartel three times a week, while Marilyn conferred twice a week. Since no one in Group C needed multiple checkpoints, Group C rotated faster than Groups A or B. To meet current

# Table 8.2
## Conference Schedule

Groups

Each day is divided into three columns — **Silent Reading (A)**, **Word Analysis (B)**, and **Word Analysis (C)** — for Monday, Tuesday, Wednesday, Thursday, and Friday. Students marked with an asterisk (*) are scheduled that day.

| Group | Monday | Tuesday | Wednesday | Thursday | Friday |
|-------|--------|---------|-----------|----------|--------|
| **A** | *Larry | *Larry | *Larry | *Larry | *Larry |
| | Dougie | Dougie | Dougie | *Dougie | *Dougie |
| | Willie | Willie | Willie | Willie | Willie |
| | *Lavonda | Lavonda | Lavonda | Lavonda | Lavonda |
| | *John | John | John | John | John |
| | Brian | Brian | Brian | Brian | Brian |
| | Ana | Ana | *Ana | Ana | Ana |
| | Bruno | Bruno | Bruno | *Bruno | Bruno |
| | Anne | Anne | *Anne | *Anne | Anne |
| | Jimmy | Jimmy | Jimmy | *Jimmy | *Jimmy |
| **C** | Kevin | Kevin | Kevin | *Kevin | *Kevin |
| | Billy | *Billy | *Billy | Billy | *Billy |
| | Dennis | Dennis | Dennis | *Dennis | *Dennis |
| | *Cathy | *Cathy | Cathy | Cathy | Cathy |
| | *Clark | *Clark | Clark | Clark | Clark |
| | *Herb | *Herb | Herb | Herb | Herb |
| | Marilyn | Marilyn | *Marilyn | Marilyn | *Marilyn |
| | Peggy | Peggy | *Peggy | *Peggy | Peggy |
| | Shelly | Shelly | Shelly | *Shelly | Shelly |
| | Johnnie | Johnnie | Johnnie | *Johnnie | Johnnie |
| **B** | *Alfonso | *Alfonso | *Alfonso | *Alfonso | Alfonso |
| | Robbie | Robbie | *Robbie | *Robbie | Robbie |
| | Kenny | Kenny | Kenny | *Kenny | *Kenny |
| | *Stanley | *Stanley | Stanley | Stanley | *Stanley |
| | *Randy | *Randy | Randy | Randy | Randy |
| | *Ellie | *Ellie | Ellie | Ellie | Ellie |
| | Joanna | *Joanna | *Joanna | Joanna | Joanna |
| | Alva | *Alva | Alva | *Alva | *Alva |
| | George | *George | *George | George | George |
| | *Francie | *Francie | Francie | Francie | Francie |

needs and insure a more equitable rotational schedule, Ms. Bartel changed group composition once a month. She tried carefully not to get too many weekly multiple-checkpointers like Larry and Kevin in one group. The group changes also allowed the children to work with a broader range of classmates, other than the 10 from their original groups.

About half of Ms. Bartel's class, as you recall, was under grade level in overall reading. To meet the instructional needs of her students, Ms. Bartel had several more reading times up her instructional sleeves. She used cross-age tutors right after lunch for decoding and provided comprehension activities during the story time. During the reading period, Ms. Bartel had sixth grade students tutor many children. Tutors were assigned a child and an agenda and had approximately 15 minutes with their assigned students to practice proficiency in specific areas.

In the 12:30 to 1:30 word analysis block, Ms. Bartel devoted her time to small group instruction. She divided her class into three groups: beginning phonics, structural analysis, and beyond phonics. The beyond phonics group had no major instructional need for word analysis. Since these children needed more sophisticated activities with prose materials, Ms. Bartel had them learn how to write outlines and book reports for research topics. Ms. Bartel turned over the objectives for this group and the instructional responsibility to the school librarian. Everyone was pleased, for the librarian could finally work with students instead of acting as a student monitor.

With the class reduced by six, Ms. Bartel had two small groups left. While the composition of a group is never homogeneous, the skill range was nevertheless more manageable. Two half-hour periods provided equal time for each group. The unattended group worked on practice activities related to a particular skill. The assignment itself was in addition to the word analysis activities completed during the morning's reading period.

Because of Ms. Bartel's class composition, word analysis skills were the most critical for advancement in reading. Other classes, especially in the upper and middle grades, will most likely need to concentrate on reading comprehension skills. Ms. Bartel's reading class schedule can easily accommodate social studies, science, or any reading-based content area. The reading areas would essentially stay the same, but the materials would reflect the content being taught, e.g., instead of a basal reader, a social studies text. Written stories would be about specific social studies concepts or events.

Did Ms. Bartel forget to teach comprehension skills? Hardly, not when she scheduled these major timeframes to check format. The first time was conference time, when she checked to see if the child knew the main idea and could sequence the passage. She also quickly asked "who, why, what, where, when, and how" and identified her students' strengths and weaknesses. The second comprehension check occurred during story reading time. Before she began the day's reading, the entire class responded to a questioning technique in a review of the past day's reading. It was similar to her conference sessions. Ms. Bartel asked the whole group for main ideas, sequencing, and "who, why, how … ." The third specific comprehension skill occurred during social studies time. Ms. Bartel used social studies material as the information base for teaching comprehension skills. Small and large group instructional units were formed. The large group would discuss a particular topic. The small group, which was heterogeneous in skill-level composition, would then use that topic in conjuction with specific comprehension instruction.

## SUMMARY

This chapter has reviewed reading techniques that assist both good and poor readers. The emphasis was on approaches and materials, without regard to handicapping conditions. Three major teacher-controlled reading variables were outlined: direct instruction, time on-task, and class management. Specific approaches were emphasized because their proper use will increase students' reading achievement. The approaches were presented within the framework of a classroom of about 30 children with a skill range of at least three grade levels. Contrasts between good and poor readers were also presented, as well as specific activities for assisting poor readers.

Finally, a model of a reading program was outlined. The model represents an eclectic approach to reading. Word recognition, word analysis, oral reading, and reading comprehension were developed in this model, as well as the teacher's time management system for large group, small group, and one-to-one instruction.

# 9
# Reading for Special Populations

In preparation for the launching, Michael abandoned his desk for a preferred station at the table next to Joey. Their space-age project was almost ready for take-off, at least on paper. Even Sue's burst of giggles did not interfere with the boys. They just scrambled to finish the last sentence of their report while Sue closed the book on the final page of her story.

Elaine, Fredrico, and Rusty, the eighth grade tutor, circled closely over a word game. Neither Josh nor Lenny so much as winced when Fredrico blurted out "Bingo!" The two young scholars' search merely continued along the mysterious depths of many oceans with books and charts spanning two desks.

Other books in the room were opened. Pencils everywhere were writing. All 30 students were busy with their personalized selection of books, pencils, papers, charts, maps, newspapers, etc. And everyone was reading something.

No one would know from observing the classroom that Joey is mildly learning handicapped or that this is Sue's first year of placement in a regular classroom. Elaine's wheelchair is the only visible clue to her disability. As for our oceanic explorers, they're just about ready to submit their entry to the science division of a national competition designed for gifted and talented children. This classroomful of readers with various levels and handicapping conditions raises some interesting questions.

# SUCCESSFUL READING PROGRAMS

## PRACTICAL CLASSROOM PRACTICES

What makes this class so special? Why does this room succeed in reading instruction while other similar ones fail? How are these students' needs for different reading skill levels met? The answer to all these questions is the teacher's use of three techniques:

1. Obtain maximum time on-task for each child by implementing an effective behavioral management system.
2. Insure that each child has daily reading success and give frequent positive reinforcement.
3. Provide each child with daily reading material at the appropriate reading level.

All children, handicapped or not, make the most progress when they are taught by a teacher who uses these techniques (Gaskins, 1982).

Adults have been asked to evaluate pro and con reading experiences of their childhood (Callaway, 1981). Their responses suggest practical and realistic classroom practices. When they were asked to rate round robin oral reading, not one single positive statement could be found. (Other statements, which will not be printed here, were readily available.) Other sources of aversion to reading include difficulty of material (too difficult, therefore, unpleasant), boring material, isolated drill, and material that was irrelevant or biased. In eliminating these unproductive, nonmotivating factors, the teacher tries to fill the void with opposites. To excite and motivate students to read, the teacher substitutes interesting and child-relevant materials for boring ones.

## High-Interest Materials

Children, especially boys, perform better reading high-interest rather than low-interest materials (Asher, Hymel, & Wigfield, 1978). Even drill can become challenging and engaging if related to the larger picture of reading. Just like an isolated piece of a puzzle, reading drill becomes interesting only when the activity can be related to the whole reading puzzle.

The circumstances, coupled with personal purpose and predilections, may dispose readers either to engage themselves in their reading or to detach themselves from the task (Hayes & Diehl, 1982). If a child is asked to read the next story in the basal to complete the reading assignment, i.e., to read for the sake of reading, then the motivation and degree of involvement may be somewhat limited. But if the teacher directs the child to the same basal and provides some sort of incentive, involvement may be greater. The incentive may be as simple as reading to discover who certain people are in the story. The student would receive a list of special events or people and, like a detective, set out to discover who or what these people and events have to do with the story. The teacher can also lay the groundwork for relevancy and purpose by having the children relate the story to some real or imagined personal (meaningful) experience. If the story is about a deaf child, the normally hearing children could write about how the deaf child's experience was similar to one that had happened to them or to someone they know.

## Active Reading Involvement

By allowing children to choose their own reading materials, the problem of active reading involvement is lessened. The simple act of choosing predisposes the child to a favorable attitude toward the reading material. Children (and adults as well) typically choose reading material that fits some need. The needs can vary from getting information to pure entertainment. Reading rate will vary as a consequence of the reader's need, but the active level of the reading process will remain the same. In a successful classroom, the teacher appreciates that both rate and understanding of the reading material will vary from one reading situation to the next. The teacher should be more concerned about the "appropriateness" of the reading rate and the understanding than about the actual rate or understanding.

## MYTH OF READING READINESS

### Entry-Level Instruction

One final general statement about the successful reading program in the regular classroom remains to be stated. The classroom teacher should not wait for the child to acquire reading skills, to produce particular language skills, or to demonstrate some particular state of cognitive development. Rather, the classroom teacher should teach reading skills beginning at the entry level of the child. The reading teacher who hesitates to teach produces children who are lost in reading. Acquiring reading skills has not been "empirically proven to be, and probably is not, intrinsically connected to a particular stage of development of cognition and language skills" (Doehring & Aulls, 1979, p. 30). Surely, if pigeons can be taught to discriminate the letters of the alphabet in about 4 months time (*Science 82*, 1982), children do not need to learn how to be pigeons before they are allowed to be taught reading.

### Teach to Skill

In other words, successful classroom teachers don't spend a great deal of time getting the children ready to read. Instead, they spend it engaging the children in the reading activities of word analysis, word recognition, oral reading, and reading comprehension.

Take the example of Ronnie. Ronnie is in the third grade. He is still using telegraphic speech, i.e., two-word sentences. His language development is very similar to a successful 2-year-old's. Granted, Ronnie should be receiving some special assistance, but the reality is that the only special assistance available is a speech and language teacher. While very good at speech and language, his teacher cannot make the time in her rather frantic schedule to put a great deal of focus on reading instruction.

Judging from Ronnie's current rate of language development, he would be about 14 years old before he would be functioning at the 8-year level typically found in a third grade class. (Actually, no one can predict Ronnie's rate of linguistic development; when he is 14, it could be anywhere in the range of 2 to 14 years old.) His classroom teacher didn't particularly feel like waiting for Ronnie to perform at the level of an 8-year-old before she began reading instruction. (Besides, by the time he had reached grade-appropriate level, the desks would probably be way too small. Furniture acquisition is such a trauma!) She analyzed what Ronnie could do with language. Her analysis of his entry skills led her to begin sight vocabulary instruction from his language experience stories. Although the first few stories weren't very long—just two or three words at the most—the stories and their words had meaning for Ronnie. As his sight vocabulary grew, his reading level improved. Ronnie's teacher also began instruction in phonics. For phonics practice, Ronnie completed many worksheets that required matching a picture or pictures with sounds. As his phonics skills grew, his vocabulary also began to expand.

At the end of the third grade, Ronnie had acquired all the consonant letter sounds as well as the consonant blends. He was able to read all the short vowels except for short *e* and was proficient at recognizing words containing a medial vowel and a final *e*, such as *rope, cute, tire*. By no means was Ronnie reading at fourth grade level. However, he had been successful in acquiring reading skills during his third grade year. Better yet, he had spent a productive year acquiring some very basic reading skills. Now instead of sitting in the back of the room coloring pictures and matching shapes, Ronnie could read, though he was somewhat limited. He could read because his classroom teacher couldn't wait to teach him. Funny thing is, Ronnie couldn't wait to read either!

# TECHNIQUES FOR READING DISABLED CHILDREN

## DEFINITIONS

Reading disabled children are typically those children who are functioning about 2 years below grade level in one or more of the areas of word recognition, word analysis, oral reading, and reading comprehension. While this definition generally holds true, multiple exceptions abound. The gifted child (as measured by an individualized IQ test) who is reading at or near grade level is an exception to the rule. The entire elementary school located in an urban inner-city poverty belt is another exception. José, Tung-Lee, and Gunther, whose respective native languages are Spanish, Thai, and German, and who have recently arrived in this country, also represent cases in which the rule does not hold.

## RESEARCH FINDINGS

But for those cases when the rule does hold, research has very little to tell the working reading classroom teacher. No one has yet clearly proven that any particular type of reading disability consistently responds best to any particular method of teaching (Harris, 1982).

## Diagnostic Teaching

The most progress in diagnostic and remedial work with disabled readers occurred in the early twentieth century. A great deal of growth was made in early test development and diagnosis. Unfortunately, the development of remedial reading approaches or methods used to solve the problems associated with learning to read did not keep pace. There has been very little fundamental change in remedial work with disabled readers in the last 30 years (Pelosi, 1981). As for what the teacher is to do, regardless of the reading disability, all is not vague. According to Harris (1982), "For now concentrate on educational diagnosis, using formal and informal lists of word recognition, decoding and comprehension to develop tentative plans, and then employ intelligent trial and error to modify the program as needed" (p. 460).

## Intelligent Trial and Error

Thus the onus of responsibility for "intelligent trial and error" is placed squarely in the hands of the teacher. For the most part, these are the best hands for teaching responsibility to be in. The key word is *intelligent*, which implies *informed*. A rather brief overview of reading disabilities as related to good and poor readers, dyslexics, and special populations may support the intuitive and experiential intelligence found in so many skilled regular classroom teachers.

## DIFFERENCES BETWEEN GOOD AND POOR READERS

## Heterogeneity of Poor Readers

First and foremost, the stereotyped notion of "poor reader" needs to be discarded. Reading disabled students are a heterogeneous group. There is no evidence supporting any one factor or characteristic that applies to all children who exhibit intellectual reading problems (Wallbrown, Vance, & Blaka, 1979). Not only are there at least four major skill areas in reading, but children can have difficulties in learning in any, all, or combinations of these areas. Morris has problems with decoding. Richard isn't sure of anything he's ever read. Donald can't remember old words or even begin to figure out how to approach them. While poor Nettie has excellent comprehension when she attends to the story, she tends to embellish once her attention has wandered from the text. Even so, unless told a word, Nettie can't sound out new ones.

## Characteristics of Reading Behavior

Certain characteristics have occurred across sets of poor readers. While not all poor readers have these problems, a good teacher will be sensitive to them. Some researchers have suggested that good and poor readers differ in their ability to effectively and actively select, organize, assimilate, or process information in the context of distracting stimuli (Cotugno, 1981; Santosstefano, 1978).

**Focusing attention**—Poor readers, in other words, are sometimes not able to zero in on the important aspect of the reading task. All information competes with the poor reader's active attention. Techniques that enhance or focus a reader's attention could be most valuable for a child who is having problems learning to read. By screening out irrelevant stimuli, the student has better access to the relevant stimuli. Better access can lead to a greater ease of learning and a higher rate of achievement. Fairly detailed techniques for focusing attention are found in chapter 7.

**Using feedback**—Closely related to focusing attention is feedback. (General techniques for appropriate feedback in the classroom are presented in chapter 7.) In general, there are two types of feedback: reinforcement and correctional information. With both types the teacher gives a student information about his or her performance. In reinforcement, the children are given praise for correct work. In correctional or corrective feedback, the child is literally corrected on some or all errors. For many readers both types of feedback are educationally useful. The two types of feedback provide the reader with different kinds of information. Reinforcement gives the reader a small pat on the back for demonstrating excellence. Corrective feedback lets the reader know that something is amiss in the reading process. In effect, reinforcement feedback tells the reader what he or she knows while corrective feedback tells the reader what still needs to be known.

For readers to learn the most from corrective feedback, a delay in feedback seems to be most valuable for learning the correct response (Burdwell, 1981). If, for example, Terrance is having problems reading, then delayed feedback will be more useful to his reading behavior than immediate feedback. If he were immediately corrected for miscalling a word, e.g., *turkey* for *termite*, he would be likely to confuse his error (*turkey*) with the correct word (*termite*). If, on the other hand, Terrance received correction after the entire passage had been read or even received help on missed words the next day, the odds of him acquiring and remembering the correct response go up. The theory behind this practice is that the delayed feedback (*termite*) doesn't become confused with the incorrect response (*turkey*) because Terrance has already forgotten his error; i.e., he forgot that he misread *turkey* for *termite*. When Terrance is presented with *termite*, the corrective feedback is almost like teaching the misread word as a brand new one. If you must choose between giving immediate feedback or giving delayed feedback, you should opt for delayed feedback. Fortunately the either/or situation rarely occurs. Usually you can provide both immediate and delayed corrective feedback.

The question then arises, should all readers be provided with the same amount of feedback? In fact, some evidence points to the notion that not all readers benefit equally from corrective feedback. Normal or good readers may not even need systematic corrective feedback, while poor readers may actually thrive on it. With respect to reading comprehension and word accuracy, Pany and McCoy (1983) found that average third graders achieved similar levels of performance with or without immediate corrective feedback. With poor readers (in this case learning disabled children), word recognition and comprehension scores increased in proportion to the amount of feedback received. The learning disabled children read and remembered what was read best if every one of their errors was corrected. Even when only selected errors were corrected, the learning disabled students had better word accuracy and comprehension than when none of the errors were corrected. This evidence suggests that learning disabled poor readers, and at the risk of over-generalization, perhaps all poor readers, may profit from corrective feedback during reading instruction.

## DYSLEXIA

Good and poor readers present one kind of challenge to the classroom teacher. The implication is that poor readers, however diverse, can at least read. What about those children called *dyslexic* who enter the regular classroom? Can a regular classroom teacher teach a dyslexic child? As a matter of fact, just what is a dyslexic child?

### Variability of Definitions

*Dyslexia* is one of those often heard and often misunderstood terms used to cast fear into the heart of the educator and status into the field of reading. (Medical terms like *dyslexia* make some frustrated educators feel more like M.D.'s. Whether justified or not, the professional glamour of an M.D. is somewhat more shining than that of an educator.) Presently, *dyslexia* is the term used at one extreme to describe a somewhat variable syndrome based on constitutional neuropsychological deviation and at the other extreme to describe a nonspecific syndrome of reading disability (Harris, 1978-79). Dyslexia, by anyone's definition, describes the failure to learn to read in spite of apparently adequate intelligence, educational opportunity, and lack of physical limitations. Are all poor or nonreaders dyslexic? If you want to use the term, then feel free to answer yes. Actually only about 1 to 3% of problem readers should probably be classified as dyslexic, and these folks are likely to have neurological deficits that impair (not destroy or eliminate) their reading performance. More than likely, the vast majority of people who experience "severe" (let us note the term *severe*) reading problems can achieve reasonable levels of reading literacy (Gentile, 1981).

## Classroom Implications

A couple of studies might relieve the heart palpitations of the classroom teacher who is about to enter a class with a known dyslexic. Taylor, Satz, and Friel (1979) compared 80 second grade disabled readers to a matched set of 80 normal readers. Half (50%) of the disabled readers were classified as dyslexic. When the dyslexic children were compared to the nondyslexic disabled readers, no differences were found. Either the concept of dyslexia needs revision, or *disabled readers* is simply a synonym for *dyslexics*. While teaching a disabled reader is not quite as exciting as teaching a dyslexic, it is a lot less threatening.

Study two is brought to us again by Taylor, Satz, and Friel (1978). In this study, poor readers were divided into two groups. Group 1 consisted of those who met the conventional criteria for dyslexia. Group 2 was composed of the remaining poor readers, i.e., those who did not meet the conventional definition of dyslexia. Upon rather long-term and careful inspection of the two groups, Taylor and colleagues found that "reading failure associated with low intelligence, sociocultural inopportunity, emotional disturbance, or physical handicaps may be no different than reading failure in the absence of these factors." Their bottom line is that dyslexia is a nonspecific concept of little value. If it makes you feel better and doesn't interfere with the child's reading progress, feel free to use the term. But be careful not to confuse the concept of dyslexia (poor reading) with the notion of causation. The concept of dyslexia is purely descriptive. Care must be taken that well-intentioned psychologists and educators do not imply causation (Valtin, 1978-79).

No one would argue that removal of a portion of the brain or a well-placed smash on the skull can (but may not) impede reading. Similarly, no one would argue that some children simply do not learn to read as quickly or as efficiently as others. These readers can be called *disabled, handicapped, slow,* or *dyslexic*. The choice is open. What cannot be said about these readers is that their dyslexic condition is the cause of the reading problem. The dyslexic condition *is* the problem. How to remediate the condition of poor reading is as variable as remediating any other heterogeneous group.

# POOR READING PERFORMANCE AND SPECIAL POPULATIONS: POINTS TO REMEMBER

## ACADEMIC PERFORMANCE

Because reading skills are so much a part of the school day, problems in reading are usually the first sign of academic discomfort or failure. Very often children who display no sensory disability such as visual impairment or hearing impairment are referred for special services because of poor performance in reading.

### Special Services

Some of the referred children are accepted into special programs, e.g., remedial reading, learning disabilities programs, behavior disorder classes, and programs for the educable mentally handicapped. Some of the referred children don't qualify for any extra assistance and are returned to the regular classroom. Even many of those children who receive special reading instruction spend most of their academic day in the regular setting. What are they doing? They are, we hope, reading science, social studies, health, and arithmetic materials.

Other special populations, those typically categorized as sensory and health impaired, also need to perform well in reading. These children—visually impaired, hearing handicapped, or physically disabled—while typically receiving special educational services, are very often found in the regular classroom. Reading for these children is an integral part of their classroom day. Success in reading is clearly one more step to success in the regular classroom.

### Regular Classroom Success

Perhaps the one safe generalization about reading and exceptional populations, slow learners included, is that they must be able to read if they are to succeed in a normal classroom. If the child cannot read, then the classroom teacher must teach reading skills. The child need not be taught grade-level skills. Each child must be taught reading skills commensurate with his or her entry skills. (Chapter 7 describes organizational schemes for dealing with multilevel entry skills in a regular classroom.)

If a special teacher can be called for assistance, teachers can consider it a bonus brought by Public Law 94–142. For those children who do have special teachers, coordination between the regular classroom teacher and the specialist can extend to all reading-based areas, not just formal reading instruction. In fact, for some children with sensory impairments, the teacher and specialist automatically join in searching for appropriate material and equipment. For the less obviously handicapped, e.g., the learning or socially disabled child, the use of appropriate materials and the setting of realistic expectations should also be shared by the regular and special teachers.

## GUIDELINES FOR TEACHING EXCEPTIONAL CHILDREN

With or without the assistance of a specialist, the regular classroom teacher does have a few safe guidelines to use in teaching exceptional (and not so exceptional) learners.

### Guideline 1: Scope and Sequence

Scope and sequences that are complete and logically planned are particularly important in teaching exceptional children. Exceptional children with learning problems are not likely to learn reading skills from inference. They typically need explicit instruction in all essential component skills in reading. This explicit instruction needs to build upon a carefully conceived sequence of skills (Samuels, 1981). The use of scope and sequence does not rule out additional instructional activities that draw upon inference or child-centered techniques. The emphasis or instructional focus is, however, placed upon a teacher-centered approach to reading instruction. If only one approach is possible, teacher-centered would be the choice. The preference for most classrooms, especially those with a high percentage of exceptional students and slow learners, would be to stress teacher-centered reading approaches while simultaneously using child-centered methods.

### Guideline 2: Language of Instruction

Technical terms, such as *sentence, word, paragraph, third,* and so forth may be unknown to the children. These kinds of terms need to be taught or the children's knowledge of them needs to be established before they are used in instruction. The lack of true understanding of these commonly used instructional terms probably accounts for many of the mistakes that children make on reading tasks (Samuels, 1981). Take no knowledge for granted when working with any exceptional student (or any student, for that matter). Teaching reading skills with a potentially unknown vocabulary is like building a castle on sand while waiting for the tide to come in.

### Guideline 3: Self-Management and Self-Regard

Often, through whatever events, handicapped children come to believe or accept that the responsibility for paying attention and receiving payment for appropriate behavior is somehow beyond their control. This sense of helplessness or lack of control often generalizes to the child's approach to reading and mathematics (Thomas, 1980). Children who have this perception need to be shown how to manage their own behavior. They need to be taught how to take responsibility for success and failure in their reading activities. Instead of accepting phrases like "I don't know" or "I can't do this" when approaching a reading task, the teacher needs to encourage a positive attitude. The teacher also needs to remind the child in a supportive manner of his or her past successful performance in reading. In a teacher-centered approach to reading, the teacher still needs to account for the child's effort and success on a learning task.

### Guideline 4: Basic Reading Skills

Basic skills in reading consist of word analysis, word recognition, oral reading, and reading comprehension. Special students need these basic skills in order to read. They do not need special skills. Perhaps they need special materials or materials used in special ways, but they need the basic skills and no others in order to learn to read. For at least 15 years there has been a continuing debate between people advocating the training of specific perceptual, motor, and cognitive skills and people advocating attention to the carefully individualized teaching of basic skills (Harris, 1978-79). This argument has been especially insidious in the field of learning disabilities. Well-intentioned but rarely empirically supported theorists and practitioners have spent long hours "training" skills assumed to underlie reading. Children were taught to walk balance beams, guide rabbits through a maze, and put myriads of puzzles together. All these activities were felt to be prerequisite to reading instruction. Not too surprisingly, time spent in teaching sounds, words, letters, and pronunciation has had a much greater effect on children's learning to read than the aforementioned activities. In effect, neither theoretical nor empirical evidence can be found to support the transfer of learning from specific perceptual, motor, or cognition skills to empirical reading (at least for LD children) (Valtin, 1978-79). What's not particularly useful for learning disabled students is more than likely not particularly useful for any other poor reader either.

In general, then, when instructing poor readers or exceptional children who have reading difficulties, only a few guidelines need to be considered. First and foremost, the teacher needs to teach reading skills. Beyond this, the reading skills are best taught in a logical and systematic scope and sequence. The language of instruction needs to be composed of vocabulary that has meaning for the students. Children must be encouraged to accept responsibility for their own learning and that which they are learning should be composed of word analysis, word recognition, oral reading, and reading comprehension skills.

# PHYSICALLY AND SENSORY DISABLED STUDENTS: READING CONSIDERATIONS

## PHYSICAL DISABILITIES

Any child who is ill for extended periods of time, who tires easily, or who has chronic problems such as diabetes, a glandular dysfunction, or circulatory or nutritional malfunctions has an increased chance of academic difficulty. The difficulty will be most prominent in reading and reading-related content. The problem stems primarily from school absenteeism rather than from any particular learning handicap. There is no evidence that specific reading disability occurs because of such physical problems (Turnbull & Schulz, 1979).

### Combatting Absenteeism

Combatting the absentee problem is a fairly straightforward task. That old friend organization once more appears to save the day and the child's reading performance. In the case of the chronically absent child, a clearly stated sequence of reading skills accompanied by a simple entry-level check will help the teacher pinpoint the appropriate instructional teaching spot.

Suppose little Harry had been absent about two-thirds of the month. He would come to school for 1 or 2 days a week, be gone for 5, then show up again for 3. Instead of sadly shaking her head and adopting a "poor Harry can't read because he's absent so much" attitude, his teacher has kept a dated record of Harry's progress. His record is nothing special, just a part of the total class record. Harry's teacher casts a quick glance at her chart (Figure 9.1) and sees that the last sound introduced was *f* and the last sound mastered was *c*. She checks Harry's recall of the last sound mastered. As Murphy's Law would have predicted, Harry can't remember the *c* sound. The teacher then checks the next two mastered sounds in the sequence. Harry has retained these sounds. His teacher has a beginning place, the *c* sound, for instruction. Her checkpoint consisted of Harry naming the sound from a set of sound cards. Would that all reading instruction problems for physically disabled children were as simple as Harry's!

### Multiple Handicaps

Some physically disabled children have multiple handicaps. For example, neuromuscular involvement can affect speech production. Visual and auditory complications can also be present. For the multiply handicapped child, potential chronic absenteeism and fatigue are complicated by the additional disability. For the multiply physically handicapped child, the specific impairments must be analyzed to determine if the required responses are within the child's physical capabilities. The specialist and the regular teacher will need to identify materials, techniques, and task requirements. Chapter 4 pro-

**Figure 9.1**
Skill Record Form

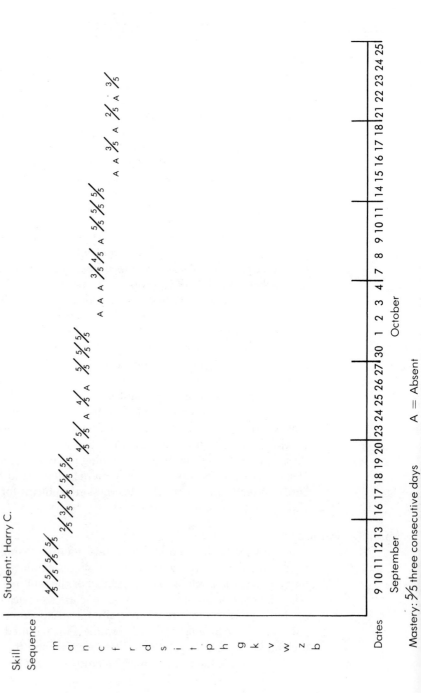

Student: Harry C.

Skill
Sequence

m a n c f r d s i t p h g k v w z b

Dates    9 10 11 12 13 | 16 17 18 19 20 | 23 24 25 26 27 | 30   1  2  3   4 | 7   8  9 10 11 | 14 15 16 17 18 | 21 22 23 24 25 |

September                                                                October

Mastery: 5/5 three consecutive days          A = Absent

Some specific tips (Love, 1978) to use when teaching reading to physically handicapped children are:

1. Use the reading method that works with the child. No single best method of teaching reading has been identified for the physically handicapped. Provide adapted materials when appropriate.

2. Extreme weakness, such as can be found in children with muscular dystrophy and atrophy, may require some form of arm support for holding books.

3. Allow for individual differences. Length of assignment and time allowed to complete the reading task can be varied according to the child's physical strength and vitality.

4. Do not be distracted by lower limb involvement. The loss of the use of lower extremities presents no special difficulty in reading.

## HEARING IMPAIRMENTS

As we saw in chapter 4, the term *hearing impairment* is a generic one, referring to all degrees of hearing loss. To understand the instructional implications of hearing impairment, the teacher needs more specific information about an individual child's condition. Areas that will affect teaching style or reading method are usually centered around (1) degree of hearing impairment, (2) age of onset of hearing impairment, (3) type of hearing impairment, (4) etiology of the hearing impairment, and (5) child's innate abilities (Katz, Mathis, & Merrill, 1978). (A more complete discussion of these characteristics and educational implications is found in chapter 4.)

### Availability of Language

With respect to reading instruction, a distinction can be fairly clearly drawn between deaf and hard-of-hearing individuals (less than 90 dB loss). Reading seems to be a communication system founded upon spoken language. It appears to be based upon cognitive experiences that are represented by a symbolic system. For children who are hearing impaired, the question is one of determining how much of the spoken or audition system is open to them. If very little is available, then the teacher must recognize that the "language" or "symbolic" system used by normal hearing children or even hard-of-hearing children is not open to the deaf child.

### Reading Instruction with Deaf Children

The symbolic system used to teach the deaf child to read will of necessity be different than that of the hard-of-hearing and normal hearing child. Perhaps vides general guidelines for the classroom teacher. These guidelines can be followed when teaching reading as well as any other classroom subject.

for the benefit of both the deaf child and the classroom teacher, only a very small number of deaf children are being fully mainstreamed. More than likely, many more hard-of-hearing children are being mainstreamed but mistakenly viewed as deaf (Quigley & Kretschmer, 1982).

This section briefly describes reading instruction for the deaf. It is primarily for general information. If you, as a regular classroom teacher, find yourself responsible for the education of a deaf child (or even a hard-of-hearing child), take yourself post haste to the nearest hearing specialist in your school, district, or state. As you will soon see, teaching reading to a deaf child is no simple task. Specialized skills are the order of the day. Unless you are well versed in American Sign Language (ASL), total communication, cued speech, and neo-oralism, your value as a teacher of reading to the deaf child is truly limited at best and possibly harmful for development. (ASL, total communication, cued speech, and neo-oralism are specific communication or language systems used by deaf persons. A description of each of these systems and their relative merits is beyond the scope of this text, but could be found in almost any introductory book on deaf education.) To teach reading to the deaf, the language of the child must be the first basis for instruction. Standard English as perceived by the normal hearing and hard-of-hearing is simply not the first language of the deaf child. Once the child has learned the reading process in the first language, then he or she can begin to transfer reading skills to a second language. In the case of the deaf child, the second language in the public schools will be English.

**Reading tests for the deaf**—At present, no reading tests have been developed and standardized for deaf students, so information regarding their reading achievement level is derived from studies that use reading tests developed for hearing children, or specially constructed but nonstandardized tests (Quigley & Kretschmer, 1982). Based on these tests, the overall results are not positive. Congenitally deaf children show very little reading progress beyond that of a 9-year-old hearing child (Trybus & Kerchmer, 1977). The third- to fourth-grade level of reading achievement, as measured by the available tests, seems to be reached or maintained by early adolescence.

Caution must be taken not to confuse low reading scores with intellectual potential. Recall that these reading scores are based on Standard English. Standard English may not have been adequately developed enough by deaf people to be used to test proficiency in reading (Moores, 1978). The reading behaviors found to be adequate were essentially the basic or mechanical skills taught in the primary grades. The basis of the deaf reader's difficulties seems to be at the "higher" levels of reading. At these levels, linguistic deficiencies probably disrupt processing such activities as single sentence analysis and prose comprehension (Quinn, 1981).

An additional factor may also need to be considered when examining the low reading achievement scores of the deaf. It is likely that their reading instruction has been somewhat limited. Traditionally teachers of the deaf have been expected to teach language and speech and have accordingly spent much time in speech and language remediation (Moores, 1978). Time spent in speech and language remediation is not necessarily the time spent on reading instruction or any other content matter. If you, the regular classroom teacher, find a deaf child in your class for part or all of the day, recall that this child has not had the same educational experiences and opportunities as your normal hearing students. Be careful not to confuse lack of knowledge with lack of ability.

**Appropriate materials**—The need for appropriate materials has been well documented. When deaf students are permitted to capitalize on their knowledge of the structure of stories, their past experiences, and their desire to make sense of the world, their reading behaviors can be remarkably similar to those of hearing readers (Ewaldt, 1981). One of the basic problems with reading instruction for deaf students is that the "vocabulary, syntax, and inference levels of commonly used reading materials are too complex" (Quigley, 1982, p. 104). Reading materials for the deaf need to provide systematic and repeated exposure to graded language structures and vocabulary.

## Reading Instruction with Hard-of-Hearing Children

The hard-of-hearing child, in contrast to the deaf, can use the auditory channel, which is affected but functional, as the primary modality for language development. Children in this category usually suffer a 35 to 69 dB loss. Up to about a 54 dB loss, the children routinely do not require special class or school placement. They do, however, typically need special speech and hearing assistance. Some children with a 55 to 69 dB loss will need special class placement and most will require speech, hearing, and language instruction (Moores, 1978). Children with hearing losses greater than 69 dB will more than likely be found in special schools and are not as likely to be found in the regular classroom.

Because the hard-of-hearing (defined here as a 35 to 69 dB loss) child can use the auditory system for some language learning, it is easy to consider the handicap more as an irritant than a true disability with respect to reading instruction. The misarticulations that characterize the child's speech are also found in the child's reading performance. A child with a serious loss may omit the last sound(s) in a word. Often a hard-of-hearing (HH) child may substitute one sound for another. Charlie, a 10-year-old with a severe loss, might read, "That moy hit me on by dee" for "That boy hit me on my knee." The sounds most likely to be omitted or replaced by other sounds are, naturally enough, sounds not heard by the HH child (Seward, 1982). As long as the misarticulations don't interfere with comprehension, the reading problem is not truly significant. If misarticulations interfere with comprehension, then it is another matter. Attempts to correct this should be coordinated between the speech-language therapist and the regular classroom teacher.

**Linguistic skills**—Of greater significance to the classroom teacher is that a major factor in the poor reading performance of many HH children is their linguistic skills (Leeding & Gammel, 1982). While basal readers are commonly used in the regular classroom, their usefulness in teaching reading to the HH child is somewhat questionable. The typical HH more than likely has not mastered the syntactic forms commonly found in basal readers (Cornett, Knight, Reynolds, & Williams, 1979). The linguistic code in the basals is too complex and contains too many abstract vocabulary terms. Before you begin to chastise yourself for lack of knowledge, be prepared to join the group. One survey of teachers of reading to hearing impaired children (Brockmiller & Coley, 1981) showed that the primary material used to teach reading is the basal

**Reading techniques**—As with most children having difficulty learning to read, but especially for the HH, controlled vocabulary, appropriate language levels, and reasonable phonetic emphasis are the cornerstones of a suitable reading program. When these three factors are kept in mind, there is no compelling evidence that any one reasonable method of teaching reading will yield results that are significantly better than any other method (Clarke, Rogers, & Booth, 1982). The best advice for teaching reading to the HH is that if one method doesn't succeed after a reasonable length of time, another approach should be tried (Rudloff, 1966).

To the extent that teachers can build HH children's vocabularies by capitalizing on the child's most successful reading method, they can at least develop some of the building blocks necessary for future reading skills (Hirsch-Pasek & Treiman, 1982). Word identification is important in building the HH child's vocabulary. Three teaching strategies that could be employed to develop vocabulary are contextual analysis, semantic mapping, and semantic feature analysis. These techniques have been described elsewhere in depth by Johnson, Toms-Bronowski, and Pittleman (1982).

*Contextual analysis* is based on the premise that words (and word identification skills) gain meaning from their context. An individual word can be deduced from the words that surround it or from the larger meaning of the passage. Suppose Wyland is to learn the word *itinerant*. If he knows how to read from context and if he knows the meanings of the other words in the sentence, he should need little or no help in arriving at the word meaning. The sentence Wyland reads is "My uncle, an itinerant preacher, traveled constantly and was always on the road." The words *traveled* and *on the road* help Wyland figure out the meaning of *itinerant*.

The key, then, to using contextual analysis with a HH reader (or any other child) is to have materials that contain a low proportion of unknown vocabulary terms. An instructional level or independent reading level based on vocabulary meaning needs to be established for reading material. Establishing a meaning level can be done just like establishing a word recognition level (see chapter 8). In place of word identification, the child is asked to give word meaning. The percentages can parallel those for word recognition, i.e., 98% (independent level), 95% (instructional level), and 90% (frustration level).

*Semantic mapping* requires children to relate new words in graphic form to their own experiences and knowledge. Johnson et al. (1982) have provided a semantic map of the word *conservation* (Figure 9.2). The map is graphic and drawn from one, several, or all members of the class. The basic instruction sequence for this map is:

1. Select a word (or topic). In this case *conservation* was chosen on the basis of classroom interest and need. *Conservation* was central to a story being read.
2. Write the word *conservation* on the chalkboard.
3. Ask the group to think of as many words as they can that are somehow related to the chosen or targeted word. Have the children write their words in categories on paper.
4. Have members of the group verbally share the words they've written. As the words are spoken, try to put them into categories on the board.
5. Number the categories and have the children name them.

Student discussion is a key feature of semantic mapping. Through this process, the children learn the meanings and uses of new words. In addition, they may learn additional meanings for old words or see relationships between words.

Semantic mapping can be especially helpful for HH children because the process helps them to build upon their own meaningful vocabulary. Sander has the terms *spoil* and *squander* in his vocabulary. Through the use of the heading "Bad things that can happen to our environment," he was able to add eight new terms. While he may not learn the precise meaning for each of these eight terms, he will at least have a reference point.

Because of the time involved in developing a semantic map, the procedure is most efficient when used with a small to large group of children. Semantic mapping is most critical for those children who need instruction in

**Figure 9.2**
Semantic map: **Conservation.**

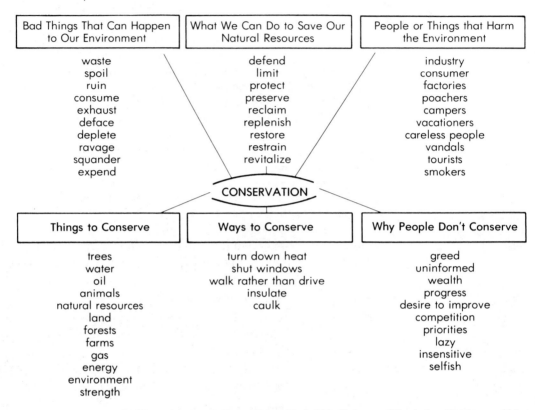

| Bad Things That Can Happen to Our Environment | What We Can Do to Save Our Natural Resources | People or Things that Harm the Environment |
|---|---|---|
| waste | defend | industry |
| spoil | limit | consumer |
| ruin | protect | factories |
| consume | preserve | poachers |
| exhaust | reclaim | campers |
| deface | replenish | vacationers |
| deplete | restore | careless people |
| ravage | restrain | vandals |
| squander | revitalize | tourists |
| expend | | smokers |

CONSERVATION

| Things to Conserve | Ways to Conserve | Why People Don't Conserve |
|---|---|---|
| trees | turn down heat | greed |
| water | shut windows | uninformed |
| oil | walk rather than drive | wealth |
| animals | insulate | progress |
| natural resources | caulk | desire to improve |
| land | | competition |
| forests | | priorities |
| farms | | lazy |
| gas | | insensitive |
| energy | | selfish |
| environment | | |
| strength | | |

Source: D.D. Johnson, S. Toms-Bronowski, & S.D. Pittleman, "Vocabulary Development." In R.E. Kretchsmer (Ed.), *Reading and the Hearing Impaired Individual* (Monograph). *Volta Review*, 1982, *84*, 11-24.

vocabulary development. Yet a mixed skill level group is likely to produce a broader and wider range of vocabulary terms and categories. Semantic mapping can be done with the context of any lesson, e.g., science or social studies, that is reading-based.

*Semantic feature analysis* displays the relationships between words as well as the finer conceptual shades within and between words. The display is also graphic and takes the form of a grid. An example of a partially completed semantic feature analysis grid for *shelters* is presented in Figure 9.3. The basic instructional sequence for semantic feature analysis is:

1. Choose a topic—in this case, *shelters.*

**Figure 9.3**
A partially completed semantic feature analysis grid: **Shelters.**

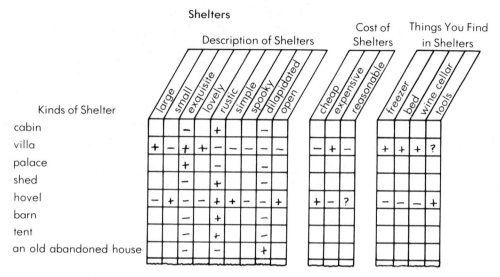

Shelters

| Kinds of Shelter | large | small | exquisite | lovely | rustic | simple | spooky | dilapidated | open | cheap | expensive | reasonable | freezer | bed | wine cellar | tools |
|---|---|---|---|---|---|---|---|---|---|---|---|---|---|---|---|---|
| cabin | | – | | | + | | – | | | | | | | | | |
| villa | + | – | + | + | – | – | – | – | ~ | – | + | – | + | + | + | ? |
| palace | | | + | | – | | – | | | | | | | | | |
| shed | | – | | | + | | – | | | | | | | | | |
| hovel | – | + | – | – | + | + | – | – | + | + | – | ? | – | – | – | + |
| barn | | – | | | + | | – | | | | | | | | | |
| tent | | – | | | + | | – | | | | | | | | | |
| an old abandoned house | | – | | | – | | | + | | | | | | | | |

*Columns grouped as: Description of Shelters (large, small, exquisite, lovely, rustic, simple, spooky, dilapidated, open); Cost of Shelters (cheap, expensive, reasonable); Things You Find in Shelters (freezer, bed, wine cellar, tools).*

Source: D.D. Johnson, S. Toms-Bronowski, & S.D. Pittleman, "Vocabulary Development." In R.E. Kretchsmer (Ed.), *Reading and the Hearing Impaired Individual* (Monograph). *Volta Review*, 1982, *84*, 11-24.

2. In a column at the left, list some words that are related to the topic (*shelters*).
   *cabin*
   *villa*
   *palace*
   etc.

3. In a row along the top, list general features related to the topic, e.g., *Descriptions, Cost of shelters, Things you find in shelters.*

4. Break the general features into more specific terms. For example, break *Description of shelters* into terms like *large, small, exquisite,* etc.

5. Next have the students put pluses or minuses in the grid to show which of the attributes are or aren't associated with the terms. Refer to both *villa* and *hovel* in Figure 9.3.

6. Hold a group or class discussion about each word as reflected by the pluses and minuses on the grid.

As with semantic mapping, this procedure lends itself to small or large group discussion. The topic must be chosen with care. Not every word needs or deserves this much attention. For those key or critical concepts, semantic feature analysis can be a valuable technique for expanding vocabulary and increasing a HH student's ability to comprehend a concept.

These three techniques, while time consuming in the short run, may be time saving in the long run. As has been mentioned before, language seems to be the basis for much school learning. Reading and writing are built upon the foundation of language. Progress in social studies, science, mathematics, and other subjects often hinges on the child's reading skills and the rate at which concepts, vocabulary, and language patterns are mastered (Katz et al., 1978).

Problems of poor word identification skills and insufficient written vocabulary have been found to be hindrances to reading progress. A number of studies have shown that hearing-impaired individuals have very limited written vocabularies (Hirsch-Pasek & Treiman, 1982). Written vocabulary is often a reflection (barring spelling and motor skills) of the child's oral vocabulary. Language, like most activities, is best learned through active participation. One such reading approach that has at its very core "action participation" is the language experience approach (LEA) (described later). Stories can be developed around the deaf child's interests. The LEA approach is a good strategy for teaching reading to HH because it stresses the importance of the relationship between the reader's experiences and written language (Gormley & Geoffrin, 1981). Gormley (1981, 1982) has compiled some specific tips to use when teaching reading to hard-of-hearing children.

1. Reading materials need to be selected according to the child's interests and experience.

2. The teacher must develop the reader's background before the child actually reads the materials.

3. Especially at the beginning stages of reading development, the written text must be familiar and highly predictable.

## VISUAL IMPAIRMENTS

To recap, the term *visually handicapped* refers to people who have severe vision problems. Usually this group is subdivided into individuals with low vision and those who are blind. Low vision or partially sighted children typically require special aids such as large type, magnifiers, and special lighting in order to complete work that requires detailed vision. Blind children, in contrast, may have no useful vision or may be able only to distinguish between light and dark. For the classroom teacher the important educational difference is that children with low vision may be able to read through visual experience if adjustments are made, whereas blind children will probably need to rely on auditory and tactile input (Ward & McCormick, 1981). These differences suggest that different types of teaching accommodations are necessary for various visual impairments. Depending on the degree and type of loss, some students may require a combination of approaches (Glass, Christiansen, & Christiansen, 1982). In any event, the efficiency with which visually impaired children use their vision, however limited, depends a great deal on the amount of light, the task requirements, the amount of contrast, and the size of print (Barraga, 1976). (A more complete discussion of the visually impaired and educational implications is found in chapter 4.)

### Role of the Specialist

If a child is unable to use the visual system for reading, a specialist will be assigned to teach a tactile system for some components. These components are likely to involve word analysis and word recognition skills. The classroom teacher will still be responsible for helping develop vocabulary meaning and comprehension skills. Lo-Tsen may go for braille instruction with the itinerant teacher. She should be reading the same material as her sighted classmates. Her classroom teacher can instruct her during both the vocabulary and comprehension lessons held in the regular classroom. The classroom teacher need only be sensitive to the clarity of her auditory demands and explanations.

### Regular Class Instruction

The question of which reading approach to use with low vision children is easily answered. The same reading approaches that are used with sighted children can also be used with low vision and blind children. Language experience, phonic, linguistic, eclectic, whole-word, and most other methods have all been used to help low vision and blind children read (Ward & McCormick, 1981). To routinely place partially sighted children in segregated classrooms for most or all of each day is inappropriate because the methods used for instruction for the partially seeing are essentially identical to those used with normally seeing children (Hanninen, 1975). Naturally enough, certain modifications in the materials may occur as a function of the handicapping condition.

### Fatigue

The most commonly stated educational problems of visually impaired children are fatigue, the need for rest periods, and restriction in eye use (Birch, Tisdall, Peabody, & Sterrett, 1966). When the handicapping condition is considered, these problems are neither surprising nor insurmountable. Visually handicapped children with limited eye scan or those with optical aids that permit them to see only one or two letters at a time have a greater demand on memory than children with normal vision.

**Memory demands**—A child using a magnifier or low vision aid to reduce focal length or one who must hold the material close to his or her eyes may become fatigued because of the tension of concentrating or even because of poor body posture. Because reading instruction requires a lot of use of the eyes, the classroom teacher can reduce or eliminate the kinds of tasks that produce fatigue by understanding the child's eye condition. This understanding as related to school and reading tasks can help the teacher improvise solutions for potential reading obstacles.

**Fatigue reduction**—For example, if the condition causes the print to be too small to read, the teacher can help set up a comfortable reading distance for the child by (1) moving the materials closer, (2) using large print books, (3) providing a volunteer reader, (4) making recorded material available, or (5) utilizing closed circuit TV (Lagrow, 1981). An understanding of the vision condition and how it affects the child physically and mentally is certainly the first step the classroom teacher needs to take in setting up an appropriate teaching environment.

The most obvious areas of fatigue reduction include procuring appropriate materials and equipment. Not so obvious is the effect of some of these materials on the child's physical and mental stamina. Children who can see only one or two letters at a time are bound to have fluency problems (Chapman, 1978). The limited eye scan, then, can not only produce fatigue, but can also affect the child's reading performance. Because some low vision children can see only a small portion of a page or even a word at a time, the child's reading speed may be slower than that of the other children in the class. The classroom teacher needs to account for the length of time allotted to the low vision child for completing work. A low vision child who consistently does not complete assignments may not be recalcitrant, but may actually be asked to do an impossible task. Signs of reluctance to complete a reading activity may also be a reaction to a punitive situation. The child may feel obliged to complete the assignment in the required time, but the stresses involved are great and physically punishing. If you have a low vision child who displays these problems, adjust your program demands somewhat until you can confer with the vision specialist.

## Reading Achievement

**Intelligence**—Visually impaired children are often 1 to 2 years behind in reading achievement since the typically partially sighted child is apparently of at least average intelligence (Birch et al., 1966). This lag is not related to intelligence, though the percentage of children in the upper IQ range (110 and higher) is greater in local public schools than in residential schools (Lowenfeld, Abel, & Halten, 1969). For those children who use braille, the rate of development of braille reading also lags behind print reading. This lag is in part because braille contractions are not logical and do not consider phonetic or structural elements. The braille contractions actually can prevent auditory analysis and may lead to problems in syllabification (Hanninen, 1975).

**Incidental learning**—In addition, a lag in reading achievement for visually impaired children may, in part, be related to restricted visual experiences. Both blind and low vision children may have a smaller conceptual range of background experiences. Incidental learning may limit the visually impaired child's ability or depth of concept learning.

Take the common occurrence of the field trip. Bob, who is sighted, and Dimitri, who has low vision, both go to the fair. Both Bob and Dimitri learn about lambs, pigs, and cows. They both learn that lambs are woolly and say "bah," that pigs are furry and smell bad, and cows have horns and four feet. Dimitri is limited to learning what he can from his senses of sound and touch. Bob has the additional advantage of sight. He has direct experience with the size and shape of the animals. Dimitri must depend on his teacher for this information. Bob and Dimitri will go back to school and read a story about farm animals. Unless Dimitri has a very skilled teacher, he and Bob will have a far different understanding of the vocabulary terms and comprehension level of the story.

## Listening Skills

Because of the incidental learning level, blind and low vision children find listening skills to be an important aspect of learning. Regardless of the visual handicap, the complex process of reading for the visually handicapped child, as well as for other children, will be based on speaking and listening. Listening to stories, retelling them, and even acting them out can enhance the child's ability to develop meaningful language (Chapman, 1978). Using props can also help the child develop vocabulary and a broader conceptual base. A situation in a story may be funny because a character might be dressing his pet dog in raingear. The teacher can dress up a toy dog (or even a real one if dog and district approve) in boots and permit the child a better sense of the ridiculousness of the situation.

Background experiences are important for children, visually impaired or not, to be able to read with understanding. For the visually impaired child, verbal descriptions allow for experiential growth. For the blind child, verbal descriptions can be associated with a sequence of events. For the low vision child, verbal descriptions can help clarify interpretations of distorted or indistinct visual images (Ward & McCormick, 1981).

Verbal descriptions can even help the blind child learn about color. Color words are an important and necessary part of any child's reading vocabulary. Through semantic mapping or semantic feature analysis, blind children can learn, for example, that snow is white and that grass is green.

Sometimes verbal descriptions can be presented on audio-tapes. We have evidence that "reading" or listening to speech is more efficient, in terms of both speed and comprehension, than reading braille (Barraga, 1976). However, caution must be sounded. Without special devices for slowing or accelerating the rate of taped materials, the listener has no control over the speed at which he or she "reads." Taped materials can also present some difficulty in listening ahead or going back over previous material. Reading for context is also somewhat limited.

**Specific tips**—Here are some specific tips to use when teaching reading to visually impaired children.

1. Reading materials need to reflect the child's background and interest.
2. Factors that contribute to physical fatigue should be reduced or eliminated.
3. Reading methods used with sighted children are used successfully with low-vision and blind children.
4. Verbal descriptions should accompany instructional events.
5. Some visually impaired children may require more time than their sighted peers to complete a reading rask.

## LEARNING AND BEHAVIOR PROBLEMS

Children with learning and behavior problems make up the greatest number of handicapped students in the regular classroom. These children are typically subclassified into the categories of learning disabled, mentally retarded, and emotionally disturbed. Within each of these categories, there is a continuum of handicap from severe or profound to mildly impaired. At the mild end of the continuum, the behavioral and educational differences between the three groups are blurred at best. In general, members of all three groups underachieve academically. In fact, the overlap of underachievement and social/emotional problem behavior commonly found in mild and moderate learning disabled and emotionally disturbed students makes differentiating between the two groups sometimes little more than the flip of a diagnostic coin (Edwards & DePalma, 1982). With respect to reading behaviors, similar difficulties occur. In one review of reading research literature (Kirk, Kliebhan, & Lerner, 1978), the authors intermingled the findings of slow (retarded) and disabled readers (learning disabled). The research findings were collapsed because "the characteristics, learning patterns and diagnostic and teaching procedures for these two groups of children overlap to a great extent. The research findings for one group have obvious implications for the other" (p. 198).

## Slow Learner/Remedial Reader

To this group can also be added the nonlabeled slow learner and the remedial reader. Within this rather mixed-up group will be children who display various shades and degrees of educational problems but who, for the most part, would otherwise be called *normal*. Yet, for obvious reasons, these children do not profit from the regular curriculum to the same extent as do children labeled *normal*. For those children labeled learning disabled, the greatest academic need is improved reading (Kirk & Elkins, 1975). The behavior disordered and the retarded child also need reading instruction. The children who fall into this category are more often than not those who have failed to learn "intuitively, inductively and incidentally." They have not acquired the facts, concepts, and generalizations that most children seem to acquire without any specific instruction (Hammill & Bartel, 1978). This description applies to the area of reading as well as to most other academic and social situations. For the purpose of this book, reading methods and procedures and research findings, unless otherwise stated, are applied equally to all three groups. For convenience (and publishing costs) these children will be called Learning and Behavior Problems (LBP). (More detailed descriptions of each of the subcategories can be found in chapter 3.)

## Successful Reading Programs

In general, four statements can be made about reading instruction for LBP children.

1. LBP children are likely to read better with a structured approach.
2. LBPs tend to ascribe reading success or failure to external causes.
3. LBPs need to have realistic and obtainable reading goals.
4. No one accepted method has been indicated as better than another.

**Structure**—Children who have trouble learning to read perform better with a method in which a sequence of specific tasks is accompanied by explicit instruction and extensive practice (Bateman, 1979). Materials need to be presented at an appropriate pace, i.e., neither too fast nor too slowly. Material presented too quickly is called *staging*—never reaching the fluency stage. Material presented too slowly is that which has been instructed beyond the point of overlearning. LBPs should be instructed systematically, one step at a time. Each step should be made clear and the child should practice until fluency level is reached.

**External control**—Many, though not all, LBP children feel that success or failure in reading is the result of some external event. A teacher, a situation, the draw of the cards—all may have perceived control in causing the LBP child to succeed or fail in reading. To the extent that the teacher can teach the LBP child to take more responsibility for learning to read, the task of teaching reading will be easier. One of the most important aspects of learning is action involvement. Employing strategies that encourage students to take responsibility for learning is helpful in reading achievement. A simple but effective technique for transferring learning responsibility to LD students was demonstrated by Pascarella and Pflaum (1981). These researchers directed children to determine for themselves as individuals whether they made a good guess or a serious meaning change error, e.g., "Do you think that reading *shopping* for *shipping* changes the meaning of the sentence?" By asking questions like this, the feedback received is both orderly and straightforward. The decision-making responsibility is also given to the child. Neither the task difficulty nor the teacher become the central actor in the reading act.

**Obtainable goals**—For children who read well, reading itself can be rewarding. For LBP children, reading can be punitive. For some LBP children, initial movement toward reading goals may need to be coupled with extrinsic reinforcers (Ross, 1976). These extrinsic reinforcers (e.g., a star, a game, free time) must be within the ready reach of the child. The first reading goals for the LBP child should be of short duration. The goals need to be explained to the child, and techniques and rewards associated with the goal should be stated clearly. The child should also be able to determine when the goal has been met (Warncke, 1981).

Suppose Bruce has been having problems with reading. He refuses to complete his assignments and makes comments like "I hate reading," "Reading is dumb," and "Reading stinks" (or some such term). The teacher strikes a deal with Bruce. The trade-off is that if Bruce learns five new sight words, he can play one Pac-Man game. (The goal and the consequence have been stated.) Bruce is to demonstrate that he has learned the words by using each word in a sentence, writing each one three times, and having his friend Marty drill each word with him. (The procedures used to learn the goal have been explained.) When Bruce thinks he knows the words, the teacher will check them on flashcards. (The means of measuring the goal has been stated.) Confirmation by the teacher lets Bruce know whether his goal has been reached.

**Method of instruction**—As mentioned before, LBP children typically learn to read best in a structured approach. For most of these children, unstructured and wholistic approaches used as the primary reading approach have been unsuccessful (Hammill & Bartel, 1978).

A cautionary note must be sounded about modality-linked reading methods. Modality-linked methods are those that attempt to match a sensory modality (e.g., usually vision or hearing) to a child's preferred or "identified" learning style. At this point in history, there is *no* sound empirical evidence for the idea that different reading approaches are differentially effective for children characterized as "visual" or "auditory" learners (Williams, 1979).

With the exception of unstructured and modality-linked techniques, the methods of reading instruction are open to the teacher's discretion. No one method of teaching reading to atypical children has been demonstrated to be superior to another (Kirk et al., 1978). As long as the primary approach is systematic and structured, LBPs have a good chance of learning to read. The primary structured approach can certainly be supplemented by less direct and more open-ended instruction.

# GOOD READING PRACTICES

No matter what the handicapping condition, the teacher needs to incorporate the following five factors into the reading program: (1) furnish practice, (2) assist the child to organize information, (3) provide instructional feedback, (4) set expectancy, and (5) deliver systematic incentives or consequences. These factors, discussed at length in chapter 4, are applicable to any approach or combination of approaches.

The final section of this chapter is intended to provide a very brief description of some reading practices related to specific areas of reading. An exhaustive description of reading methods or practices is beyond the scope of this book. Detailed descriptions of reading techniques and materials can be found in textbooks designed for that purpose. Kits, programs, and classroom texts are also available for inspection through your district, state curriculum library, or various curriculum fairs. With most mainstreamed children, the materials found in the regular classroom, with some modifications, are the most appropriate to use.

## WORD ANALYSIS IN BRIEF

### Phonemic Analysis Skills

Item order and phonetic recording are two major aspects of word analysis. Poor readers don't appear to have problems with remembering item order, but do seem to have a general problem in phonetic coding (Katz, Shankweiler, & Libermen, 1981). Poor readers need to be taught the efficient use of strategies when learning phonemic awareness skills, vowel sounds, and visually and auditorily similar letters (*b,d*) or words (*saw, was*).

Phonemic awareness skills are important primarily because of their relationship to decoding (Lewkowicz, 1980). The basic phonemic awareness skills are blending and segmentation. Blending is the process whereby the child supplies the missing bonds between sounds. Segmentation is the act of isolating the sounds, e.g., as in CV, VC, or CVC segmentations of words. The following are descriptions of various techniques for teaching isolated sounds and phonemic awareness skills (Lewkowicz, 1980).

**Isolated sounds**—Two main methods for focusing attention on the initial sounds are:

1. Stretching or prolonging the initial sound while pronouncing the word.
2. Repeating or iterating; repeating the initial sound two or three times before pronouncing the entire word, e.g., *p-p-p-palace*.

**Phonemic awareness skills**—

1. Teach both CV and VC segmentation before introducing CVC segmentation.
2. Smooth transition from CV and VC to CVC by starting with CV–CVC, or VC–CVC pairs in which the three-phoneme word is identical to the two-phoneme word except for the added consonant (e.g., *bee–beep, age–page*).
3. Introduce blending when the children have a good understanding of segmentation and are practicing segmentation activities intensely.

**Vowel sounds**—Teaching vowels is one of the most difficult skills in teaching beginning reading. There are essentially two schools of thought regarding teaching vowels:

1. Vowels are taught in isolation, i.e., the single phonics method. In this approach the child learns each sound and then blends them to form a word (*j-a-r*).

2. Vowels are taught by phonograms or word families. In this method, the child learns familiar word parts and then blends the initial consonant with the ending (*j-ar*).

Recent research (Neuman, 1981) suggests that the two methods have different effects on poor and average readers. Readers in the lowest quartile of achievement score higher when using the vowel-in-isolation approach. Readers in the middle levels of achievement score higher when using the phonogram method. Interestingly, children who received either the vowel-in-isolation approach or the phonogram approach benefited more positively from instruction than children who received the typical basal reading program. The results of this study suggest that an overall reading program for lower achievers could be based on the phonogram technique with supplemental vowel-in-isolation instruction.

## Visually and Auditorily Similar Correspondence

**Reversals**—In the written and spoken symbolic system of the Engish language, some letters and words are very similar in appearance or sound. These are often confused by poor and beginning readers. Often words or letters are reversed, e.g., *b* for *d* and *was* for *saw*, or substituted for one another, e.g., "I sleep in a deb." Reversals appear to be a developmental phenomenon and seem fairly normal up to the age of 8 or 9. Even though a child may have had many chances to learn, reversal tendencies can continue to persist beyond the expected age. In fact, most people, under certain conditions (often associated with stress), tend to reverse. Reversals in and of themselves, then, are not necessarily a sign of a pathological condition (Heydorn & Cheek, 1982).

Problems with words and letters of this sort can be reduced through the manner of instruction. If, for example, *was* and *saw* are taught simultaneously or introduced in close temporal proximity, the odds are higher that the child will become confused. Carnine (1981) has described a system for teaching *b*'s and *d*'s that reduces confusion.

> If "b" was introduced six weeks ago and "d" is to be introduced today, do not begin instruction with examples of just "b" and "d" and require the students to identify them. The preferred method is to 1) present "b" and "d" but tell the students to identify "d" as "not b." 2) Present "d" along with other letters that are not similar to "d." 3) Present "d" with lots of letters, one of which can be "b" (p. 276).

**Teaching format**—The teaching format described by Carnine can be adopted for any visually or auditorily similar letters or words. The basic pattern has three parts. (1) Present the two visually or auditorily similar terms, but teach the meaning for only one of the terms. Do not teach the second term. Refer to the second term and any other word as a "not-(first term)." (2) Present a lot of other letters or words that are also "not-(first term)." The child will then realize that a lot of words are "not-(first term)"—not just the similar one. (3) After the child can identify the first term, present the second term and other letters or terms.

In essence, you have stressed identification of a particular term. You have avoided making a single and easily confused discrimination, and you've bypassed making a big deal about words or letters that are often confused.

### Dialect and Word Analysis

Sometimes teachers confuse a dialect problem with a decoding problem. Generally speaking, the role of dialect interference in reading is unclear, and some of the findings are contradictory (Harber & Bealty, 1978). The fact that a child drops final consonants when speaking does not mean that he or she ignores the consonants while reading. In a study examining Black English (BE) and reading (Hart, Guthrie, & Winfield, 1980), children who spoke BE used the final consonants to assist them in decoding words. So, while a child may not be pronouncing a sound due to dialect, the sounds may still have phonological meaning. Meaning, of course, is the crux of reading. When dialect speakers' miscues were analyzed relative to comprehension, the findings indicated that the speakers' miscues didn't affect their ability to comprehend instructional-level prose material (Eberwein, 1982). Rather than becoming a speech therapist, downplay dialect differences. Maintain watchful care that the child is obtaining meaning from the letters or words.

### Decoding and Comprehension

Beginning readers (or poor readers) often resort to a strategy of directing all of their attention to decoding and then to comprehension. Giving alternative attention to decoding and to comprehension allows readers to understand the materials, but the switching is slow and laborious and makes heavy demands on memory and attention (Samuels, 1981). The skill with which decoding is taught can reduce some of the attention and memory demands. Reading specialists, for example, feel that if readers are taught to decode well, comprehension will become automatic. The idea is that becoming proficient in decoding enables the reader to comprehend text material about as well as spoken language (Jenkins, Stein, & Osborn, 1981).

Speed of decoding may be related to comprehension. According to Guttenberg and Haith (1980),

> During the early stages in learning to read the ability to process letters automatically develops either before, or simultaneously with, the develop-

ment of the ability to read printed words rapidly, a pattern that is consistent with the hypothesis that automatic letter processing is necessary for rapid word processing. (p. 705)

The effect of training in rapid decoding on poor readers' comprehension has also been studied (Fleisher, Jenkins, & Pany, 1979). Training in decoding, whether centered on isolated words or phrases, significantly increases the speed of decoding single words, though phrase training is not quite as effective as single word training. More importantly, poor readers who received training in decoding actually performed no better on comprehension measures than did poor readers without training. Fleisher et al. concluded that word practice does not generalize to reading in context. They caution teachers to provide speed reading practice of words in context, i.e., a story or passage, rather than in isolation.

Samuels (1981), among others, has made some fairly important generalizations about decoding skills. It is his belief that weak decoding skills require attention during the reading act. Thus, because attention is focused on decoding, attention for comprehension is proportionately reduced. With practice in decoding and more accuracy of letter recognition, readers are freed to concentrate more on meaning. Accuracy with letter recognition seems to be relatively easy to master, but rapid recognition may take somewhat longer. Teachers need to be aware that accurate letter recognition does not automatically lead to rapid recognition. A student with accurate letter recognition may still be concentrating on decoding rather than on comprehension.

There is a final point to remember when teaching phonics. Children need to know the rules of phonics, but not at a well-articulated conscious level (Rosso & Emans, 1981). That is, Vasili does not need to be able to recite specific phonic rules, but he does need to be able to use them. Vasili, like many other readers, should be able to use phonic generalizations without being able to state them. Incessant drill on rules is not likely to help anyone learn to read. Active practice—applying rules to read—is the key to learning the phonics generalizations.

## WORD RECOGNITION/ORAL READING: IN BRIEF

### Specific Remedial Reading Approaches

The fluent and automatic processing of words is the major aim of instruction in word recognition and oral reading. Many reading approaches used with normal children are described in basic introductory reading methods books. Four approaches that have been gaining popularity for use with poor readers but that may not be found in the typical reading methods textbook are the imitative reading, repeated reading, impress, and mastery learning approaches. Ashby-Davis (1981) has written an excellent critique of the first three methods. The following is a synopsis of her description.

**Imitative reading**—In the imitative reading method, the child reads along silently or aloud with a recorded text. After "reading" the passage once, the child is asked to respond to written or oral comprehension questions. The effectiveness of this method relies a great deal on the reader's previously acquired word recognition skills. For example, Anthony is presented with a passage written in English and a recording of the same material. He is told to read along with the text. Unfortunately, Anthony has limited skills and a very restricted sight vocabulary. He starts out "reading" with word one, but because he can't relate the words from the recording to the word in print, we soon find him on page two of the text while the recording is on page five. Because Anthony doesn't know which symbols on the page match the sounds he's hearing, he can't really judge where words begin and end. Reading along with the text becomes impossible for Anthony.

If, on the other hand, a child has a fairly large sight vocabulary or at least has the vocabulary used in the text, the imitative method can be quite helpful. For children who tend to sound out the printed sentence word by word, this method can help develop fluency in oral reading. It can also be worthwhile in teaching good interpretive oral reading.

**Repeated reading**—In the repeated reading approach, children are given a printed passage and asked to read it aloud to the teacher. The reading is timed. Then the students are given a recording of the same passage and instructed to practice reading the passage over and over. When the child feels ready to read the text with greater ease, he or she returns to the teacher to be retimed and tested on comprehension. The child receives a new passage only if the second timing shows improvement. If no improvement occurs, the student continues the process with the same passage.

This particular approach makes instructional sense if the child needs greater fluency in processing an entire text. The method should be used only after word recognition skills are well established and sight vocabulary is parallel to the text being repeated.

**Impress method**—The impress method is designed to help readers understand the relationship between spoken words and the symbols that represent them. In this method, the reader sits close to the teacher, who reads a passage orally. The student reads aloud along with the teacher. A couple of variations are common. In one, the teacher passes a finger under the words as they are read, indicating where they begin and end. In another, the child moves a finger under the words.

The impress method has several features thought to be helpful for poor readers. First, the teacher speaks fluently while reading the text. Second, the moving finger can help demonstrate when words begin and end. It also teaches the child that the eye sweeps from left to right and then down-left. The biggest problem with this approach is that using the moving finger slows the oral reader. If employed while reading silently, it may slow readers to oral reading speeds.

**Mastery learning**—Mastery learning is based on two basic premises. First, the child must be given enough time to master (become proficient in) every learning step in an instructional sequence. Second, the learner must be given appropriate remedial help on any step that is not at mastery. Mastery learning is basically teacher-directed group instruction, with the amount of practice and feedback tailored to the individual student's needs (Bloom, 1977). It is extremely useful in teaching basic skills to slow learners or children who do not learn independently (Mueller, 1976). The seeming Catch-22 of mastery learning lies in the amount of time each child may need.

The problem of providing reading instruction to all children within a 45- or 50-minute class period can be addressed in the mastery learning model. In one study (Bryant, Fayne, & Gettinger, 1982), LD children used mastery learning to learn basic sight words. The children were taught in groups of two to five, 3 days a week, in 30-minute lessons. The basic lesson format consisted of having the children read each word from a card while the teacher recorded the number of times each child needed to reach criterion. When a child made an error, the teacher recorded the incorrect response and gave the correct word. The child immediately repeated the correct word. Once the child read the word correctly, it was dropped from the child's list, but reviewed in a subsequent lesson. Children reviewed words in two-word and three-word phrases and finally in sentences. The children also received silent and oral reading practice along with comprehension exercises on short stories containing the sight words. The children were taught 10 sight words a week this way. In this study, training words were introduced one at a time, practice was provided on all the words throughout each lesson, and corrective feedback was given.

The results of the study led to the conclusion that mastery learning as presented in group instruction was effective for LD students. Better yet, it brought the majority of the LD children to a high criterion level (80%) within a reasonable instructional time. Thirty new sight words in 9 half-hour lessons delivered over a 3-week period is no mean feat for LD children (or any other readers, for that matter).

## General Teaching Practices

**Choosing words to teach**—The first decision to make in teaching word recognition and oral reading is the content. Which words do you want the child to learn? If you have a choice (and district-mandated word lists or not, you do), the results of at least one small-scale study (Noble, 1981) show that disabled readers are more likely to learn words that they themselves choose to learn. This doesn't mean that the child is allowed to flip through the dictionary, basal reader, or Dolch word list and randomly point to interesting words. Child-chosen words can be derived from life experience stories or "plain world experience." Plain world experience simply entails engaging the child in conversation and capitalizing on his or her interests. If Janek is interested in spies, let his word recognition vocabulary reflect this interest. Build from it and extend his vocabulary by adding new words to his basic ones. Janek's orally chosen words may be *spy*, *destruction*, and *assassins*. You can supplement these words by providing some exciting and appropriately useful verbs, adjectives, and adverbs, such as *informed*, *clandestine*, and *presumably*. While these words may not appear on the top 10 word list of academia, they do provide a basis from which either top-down or bottom-up reading instruction can build.

**Isolation or context?**—How to teach words is another point of teaching concern. While research has shown that some poor readers can use contextual information, research has also found that poor readers can identify words in isolation but can't seem to recognize the identical words embedded in context (Allington, 1978). On face, then, teaching words in isolation is somewhat suspect, while teaching them in context seems valuable if the child knows how to use contextual clues.

Yet another interesting and teaching-related idea has been put forth. The type of word instruction, i.e., isolation or context, may result in different learning. Possibly the best method for learning decoding and spelling is by learning words in isolation, while the method for learning words through context is in meaningful sentences. Ehri and Wilce (1980) caution the teacher to consider the purpose of instruction, i.e., which aspects of the words are to be learned? How obvious are the word meanings out of context? Are the words easily guessed and passed over when found in meaningful contexts? Ehri and Wilce suggest that the best approach to teaching words is to present both types of word-reading practice, i.e., words in isolation and words embedded in meaningful sentences.

**Dependent practice activities**—Various feedback techniques have been used to increase word recognition and oral reading scores. For beginning first-grade problem readers, correction techniques helped during practice activities, but didn't increase the actual number of words remembered or acquired (Kibby, 1979). For beginning readers the acquisition of words seems best done throught a phonetic approach. Yet sight word learning can be facilitated in ways other than phonics for at least some other children. Pany and McCoy (1983) found that corrective feedback significantly helped LD children acquire sight words, but didn't affect the number of sight words learned by normally reading third grade children. When learning disabled children are corrected on each error made during oral reading, they retain and acquire these words better than when they are not corrected at all or are corrected only on critical meaning-based terms such as nouns, verbs, and selected adjectives and adverbs. Normally reading third graders don't show any particular gain under all, some, or no feedback during oral reading.

## Word Recognition, Feedback, and Comprehension

**How feedback affects comprehension**—The reading field is still undecided as to the relationship between word recognition and comprehension. Some feel that the two are closely related (Becker & Engelmann, 1977); others are not convinced. Perhaps of more importance to the teacher is the question of feedback during word recognition or oral reading practice and how it affects comprehension. This question, too, is hotly debated. The few empirical investigations available have produced inconsistent results (Niles, Graham, & Winstead, 1979; Pany, McCoy, & Peters, 1981; Pehrsson, 1974).

Following instructional recommendations from past studies is confusing at best. The children studied differ in age and ability. Types of reading materials vary, and different types of comprehension measures are used. In an attempt to examine the relationship between oral reading feedback and reading comprehension with good and poor readers, Pany and McCoy (1983) conducted a study. The results of the study indicated that corrected feedback and even selected feedback (i.e., feedback on only some words read in error) benefitted learning disabled students. In contrast, average readers performed about the same with or without feedback on comprehension measures. Teacher-supplied feedback does not appear to interfere with comprehension for any student. In fact, the study showed that the more the teacher supplied feedback for LD students, the more likely it was that their comprehension would increase.

**Using pictures**—Sight word learning has also been taught with the use of pictures. When pictures are used to teach sight words, the teacher typically shows the child a printed word and a picture represented by that word simultaneously. In a fairly recent study (Singer, 1980), variations of this picture/

word association technique were examined and compared with the word-alone technique, sentence-plus-word technique, and sentence-plus-word-plus-picture technique. In all conditions or variations, the teacher said "right" if the response was correct and went on to the next word. If the response was wrong, the teacher provided the correct one and had the child repeat it while looking at the printed word (if in the printed-word-only variation). In the other variations, the child not only looked at the word but also at the picture and/or sentence. This study and many others found that feedback with printed word alone is significantly better at teaching sight words than the other variations (which is just as well, since finding appropriate pictures these days is more difficult than finding scenes of pastoral life in *The Daily Enquirer*).

**Reducing word errors**—Reading practice through oral reading has the basic purpose of reducing word errors. Three types of reading practice—(1) unison, (2) silent, and (3) reading orally to partners—have been examined. Cox and Shrigley (1980) looked at the effect of all three methods on normally reading second and third graders. They found that all three methods reduced oral reading errors, but unison and silent treatments were a little more effective at error reduction than reading orally to partners. Whether the same results would be found for poor readers is not known. As a classroom teacher, you will need to determine, through pre- and posttesting, which of the three techniques is the most effective for each of your slower readers.

## Word Recognition, Context, and Comprehension

**Using contextual information**—Kendall and Hood (1979) identified two types of poor readers: those with good comprehension but poor word recognition and those with poor comprehension but adequate word recognition. Kendall and Hood found that the good comprehension plus poor word recognition readers didn't use contextual information as well as and corrected fewer errors to identify words than did the poor comprehenders with adequate word recognition. Yet when comprehending the meaning of the story, the high comprehenders somehow managed to use the context of the story in spite of the fact that they could identify fewer individual words. Results of this work suggest that comprehending text material is much more involved than simply identifying the individual words in the story.

Teaching poor comprehenders how to use context seems like a good teaching strategy that does not seem to be used much. When teachers have been observed responding to miscues during oral reading, they don't seem to capitalize upon the "teachable/contextual moment." Teachers rarely ask children to use meaning as a cue to word identification or to test the correctness of their response (Spiegel & Rogers, 1980). By asking the child to check the meaning of the word read against the meaning of the rest of the sentence or story, you teach the child that written words have real meaning not just in and of themselves but also in relation to each other.

Bray is a child just beginning to realize that words come together in sentences to convey meaning. When Bray first started to read, his errors showed that he was reading word by word. He could read the sentence "The brown and white dog has spots on his nose" as "The brown and white horse had spots on the now." Even though Bray knew the story was about a dog (his teacher had prepared him), he did not let that knowledge interfere with his need to read each word. At his current reading stage, Bray is beginning to be more aware of the context of the words as they relate to the sentence and the story. He is now more likely to read the sentence as "The brown and white pup had spots on the nose." His teacher is helping him by guiding him to use his skills in phonics, structural analysis, and use of context. We can hope that in the near future Bray will read the sentence with both the correct words and the correct meaning.

**Word meaning**—In a landmark study (Davis, 1942), two components of reading accounted for about 89 to 90% of children's success or failure. These two components are word knowledge (recalling word meaning and reasoning) and weaving together ideas to draw inferences from the context of the story. There appears to be a causal link between vocabulary and comprehension, with vocabulary causing the comprehension (Yap, 1979). When children's errors are analyzed, the difference between good and poor readers turns out to be their respective behaviors regarding misread terms. Good readers seem to correct errors that distort meaning much more effectively than do poor readers (Malicky & Schienbein, 1981). Perhaps poor readers can profit from being corrected on their miscues.

By their very definition poor readers are likely to make a number of errors. A little discrimination on which errors are best corrected might be useful. Almost half the errors made by readers are substitutions (Beebe, 1980). Substitution errors seem to be a good place to start error correction. They can easily be classified into three types; those which are (1) self-corrected, (2) syntactically and semantically acceptable relative to the meaning of the passage, and (3) syntactically and semantically unacceptable relative to passage meaning. According to Beebe (1980), middle-grade teachers need to be concerned only about syntactically and semantically unacceptable errors. If the errors don't interfere with comprehension at the middle stage of learning to read (skills acquired in fourth through sixth grade), then bypass correction. Concentrate instead on errors that affect the meaning of the passage. Beebe's suggestion in no way applies to the beginning reader, but rather focuses on the reader who has had instruction in the basics and reads well at a low skill level, but who continues to make errors in comprehension. Miscues that don't change meaning may be acceptable if they indicate that the child is anticipating the appropriate meaning (Wanberg & Thompson, 1982). Toni's error "The 'home' [house] is cheerful and warm" is just such an acceptable error.

It is hard to argue with the concept that children are helped to comprehend a passage if someone explains the meanings of unfamiliar words (Anderson & Friebody, 1979). Teaching word meaning to children with sensory handicaps has been discussed elsewhere in this book (see the section on deaf and hearing impaired, chapter 4). For nonsensory-handicapped children, the techniques remain essentially the same. Children can learn word meaning ing through association, category tasks, or concept development tasks. Ludia could learn the word *prompt* by having it presented with the phrase *on time*, i.e., through association. She could also learn *prompt* by including it in a hierarchy composed of similar-meaning words, e.g., *on time, punctual, done without delay*, etc. Finally, she could work through a concept development task in which *prompt* is defined, examples provided, and application activities undertaken. For both poor and good readers, the concept development task approach seems most useful for vocabulary expansion and retention (Gipe & Arnold, 1979). Associating new words with familiar synonyms is also valuable, whereas using category labels and dictionary practice is not particularly helpful in vocabulary development (Gipe, 1978-79).

**A caution**—One small note of caution must be sounded in the symphony of "context approach to learning vocabulary" praise. Prior reading achievement may counterpoint it. In one study, LD children whose frustration scores are at least at grade three or grade two instructional level seem to do very well by using context to maintain meaning while reading orally. Those whose instructional level is lower than second grade do not gain much in reading achievement by using the context to gain meaning (Pflaum & Pascarella, 1981). The message to the classroom teacher may be that readers must have working skills up through about the second grade level before vocabulary development through context will be profitable.

Even for those children whose instructional level is lower than second grade, vocabulary development is still quite necessary. The technique may be slightly shifted. Enter the Language Experience Approach (LEA). The teacher can increase vocabulary by capitalizing on basic story dictation. Words (or selected words) from the story can form the basis of vocabulary development. To insure the vocabulary growth, the story must be complemented by a structural procedure focusing on the words in the child's word bank. Words in the bank that one systematically reviews are retained at higher levels than vocabulary terms found only in the dictated portion of the story (Reifman,

Pascarella, & Larson, 1981). LEA by itself can aid in vocabulary growth, but to make a much greater impact, the words from the story must be systematically reviewed.

## COMPREHENSION OVERVIEW

### Language Comprehension

Many reading comprehension problems may be described as language comprehension problems. Even with successful decoding instruction, a child with language problems may not be able to comprehend written material past his or her listening comprehension level (Jenkins et al., 1981). Some poor or transitional readers may need very early reading instruction that includes an awareness that language has a characteristic group of patterns. Activities that let children expand or transform sentences can enhance linguistic awareness. Sentences can be expanded by adding words or phrases or even combining with another sentence. They can be transformed by rearranging words, perhaps changing a simple declarative statement to an interrogative.

**Basic mechanics of grammar**—At an even simpler level, some children need to know the basic mechanics of grammar. They need to learn the significance of uppercase and lowercase letters and understand that the various punctuation marks are signals that help make the written language more like spoken language (Samuels, 1981). A popularly accepted and well-documented finding is that reading comprehension is an active intellectual process (Tuinman, 1980). The process of reading comprehension to create meaning entails the use of both the text (structure, organization, etc.) and the reader's own knowledge (Adams & Collins, 1979). Comprehension of any written material relies heavily upon the reader's skill in relating new information in the text to previously acquired knowledge (Christopherson, Schultz, & Warren, 1981; Jenkins et al., 1981). This knowledge includes both that of the structure of language as well as prior ideas or general background information.

**Use of prior knowledge**—Some poor readers may have problems comprehending because they either lack the ability to use background knowledge or they simply do not have relevant background experience upon which to draw. Some children need to be taught how to relate background knowledge to text material.

### Activation of Prior Knowledge

Activation of previous knowledge prior to reading can help the poor comprehender (Beck, Omanson, & McKeown, 1982; Bransford & Johnson, 1972).

Previous knowledge can be drawn out from the child, and the teacher can relate the child's statement to the main ideas and story content of the material about to be read.

**Developing background knowledge**—For the child who lacks relevant background information or the teacher who chooses to take no chances in ensuring comprehension, activities are available. The teacher can spend time developing background knowledge before reading (Pearson, Hansen, & Gordon, 1979). Background knowledge can be taught directly. A teacher can teach relevant conceptual information as well as basic reading skills (Stevens, 1982). Reading related stories, showing films, and bringing guest speakers to the classroom all contribute to background knowledge. Yet these experiences are not enough for some children. The teacher must literally remind them of the story, film, speaker, etc., and draw out relevant information to the story or material about to be read. Enhancing a learner's prior knowledge is an old learning theorist's trick (Thorndike, 1913) that fits well into any classroom teacher's comprehension magic show.

**Keeping knowledge memorable**—Another slight-of-hand comprehension technique is to keep background memorable by making the information as personally meaningful as possible (Ausubel, 1968). As a teacher you may use information gathered about your own students' interests to promote meaningful comprehension. Information can be gathered from interest inventories, questionnaires, or writing samples (Shuman, 1982). The information can be used as the focus of class content. Reading materials can be gathered that center around the student's stated interests. If you already have particular topics that have been designated, relate the children's interests to those topics. Granted, your creativity may be a little strained associating "Donkey Kong" to the glories of the solar system, but where there's a will ... .

In any event, a great deal of information has been written to show the relationship between a readers' background knowledge and the ability to comprehend new knowledge from written material. Claxton (1980) has summarized the volumes of knowledge into four succinct statements:

1) What a person knows influences what s/he learns.

2) What a person expects and knows influences what s/he sees.

3) How deeply a person understands something influences how much s/he remembers of it.

4) The context in which a person learns something influences how s/he remembers and recalls it. (p. 415)

## Practices to Enhance Comprehension

**Focus on good reading practices**—Readence and Harris (1980) identified skills necessary for the acquisition of reading comprehension. These skills were achieved by almost all good readers, but not poor readers. They include (1) identification of main ideas, (2) drawing conclusions, (3) determining sequences, (4) identifying pronoun referents, and (5) deriving meaning. While these skills were found in good sixth grade readers, nothing should prevent teachers at any level from developing these skills in their remedial and non-remedial students.

Surprisingly, less than 10% of classroom reading time is spent in direct teaching of comprehension (Durkin, 1977). One explanation may be that comprehension occurs so naturally with many children that it is thought to be an inherent and thereby an untaught or unteachable skill. The plain truth is that comprehension is a skill; like any other skill, the more appropriate the experience, the better the skill becomes. Sometimes teachers accept a student's response at face value, especially if the response is correct. If the teacher had probed a little deeper, he or she may have found that the underlying process was not correct. The answer is right, but for the wrong reason—a reason that may show a decided lack of text comprehension. To check and insure that underlying reasoning processes are logical and based on prose material, the teacher needs to allow students to discuss the reasons for their responses. Students also need a chance to compare their responses with those of their peers and to generalize their way of responding to new situations (Howell & Riley, 1978).

At a minimum, the teacher can center discussion around five aspects of the material read, identifying (1) the main idea, (2) the person communicating the passage, (3) the audience to which the message (idea) is communicated, (4) the circumstances under which the message is transmitted, and (5) the reason for transmitting the main idea(s) (Giordano, 1982).

**Text difficulty**—Not surprisingly, text difficulty influences the types of errors students make in oral reading (Tamor, 1981). Vocabulary level, syntax and grammar, and level of reading all contribute to text difficulty. Easy vocabulary words coupled with redundant information in a text help students improve in both comprehension and recall (Kameenui, Carnine, & Freschi, 1982). Translated for practical classroom application, this suggests teaching comprehension skills by using materials on the independent reading level—which is not so complicated once the independent reading level has been established.

Three basic strategies have been identified that appear to facilitate children's memory and comprehension of written materials. These strategies include manipulating objects that represent characters or concepts in a story, using pictures and illustrations that represent the main idea of the material (Peng & Levin, 1979), and using some kind of organizing, usually the author's, to aid recall of the content (Elliot & Carroll, 1980). Using the first two practices in comprehension lessons requires very little imagination. The third strategy, i.e., teaching the student to use some kind of organization, is somewhat more sophisticated, but well within the realm of the regular classroom. In fact, teaching poor readers to organize input may be a major task of the regular classroom teacher. Techniques used to teach organizational strategies run the gamut from the very simple to the highly complex.

**Chunking**—One of the simplest techniques is called "chunking." Chunking involves breaking sentences into meaningful subparts, or chunks. Take the sentence "He sat there for almost two hours while the noise from the unruly group died slowly in the midafternoon." As a good reader you have automatically (and imperceptibly) provided meaningful stopping points in the sentence. You didn't read the sentence as a whole, but rather as tiny meaningful phrases linked to the greater meaning of the total sentence. The natural chunks in the sentence are: He sat there/for almost two hours/while the noise/from the unruly group/died slowly/in the midafternoon. Children who can't chunk comprehend very little. Even if they can read the words, they won't be able to understand the sentence meaning until they can organize the material (Stevens, 1981). In one study (Cromer, 1970), when reading material was organized in prephrased or chunked meaning units, poor readers made significant comprehension gains. In fact, when given chunked material, some poor readers with adequate vocabulary skills could comprehend as well as good readers. The lesson to be learned is that teachers need to teach phrasing. They should encourage their readers to attend to it.

**Mapping**—A little farther along the continuum of organizational strategy teaching is mapping. Mapping consists of presenting a fairly extensive written outline of the material after it has been read. To construct a map, someone (teacher, students, or any combination) lists the major events and ideas in sequence. Implied ideas that are part of the story but not part of the text and the links between ideas are also listed.

**Study procedures**—Other study procedures that can assist students to comprehend better are GRP (guided reading practice), GRS (guided reading strategy), and SQ3R (survey, question, read, recite, and review). All of these approaches require some sort of prereading overview, active response to the overview, silent reading, and comparision of prereading information with total text reading. Within each of these systems, the reader begins with a pre-reading hunch about the content. The teacher essentially sets a purpose for reading by having the reader verify the correctness of the hunch by reading the text. Active involvement is at the basis of these methods, but it is guided by teacher-directed activities.

GRS (Bean & Pardi, 1979) is an extension of GRP (Manyo, 1975). GRP is a developmental strategy that essentially focuses upon independent silent reading and class discussion. GRS is a little more directed. In GRS the students complete the following sequence:

1. Survey a section of a text by reading only: titles, subtitles, vocabulary lists, graphs, charts, maps, and chapter questions.
2. Close books and orally state as a group everything remembered from the survey.
3. Students then recheck the chapter briefly for any missing information.
4. Missing information is listed on the chalkboard.
5. Teacher and students organize the information into a topical outline on the chalkboard.
6. After the survey, retelling, and outlining steps are completed, students read silently. (p. 146)

The SQ3R technique (Robinson, 1970) follows the procedure defined by its name:

1. The student surveys all titles, headings, and subheadings.
2. While surveying the student forms questions and hunches about the titles. For example, given the subheading "Birds of Prey," the student might guess that the section is about hunting birds or might simply note that he'll learn what "birds of prey" are by reading the section.
3. The student then reads the material silently.
4. After reading the materials the student tries to provide answers to the hunches.
5. The final step is to review the material. The overview allows the student to accept or reject answers to the original questions asked by verification from the text.

The SQ3R method contains both practice and repetition. Perhaps its greatest strength lies in the fact that the reader is forced to read a passage thoroughly and purposely (Graham, 1982).

## SUMMARY

Throughout this chapter, four aspects of reading instruction have been emphasized: word analysis, word recognition, oral reading, and comprehension. Techniques to teach reading used with various handicapped populations were described. As in any other subject area, teaching reading to handicapped students requires remembering that each student is an individual student first and handicapped second. Not all handicapped students are poor readers. For the great majority of handicapped readers, the reading techniques used with nonhandicapped readers are the most appropriate ones. Sensory disabilities, however, may require modification of materials and methods to some degree.

For those handicapped students who are poor readers, a more structured and systematic approach to reading instruction seems to be the most effective. Structured approaches such as those found in direct instruction and mastery learning are beneficial for most poor readers, labeled or unlabeled.

The final selection of this chapter presented strategies for teaching reading that seem helpful for poor readers. These strategies are complements that can be attached to the regular reading program in the classroom.

# 10
# Language Arts

*Stephen Isaacson*

Children with learning problems almost always have difficulty in one or more of the language arts skills. A student with a reading problem may also have difficulty spelling, writing a simple sentence, or using correct syntax when speaking. Many reading specialists assert that the language skills are all related. Logically, this would seem so. Reading and writing are part of a larger communication process; in other words, what is read has been written by someone, and anything written is usually written to be read by someone.

Assumptions about these relationships are often used as arguments for approaches that attempt to integrate the various language skills. After looking at the research, however, the most that can be said is that some language skills are related and others do not seem to be (Spearritt, 1979). Practice in one skill will not automatically lead to improvement in another.

Nevertheless, a language problem, whether oral or written, is often a signal to the classroom teacher that a child may have other academic problems in the future. It is frequently a student's poor handwriting or inability to speak or write a good sentence that prompts a referral to special education. Similarly, children with learning problems who are integrated in regular classes for science or social studies may do quite well in discussions, but have a hard time with projects, reports, or tests that require written responses.

You may have the opportunity to work with a speech-language specialist or a resource room teacher in planning and implementing a language arts program for your students. On the other hand, you may find that resource help is not readily available. In either case, knowing about language problems will help you as you take responsibility for some—if not all—of the students' language arts instruction.

## ORAL LANGUAGE: LISTENING AND SPEAKING

Many educators believe that language is the single most important tool a child can have. It is important for several reasons. First of all, it is an important social skill, the means by which a child can communicate—and thereby build relationships—with other children. It is also crucial to extended thought, the means by which we store and recall information and manipulate abstract concepts. As parallels between language and other areas of cognition are revealed, there is greater reason to believe any language skill that children acquire is only one aspect of more general cognitive abilities (Moskowitz, 1982).

For the most part, teachers have the opportunity to teach only the subtle refinements of language; the greater part of the language acquisition process has been completed by age 5 (Moskowitz, 1982). Unfortunately, it is this small proportion of subtle details that distinguishes an articulate student from one who has trouble speaking.

## REASONS FOR LANGUAGE DELAYS

There are several reasons for delay or difficulty with language. Impaired hearing that is not detected until the child is several years old may interfere with correct perception of speech sounds. Children who do not hear sounds correctly will not learn to produce them correctly. If the hearing loss is great enough, the child may not hear whole words or phrases, preventing the learning of the structure and the rules by which words are put together.

Be alert for signs of a possible hearing loss:

- A child who is easily irritated or frustrated when directions are given
- A child who acts "lazy" and begins an assignment only after everyone else has begun
- Any child with a speech problem
- A child who is "too attentive" and strains to "see" what is being said
- A child who cannot sit still during an activity that requires listening
- A child who frequently asks for instructions to be repeated

Never hesitate to refer a student for a hearing test if any of these behaviors occur.

Language problems can also occur in children who have adequate hearing but who are raised in households where not much language is exchanged. Some children receive insufficient language stimulation or may not be encouraged to talk. Bilingual children, learning different syntactic rules for each language, may also have problems.

## IDENTIFYING LANGUAGE PROBLEMS

Occasionally all of us become confused while we talk or express ourselves awkwardly. A real language problem is when the quality or quantity of a person's speech is so low that it consistently interferes with communication and the maintenance of normal relationships with peers. Students can have problems understanding language coming to them ("language-in") or problems expressing themselves to others ("language-out"), or both.

### Receptive Problems

Here are a few ways to identify students who have receptive, or "language-in," problems:

1. Look for the student who is easily confused when a two- or three-step direction is given.
2. Notice the student who doesn't understand common idioms, such as "Time to get the lead out," or takes them literally.
3. Test relational concepts with riddles like "Dan stood in back of Beth. Who was in front?" or "What is the day after tomorrow?"
4. Say something absurd and see if the child reacts to the absurdity.

### Expressive Problems

Here are a few ways to spot expressive, or "language-out," problems:

1. Listen for confusion or inconsistency in the use of tense, such as "John slugged me, but I don't hit him back."
2. Listen for telegraphic speech, the omission of articles and words like *is*.
3. Notice the child who starts to give an answer but interrupts it with "you know" or "I don't know."
4. Notice the student who confuses pronouns, such as *he* instead of *she*, or utters sentences such as "Her washed her hair."
5. Listen for words in mixed-up order within a sentence, such as "The teacher took away it."
6. Take note of children who speak in a monotone or with a broken, irregular rhythm.
7. Don't overlook the student who is shy in school, but seems to talk a lot to parents or one special friend.

### Articulation Differences

Again, keep in mind that everyone makes mistakes in speech now and then. However, if a child seems to exhibit the same problem consistently and to the degree that it diminishes his or her social acceptance and academic success, then language should be a primary concern.

It is also important to distinguish between language problems and articulation problems. Articulation problems are difficulties only in producing the right speech sound. Many children in the primary grades have lisps or substitute *w* for *r*. In most cases as the child matures, the problem disappears. Articulation problems are not usually serious and seldom detrimental to the child's school success, as language problems are.

Do you need to correct every language mistake you hear? No, some problems you should leave to time to change. Sentences like "Her washed her hair" are not unusual for a 2- or 3-year-old, but definitely should be a concern when the child is 6 or 7. Also proceed cautiously with bilingual children. Opportunities to practice English and exposure to good language models will result in better speech by and by.

From the linguist's perspective, Black English is another dialect, no better or worse than Standard English. It has its own grammatical rules and is just as effective in conveying the speaker's message as any other dialect. However, from another perspective, Cazden (1972) reports that Black parents feel that BE has no place in school and prefer that their children be taught Standard English. Standard English is the dialect that carries prestige and is used by those with power and influence in our society.

## TEACHING AREAS

In most school districts speech-language clinicians are spread too thin over several schools and many children. Some therapists see their clients as little as 15 or 20 minutes a week. Even if a child receives speech service for two or three times that length of time, it may have little effect on changing patterns that have been practiced for many years. Another problem many speech-language clinicians find is unsatisfactory carry-over from the therapy session to the classroom. Although the child learns to say a sentence correctly in a one-to-one session with the clinician, he or she may forget to do so when caught up in classroom activities or playing with friends after school. The ideal program is one in which you, the classroom teacher, can listen for and reinforce the same things the clinician is teaching. You may want to ask the clinician for recommendations to give the parents, too. Consistency across all settings will improve speech and language skills much faster than just a few minutes per week in one small room with a clinician.

Children are often fairly impervious to correction of their language by adults, since each child's utterances at a particular stage of development are from his or her own point of view grammatically correct (Moskowitz, 1982). Children often do not understand exactly what it is the adult is correcting.

### Techniques for Nurturing Expressive Language

A teacher can help by establishing a classroom environment in which language expression is nurtured and by directly teaching important language skills. Here are a few tips to encourage language development in your classroom.

**Interactive environment**—Talk a lot with your students. Describe and discuss everything you do as a class as you are doing it. Schmid–Schönbein (1979), a German educator, talks about a "language bath" where a child is immersed in language in a relaxed, warm atmosphere. Sister Barbara Louise (1982), a teacher of hearing impaired children, incorporates language practice by dramatizing everyday routines. Here is an example of what she might do to stimulate language practice:

> "Who will feed our rabbit?"
> (Student volunteers.)
> "John will feed our rabbit today."
> "Is the rabbit hungry? Ask the rabbit."
> (Student talks to the rabbit.)
> "What did the rabbit say?"
> (Student reports what the rabbit would say.)
> "Ask the rabbit what he'd like to eat."
> (Student speaks to the rabbit again and reports what the rabbit would say.)

This teacher stimulates language by giving the students many opportunities to speak, while she herself provides a good language model.

**Reading to students**—Cazden (1972) points out that literature is also an important part of a child's linguistic environment. Reading may be a particularly potent form of language stimulation. The language in books is different in content and function since the events are removed in time and space. It is qualitatively different in its structure than conversational language. Keep in mind that listening skills have a close relationship to reading comprehension (Spearritt, 1979). If children are to understand what they read, they must first be familiar with the language in which it is written.

**Converse with students**—Keep your conversations warm and enthusiastic. As a teacher, realize that you are an external source of stimulation and reinforcement for the child who is learning personal expression. Make your students regard talking to you as motivation for speaking. Enjoying the conversation will make the child more likely to want to speak to you again. Give children plenty of time to answer, and praise them for their contributions to discussions.

**Be sensitive and discreet**—Do not correct a child's speech in front of other students. Be very careful not to make the child more self-conscious about speaking. Avoid practice activities that will put the spotlight on the child's weaknesses, and do not pressure students into activities they may not have the confidence to attempt.

### Language Dimensions

Language has three dimensions (Bloom & Lahey, 1978): (1) form—saying the correct sounds, attaching the right inflectional endings to words, and putting the words in the right order to make an acceptable sentence; (2) content—the meaning that is conveyed as we listen or speak; and (3) usage—the practical, day-to-day functions of language.

**Form**—Learning the form of language does not mean learning rules of textbook grammar. There is no evidence that knowing parts of speech or diagramming sentences make any difference in verbal performance, oral or written (Straw, 1981). Trying to differentiate adjectives from adverbs will probably only add to Jane's frustration with language, and she will not be a better speaker because of it.

One good way to teach correct form is to expand and elaborate whatever is expressed by the child, carefully modeling correct word endings and word order as you speak.

Teacher: "So what happened at recess?"
Student: "Well, Billy ... he jump on the board and fall off."
Teacher: "Billy jumped on the board? What board?"
Student: "The board the men leave ... by dirt pile."
Teacher: "Do you mean the construction men who've been constructing our new play equipment?"
Student: "Yeah—the construct men."
Teacher: "Where is this board?"
Student: "The board by dirt pile ... by the fence—the other fence."
Teacher: "It was a dirt pile by the fence. Tell me what happened to Billy."

Another technique for teaching form is modeling for imitation. A child's ability to imitate is strongly related to other measures of language ability (Mittler, Jeffree, Wheldall, & Berry, 1977). Since imitation seems to play a minor role in a child's acquistion of language, many educators doubt its usefulness as a remedial technique. However, several behavioral language programs, such as DISTAR and Monterey Language, incorporate patterned modeling in combination with reinforcement for correct responses. The success of these techniques with handicapped children demonstrates their worth.

One way to make an imitation activity more fun is to use silly sentences, such as "My goldfish is eating my clothes." Begin by having the child imitate short, simple sentences after you say them. Choose sentences with grammatical structures that are a special problem for the student. For example, if Manuel says "I seen" intead of "I saw," your sentences would begin with:

> I saw a purple dog.
> Mary saw the sky fall down.

As Manuel learns to correctly repeat simple sentences, gradually increase their length and complexity.

> I saw a dog.
> I saw a purple dog.
> I saw a purple dog in the sink.
> I saw a purple dog riding a bicycle in the sink.

Don't spend too long on the activity; keep it light and success-oriented.

**Content**—Content is an important dimension of language. As part of language-in abilities, the child must understand the meaning of the words and phrases that other people use. Take time at the beginning of your science or social studies lesson to introduce a new word, and look for opportunities throughout the day to use it. Words can be chosen from current events as reported on the radio or in the newspaper, e.g., *economy, ballot, veteran, environment, promotion, demonstration, toxic.* Learning new meanings of words that have multiple meanings is also valuable.

Point out the ways in which words and the ideas they represent are related to each other. Words are related to different words that mean approximately the same thing (synonyms) and to words that mean the opposite. Words represent objects or ideas that are part of a larger class. When reading a story about penguins, for example, stop and talk about the way penguins belong to a larger class of animals—birds. In what ways are penguins like other birds? In what ways are they different? What does a penguin have that makes us think of it as a bird? Objects and ideas are also composed of smaller parts. For example, a discussion about a bicycle can lead to discussion of its components and introduction of still more vocabulary.

There are several ways to teach your children to listen for the content in what they hear. Riddles do just that and are a lot of fun.

> If an airplane crashed on the U.S.–Canada border, where would they bury the survivors?

In a social studies lesson, deliver a brief monologue to the students and have them guess the historical character by what you are saying. On the basis of an oral description, have your students draw the character or the scene described.

Activities that require students to follow directions are also a good way to teach them to listen for content. Arts and crafts projects require listening for content in order to produce the desired product. Direction games are also fun. Try the Shopping List Game: Send Caroline around the room, giving instructions to "get Sally's pencil ... get John's shoelace ... get Philip's science book ..." as she puts it all in a large shopping bag. When Caroline returns to the teacher, she must try to name everything before it is unpacked. As previously discussed, reading to students is also important. Appreciating the sentiment in stories or poems requires listening for content.

Hearing impaired children have a particular problem understanding the figurative uses of language (Rittenhouse & Stearns, 1982). To many deaf students, something is either literal or absurd and, therefore, insignificant. This problem contributes to poor reading comprehension. Rittenhouse and Stearns reported extensive use of idiomatic expressions and similes throughout children's fiction and basal readers, mostly related to key ideas. Rittenhouse and Stearns demonstrated that even 10-year-old deaf children could begin to understand metaphors if they clearly understood what was expected of them through careful teaching. Children in the study were asked to read a short one-paragraph story and then select the metaphor that most closely expressed the idea of the story. After the story was read, the following teaching steps were used.

1. The teacher showed the accompanying picture and asked the child to explain it.
2. The teacher reinforced the idea that the picture was related to the story.
3. The teacher explained that only one of the sentence metaphors below the story was related to it.
4. The child chose and explained an answer.
5. The teacher gave the correct answer and explained the analogy.

Hearing impaired and other language-disordered children may have trouble understanding meaning in sentences in which the syntax, or order and arrangement of words, does not follow the usual simple sequential rules (Bishop, 1982). Passive constructions are an example of this problem:

The angry boy was scolded by the old woman.

Some children tend to treat all sentences as straight subject-verb-object constructions. If you asked, you might have an exchange like this:

Teacher:  Who was scolded?
Student:  The old woman.

Teacher: Who scolded her?
Student: The boy.
Teacher: Tell me what happened.
Student: The boy scolded the old woman.

Similar problems occur with postmodified nouns.

The chicken in the box is red.

The adjective is usually assumed to refer to the noun closest to it.

Teacher: What is red?
Student: The box is red.

Dealing with problems like these requires the same approach as teaching metaphors: careful explanation, corrective feedback, and practice from time to time. There are no magic remedies.

Teachers can also enhance a child's language-out expression of meaning. In a science lesson give your students the opportunity to describe the attributes of something observed. Children should also be able to describe something in terms of its function. Bring to class an unusual tool and have your students invent as many possible uses for the object as they can imagine. One popular game is to have a child reach into a grab bag, select an object, and describe it in as much detail as possible without the other children being able to see it. From the description, the others try to guess what the object is.

Pictures from magazine ads, especially humorous ones, provide an excellent stimulus for children to describe events. After the student has described the situation in the picture as it exists, ask him or her to tell you what happened just before the picture was taken or what will happen immediately after. Stories can also be invented by the children after listening to tapes with assorted sequences of sound effects.

It is important for a child to be able to report events in sequence. A good way to provide opportunities for the student to do this is through *how* questions:

Tell me how ...
    you tie your shoes.
    you come to school.
    your father washes his car.

To point out cause-effect relationships, ask *why* questions:

> Tell me why ...
> > you tie your shoes.
> > you come to school.
> > your father washes his car.

Remember not to make the routine a grilling inquisition. Questions should be used to stimulate conversation and create an interactive environment.

**Function**—The third dimension of language to teach is function. Teaching function means stressing the uses of language in day-to-day events: giving and following directions, making phone calls, chatting with friends, asking for information. To use language functionally, the child must learn to act as both a sender and receiver of information. The best way to teach this is through simulated practice and role-playing. Here are a few ideas for simulation games.

1. Make phone calls in response to an ad.
2. Take a message when answering the phone.
3. Act as a seller of pens and pencils (or other "products" you find in the classroom).
4. Act as a person at home trying politely to get rid of the pencil seller at the door.
5. Give directions to help another find hidden treasure in the room.
6. Find hidden treasure by following another's directions.
7. Be a TV talk-show host (learn how to maintain a conversation through the use of questions).
8. Make introductions at a party.
9. Play the hidden treasure game by using only hints and indirect statements. ("Have you thought of looking in other cupboards?" versus "Open the cupboard door below the sink.")
10. Build conversations by expanding and elaborating the statement of the previous speaker.

For some students, acting out these activities with a tape recorder may be more motivating and less threatening than doing them before other students.

# WRITTEN LANGUAGE

## DEVELOPMENT OF WRITTEN EXPRESSION

Although written expression develops in much the same way as oral language, it is much more complex and does not develop as soon or as fast. According to Vygotsky (1962), there is a lag of as much as 6 to 8 years between a child's *linguistic age* in speaking and in writing. Writing requires a solid base of language-in and language-out knowledge but, in addition, it requires good visual abilities integrated with the fine motor skills necessary for the physical task of writing.

The difference between speaking and writing, however, is not just due to its mechanical aspects. Written expression is a separate linguistic function different in both its structure and style. Vygotsky (1962) pointed out several unique aspects of writing, among them:

- It is more abstract because it lacks the intonation and body language components of spoken language.
- A child must disengage from the immediate sensory aspects of speaking and replace words with graphic images of words.
- The writer does not have an interlocutor (or immediate responsive recipient); the recipient is either absent or imaginary.
- Writing does not carry the same motivation as speech, which is more immediately useful.
- It is detached in time and space from the real event it seeks to recreate; the writer must create the situation in his or her own mind.
- Writing is deliberate and analytical; speech is spontaneous.

## ASSESSMENT OF WRITTEN LANGUAGE

There are five basic components of written expression that combine to make a good composition: fluency, syntactic maturity, vocabulary, content, and conventions.

### Fluency

Fluency is the child's ability to generate written language from his or her own inner language and to do so in complete sentences. To evaluate fluency, the teacher looks at quantity, i.e., the number of words the child can write and, later, the number of words per sentence. Cartwright (1969) reported that the average 8-year-old can write about eight words per sentence, the average 9-year-old about nine words per sentence, and so forth, gaining about one word per year until around age 13. These are not exact standards; falling short by a word or two is within acceptable limits.

Here is an example of how a child's paragraph can be analyzed according to fluency. Billy wrote this paragraph about his favorite TV show:

> After dinner me and my brother like to watch Mathew Star. My favrite show. Mathew cames from outer space. He does magic things. He makes things fly across the room. He saves people.

If our objective were simply to get Billy to write more and practice putting his thoughts on paper, we would only look at fluency. First, let's just count the words: there are 33. We might gently encourage Billy to increase the length of his compositions, and eventually he might write stories of 50 or 60 words. Several of his sentences are very short; the average length is about five words. [To get the average sentence length, we divide the number of words (33) by the number of sentences (6).] Since Billy is 10 years old, his sentences are rather short for his age. This is a clue that he might have low syntactic maturity, as well.

## Syntactic Maturity

Syntactic maturity refers to the type of sentence the student writes. Beginning writers write simple subject-verb-object sentences. Mature writers create more complex, interesting sentences. For example, a 7-year-old may write the sentences:

> She saw the dog.
> The dog was running to the gate.

An 11-year-old will usually combine these two sentences into one more like this:

> She saw the dog running towards the gate.

A simple way to evaluate syntactic maturity is to count the number of sentences that fall within the following categories to see which type is most predominant in the composition:

> Incomplete sentences
> Simple sentences
> Compound sentences
> Complex sentences

Let's assume that Billy's compositions are long enough and the next component we want to assess is syntactic maturity. Out of his six sentences, which type is prominent?

> After dinner me and my brother like to watch Mathew
>     Star—*Complex*
> My favrite show—*Incomplete*
> Mathew comes from outer space—*Simple*
> He does magic things—*Simple*
> He makes things fly across the room—*Complex*
> He saves people—*Simple*

Billy usually writes in simple sentences (i.e., subject-verb-object or subject-verb-adverbial phrase), though he can use more complex structures. (He used no compound sentences.) Billy's teacher could show him how to combine some of his sentences into compound sentences,

> Matthew comes from outer space and he does magic things

or into complex sentences

> He does magic things, such as making things fly across the room.

## Vocabulary

Vocabulary is evaluated by looking at the diversity in the student's choice of words. Some students may be able to write sentences fluently to form a simple composition, but may tend to overuse certain words and phrases. Look for these two things when assessing vocabulary:

1. The number of repeated words
2. The number of unusual or new words

Notice whether the student incorporates new vocabulary introduced in the science or social studies lessons. Compare other key words used with grade level word lists, such as Dolch.

Evaluating Billy's vocabulary begins with counting the number of repeated words.

> After dinner me and my brother like to watch Mathew Star. *My* favrite show. *Mathew* comes from outer space. He does magic things. *He* makes *things* fly across the room. *He* saves people.

There are not many repeated words. Using more complex sentences would eliminate several repetitions of *he*. As Billy's vocabulary increases, there might be several words he could substitute for *things*.

## Content

Content is the most difficult aspect of a composition to evaluate objectively. The primary question asked by the evaluator is: Did the student creatively and clearly express what he or she intended to say? A checklist is probably the best way to look for the important content components. Cooper (1977) suggests six general qualities to be assessed:

1. Author's role: keeping the correct role of either the participant or the observer throughout.
2. Style or voice: stating what he or she really thinks in a personal, interesting way.
3. Central figure: describing the character in such detail as to seem real.
4. Background: describing the setting, giving the events a real place in which to happen.
5. Sequence: making the order of events clear.
6. Theme: holding it all together by choosing incidents and details that relate to the subect matter or purpose.

Cooper's six attributes apply best to narrative compositions. In descriptive or expository writing, attention should also be given to elements of accuracy, relevance, and clarity.

Let's use Cooper's checklist to evaluate the content of Billy's paragraph.

| | |
|---|---|
| Author's role: | Billy begins as the participant, but soon changes to an observer. |
| Style or voice: | The first two sentences share personal feelings, but the last four are written without much feeling or interest. |
| Central figure: | Billy does not describe Matthew's appearance or personality. |
| Background: | The background seems adequate in proportion to the size and scope of the paragraph. |
| Sequence: | This too is adequate, considering the paragraph is *descriptive* rather than *narrative*. |

| Theme: | Incidents are presented rather randomly. There is no central event or attribute acting as a focus for the detail. |

Billy's content is somewhat restricted by his limited fluency and vocabulary, which are more appropriate objectives to work on.

## Conventions

The conventions of a composition are made up of the mechanical aspects of writing: correct grammar, punctuation, spelling, and so forth. They reflect how well a student can recognize his or her own errors and rely a great deal on reading, spelling, and oral language skills. Though this is the polishing touch to written expression, it receives a disproportionate amount of critical attention from teachers. When the other facets of writing have developed and conventions become the primary objective, they can be evaluated by a checklist or scoring sheet such as the one shown below.

*Paragraph Conventions*

| Words | 10 minus number of errors |
| --- | --- |
| Word usage (subject-verb agreement, pronoun agreement, etc.) Spelling | |
| Margins | 10 minus number of errors |
| Left margin, right margin, name, date, skip a line, title centered, indent. | |
| Punctuation | 10 minus number of errors |
| Capitals, periods, question marks, quotation marks, etc. | |
| Handwriting | 10 minus number of errors |
| Touching the lines, formed correctly, legible. | |

Total Score
(90% criterion)                                     (36 points)

Let's look at the mechanical structure of Billy's paragraph. Here is his score sheet:

| Convention | Points | Explanation |
| --- | --- | --- |
| Words | 8 | −1 for "*me* and my brother ... " and −1 for misspelling *favorite.* Subject-verb agreement is good and he is consistent in his use of tense. |

| Margins | 9 | − 1 for forgetting to indent. |
|---|---|---|
| Punctuation | 10 | Capitals and periods are all there. We haven't taught him about quotation marks. |
| Handwriting | 9 | − 1 for a poorly formed letter. |
| Total Score | 36 | 90% (Billy deserves a pat on the back!) |

Notice that we didn't take off a point for misspelling the proper noun *Matthew*; "Mathew" is a very good attempt. Actually, Billy's teacher may not even want to score conventions until fluency and vocabulary have improved.

## INCREASING WRITTEN LANGUAGE SKILLS

Deciding what to teach depends on which component of written expression is the greatest problem. Billy, for example, needs to expand his fluency before his teacher can fairly evaluate the content of his work. Basal language arts texts are not always helpful either. Most deal with a wide range of language and study skills and give the student relatively little opportunity in actual composition. It is best to look at one component at a time. Let's take them in the same order in which they were evaluated.

### Increasing Fluency

**Relationship to reading**—It isn't necessary for children to be proficient readers before they begin to write. Some children write words and short messages in their own invented spellings for up to a year before they begin to read (Chomsky, 1969). Writing with invented spelling is a more concrete, accessible skill than reading. The words and messages are already known to the child as he or she communicates. The need to identify a message written by someone else is a significant extra step. Maria Montessori (1964) had this to say about it: "Experience has taught me to distinguish clearly between writing and reading and has shown me that the two acts are not absolutely contemporaneous. Contrary to the usually accepted idea, writing precedes reading" (p. 296).

First, a child must learn the function of language in communication, i.e., what is read has been written by someone, and what is written will be read by someone. The awareness of written language often first comes about by exposure to environmental print: TV captions, names of products, signs, etc. Unlike most written language, environmental print is immediate to the situation in which it occurs. Many primary teachers use environmental print by labeling items in the room, using charts to convey information, and writing simple directions.

**Activities for increasing fluency**—Here are some activities that will reinforce this idea of language's function.

1. Have the child color a picture and label its various parts: "house," "tree," "Mom," etc. Spell the words for him or her only if you are asked for help; if not, accept invented spellings.

2. Have the child make a little book or diary in which to draw pictures and write a few words every day. (One day Joey asked his teacher how to spell *baby* and *sister*; his mother had just given birth to a baby girl. All Joey wrote in his book that day was "baby sister baby sister baby sister baby sister … " but those were two words he never forgot.)

3. Attach a message pocket to your student's desk and one to your own. Leave simple messages for the student, like "I'm glad you're here today" or "You did a good job on your math." More importantly, encourage the child to leave messages for you.

There are several ways to teach a child to write a sentence. The five basic kernel sentence types (Phelps-Gunn & Phelps-Terasaki, 1982, p. 64) are:

1. Subject-verb—"The boy ran."
2. Subject-verb-object—"Sally kicked the ball."
3. Subject-state of being verb-adjective—"That woman was angry."
4. Subject-state of being verb-predicate noun phrase—"Mr. Green is a poor farmer."
5. Subject-state of being verb-adverbial phrase—"The king is on his horse."

Begin with the simplest type of sentence (subject-verb) and use one or all of these ideas.

1. Write simple words from the student's reading vocabulary on colored index cards, e.g., pink for subject cards, blue for verb and state of being verb cards, yellow for objects, adjectives, etc. Put them in

an envelope with the color pattern of the sentence on the front. Have the student draw cards from the envelope according to the color pattern, making a simple sentence. The student then copies the sentence on paper and draws different cards (Figure 10.1). If the student cannot read the words, paste or draw simple pictures on the cards to convey the meaning of the words (Figure 10.2).

2. Using word charts with words that are "people namers," "action words," etc., have the student choose and copy words following a *sentence map* (Figure 10.3).

3. Write longer sentences on strips of tagboard. Cut them up between words and give them to your student to unscramble and copy on paper. Point out that capital letters and periods give clues to the beginning and ending of the sentence.

4. In a slightly more difficult variation of #3, write scrambled sentences that the student has to unscramble and write in the correct order. (The student does not have manipulative parts to move and must use memory and cognitive sequencing skills to unscramble the sentence.) The easier unscrambling tasks are those in which phrases are kept intact:

kick the ball.     a girl     He saw

**Figure 10.1**
Writing Sentences from Word Cards

**Figure 10.2**
Word Cards with Illustrations

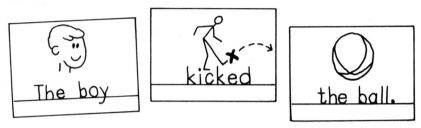

**Figure 10.3**
Word Charts and Sentence "Maps" Using Symbols from SIMS Written Language

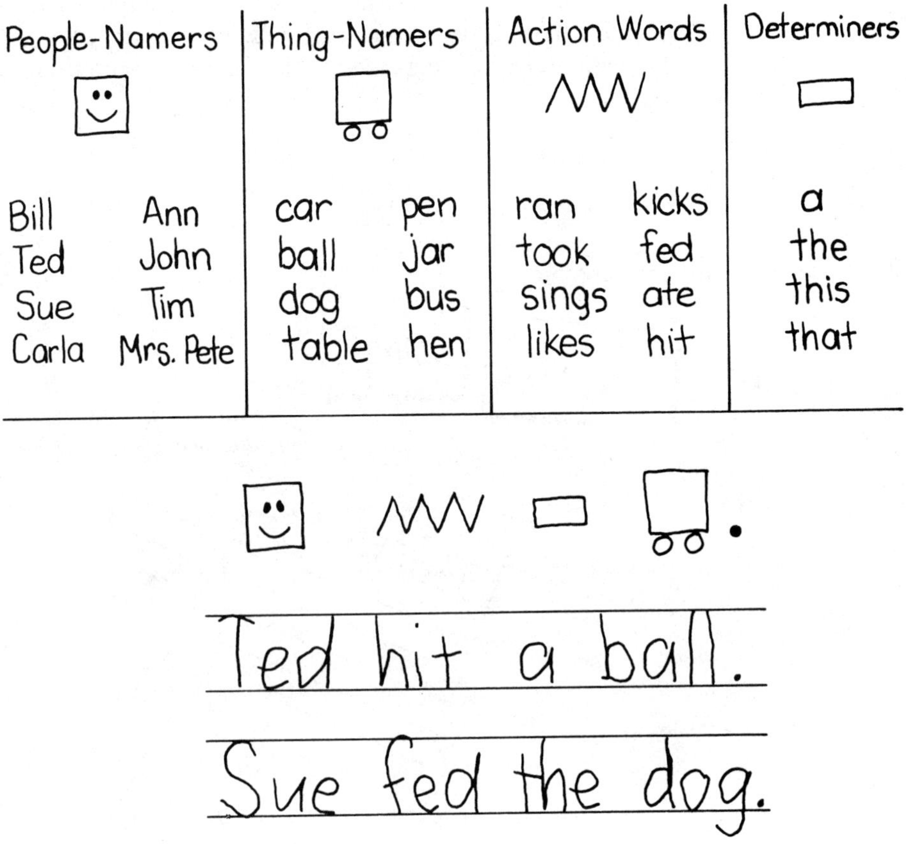

| People-Namers | Thing-Namers | Action Words | Determiners |
|---|---|---|---|
| Bill    Ann | car    pen | ran    kicks | a |
| Ted    John | ball    jar | took    fed | the |
| Sue    Tim | dog    bus | sings    ate | this |
| Carla    Mrs. Pete | table    hen | likes    hit | that |

Ted hit a ball.

Sue fed the dog.

A child also must be able to think of and write his or her own sentences. This can be done in many of the same ways recommended to elicit oral language.

1. Ask the child to describe in one or two sentences an action photograph, illustration from a text book, or humorous ad from a magazine. First give the student time to talk about it and think about it.

2. Give the student a one- or two-paragraph story in which the last sentence has been left out. The child can finish the story by writing the last sentence.

> Buzz had a fussy dog. His dog, Zip, didn't like dog food. It was time for Zip to eat, and Buzz wanted to fool him. When he put the dog food in the dog dish, he had an idea. He did something to Zip's dog food and took the dish out to Zip. _____
>
> _____
>
> _____

(The story can be read either by the student or the teacher.)

3. Have the student write sentences as answers to direct questions about himself or herself.

> Tell about something that really makes you mad.
> What do you like best about school?
> When do you feel proud?

4. Instead of having the student answer several questions at the end of a social studies chapter, have him or her write one or two sentences about its most important points.

## Developing Syntactic Maturity

As the student masters the spelling of many frequently used words and writes original compositions with gradually longer sentences, your goal will be expanded, more complex sentences. In the past 15 to 20 years, several researchers have discovered the dramatic effects of sentence-combining practice on increasing the complexity of sentences written in compositions. Sentence combining is the process by which complex sentences can be made from simple kernel sentences.

**Sentence combining**—There are several ways in which sentences can be combined. The easiest is by *conjoining*, the union of two sentences by a conjunction.

> The man is in the kitchen.
> He is baking cakes.
> The man is in the kitchen *and* he is baking cakes.

Combining also can be done by *coordination* of either two subjects or two predicates, deleting the redundant words.

> Sally will wash the car.
> *Sally will* drive it home.
> Sally will wash the car and drive it home.
> The fat girl liked to eat ice cream.
> Her dog *liked to eat ice cream.*
> The fat girl and her dog liked to eat ice cream.

Sentences can be combined by *connecting*, using a semi-colon and connecting words such as *however, nevertheless, therefore,* and *moreover.*

> I didn't go to school.
> I saw John after school.
> I didn't go to school; *however,* I saw John after school.

*Subordinating* is another way in which sentences can be combined. Subordination gives more importance to one message and less importance to the other by attaching subordinators such as *if, unless, because, until, when, whenever, wherever,* and *since.*

> I go to school.
> I will see John.
> *If* I go to school, I will see John.

Another mature type of combining is when kernel sentences are *embedded* as phrases or clauses within another sentence.

> The man is in the kitchen.
> He likes ice cream.
> The man *who likes ice cream* is in the kitchen.
> The man is in the kitchen.
> He likes ice cream.
> He is baking cakes.
> The man who likes ice cream is in the kitchen *baking cakes.*
> The man is in the kitchen.
> He likes ice cream.
> He is baking cakes.
> He is fat.
> The *fat* man who likes ice cream is in the kitchen baking cakes.
>    (embedded as a pre-nominal adjective)

Strong (1983) begins teaching sentence combining with just two sentences in each problem.

The girl is singing.
She is baking a cake.

When several such pairs of sentences are combined, they form a complete paragraph. Keep in mind that there are several acceptable ways of combining the kernel sentences.

The girl is singing and baking a cake.
The girl is singing while baking a cake.
The girl who is baking a cake is singing.
The singing girl is baking a cake.
The girl singing is baking a cake.

If the student favors one combination almost exclusively, other types of transformations can be encouraged through patterned models, such as those by Hunt and O'Donnell (1970).

Model:    1. The monkey eats bananas.
          2. The monkey is in the tree.
             The monkey in the tree eats bananas.
Exercises: 1. The old woman cried.
           2. The old woman is in the shade.

Mellon (1969) went even further in structuring the combining task. His curriculum consisted of a series of short sentences to be combined in a certain way signaled both by indentation and symbols.

Mother wondered *SOMETHING.*
    Sally would come home from school sometime. *(WHEN)*
Mother wondered when Sally would come home from school.

Perron (1974) suggested several exercises and games to increase skills in creating syntactically complex sentences. Four of them are given here as examples.

1. To demonstrate ways of extending sentences without the use of *and*, students are given writing practice with sentence-starters such as:

   I had a dog that _____.

   My friend saw it after _____.

   The sidewalk cracked when _____.

   Joe is the guy who _____.

   (Each sentence ends in a word that is used as a cue in sentence-combining lessons.)

2. Students write poems using sentence-combining words such as *who*, *that*, and *before*. Perron first has the children assemble prewritten poems, written on 3 × 5 index cards, one line per card. However, students could also write their own poems following the same format.

   > I know a boy
   > *Who* sleeps on a toy
   > And falls to the floor
   > *Before* his first snore
   > *Which* echoes through the house
   > And wakes up a mouse ...

3. Sentence puzzles are rows of boxes each standing for a word that fits in the combination of two given kernel sentences. The two sentences and the puzzle boxes are written on a 5 × 8 card. On the opposite side is the answer, written in boxed form.

4. On 8½ × 11 sheets of paper, sentence-combining problems are written out and illustrated using three kernel sentences.

   > The (picture of bird) likes to sing in the (picture of tree).
   > The _____ is noisy.                    The _____ is tall.
   > (Solution: The noisy bird likes to sing in the tall tree.)

Syntactic maturity is not the only benefit to be gained from sentence-combining practice; Hughes (1978) reported several studies (including his own) that also showed significant gains in reading comprehension. This should not be surprising since both concern the structure of meaning.

## Increasing Vocabulary

A child's written vocabulary can be developed in many of the same ways as oral vocabulary. In addition to those ideas, here are a few more that pertain to written expression in particular.

**Paradigmatic responses**—Baines (1975) examined children's skills in supplying paradigmatic responses to single-word stimuli. His review of research revealed that the proportion of paradigmatic responses increased with grade level, the most marked increase occurring between the ages of 6 and 8. This increase was also parallel to the increase in the use of differing syntactic structures. Controlled composition exercises, which have been used for many years with English as a Second Language (ESL) and adult education programs (Hashimoto, 1982), require paradigmatic responses in a variety of word classes to create new sentences of the same structure. An example by Swan (1968, p. 124) is given below:

Repeat: I'm in the taxi. (Student repeats.)

| Teacher | Student |
|---------|---------|
| bus | I'm in the bus. |
| street | I'm in the street. |
| shop | I'm in the shop. |
| You | You're in the shop. |
| teashop | You're in the teashop. |
| He | He's in the teashop. |

**Verbal labels**—Supplying verbal labels is also a useful and possibly very important vocabulary skill. Torgeson and Kail (1980) suggested from their review of the research that the slow naming speed of poor readers interferes with their ability to process information efficiently. Supplying word labels is a language process that is important to composition, also. Exercises can take the form of supplying one-word or phrase descriptions of novel line patterns or pictures depicting scenes of various kinds. Writing titles is a form of verbal labeling, requiring the naming of complex, abstract information.

**Ideas for developing vocabulary**—Here are some other ideas for providing practice in vocabulary skills.

1.  Set up a writing center in a corner of the room supplied with pencils and lined paper. In the writing center have a few charts for synonyms, antonyms, and frequently misspelled words. At the top of one chart write *said*, a word that is frequently and excessively repeated in children's writing. Under the word *said* list several words that can be used in its place, e.g, *asked, declared, exclaimed, reported*. A similar chart can be made for other frequently overused words, such as *nice*.

2.  Give the student a short passage in which several words are underlined. Have the student substitute the underlined word for a more colorful or interesting one that fits the context of the passage.

3. Play "mad-libs," a game in which randomly chosen words are inserted into a short story or anecdote with usually hilarious results. First have the group generate lists of words that will be needed, i.e., a list of "people namers" (or *proper nouns*, if they have learned that term), a list of "thing namers," a list of action words, and so forth. Then have the participants take turns choosing a word from the list as you fill it in the appropriate blank. After all the needed words have been supplied, read the story and enjoy the laughter.

4. Play "Facts in Five" on a large 5 × 5 grid (see Figure 10.4). First the student draws five category cards that are placed to the left of the grid, one card per row. Then one letter card is drawn for each of the five columns. A timer is then set for 3 minutes, and the student tries to fill in as many squares as possible, finding words that match the appropriate category and begin with the letter at the top of the column. The game can be played orally, putting markers in the squares, if the child is a slow writer or a very poor speller (Bailey, 1975).

5. Simple crossword puzzles can be fun to do if the student is allowed to ask others for help when stuck.

**Figure 10.4**
"Facts in Five" Game

| | h | p | t | c | b |
|---|---|---|---|---|---|
| musical instruments | horn | piano | | | bassoon |
| clothes | hat | | tie | coat | |
| pets | | | turtle | cat | |
| food | hamburger | peas | | | bread |
| vehicles | | plane | train | car | boat |

## Enhancing Content

**Using expressive writing**—Britton (1970) believed that the starting point for developing content should be *expressive* writing that focuses on the speaker's experiences and feelings. Teaching a student to develop style starts by focusing the child's development as an observer. Warm-up may include leading the student through an observation exercise, talking about personal perceptions. Start with topics that evoke strong feelings, e.g., losing an important game, the scariest dream the child has ever had, a favorite TV show, having a fight with a friend, things parents do that make kids angry, and so forth.

The planning stage of the composition process is very important to content. Marcus (1977, p. 146) stated that the essential factor in helping students make decisions about content is exploratory talk preceding actual writing. These discussions are "shaping" experiences that convince the child he or she has an ample stock of ideas and experiences related to the topic.

**Ways to enhance expressive writing**—Here are some ideas to use in leading a student to look at situations from other points of view, moving from descriptive to narrative and, eventually, expository themes.

1. Use "bird at the windowsill," "mouse in the corner," or "fly on the lampshade" types of discussion games to describe familiar scenes at home or school. Start with "Pretend you are a bird (mouse, fly) ... ." Some students won't have much to say about what the bird saw at home, but may love to describe what the bird saw at a ball game or party.

2. Polloway and Smith (1982) have suggested journal writing as a way to increase expression and ideation. They claimed that journals or diaries can significantly increase interest and competency in writing, especially when tied to reinforcement for length and improved quality. Teachers should make it clear that these are not confidential diaries, but interactive journals that the teacher will read and respond to with written comments. However, the teacher should encourage expression and *not* correct for spelling, grammar, or punctuation.

3. The "Matrix of Three" technique is a discussion game that prepares the student to write a story (Marcus, 1977). Introduce the activity by saying something like: "On your way to school today you saw many

things. Tell me what you saw as I make a design out of it." As the student tells you things, write them in a 3 × 3 matrix.

| cat | bird | tree |
|---|---|---|
| lost shoe | police- man | lady |
| car | dog | bus |

Have the student choose a line of three items, horizontally, vertically, or diagonally (like "Tic-Tac-Toe"). Then set up the situation: "Can you think of a situation in which we could find a lost shoe, a policeman, and a lady?" Establish a setting, set up a problem, and have the student find a solution to the problem.

4. Teach the importance of correct narrative sequence through the use of short action cartoons or picture sequence cards used in early childhood language programs. Read and talk about the cartoon together. Then have the student write about it, using sequence words like *first*, *then*, *next*, and *finally* (see Figure 10.5).

5. Use literature as a stimulus for creative writing, letting children borrow heavily either the content or style of the story they have heard. For example, using the story of the three little pigs, have them write a story about the three little *fish*. Who were they pursued by? What did they do to protect themselves? Did their enemy outwit them or did they outwit their enemy? Remember that almost all the great artists, composers, and writers borrowed heavily from the style of those they admired early in their artistic careers, long before developing a style of their own.

6. Mercer and Mercer (1981, p. 372) suggest reading to the students letters like those that appear in advice columns in the newspaper. Have the students give advice by writing responses to the letters. The responses can be shared with classmates or compared to actual newspaper replies. Practice in writing letters reinforces the awareness of the function of language. Students could also write to real columnists about real or imaginary problems.

Assign expository themes as the student develops fluency and confidence. While most assigned writing is descriptive (Petty, 1978), telling about a pet, a favorite place, an Indian custom, much of children's own writing is

**Figure 10.5**
Using Sequence Words

narrative, telling a story or relating personal events. Expository writing, on the other hand, explains *how* something works or *why* something is the way it is. It can be compared to investigative reporting.

Descriptive and narrative writing may result in more sentences and is good for building confidence and fluency. However, these kinds of sentences will be significantly shorter and less complex than expository ones. Writing maturity is developed more rapidly through expository themes (Heil, 1976). Expository writing is the content of newspapers and instructional manuals that the student will need to understand as an adult.

### Increasing Correct Use of Conventions

Basal language arts texts are full of exercises to teach the formal or mechanical components of composition. However, learning to capitalize, substitute pronouns, or identify incomplete sentences may be putting the cart before the horse if the student cannot yet write more than a labored sentence. When the student is beginning to write a fairly good paragraph and is ready to tackle indentation, punctuation, and the finer points of grammar, there are two tips that will help teach conventions to the child.

1. Employ a *verbal mediation* strategy by teaching students a simple rhyme or rule to remember as they write, such as
     "Name, date,
     Skip a line, title,
     Skip a line, work."
   Make up your own for teaching other skills, such as capitalization:
     "Names of people, names of pets,
     Titles such as Mrs.,
     Special places, months, and days
     First word in a sentence."
   (No, it doesn't really rhyme, but the rhythm is catchy.)

2. The reviewing stage of the writing process is important to a conventionally correct paper. Always have the students *edit* and correct their own work. Since there are many things to look for, a simple checklist will help the student remember what to check. Some teachers attach a small self-check slip of paper to each page of work, and the student can mark each item as it is checked (see Figure 10.6).

### Practice Practices

Whatever the skill, give the student plenty of practice. According to several researchers, a student's active time on task is the first major predictor of achievement (Rosenshine & Berliner, 1978). This seems to be just as true for writing as for other subjects. Unfortunately, teachers who describe writing as

**Figure 10.6**
Self-Check Slip for Conventions

Make a 🙂 or a 🙁

Name and date ◯

Margins ◯

Tricky spellings ◯

an important area of the curriculum also often indicate that as little as 30 to 60 minutes of class time per week is spent on writing instruction (Hughes, 1978).

**Time on-task**—In a study of 8- to 11-year-olds in the United States and England, Hughes (1978) found that British children averaged 9½ hours per week in written composition while U.S. children spent an average of 1½ hours per week, some as little as ½ hour *per month*. The difference was apparent in measures of ability. In measures of sentence complexity, British children showed significantly higher maturity. As to fluency, U.S. children produced less than half the average number of words as British children per composition. And in a subjective evaluation of quality, British children had a better sense of organization, with a definite beginning, middle, and end to their compositions. In writing, as in other subjects, there is no substitute for practice.

**Feedback**—A very sensitive and important part of teaching is the type of feedback given to a student learning to write. To a child painfully aware of a literacy problem, insensitive correction can be perceived as criticism and detrimentally affect the child's attitude toward writing. Polloway and Smith (1982) recommend a technique of *selective checking*, whereby a teacher avoids excessive correction by selecting just one particular skill to reinforce and one to correct. The skill you choose to work on should relate directly to your evaluation of the student's abilities in each of the five basic components, as described earlier in the chapter.

In a study of fourth grade boys, Taylor and Hoedt (1966) compared the effects of teacher praise without correction to criticism. Both praise and criticism took the form of written remarks in red ink on the student's work. The group that received only praise increased significantly more in fluency and maintained stronger motivation than the group that received criticism. Quality improved equally in both groups.

Kitagawa (1982) beautifully described the way in which Japanese elementary teachers use positive comments on a child's paper to teach the elements of good writing. *Sei katsu tsuzuri kata* is a philosophy of writing education that uses teacher–pupil dialogue to promote a child's own style in expressive writing. The teacher joins the child in the spectator's role and reinforces keen multisensory perception with remarks such as:

> You are recalling the cat's behavior very well here.
> Here you are remembering just what went through your mind.
> You are recalling subtle details very clearly.
> Strong feeling, directly expressed.
> You use the present tense for a feeling of *now*.
> Your writing really makes us see the cat's behavior.

## SPELLING

Spelling is part of the conventions component of writing, and most children with learning problems have difficulties with spelling. Some cannot even demonstrate basic sound-symbol correspondence as they write two- and three-letter words. Others may practice for hours at home with their parents, only to forget almost all the words a week after the Friday test.

### BASAL SPELLERS

#### Content

There are a few things to keep in mind when using a basal spelling text with a student with learning problems. The first is that many of the activities in a spelling text are not really spelling. Copying or alphabetizing words, doing crossword puzzles, or looking up definitions may have value for certain study skills, but these activities are not spelling. Spelling is writing a word after hearing it (in your head or when spoken by someone else) without a visual cue. This is the skill that must be taught and practiced.

#### Sequence of Skills

A second thing to keep in mind is that not all basal texts are sequenced very well. It is terribly confusing for children just learning to spell to have to sort out whether to use *ir*, *er*, or *ur* when they hear them all presented together. Being able to discriminate which one to use is important to a good speller, but discrimination should come later. Any possible confusion should be avoided when words are first introduced.

#### Amount of Review

Insufficient review is another problem in basal texts. The authors of many basal texts make the class wait 6 or 7 weeks before providing review units. A child who could barely remember 15 words long enough to spell them correctly on Friday will be hopeless at keeping them in long-term memory for 6 weeks without any practice.

### ASSESSING SPELLING PROBLEMS

#### Error Analysis

The first step in helping a student with a spelling problem is to look at the type of mistake most frequently made. Do spelling errors most frequently occur at the beginning, the middle, or the end of the word? Is the problem usually with vowels, consonants, or those funny vowel–consonant clusters like *igh*, *alk*, and *ough*? Often the problem lies in knowing an important rule, like doubling the final consonant before adding the suffix, or dropping the silent *e* before adding *-ing*.

Let's use Millie as an example. Although Millie did fairly well the first 2 or 3 weeks of school, she soon began doing very badly on spelling tests, even with help from her parents in the evenings. It soon became clear to her teacher that Millie could not keep up with the rest of her class. The teacher was prepared to put her on an individualized spelling program, but didn't know exactly where to start her. She decided to informally test Millie, selecting one or two representative words from each lesson, going back to the beginning of the book. She made an answer sheet for Millie like the one shown in Figure 10.7. She gave Millie 10 to 15 words each day until she felt she had a good enough sample to appropriately place her in an individualized program.

**Figure 10.7**
Informal Spelling Assessment for Millie

Spelling Test

|   |   | Vowel | Consonant | Cluster | Irregular Word | Rule |
|---|---|---|---|---|---|---|
| c | 1. Said |  |  |  |  |  |
| ✓ | 2. bot (boat) | oa |  |  |  |  |
| ✓ | 3. site (sight) |  |  | igh |  |  |
| ✓ | 4. enof |  |  |  | enough |  |
| ✓ | 5. babys |  |  |  |  | y→i |
| ✓ | 6. wich (which) |  | wh |  |  |  |
|   | 7. |  |  |  |  |  |
|   | 8. |  |  |  |  |  |
|   | 9. |  |  |  |  |  |
|   | 10. |  |  |  |  |  |

From her informal assessment, Millie's teacher identified five spelling objectives to work on: (1) words with the vowel combination *oa*, (2) words beginning with the digraph *wh-*, (3) words with the *igh* cluster, (4) two or three irregular words like *enough*, and (5) the spelling rule about changing *y* to *i* before adding the *-es* suffix. It was easy to find words for each objective in the basal text. The teacher decided to quickly look through a lower level spelling book as well to find a few more words that would fit the objectives for Millie.

## Individualized Spelling

There are two ways spelling words can be given to students: in a fixed list, which is a fixed group of related words that a student must learn in its entirety before going on to the next group; or a flow list, where new words are added to the list one at a time and other words are dropped one at a time as they are mastered. A flow list changes every day as words are dropped and added.

**Fixed list**—Let's begin with a fixed list contract. Each week's word list can be chosen from the problems identified through the informal assessment. They may be grouped according to a common phonic element, e.g., *oa* or *wh*, or they may be simply a list of various misspelled words in the order they were given on the test. If the student had trouble mastering 15 to 20 words per week, the contract should start with only 5 to 8 words per week. If the student spells all eight correctly, he or she can then tackle 10 words per week, then perhaps 12, and so forth. In addition to the words the teacher chooses, the student may want to choose some words, vocabulary from a reading or social studies lesson. The teacher also may want to add one or two words misspelled in the student's written composition. Figure 10.8 is an example of a weekly fixed list contract from which the student can choose a variety of practice activities.

There are several things to notice about the spelling contract in Figure 10.8. First of all, the student is tested on the words every day; every day the child must *spell* the words. The practice activities are useful reinforcement of spelling skills, but they are not intended as a substitute for the actual exercise of hearing the word and writing it without a visual cue. Words can be dictated by another student as well as by the teacher. Second, the student corrects his or her own words after the test. The teacher—or tutor—can either spell the words out loud or write the word on the chalkboard, or both, as the child follows along comparing the teacher's spelling with his or her own. Finally, notice that review words are added to every group of words. Each word learned should pop up periodically and frequently as a review word, keeping it in the student's mind, rather than only appearing in a review test 6 or 7 weeks later.

"Copy-cover-compare" is a practice activity used frequently to improve children's spelling. First the student copies the word, saying each letter silently

**Figure 10.8**
Fixed List Spelling Contract

Spelling Contract

Name _____    Week of _____

| Tricky Words | Reading Book | Review Words |
|---|---|---|
| _____ | Choose ____ words | _____ |
| _____ | _____ | _____ |
| _____ | _____ | _____ |
| _____ | | |

Every day:

Test
Correct
Practice

Practice Activities:

☐ Write your words on the blackboard using your very best writing. Erase them and write them again without looking at your contract.

☐ Do a spelling ditto.

☐ Do Copy-Cover-Compare.

☐ Spell all your words on the typewriter.

☐ Write each word in a sentence.

☐ Spell each word to a friend.

☐ Use the tape recorder. Say the word. Look and spell. Turn your contract over and spell it without looking. Play it back to check.

and noting the word's distinctive features. Then the student covers the word and writes it again from memory. Finally, the student compares the word just written with the original to see if it is spelled correctly and corrects the errors. Have the student do this five times or more for each word. Hansen (1979) found that this method alone was sufficient for mastery learning of nearly two-thirds of all spelling lists.

**Flow list**—Words can also be presented to a student on a flow list, a list that changes every day as the student masters each word. An example of a flow list is shown in Figure 10.9. The teacher circles the number of each new word assigned to the student. A correctly spelled word is marked with a *C* and an incorrect one with a check. Words that are learned are crossed out. Millie's teacher decided that Millie should be able to spell each word correctly for 3 days in a row before it could be crossed off the list.

Even when a word is crossed off the list, however, it is not forgotten. Beginning the second week, Millie's teacher quizzed her every day on two review words from previous weeks, since Millie had a tendency to forget them. Both overlearning (spelling each word three days in a row) and periodic review are teaching strategies that increase retention.

## TEACHING CONCEPTS

There has been a considerable amount of research on methods of teaching spelling, and here are a few tips for you when you sit down to a spelling lesson with Millie.

### Amount of Instructional Time

The first recommendation concerns time: 10 to 15 minutes a day seems just as beneficial as longer periods of time (Horn, 1969). Keep the lesson short, but make sure all of that time is spent in spelling, not copying letters or answering vocabulary questions.

**Pretest**—Second, begin your lesson with a test, then teach the words the student does not know. The test-study method is more effective than the study-test method (Montgomery, 1957).

**Air writing**—Writing words in the air or writing them on paper over and over again is *not* a valuable means of helping the student learn a word or re-

**Figure 10.9**
Example of a Flow List

*Spelling List:* ___6___ *words*          Name ___Millie___

| | M | T | W | Th | F | M | T | W | Th | F | M | T | W | Th | F |
|---|---|---|---|---|---|---|---|---|---|---|---|---|---|---|---|
| (1.) coat | c | c | c | | | c | | ) | | | | | | | |
| (2.) boat | c | c | c | | | | c | | | | | | | | |
| (3.) soap | c | c | c | | | | | Review | | | | | | | |
| (4.) soapy | ✓ | c | c | c | | c | | | | | | | | | |
| (5.) road | c | c | c | | | | c | | | | | | | | |
| (6.) fight | ✓ | ✓ | c | c | c | | | ) | | | | | | | |
| (7.) fighter | | | | | c | ✓ | c | c | c | | | | | | |
| (8.) fighting | | | | ✓ | c | ✓ | c | c | | | | | | | |
| (9.) sight | | | | c | c | c | | | | | | | | | |
| (10.) night | | | | c | c | c | | | | | | | | | |
| (11.) tonight | | | | | c | ✓ | c | c | | | | | | | |
| (12.) midnight | | | | | | ✓ | c | ✓ | | | | | | | |
| (13.) mighty | | | | | | | c | c | | | | | | | |
| (14.) mighty | | | | | | | c | c | | | | | | | |
| (15.) light | | | | | | | | | | | | | | | |
| (16.) lighter | | | | | | | | | | | | | | | |
| (17.) babies | | | | | | | | | | | | | | | |
| (18.) pennies | | | | | | | | | | | | | | | |
| (19.) families | | | | | | | | | | | | | | | |
| (20.) stories | | | | | | | | | | | | | | | |

member it (Petty & Green, 1968). These practices belong to the category of teaching myths that somehow have been passed down through the years.

**Guided self-correction**—The last tip is the most important: Have the student correct his or her own spelling, under your direction. Spell the word out loud as the student points to each letter on the paper. Immediately correct misspelled words together and give generous praise for those spelled correctly.

‧     Self-correction, under the teacher's direction, is the single most important
factor in learning to spell (Christine & Hollingsworth, 1966).

## HANDWRITING

### RESEARCH FINDINGS

#### Rules Governing Young Children

Handwriting, in the manner commonly prescribed in schools, does not come
easy for any child. Most letter strokes run directly against the inclinations
children have when they copy a figure. In his study of very young children,
Simner (1981) uncovered a "grammar of action," tacit rules that guide the
way children construct geometric figures. Typically, children begin at the
topmost, leftmost point and proceed downward and around. For example,
the expected stroke for *b* is shown in Figure 10.10. This stroke pattern oc-
cured in 85% of the letters and numerals tested. When strokes from the top/
left point did not fit the figure to be copied, children selected strokes that
minimized the complexity of the copying task. Formal printing instruction
does instill new stroke patterns in many children, but Simner found second
graders who still used the predicted pattern.

#### Cursive Writing

The problem of learning new stroke patterns is further complicated when
children learn cursive writing. Several cursive strokes run opposite to manuscript stroke patterns. Using *b* again as an example, the taught manuscript
pattern begins with a downward vertical stroke followed by a clockwise circular stroke. The proper cursive *b*, however, begins with an upward vertical
stroke, comes back down to the base line, and then makes a counterclockwise

**Figure 10.10**
Expected Stroke for **b**

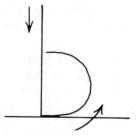

Source: Drawn from discussion in M.S. Simner, "The Grammar of Action and
Children's Printing," *Developmental Psychology* (1981), *17*, 866-871.

movement toward the midline, closer to the very young child's natural inclination. In other words, the beginning writer has to overcome natural inclinations to learn the proscribed form and then break those movement patterns to learn yet another set of movements.

## Hand–Paper Positions

In addition, most teachers insist on one hand and paper position. However, Wellman (1983) insists that this disrupts an orientation that is natural for a child's natural organization. Children often go through a range of positions that change as part of a developmental process. Wellman concludes, "It follows logically that children should be allowed to use whatever hand position is natural for them" (p. 56).

## Teaching Implications

What are the implictions of these findings for teaching? First, legibility, not esthetically pleasing form, should be the primary objective in handwriting. Cursive styles that involve ornate loops or varying letter heights are unnecessarily difficult for students who lack fine motor skills.

Second, primary students should not be taught letter strokes that will later have to be broken and relearned an entirely different way. Many districts are adopting italic or *continuous flow* scripts as a way of avoiding this problem. The D'Nealian program (Scott Foresman, 1978) is an example of continuous flow style in which both the connected and unconnected forms of writing use the same slant and letter strokes. Children with learning problems, especially, should have a program in which writing patterns are consistent as practiced throughout their school career.

Third, a teacher should meddle with a student's letter formation, slant, or hand and paper position only when these behaviors interfere with legibility or fluency. Obviously, when you cannot decipher the letters a student makes, you will have to teach the correct way to write them. When a student's writing is legible but painstakingly slow because of the hand position or the way the pencil is held, it would be in the student's best interest to demonstrate a better way. However, if a student writes as fluently as most students with a style that can be easily read, even if not pretty, leave well enough alone and concentrate on spelling, reading, or other more important goals.

## ASSESSING HANDWRITING

## Fluency

Assessing the effectiveness of a student's handwriting is a simple two-step process. First, measure how fluently—or fast—the student can write. Fluency can be informally measured by watching the student as the class copies a poem or a language experience story from the chalkboard. The student's fluency is adequate if he or she finishes at about the same time as the other students.

## Legibility

Second, compare the speed and ease with which you can read the student's writing as compared to other students' writing. Use a stopwatch if you like. If the writing sample is as easy to read as that of the other students, assume it is adequately legible. If a student's writing takes longer to produce or longer to read, look more closely at specific behaviors: position of the hand, how the pencil is held, spacing, or certain problematic letters or strokes.

## TEACHING LETTER FORMATION

There are three instructional techniques that will help a child learn better writing: a moving model, verbalized prompts, and feedback. While these are important techniques to use with learning handicapped students, they are also effective with all children.

## Moving Models

Models of letter formation depicting motion are more effective than still models. In large groups, moving models are presented using films, videotapes, or in demonstration by the teacher on the chalkboard or overhead projector. However, to accommodate individual student needs, Wright and Wright (1980) have suggested flipbooks. As a child flips through the little book with his thumb, the letter appears in cartoon-like animation. In their study of first grade children, Wright and Wright found that the group using flipbooks improved their writing significantly more than the group using traditional still models.

## Verbalized Prompts

Even more effective than the use of moving models alone is the use of auditory processes to reinforce visualization of letters. Verbal descriptions of the stroke sequence draw attention to previously unnoticed features and increase the student's memory of the sequence. In addition, Hayes (1982) found that children who were taught to verbalize the stroke sequence themselves did better at reproducing letters than those who only listened to the teacher's verbal prompts. In other words, providing children with visual and verbal demonstrations of letter motion, while directing them to say the sequence as they form the letters themselves, is the most effective strategy in teaching handwriting.

Here is an example. The lower case cursive *h* can be taught using the following verbal prompt:

> Up to the top,
> Loop down,
> Over the hump,
> Swing.

Manuscript letters that do not begin on one of the guidelines but somewhere between them always present a problem. Some teachers have alleviated this problem by teaching children to visualize a human head, using ears, top of the head, nose, and chin as guide points. For example, *c* (either upper or lowercase) can be taught as follows (see Figure 10.11):

> Start at the ear,
> Over the top,
> Around,
> And under his chin.

A tricky letter like *s* can be taught:

> Start at the ear,
> Over the top
> Across the nose,
> Under the chin.

### Feedback

Several researchers have demonstrated the effectiveness of immediate corrective feedback and positive reinforcement in improving students' handwrit-

**Figure 10.11**
Images for Verbalizing Stroke Sequences

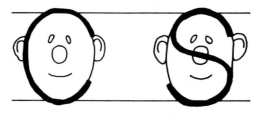

ing. Hansen (1978) found having students evaluate their own writing produced positive changes in both rate and form. She also found that "beat your rate" contests were effective in increasing writing fluency. A card was attached to a student's desk showing the average and highest daily rate for correctly written letters. Prior to each writing session, the rates were discussed and the students encouraged to "beat your rate." Teachers also have found success by using reinforcement strategies that range from giving stickers for carefully completed assignments (Idol-Maestas, 1983) to short free activity periods for those whose writing has shown improvement (Polloway & Smith, 1982).

## Reversals

The best approach to letter reversals is immediate corrective feedback followed by massed practice of the problem letter. In addition, use one of the strategies suggested by Graham and Miller (1980).

1. Have the student simultaneously say the letter name while tracing and writing it.
2. Associate the problem letter with another that does not cause confusion, e.g., *c* within *d*.
3. Give a verbal cue the child can use for correctly writing the letter (as discussed earlier).

## SUMMARY

Many children with learning problems have language problems. Language problems can occur among children with hearing impairments, children who come from language impoverished environments, or sometimes bilingual children who confuse the syntax of one language for another. The involvement of the classroom teacher in remediating language problems is important; first, to augment the limited time the speech clinician can give to the student and second, to increase the settings and situations in which new language skills can be applied and practiced.

Students can have problems with receptive language or expressive language. A classroom teacher can encourage language development by describing and discussing everything that happens in the classroom, reading to students, keeping conversations warm and reinforcing, and being sensitive to students who are self-conscious about their speech.

Written expression requires a solid base of language abilities, but it is also a separate linguistic function, requiring additional cognitive and visual-motor processes. The five components of written expression are fluency, syntax, vocabulary, content, and conventions. Five tips for teaching written language are:

1. Encourage awareness of the function of language. Draw attention to environmental print and give the student opportunities to write for others.

2. Assign expository as well as descriptive and narrative themes. Expressive writing is good for developing fluency, but it is through expository themes that students learn to use more syntactically complex sentences.

3. Encourage the use of new vocabulary. Draw attention to repetition in the students' writing and encourage them to replace old words with new ones.

4. Give plenty of practice. As in other subject areas, student achievement is directly related to the amount of time devoted to the task.

5. Reinforce the student's efforts. Use a "selective correction" procedure to give feedback on compositions. Emphasize the positive aspects of the writing and focus on the student's improvements.

Spelling is an important part of written language. Provide an opportunity for your student to practice spelling the assigned words everyday, using a test-study procedure. Allowing students to correct their own spelling is the single most effective way of increasing spelling performance. Spelling contracts, such as the examples in this chapter, are useful ways to individualize a spelling program for students who need special help.

The two most important criteria for acceptable handwriting are fluency and legibility. The most effective methods of teaching handwriting are those which include a moving model and verbalized prompts. As in every other language skill, plenty of practice, careful feedback, and reinforcement are important components of teaching the skill.

# 11

# Mathematics Skills Evaluation

No live teacher can continue to live sanely for long under the conditions of the reality of mathematics instruction; even teachers and students are allowed to dream. The math classroom, not sane, stands by itself against its textbooks, holding darkness within. The mystery of math learning has stood for many instructional years and might continue to stand for many more instructional years. Within classrooms walls continue upright, bricks meet neatly, floors are firm, and doors sensibly shut. Yet silence lays steadily against the wood and stone of the math classroom; whatever is learned there is learned alone.

Jean Monty was a doctor of philosophy; she had taken a degree in math education, feeling obscurely that in this field she might come closest to her true vocation, the analysis of the mysteries of mathematics instruction, somewhat akin to supernatural manifestations. She was scrupulous about the use of her title because, her investigations being so utterly theoretical, she hoped to borrow an air of respectability, even scholarly authority, from her education. Since she was not a begging person, it had cost her a good deal in money and pride to enter the public school math classroom for 3 years, but she expected to be compensated for her pains by the rewards that would follow the publication of her definitive work on the courses and effects of math techniques in a setting commonly known as "the public school math class." She had known about public school math classes all her academic life. When she had heard about the conditions of these classes, she had been at first doubtful, then hopeful, then indefatigable; she was not a person to let go of a problem once she had found it.

A good thing, too, that Dr. Monty is persevering. Her life's work is certainly challenging. Of all areas of academic instruction that haunt the hearts of most classroom teachers, mathematics is by far the most feared. Teachers, students, and national organizations all concur that the need for more effective mathematics instruction is long overdue. Surveys of mathematics achievement constantly remind us that most children have learned to perform routine processes well, but have no idea of how to apply these processes in new situations. As such, mathematics instruction may not be taught in a manner that is even favorable to developing intelligent learning (Skemp, 1981).

Many teachers feel that math training programs are inadequate. Teachers are especially concerned about the lack of information and guidance available for working with students who have a difficult time learning mathematics (Silbert, Carnine, & Stein, 1981).

# PROBLEM LEARNERS IN MATHEMATICS

## HANDICAPPED STUDENTS AND MATHEMATICS

Children who have problems learning mathematics can range anywhere along the intelligence continuum. Very, very bright children as well as children with known organic disorders can all have problems learning math. In fact, once children have passed beyond learning the rote skills involved in arithmetic and are asked to solve problems, the number of problem learners in mathematics increases considerably. This increase is also apparent with handicapped children.

Just as in the normal population of children, not all handicapped children have problems learning mathematics, but a great many do. Materials and techniques designed to compensate for sensory deficits, such as visual or auditory impairments, may be the only accommodations necessary for some handicapped children. For other handicapped children and many nonhandicapped children, the teacher will need to manipulate the teaching–learning situation in the ways that best fit the children's mathematical learning needs, as well as to attend to both cognitive and affective factors that influence the learning of mathematics.

## THREE FACTORS AFFECTING MATH LEARNING

To define the problem learner in mathematics, then, requires looking at the problem from at least three different and occasionally related perspectives: medical, psychological, and educational. According to Kosc (1980), problems in the three areas can be viewed in the following way:

- Medical problems deal with disturbed capacities and respective functions of the brain.
- Psychological problems deal with disturbances and disorders of mathematics abilities as functions of the personality.
- Educational problems deal with difficulties in learning mathematics content as a function of teaching.

The number of children with difficulty in learning mathematics will vary with your perspective on the problem. The smallest numbers are cited from the medical perspective and grow increasingly larger, with the psychological category reaching the high from an educational perspective. Commonly cited generic incidence numbers range from 6% (Koch, 1974) to 15% (Bennett, 1969). However, many classroom teachers, during particularly exasperating math lessons, are more likely to quote 110% math disabled, including themselves.

## The Medical Perspective

*Dyscalculia* **defined**—*Dyscalculia* is the term commonly used in medical circles to refer to a person suffering from extreme problems learning mathematics. This term implies a direct connection between a neurological condition and the inability to learn math. The term has been borrowed by some educators. However, when educators typically use the term *dyscalculia*, no neurological evidence for the problem has been found. *Dyscalculia*, as used by most educators, usually means that the child is having greater difficulty than most learning how to do grade-level math. Unfortunately, some of the problems found in neurologically based dyscalculia are found in educationally based dyscalculia, e.g., difficulty using place value and confusion of the columns (ones, tens, hundreds, and so forth) in carrying out arithmetic operations (Denckla, 1978). The true nature of dyscalculia is not clear. Much of the data is founded on observation and not the result of systematic empirical research (Kraner, 1980).

**Perceptual deficit hypothesis**—Clinical observation of dyscalculia spawned a once popular but currently declining theory called the *perceptual deficit hypothesis*, loosely based on neurological theory. The perceptual deficit hypothesis espouses the notion that many learning difficulties (including mathematical ones) stem from undeveloped or interrupted sensory-processing skills. Proponents of the hypothesis believe that children with math learning problems have directly related causal problems in one or more perceptual areas, e.g., visual closure, spatial orientation, auditory discrimination. While a certain face validity makes the perceptual deficit hypothesis somewhat appealing, the evidence supporting this position does not. Even bona fide, i.e., neurologically proven, dyscalculic children have little difficulty with most of the perceptual components identified with mathematics (Ceci & Peters, 1980). In light of this evidence, materials designed to remediate math learning problems by developing perceptual skills are indeed questionable. This is just as well since most of these perception-building materials are not found in the majority of special or regular classrooms anyway.

## The Psychological Perspective

**Math anxiety**—Isn't it surprising that a discipline often viewed as cold, indifferent, logical, and objective can generate more intense emotional response than almost any other subject area (Rosamond, 1982)? The negative response to mathematics learning has reached such a grand proportion as to merit its own label: *math anxiety*. Math anxiety is among the fairest of the equal opportunity phobias. It is a fear of math that occurs across boundaries of sex, race, age, and intelligence. All who suffer from math anxiety—and not all suffer equally—can exhibit such subtle behaviors as the avoidance of mathematics or anything to do with numbers to a very real physical reaction such as heart palpitations or sweaty palms when in the proximity of quantitative subject material (Ben-Jacob, 1981). Needless to say, people who suffer from math anxiety have shared many of the same negative experiences in mathematics instruction. Some commonly experienced negative situations can be found with impatient parents or teachers who "helped" the child through sarcasm, patronizing, and sometimes pejorative statements such as "Think!" "Try harder!" and the ever-popular "How can you be so stupid!" Another source of math anxiety stems from buying into various false indoctrinations like "math takes a 'special mind' " (one wonders if the notion of a special mind had been the brain child of some rather uppity mathematicians themselves!) or "Mathematics is only for 'good students.' " Yet a good student will not necessarily be a good student in math. While students bring inclinations to learn, they also respond to the classroom. What they bring to the classroom in terms of affective responses interacts with the instructional procedures (Morse, 1981).

**Math self-concept**—Self-concept with respect to mathematics ability is well established in the early school years. Even the best of teachers (Norton, 1973) finds it very difficult to modify self-concept positively to any degree. As early as fourth grade, fatalism toward math achievement begins to rear its negative head. The power of fatalism grows steadily with each succeeding grade level. This attitude is consistently greater for girls than for boys (Shaughnessy, Haladyna, & Shaughnessy, 1983) until about junior high level, when many boys and girls feel equally helpless towards mathematics (Haladyna & Thomas, 1979). With the stereotype of boys preferring mathematics galloping off into the sunset, we are left with students' perception of mathematics as being something bizarre over which they have very little control. So much for active learning/engagement in the task. A little anxiety may stimulate learning, but too much tends to be disorganizing and disturbing. Too much anxiety is especially problematic to children with learning problems, who are often low on persistence to begin with (Morse, 1981).

Math anxiety itself is very often a response to self-concept of ability. Many math-anxious children view themselves poorly and feel that they have low ability. We can easily deduce that comments like "I don't care," "Math is dumb," and "I hate math" are reflections of upset and defensive children who feel unable to use mathematics meaningfully (Meece, 1981).

One educational researcher (Hoyles, 1982) collected stories from more than 300 14-year-olds about how they viewed math learning. The students had various reasons for wanting to learn math. Some wanted to know "why" as well as "how"; others were happy if they could just reach the right solution. The view the students held was apparently influenced by failure to reach the goal. Failure to reach the personal goal—whatever that goal might be—negatively influenced the students' self-perception of being able to do math. The stories also revealed another common theme. Feelings of inadequacy and shame were often associated with bad experiences in learning math. Many reported being resentful and frightened of teachers who appeared to impose any additional mathematical demands on them. Hoyles suggested that pupils seemed to want teachers to "make it easy" or "tell them the way," possibly to relieve any tension the students might feel in learning mathematics.

**Learned helplessness**—The need to relieve the tension surrounding math learning is closely related to the psychological term *learned helplessness*. In learned helplessness the critical factor is not the aversive event or situation (in this case math learning), but rather the perception of feeling surrounding the relationship between the learner's behavior and the occurrence of math instruction. If learners interpret failure in one or many math problems as inevitable, they can feel that learning mathematics is beyond or out of their control. The child who experiences repeated failure with no expectation for success, no matter how hard he or she tries, is likely to give up in the face of new situations. In effect the child has learned to become helpless and may not even attempt to solve problems well beneath the already established skill level. A child who is characterized by learned helplessness is likely to give up in the face of failure when compared to the more persevering child, who like "Little Toot" believes he can make it up that mathematical hill (Diveck, 1975). Many normal children as well as special ones can be characterized as showing learned helplessness to a greater or lesser degree in mathematics. Remediation is important. Without the belief that math can be controlled, the learner cannot loose these psychological constraints. Successful completion of a mathematically challenging problem can then be paired with the phrase "I knew I could! I knew I could!"

**Personality characteristics**—Individual differences in learning mathematics are sometimes attributed to personality characteristics as well as cognitive aptitudes (McLeod & Adams, 1980/81). One of the most widely investigated personality variables is field dependent versus field independent. A field-independent cognitive style is described as being analytic. A field-dependent style is global, i.e., influenced by the total context of a situation. By about third or fourth grade, children who are described as field independent seem more likely to be successful in mathematics than children who are field dependent (Vaidya & Chansky, 1980). Fortunately, with a little bit of help from a skilled teacher, all mathematics learning is not lost for the postsecond grade field-dependent learner. While field-independent learners may learn best with a minimum of guidance and maximum opportunity to discover, field-dependent students perform well with a lot of guidance (McLeod & Adams, 1979/80). In other words, field-dependent students need to be taught, i.e., typically taught in a direct and structured style. Instead of waiting for the field-dependent child to "find" or "discover" the critical features of a problem, the teacher can simply provide the child with a means to identify the pertinent information. Bien (1974) has clearly demonstrated that field-dependent and field-independent students perform equally well once the field-dependent student is given an external guide. In Bien's study, the external guide was simply providing the students with structure by circling the relevant information in a word problem-solving task.

Regular and special students can be cast either field dependent or field independent. Various tests can indicate cognitive preference. More than likely, as a regular classroom teacher you will not have access to any of these tests— not to mention time to administer them. Before you bring your mathematics instruction to a screaming halt for fear of a mismatch between your teaching style and the students' learning style, take heart. If your students are learning well, don't worry; proceed as before. If some of your students are not learning math very well, alter your style for them and analyze their math progress under the old and new teaching styles. If no improvement occurs, refer the child for outside testing. If all of your students are doing poorly in math learning, have an immediate heart-to-heart talk with a trusted and time-proven successful math teacher.

**Teacher attitudes**—The classroom math environment has an effect on a learner's math performance and interest, and one of the most significant people there is the teacher. To truly understand mathematics education, the effect of the teacher's attitudes must also be considered (Bishop, 1980). Interestingly enough, some research (Schofield & Start, 1979) suggests that a teacher who is highly skilled in math is likely to produce high pupil achievement in math. Even though the teacher may enjoy mathematics, this enjoyment is not particularly transferred to the students. In fact, some teacher behaviors that advance the learning of mathematics skills may actually conflict with behaviors that enhance the development of positive attitudes toward math. Math teachers who invite the students to have challenging problem-solving experiences and who foster independent exploration and application of old principles to new situations while increasing students' skills may in fact actually be diminishing the students' desire to use these very skills. The balance between skill acquisition and attitude towards math is at best very precarious. Some teachers who are skilled mathematicians may themselves need a brush-up course on the psychology of human motivation and emotions. They may have the content mastered, but not the "warm fuzzies" so often needed by math learners.

And the greater number of elementary teachers, we discover with no particular surprise, view mathematics as a necessary evil at best (Bulmahn & Young, 1982). Attitudes of strain, dislike, fear, insecurity, and confusion when confronted with mathematics are found in prospective teachers as well as long-established teachers (Clark-Meeks, Quesenberry, & Mouw, 1982). As the good ship of mathematics instruction is about to collide with the inevitable iceberg, a lighthouse of hope shines forth an optimistic, if not entirely safe, passage. We cannot assume that

> all teachers who dislike mathematics as students, or even those categorized as math anxious, dislike teaching mathematics. Many in fact, seem eager to break the cycle of poor attitudes engendering poor attitudes and are determined to provide their pupils with positive experiences in learning mathematics. (Widmer, 1980, p. 351)

Perhaps identification with the personal stresses sometimes encountered when learning mathematics accounts for the teacher's empathy. While empathy cannot make up for lack of content, the odds are high (and research-supported!) that teachers, though not demonstrating high levels of math skills (but at least a minimal level of competence), can indeed foster positive attitudes towards math.

The presence of a supportive teacher is truly a vital component of a healthy classroom atmosphere. Anxiety can be reduced by manipulating the social climate of the classroom. Openness to learning mathematics is quite rightly the first step toward high-level skill acquisition.

Students appreciate teachers who provide secure and encouraging math lessons. These lessons are structured in a logical progression and coupled with plenty of patient explanation, encouragement, and friendliness (Hoyles, 1982).

**Grading style**—Grading style also plays a key role in shaping students' feelings about math learning. Mathematics achievement, probably more than any other subject, has been viewed in very simplistic terms. For most teachers math answers are graded as either right or wrong. Partial credit in the land of mathematics is indeed a rare visitor most often not seen until junior high. No wonder students confronting such an unforgiving grading system often feel helpless. Repeated exposure to an either all right or all wrong system surely must play a major role in developing motivation and attitudes toward mathematics (Head, 1981). Teachers can institute a grading procedure that accounts for partially correct responses. The system could grade the choice of operation, the procedure used, even the orderliness of the work. The correct answer could be just one component of the many that entail calculating or problem solving. By encouraging students through use of a partial credit system, the sense of failure is decreased and opportunities for skill development are enhanced. Motivation to use skills can remain strong, even if the skill levels are not initially high (MacKennin, 1982).

Teacher attitudes that are especially relevant to handicapped children focus on expectations. By attributing success or failure in mathematics to labels and associated characteristics in ability, the teacher may be inadvertently creating an environment of failure. A teacher's image of the child's low ability is quite likely to end up in an unwillingness to interact with or even help the child because of the belief that the child can't learn. If, in contrast, the teacher views the child's math learning problem as rooted in some modifiable problem, willingness to help and interact is quite likely (Lorenz, 1982). By viewing a child, handicapped or not, as lacking in motivation, fearful of failure, or even math anxious, the teacher can provide additional help to these real but fixable problems.

## Teaching Perspective

**Negative learning styles**—Failure to learn mathematics can also be attributed to the type and amount of instruction the child receives. Granted, emotional maladjustment and mathematics prowess can be related. However, the teacher is still basically responsible for providing the learning environment. Children who are very stable can have negative and extreme reactions to failure that are confined solely to the classroom mathematics situation. A major implication for teachers is to reduce the amount of mathematics failure substantially by identifying causes of behavior disturbance that impede learning. In addition to early identification of situations that lead to a child's negative emotional responses, the teacher must also attempt to alleviate the problems. Any activities that encourage confidence, stimulate motivation, and reinforce attention and reflecting are necessary teaching artillery in the arsenal of mathematics instruction.

In a recent study by Stott (1981), six types of disturbed behavior that lead to learning failure were identified. While Stott's primary questions focused on children labeled *behaviorally disturbed*, his findings may have practical applications for any child who fails to learn mathematics (or any other subject) as a function of some specific sort of behavior disturbance. Identification of one of these styles in a slow mathematics learner may let the teacher create a more positive learning environment. The six styles and the questions Stott used to identify them are presented in Table 11.1.

Encouraging the child who exhibits temperamental timidity to become more willing to attempt responses is a teacher responsibility. The teacher needs to recognize that unresponsive behavior is not necessarily a sign of dullness but may in fact be a maladaptive emotional response to failure. The child who is emotionally distant deals with potential failure by withdrawing from the teacher's cognitive stimulation. Lack of an interactive teacher/child environment is very commonly associated with poor academic performance. One of the most easily identified, the hyperactive child needs an environment that allows the formation of a system of self-control. Constant unfocused activity, be it mental or physical, can certainly reduce learning. The temperamentally impulsive child has problems learning because very little or no time is given for the perception of relevant task features or reflection of how new knowledge may be related to past experience. The hostile child will perform poorly as a function of seeking rejection. Hostile children may do badly in order to insult or offend the teacher.

According to Stott (1981) and most anyone else who has worked with low-achieving children, these coping styles can be found in various degrees in math-fearful learners. The degree to which these styles are used will naturally affect math performance. The greater the use of the style, the less likely the child will succeed.

Table 11.1
Coping Styles Attendant to Failure to Learn

| Style | Screening Question |
|---|---|
| 1. Temperamental timidity | Is the child timid, lacking in confidence, fearful of joining activities? |
| 2. Emotionally distant | Does the child seem unconcerned about being in the teacher's "good book," never greeting or smiling or showing work for approval? |
| 3. Lethargic | Does the child have phases of lethargy and unresponsiveness to what is going on nearby? |
| 4. Hyperactive | Is it difficult to make the child settle to any activity or keep seated? |
| 5. Impulsive | Does the child react impulsively to everything—grabbing things out of turn, continually pestering, meddling, getting into temper tantrums when frustrated, and not heeding correction for more than a moment? |
| 6. Hostile | Does the child seem to make an effort to be naughty, to annoy the teacher or other children, to make provocative, rude, or nasty remarks? |

**Screening for negative learners**—For classroom teachers, identification of these styles by asking screening questions can direct how instruction is to take place. Mathematics instruction cannot take place without considering the role of the child's learning problem. Whether the child is labeled handicapped or normal, the teacher must be sensitive to the degree to which these styles influence the math lesson. Teaching should reduce the negative impact of the learning styles. Reduction of these negative styles includes applying principles of learning to each math lesson as well as maintaining a high level of professionalism. Professionalism in this case refers to the ability to not take pupil misbehavior or rejection personally. It also means knowing when to call in the special resource teaching troops if the problem is too complex to be handled in the regular classroom.

**Instilling confidence**—Attitudes of students who have little hope of succeeding in math can be turned around by appropriate teaching techniques. Trying to teach mathematics by standard class procedures to math-hopeless children apparently does not work and is not likely to work. The first step in instructional intervention must focus on the learner's readiness to believe that success in mathematics is possible. This feeling can be brought about through class management of the mathematics material itself. Children can alter their attitude toward their math ability in the context of the normal routine of the mathematics class (Smead & Chase, 1981). By manipulating the material and systematically presenting high probabilities of success, confidence and subsequent higher expectation levels can be built in the math-fearful child.

## MATHEMATICS EVALUATION

Evaluation of math skills can be an accounting of the physiological and psychological make-up of the child as well as an examination of the teacher's behavior in relation to fostering positive attitudes towards mathematics. With children who typically experience failure in mathematics, these three areas may be as important in math success as the actual content of math itself.

Attitudes and physiology aside, the entire area of mathematics content also needs to be evaluated. For practical reasons, if not necessarily mathematically precise ones, math content can be viewed from three general skill areas. These skill areas are *fundamental* or *basic facts*, *algorithms*, and *problem solving*. With due respect to the field of mathematics, each of these areas in turn can be divided many times over. Detailed descriptions of these subdivisions are best found in actual mathematics texts. We will look only briefly at content, evaluation, and remediation techniques in mathematics.

## EVALUATING FUNDAMENTALS AND BASIC FACTS

### Definitions

In essence, basic facts consist of the most rudimentary but fundamental skills upon which all further arithmetic or mathematics instruction is based. They include knowledge of basic shapes, number recognition, and counting. The basic fact area that is probably given the most instructional attention is number facts. Approximately 400 number facts are taught, 100 each in addition, subtraction, multiplication, and division (Silbert et al., 1981). These number facts and their various combinations are usually referred to as addition, subtraction, multiplication, and division tables.

Number facts, like most other basic facts, ultimately require automatic stimulus–response performance. Knowledge of basic facts in arithmetic is very similar to word recognition skills in reading. The stimulus in word recognition is the written word; in basic facts, the stimulus is the shape, the number, or the number combination, e.g., $1 + 1 = $ _____. The goal is automatic recognition that lets the learner advance to more complex activities. In reading, these activities culminate in comprehension. In mathematics, they culminate in problem solving.

Examples of basic fact tests are:

Example 1: Look at these flashcards and tell me the answers:

$3 \times 3 = $ _____     $7 \times 6 = $ _____     $5 \times 9 = $ _____

Example 2: Write the answers to these problems as quickly and accurately as you can:

$$\begin{array}{ccccc} 6 & 4 & 3 & 1 & 9 \\ +2 & +3 & +1 & +1 & +6 \\ \hline \end{array}$$

Example 3: Count out loud to 50.

As can be deduced from these examples, evaluation of basic facts can be written or verbal. It can also include the notion of rate, e.g., "as quickly as you can," "in your fastest time."

### Evaluation Components

Each additional component, e.g., written or oral, timed or untimed, gives the teacher more information about the child's flexibility in using or reading the basic facts tested. The evaluative catch is to be sure that the additional information is instructionally valuable. If, for example, you were interested in determining if a child could identify circles, squares, and triangles, you probably would design items that required the child to identify those shapes. Identification tasks usually require activities like marking, selecting, and pointing out, any of which can be done either orally or in writing. Unfortunately, because these concepts are so rudimentary, there is a tendency to complicate the child's action, i.e., "draw" a circle, square, or triangle. By changing the word *mark* to *draw*, you have asked a fundamentally different question. A *mark* question requires a simple discrimination task. A *draw* question requires the child to create some desired product. But a production task is simply not necessary if you really need a simple discrimination.

## Task Demands for Handicapped Children

Additionally, attention must be paid to the task demands relative to the skills of the child. Some handicapped and nonhandicapped children show delays in the fine-motor skills of writing; others, e.g., some cerebral palsied children, cannot write at all. Production tasks or tasks that require manual dexterity may place unrealistic demands on these children. Results from tasks that are not sensitive to the skill levels of the child most likely will result in a misleading interpretation of actual task knowledge. Knowledge of task demands, children's skill relative to task response, and specific information to be evaluated apply equally to the basic skills, algorithms, and problem-solving areas of mathematics.

## EVALUATION OF SKILL IN USING ALGORITHMS

## Definitions

Algorithms are the natural extension of basic number fact computations. While number facts require simple associations, algorithms are the series of separate steps required in more complex calculations such as long division or addition of fractions with unlike denominators. To use algorithms, children must know what steps to perform, perform them in the proper order, and recall needed number facts accurately (Resnick & Ford, 1981).

Doing problems or computations that require algorithms is somewhat similar to using phonics skills in determining a new word. Just as the individual sounds are previously learned in phonics, the number facts are already within the learner's grasp. With phonics, a reader uses systematic rules for applying sounds both in terms of the isolated sound and in an acceptable sequence for blending. The ultimate conclusion is the production of the appropriate word. So too with the application of algorithms.

Using isolated number facts, a child must also follow a prescribed step-by-step sequence to arrive at the correct solution of a complex computation.

Examples of tests using basic algorithms are:

Example 1: Solve the following problems:

$$14 \quad\quad 36 \quad\quad 930$$
$$+14 \quad\quad +6 \quad\quad -127 \quad\quad 52\,\overline{)3895}$$

Example 2: Compute the following:

$$\frac{5}{6} = \frac{}{12} \quad\quad \frac{1}{3} = \frac{}{9} \quad\quad \frac{3}{7} = \frac{}{14}$$

Example 3: Calculate the following:

$$80\% \times 50 =$$
$$160\% \times 10 =$$
$$25\% \times 73 =$$
$$9\% \times 100 =$$

Algorithms permit the user to perform those calculations that require more than memorization of a single idea or association. A lot of time is spent teaching algorithms in elementary school. Generally the teacher shows the learners a standard algorithm, e.g., carrying or regrouping in addition. The child is expected to memorize the sequence and then apply the algorithm in various problems.

## Conceptual versus Procedural Learning

Many educators have tried to differentiate between skill at using algorithms and actual understanding of the concepts involved in the algorithm. While some have felt that the teaching of understanding of the algorithm is essential for correct usage, others have not. Those who espouse conceptual understanding often stress that the abstract nature of the math relationship needs to be presented more concretely.

**Manipulatives**—To this end, manipulatives such as sticks and blocks are used to represent the arithmetic concepts. Gagné (1983), a prominent educational psychologist, believes that computation, even at the level of algorithm, is entirely a concrete task. He has written that the introduction of "sticks, blocks or other objects as a means of performing the central computational task ... has absolutely no advantage" (p. 14). He believes that the concrete materials of computational operations are the numerals and operations signs printed on the page.

Interestingly enough, from examination of children's work, the evidence is clear that children often calculate by the methods they are taught, but understand little about them (Ginsburg, 1976). Understanding, then, must not be equated with the ability to follow a predesignated sequence leading to the solution of a given problem. The ability to manipulate an arithmetic algorithm correctly, with or without specified concrete objects, can develop with or without understanding. While understanding a concept may help a child understand an algorithm, understanding of the algorithm may come later and thus would have little if any effect on the development of basic concepts (Slesnick, 1982).

**Educational implications**—The educational and evaluation implications are clear. For some children, conceptual knowledge of the algorithm may not occur with initial teaching or perhaps ever. Yet many of these children can be expected to use the algorithm in a functionally positive way. After all, how many times do you think of the concept of place value (other than the decimal point as you balance your checkbook)? To wait for conceptual understanding of any given algorithm may actually prevent the child from using that and more complex algorithms in advanced arithmetic and mathematical problem solving.

## EVALUATING PROBLEM SOLVING

### Definitions

Children use both basic facts and algorithms in problem solving. Usually the problems are called *word problems* or *story problems*. Story problems require learners to interpret the words of the problem, set up a representational mathematical calculation, and apply relevant procedures (Resnick & Ford, 1981). To problem-solve efficiently, the learner must be able to concentrate on problem-solving processes. Basic facts and computation procedures must be firmly established and readily available. Time spent on hunting down facts or on trying to reconstruct the steps of an algorithm is time wasted, especially since this time should be used to focus on the act of problem solving itself (Driscoll, 1980).

### Renewed Instructional Emphasis

Instruction in problem solving has gained considerable stature. In fact, problem solving has been earmarked by the National Council of Teachers of Mathematics as the most important target for mathematics teaching in the

1980s (National Council of Teachers of Mathematics, 1981; Newell, 1983). This newly placed emphasis has stemmed from a number of sources, not the least of which is the National Assessment of Educational Progress (NAEP). NAEP has presented strong evidence suggesting that students are unable to choose correct operations in problem solving. Computational weakness did not contribute nearly as much to the children's ability to solve problems as was expected (Zweng, 1979). The data show that "students know how to add and subtract, but not when" (p. 161) (Hodgkinson, 1979).

**Identifying critical skills**—Skills to be evaluated in solving word problems can be broadly classified into four different abilities (Ballew & Cunningham, 1982):

1. Reading the problem
2. Setting up the problem in order for the necessary computation to be completed
3. Completing the necessary computation, and
4. Integrating reading, interpreting the problem, and computing into the total solution of the word problem.

Assuming that the child can read, the results of the national survey strongly indicate that many of our children cannot perform steps 2 and 4.

What makes these findings so unpalatable is that recent research studies have shown that children can solve problems even before they come to school. Unfortunately, the introduction of number sequences, manipulative materials, and various other techniques is not always carefully considered in relation to the developmental level of the child (Suydam, 1982). As a result, problems that were intrinsically simple for a child may become confusing and complex tasks with no apparent logical conclusion—at least, none that are logical to the child. Implications for content evaluation are clearly strong for all children, but especially so for handicapped and slow learners.

**Instructional implications**—Four other points supported by research (Suydam, 1982) also have explicit instructional implications for problem solving:

1. Knowing problem-solving strategies or heuristics promotes the learner's ability to solve problems.
2. Children can complete one-step problems much easier.
3. Reading skill is related to problem solving but children may be unable to solve problems even if they know all the words.
4. Calculations can assist children by expanding their storehouse of problem solving strategies. (p. 59)

Problem solving, then, consists of more than simple memorization. It demands the use of various strategies and the ability to choose appropriate operations.

Examples of test items using problem solving are:

Example 1:
> Jem had 7 marbles. He gave 3 to his sister. How many did he have left?

Example 2:
> Scout ran 15 miles on Monday, 10 miles on Tuesday, and 7 miles on Thursday. How many miles did she run all together?

Example 3:
> Atticus collects books and puts them on his shelves. He puts 10 books on each shelf. He has 6 shelves filled with books. How many books does he have on the shelves?

To solve items like these, the learner needs carefully guided discussion, interaction among students, and an explicit examination of strategies used (Van de Walle & Thompson, 1981).


# DIAGNOSTIC MATHEMATICS TOOLS

## Conceptual Analysis

To determine the teaching needs of the child, a teacher must perform a diagnostic evaluation of math content. Instead of stating what is wrong, true math diagnosis tells you why something went wrong. For most evaluations, sadly, the focus is on the what and not the why. Both commercial and teacher-made evaluations usually account for the correctness of a response. In fact, standardized and informal tests may actually misrepresent children's competence (Ginsburg, 1976). While production of an accurate response is clearly a fundamental goal of math instruction, the logic of the child's thinking is equally important. The only way to understand the child's logic is through observing his or her responses, both successful and unsuccessful, and attempting to interpret the reasoning (Freudenthal, 1981). Analysis of the child's reasoning used to solve arithmetic computation or problems allows the teacher to determine not only the child's ability to complete math assignments, but also the degree to which the child has grasped the concept behind the solution.

Take the example of Calpurnia and Alexandra. Both girls worked the problem 17 + 26. They arrived at different answers, each of which was wrong. Calpurnia determined that 17 + 26 = 313; Alexandra computed 17

+ 26 to be 88. An analysis of their logic shows very different problems. Calpurnia simply had no regard for place value. She added 7 + 6 to get 13, and then she added 1 + 2 to get 3. Ergo:

$$
\begin{array}{r}
17 \\
+\,26 \\
\hline
13 \\
3 \\
\hline
313
\end{array}
$$

Alexandra was operating from a different card deck. She did not even understand the first phase of the algorithm, i.e., vertical computation. She could calculate only horizontally, regardless of a problem's format. For Alexandra 2 + 6 = 8 and 1 + 7 = 8; ergo 88. To be effective, instruction for Calpurnia and Alexandra will need to take into account each child's logic.

## Invented Procedures

Interestingly enough, the creative computation procedures used by Calpurnia and Alexandra were only noticed because they arrived at incorrect responses. Actually common standard algorithms are just one of the methods children use to calculate. Many children compute by using invented procedures, i.e., methods the child devises, in part, that are probably based on school learning (Ginsburg, 1976).

**Use of previous math knowledge**—Invented strategies, characterized by the use of previous math knowledge, allow the learner to assimilate past knowledge in current problem-solving or computation strategies. Awareness of a child's invented strategies can provide a successful transition to future or new math knowledge. By building upon what the child knows, the teacher can begin to show the child the relational nature of math. The teacher can also refine strategies that work well at a fairly unsophisticated level, but may actually interfere with learning at more advanced levels. For instance, addition by counting is fine for beginning computations but can be quite cumbersome for multistep algorithms like two- and three-digit multiplication problems.

**New math learning**—Basically, children gain most new mathematical knowledge by constructing for themselves new organizations of concepts and new procedures for doing mathematical operations. New information takes on significance and is likely to be retained only to the degree that it can be incorporated into the learner's organized and connected systems of knowledge (Resnick, 1980). By watching the child work and asking from time to time how he or she arrives at a solution, the teacher can get the kind of diagnostic information so crucial for math concept building.

## Error Analysis

**Reflections of conceptual strategies**—Errors in basic facts and algorithms often reflect the child's math conceptual strategies. No one sets out to teach children incorrect algorithms, yet those having difficulty with arithmetic often turn out to be using systematic routines that unfortunately yield incorrect responses. More than likely these children either forgot some part of the conventional routine or were initially confused by some aspect of the teaching of the correct sequence of operations (Resnick, 1980). Given that student errors are the result of previous mathematics experiences, Radatz (1980) has identified several trends in error research. Student errors:

- are causally determined and very often systematic;
- are persistent and will last for several school years, unless the teacher intervenes pedagogically;
- can be analyzed and described as error techniques;
- can be derived, as to their causes, from certain difficulties experienced by students while receiving and processing information in the mathematical learning process; or
- can be derived from effects of the interaction of variables acting on mathematical education (teacher, curriculum, student, academic achievement, etc. (p. 16)

Children's math errors, then, are essentially systematic, long-term (unless corrected), descriptive, and usually causally related to some aspect of math instruction. Armed with this information, math teaching can focus on error patterns with the optimistic note that proper instruction can remediate even long-term problems.

**Types of errors**—Errors can be further analyzed by type. Engelhardt (1982) has described four computational error classes used in diagnostic teaching. They are:

1. Mechanical errors—responses resulting from motor or perceptual-motor problems such as misformed symbols ꞏ9 (Is this numeral a 9 or a 7?) or misaligned symbols (e.g., $\frac{265}{+37}$ ).
2. Careless errors—responses stemming from lack of task engagement; for example, a situation in which a child is unable or unwilling to attend to the task.

3. Conceptual errors—responses derived from absent or incorrect concepts or principles. An example would be Alexandra's creative approach to addition (page 338) or an inappropriate concept of 0 ($0 + 1 = 0$, $0 + 8 = 0$, $0 + 254 = 0$).

4. Procedural errors—responses produced from misordered or inappropriate procedures, e.g., subtracting the minuend from the subtrahend (the top number from the bottom one) $635 - 87 = 652$.

These error types can be found in isolation or in combination. Much like the situations encountered by Sherlock Holmes, the problems are most often elementary in nature. The solutions, of course, are made through logical deductions, and not found on the response sheet of any particular test.

**Diagnostic techniques**—Two diagnostic techniques that can be used to identify patterns of behavior in problem solving are "think aloud" and "reflection" (Lester, 1980). "Think aloud" is just that. The child works on a problem and describes out loud what he or she is doing. "Reflection" is much the same but occurs after the problem has been completed. The child thinks back to what he or she did and then describes the math process introspectively. While these two approaches are not foolproof, they can contribute to the teacher's sense of what the child is mentally processing. With these approaches, the teacher must take into account the child's linguistic competence. For some children, oral expression is not particularly a strong point. Children who have difficulty expressing themselves may not provide a clear picture of their math processing, but every little bit of information can be of diagnostic help. Even if the verbal picture is not clear, the teacher can couple the description with information derived from written work to form at least a tentative hypothesis. The hypothesis can then be judged against teaching goals, objectives, and student performance. In other words, the greater the child's language problem, the less information you'll receive from self-report. Given this situation, you'll need to pay even greater attention to errors as they emerge over time in the child's written material.

## TYPES OF EVALUATION TOOLS

Math evaluation is an ongoing process that enables teachers to monitor and improve an instructional program while it is in process. Evaluation data routinely allow the teacher to make decisions and form opinions about student growth. Fortunately, numerous kinds and levels of evaluation materials are available: readiness tests, achievement tests, and inspection of daily class-room activities are a few of them. The tools themselves can also be catego-rized into general or survey; specific, individual, or group. The key to using evaluation data is to be certain that the tools measure what you need to know and that you can educationally do something about what you find out. More than likely the more directly you ask the evaluation question, the greater are your chances of discovering your answer. Furthermore, the more simplified the data-collection process, the more likely useful answers will be derived.

## READINESS TESTS

### Specific Meaning in Mathematics

A readiness test, by definition, should separate those learners who are ca-pable of learning a particular concept from those who are not (Hiebert & Carpenter, 1982). Because of the logical nature of arithmetic, all tests should be broadly considered readiness tests for the next concept. Yet we have spe-cial uses for the term *readiness*. In arithmetic instruction, readiness has come to focus on two somewhat different aspects of learning. One has to do with the content of arithmetic itself, e.g., the ability to count, recognize number quantities, etc. The other readiness area is related to cognitive development, usually à la Piaget, e.g., the child's ability to perform certain tasks associated with such cognitive developmental milestones as conservation and opera-tional thought.

### Skill Mastery versus Cognitive Development

Skills associated with the arithmetic notion of readiness are often taught in preschool, kindergarten, and even first grade. These skills are considered by some to be precursors of arithmetic performance. The importance of prepar-ing children for later math experiences has given a great emphasis to the readiness stage (Johnson, 1979). Items that test readiness skills are often found in the first part of basic achievement tests. The *Wide Range Achieve-ment Test* (Jastak & Jastak, 1978), for example, has a small readiness compo-nent that can be given prior to evaluating basic facts and algorithmic skills. A fairly broad list of readiness areas is presented in Table 11.2. Readiness tests accompany most preschool and first grade basal math texts. Teacher-made readiness tests can also focus on the content of kindergarten through first-grade texts.

**Timeline for skill development**—That the child needs to be skilled in read-iness areas is not debatable. What is debatable is when the child must possess these skills. How long does the child with counting skills from 1 through 20

Table 11.2
Readiness Areas in Arithmetic

Counting
Number recognition
Identification of number groups
One-to-one correspondence
Matching number symbols to objects
Recognition of number symbols

wait to add 1 + 1? The answer, of course, can be found by analyzing the minimum skills needed by the child before proceeding to the next task in the sequence. A child does not need to be able to count to 20 to be able to conceptually comprehend that 1 + 1 = 2. The child does need to know counting from 1 to 2; number recognition of 1 and 2; numerical correspondence for 1 and 2. With these readiness concepts firmly in place, the child is now prepared to learn " +," " =," and "1 + 1 = 2." Perhaps the most important point to be made in evaluating arithmetic readiness is simply to use test results as a means for determining the next teaching concept. Don't wait for readiness. As soon as the child's performance indicates mastery of one concept, it is time to teach a new one, i.e., the child is ready for teaching.

**Piagetian theory**—Readiness à la Piaget presents a different sort of problem. Piagetian theory as applied to math readiness is developmental. The theory emphasizes the interaction between intellectual activity and the kind of mental organization that characterizes children at various levels of development. The ways by which children organize their experiences develop sequentially and in progressively more sophisticated and well-defined stages. During the normal school years (K–12), children evolve through three stages: preoperational, concrete operations, and formal operational levels. Each of these stages is associated with the child's ability to learn. Different levels allow for different types of learning. Theoretically, the more advanced the child is in the three stages, the more sophisticated the learning can be. Piagetian readiness applies to all levels and focuses especially on the type of thought (preoperational, operational, or formal) demanded by the mathematics problem. Readiness in this sense is not limited to pre-arithmetic skills, but encompasses all mathematics skills. Evaluation measures for the three stages are fairly complicated and not found in typical math achievement tests. If evaluative information is desired, a chat with a school psychologist or Piagetian scholar is a good starting point.

**Research findings**—Once again, the teacher must ask if he or she needs to know whether the students are preoperational, operational, or formal thinkers. Some Piagetian scholars believe that identification of thinking levels has very important instructional implications; others are not so sure. Apparently people in all cultures sooner or later develop at least concrete operational thought, but the evidence for teaching formal thought is not yet in (Resnick & Ford, 1981). This is no doubt in part because scholars are not yet sure which tasks actually reflect formal operational thinking. If the scientists aren't clear, we teachers may not need to feel neglectful if we pass by Piagetian readiness evaluation in the regular classroom. Interestingly enough, results of several studies of concrete operational tasks (conservation, transition reasoning, and other concrete reasoning abilities), and mathematics achievement showed little relationship. These studies demonstrated that most math tasks can be mastered by children who have not yet developed concrete operational thinking (Hiebert & Carpenter, 1982). To rephrase, children who, according to Piagetian readiness criteria, were not ready to learn certain mathematics concepts, forged ahead and learned the concepts anyway. Based on this empirical evidence, waiting for Piagetian readiness does not appear to be the best use of a child's mathematical instruction time.

## FORMAL/COMMERCIAL TESTS

### Normative Measures

Formal tests are those designed to measure the child's performance against some prespecified criterion or standard. Most formal tests used to evaluate mathematics in the classroom are normative; they compare the child's performance to the performance of a typical group of children who are of the same general age, experience, and cultural background. The most common type of normative tests is the achievement test.

**Achievement tests**—Achievement tests can be given individually but are primarily designed to be given to large groups. The most commonly given ones are the *Iowa Test of Basic Skills* (Hieronymus, Lindquist, & Hoover, 1982), the *Metropolitan Achievement Tests (Comprehension Tests and Basic Skills)* (Prescott, Balow, Hogan, & Farr, 1978), and the *Stanford Achievement Test* (Madden, Gardner, & Collins, 1983). Achievement tests typically result in grade equivalence scores, percentiles, standard scores, and occasionally mental age equivalency scores. They usually provide a good classroom screening. A very high or low score is an immediate flag for additional testing.

**Mini-error analysis**—Another equally valuable use of the achievement test is analyzing individual items missed by particular children. In essence, a mini-error analysis can be completed on each child's test. Error patterns on achievement tests, while certainly not complete, can point the teacher in the direction of additional testing within a specific area. Table 11.3 shows the responses of a child on the *Wide Range Achievement Test* (Jastak & Jastak, 1978). An analysis of this protocol shows that the test, like most achievement tests, samples only a small amount of the content covered at various grade levels. Even from this small sample, the teacher can begin to get a better idea of this student's math needs. In the example in Table 11.3, the teacher can draw the following conclusions.

Student needs additional testing in:
1. Multiplication of single-digit numbers: $4 \times 2 = 6$; $23 \times 3 = 26$
2. Regrouping in both addition and subtraction:

$$\begin{array}{ccc} 28 & 75 & 452 \\ -19 & +\ 8 & 137 \\ & & +245 \end{array}$$

3. Basic multiplication and division facts: $4 \times 2 = 8$;

$$\begin{array}{r} 23 \\ \times 3 \\ \hline 26 \end{array}$$

Unless otherwise noted student needs no testing in:
1. Basic addition and subtraction facts:

$1 + 1 = 2$, $4 - 1 = 3$

$$\begin{array}{cc} 6 & 5 \\ +2 & -3 \\ \hline 8 & 2 \end{array}$$

2. Addition without grouping:

$$\begin{array}{r} 32 \\ 24 \\ +40 \\ \hline 96 \end{array}$$

Postpone testing in all other advanced areas until the student has mastered areas indicated for testing.

In the areas indicated for further testing, the teacher can expand upon both the number and type of items given in the original tests. In the example in Table 11.3, only three items required grouping:

$$\begin{array}{ccc} 28 & 75 & 452 \\ -19 & +\ 8 & 137 \\ & & +245 \end{array}$$

---

Table 11.3
Sample Math Protocol

---

| $1 + 1 = 2$ | $6$ | $5$ | $33$ | $4 \times 2 = 6$ | $23$ |
|---|---|---|---|---|---|
| $4 - 1 = 3$ | $+2$ | $-3$ | $24$ | | $\times 3$ |
| | $8$ | $2$ | $+40$ | | $26$ |
| | | | $106$ | | |

| $28$ | $75$ | $452$ |
|---|---|---|
| $-19$ | $+8$ | $137$ |
| $11$ | $713$ | $+245$ |
| | | $71212$ |

Source: J.E. Jastak & S.R. Jastak, *Wide Range Achievement Test.* Wilmington, DE: Jastak Associates, 1978.

---

The teacher can broaden the type and number of examples of regrouping problems by difficulty level. Items like $75$ (double digit plus single digit) can be expanded to include: $\quad +8$

double digit + double digit

$$27$$
$$+58$$

triple digit + single digit

$$396$$
$$+\phantom{0}7$$

triple digit + double digit

$$895$$
$$+\phantom{0}28$$

triple digit with zero + double digit

$$706$$
$$+\phantom{0}27$$

## Relation of Scores to Curricula

The degree to which the original items are expanded is somewhat related to the child's expected grade level. A second grader, for instance, may not be expected to regroup triple-digit numbers with zero, while a third grader would be expected to do the more sophisticated regrouping problems. You would also not expect a child who can't complete double digit + double digit regrouping to proceed to more advanced problems. Evaluation is, after all, information seeking, not a test of courage under overwhelming, impossible odds.

While no magic number of items is preferable, a good choice might be three items of each type. If one item is missed, perhaps a combination error is at fault, but at least a warning note is sounded. Two or three items missed is a fairly clear direction for additional instruction.

Before arithmetic tests take on the hallowed glow of math diagnostic nirvana, a few words of caution must be expressed. Freeman, Kuhs, Knappen, and Porter (1982), when examining the four most widely used tests (Stanford, Iowa, Metropolitan, and CTBS), found that all but the CTBS gradually deemphasized place value across grade levels.

1. Standardized tests at any given grade level do not all measure the same content.

2. Getting an answer correct on the one item that assesses a particular skill, e.g., division with remainders, hardly demonstrates mastery of that skill and others related but untested.

3. An incorrect answer may or may not indicate the child's knowledge. A basic fact rather than the algorithm could be the reason for an incorrect response to a three digit by two digit multiplication problem.

4. Grade equivalency scores can be very misleading. Freeman et al. (1982) state this problem very well:

> A third grade student with a grade equivalent score of 6.2, e.g., has a score which is equal to the average score on the third grade test for students in the second month of 6th grade. A common misinterpretation is illustrated by concluding that a 3rd grade student with a grade equiavlent of 6.2 is capable of doing 6th grade work. A child who scores 6.2 equivalent on a test administered in the third grade has merely demonstrated a high level of achievement on 3rd grade content. This is no assurance that this youngster can solve such problems as subtraction with remainders, or perform other operations which are typically tested at the sixth grade. (p. 54)

## Individually Administered Achievement Tests

Another form of achievement test has been designed primarily for use with individuals. These tests are more commonly associated with special education classes, but could be used in regular classes as well. The content does not differ significantly from the content of instruction in the regular class. The distinctive difference between tests designed for individual administration and those designed for group administration is the number and variety of items asked. Because individually administered tests are longer, they typically take more time to administer.

Some commonly used tests in special education that are certainly applicable to regular classroom math settings are the *Peabody Individual Achievement Tests* (Dunn & Markwardt, 1970) and the *KeyMath* (Connolly, Nachtman, & Pritchett, 1976). Both of these tests lend themselves to a mini-error analysis.

*KeyMath*—The *KeyMath* has another feature in that all the test items are coded to specific well-stated math objectives. The *KeyMath* also consists of 14 specific subtests grouped by three broad categories: content, operations, and applications. These categories are roughly analogous to basic facts, algorithms, and problem solving. Table 11.4 lists the 14 *KeyMath* subtests. Each of the subtests can be given individually and interpreted against the child's current grade level. Subtests of the *KeyMath* can be especially useful when the group achievement test omits particularly relevant areas like time or money.

**Table 11.4**
**Fourteen KeyMath Subtests**

CONTENT
- Numeration
- Fractions
- Geometry

OPERATIONS
- Addition
- Subtraction
- Multiplication
- Division
- Mental Computation
- Numerical Reasoning

APPLICATIONS
- Word Problems
- Missing Elements
- Money
- Measurement
- Time

Source: A. Connolly, W. Nachtman, & E. Prichett, *KeyMath Diagnostic Arithmetic Test.* Circle Pines, MN: American Guidance Service, 1976.

**Other diagnostic measures**—Other tests like the *KeyMath* that provide a criterion system in addition to or in place of normative information are the *Diagnostic Mathematics Inventory* (Gessell, 1977), the Math subtest of the *Brigance* (Brigance, 1977), and the *Stanford Diagnostic Mathematics Test* (SDMT) (Beatty, Madden, Gardner, & Karlsen, 1976). All of these tests assess skill development strengths and weaknesses in mathematics for the individual child. Because the individual's needs are identified, the teacher has a clearer understanding of the child's instructional needs. However, reliance on these tests alone can be somewhat misleading, too. The best use of these tests is in conjunction with teacher observation and in some cases expanded area evaluations of problems incorrectly completed.

With the exception of the SDMT, which can also be given to a large group, the individually administered diagnostic math tests would best be used with children having problems in math or performing at a math level much more advanced than most of the students in the class. Tests of this sort are really designed as a part of a system used to develop individualized math programs.

## INFORMAL MEASURES

Informal measures usually provide the teacher with comparisons of the child's work to prespecified goals or objectives. Informal math measures stem from three basic sources:

- Daily classwork
- Informal survey tests
- Informal specific tests

All of these data sources lend themselves to error analysis. The basic difference between the three measures is the type of information given.

### Daily Classwork

Analysis of daily work reveals how the child works over time and in a less supervised or time-structured situation. Problems tangential, but nonetheless relevant, to math instruction can be found and remediated by an analysis of daily work.

**Tangential problems**—Take the example of Kari Dee. Day after day she did not complete her math classwork. She took her work home every night, completed it perfectly, and continued to chatter away her math time with her desk partner. Even when moved to a desk *sans* partner, Kari Dee's math pattern continued as before. On math achievement tests she had scored well into the average and above average range. Lest one be suspicious of Kari Dee's ownership of her math work, a conversation with Mom testified to Kari Dee's honesty.

The conversation also revealed the math-related problem. As her mom explained, Kari would do a single problem, then ask her mother if the problem was correct, which it typically was. Kari Dee would then say that she couldn't do the next problem. Her mother would tell her that she could. Given this reassurance from Mom, Kari would complete one more problem. This pattern would continue until the whole assignment was completed. Kari Dee did all the work tensely and was seemingly paralyzed without continuous positive feedback from her mother. (She could complete tasks on the achievement test because the tests were highly time-structured and couldn't be taken home to be finished.) Mother and teacher both appreciated that Kari had math skills. They also recognized that her skills were not functional, i.e., the Kari/Mom math team was not a viable option for the real world. With some cooperative planning on the part of teacher and parent, Kari was systematically allowed to bring less and less work home. Mother also systematically reduced the amount of feedback given. Instead of responding to one problem at a time, Mom would wait for two to be completed, then three, then a row, and finally the whole practice page. Within about 3 weeks, Kari Dee began to find that math problems could be finished in school—which brought her both teacher praise and self-satisfaction.

**Rate of work**—A more obvious use of daily classwork is the direct relationship between the number of problems completed and the way they were completed. The number of problems refers to the rate. Assuming no other competing social problems (i.e., garrulous neighbors or politicians-in-training) or academic problems (algorithms or basic fact knowledge), a measure of rate can add valuable teaching information. In Kari Dee's case, rate seemed to be the obvious problem but was not. For other children, rate is the problem but not an obvious one. Labels like "lazy" and "disinterested" and all sorts of special education tags are often quickly given to the child who doesn't complete classwork in the allotted time.

The most common cause (barring the academic and social ones mentioned above) for slow rate is lack of familiarity with the task at hand. The child understands what needs to be done but hasn't worked enough problems to be proficient. Two solutions are to allow the child more time in the math activity during the day or to increase the number of days on which the child can practice the same activity. While both solutions involve use of more time rather than less, the sequential nature of mathematics, especially at the elementary level, demands a well-established foundation. This strong foundation will allow for better problem-solving rates later.

**Timings**

Daily or weekly timings on certain key facts or algorithms can also be a way to measure as well as increase rate. Timings are most often taken on number facts and one- or two-step algorithms. For ease of measurement and kindness to the children's system, timing (especially those involving number facts) are usually restricted to 1 minute. For more complex algorithms, timings can be extended to 5 or 10 minutes.

**Record keeping**—For ease of record keeping, children can keep copies of their work in a special folder. The folder can have the work on one side and a graph on the other. The dated chart can allow you, the child, and the parents to analyze daily or weekly progress on the timed skill.

**Criterion**—How many problems are enough to move to the next set or concept? A general rule of thumb for written number facts is the completion of one fact per second; in other words, about 58 to 60 correct number facts in one minute. This rule would vary depending on the child's response mode. A child who is motorically handicapped or who is very young may not have the fine-motor skills to complete 60 items per minute. An oral response would be faster, and more facts could be completed.

To determine the most appropriate rate for your class, time the entire class on a concept. Eliminate the five highest and the five lowest scores and average the remaining ones. The average is your "best guess rate" for your particular class. This rate can be used for all timings of material in the same class of materials. For example, if you found your best guess rate originally on simple addition facts, this rate can also be safely used in other fact areas, but not in simple algorithm areas. Table 11.5 shows how to find a best guess rate for number facts in a typical 28-member classroom.

**Fear of timings**—Care must be taken when conducting daily or weekly timings. For children who are averse to timings, you may need to assess rate in a fundamentally different format or perhaps not at all. Surreptitious rate taking can be done by noting how long a child takes to complete a task, rather than by giving a specific amount of time in which to work. If, for example, Dewey begins a 10-problem paper at 9:05 and completes it at 9:30, he has taken 25 minutes. This means that Dewey has taken about 2½ minutes per problem. If the best guess rate was 54 problems in 1 minute, Dewey would be expected to complete approximately 1,350 problems in 25 minutes (54:1 minute = 1350:25 minutes). By these standards Dewey is very, very slow. Naturally, if he was this slow, you wouldn't even bother to time him, but the principle for finding rate is still the same.

1. Find the total amount of time the child needs to complete the assignment.

Table 11.5
Finding Best Guess Rate for Classroom Data

| Student | Score |
|---|---|
| Corde | 58 |
| Minna | 46 |
| Gigi | 44 |
| Antone | 48 |
| Valeria | 55 |
| Albert | 56 |
| Rugus | 49 |
| Viorica | 60 |
| Doina | 56 |
| Cornelia | 59 |
| Sam | 48 |
| Vlada | 65 |
| Mason | 61 |
| Rickie | 57 |
| Lucas | 59 |
| Lydia | 48 |
| Elfrida | 49 |
| Max + | 60 |
| | 978 |

**Procedure:**
*1. Eliminate the 5 lowest scores.
*2. Eliminate the 5 highest scores.
3. Add the remaining scores.
4. Divide the sum by the number of scores left (18).
5. Arrive at a best guess rate for your class.
*Steps 1 and 2 are not illustrated.

Best Guess Rate = $\dfrac{54.3}{18\overline{)978}}$

2. Divide the time by the number of problems to get an average time per problem.

3. If a best guess rate or standard has been determined, compare the standard number of problems and the rate of time to an expected standard and the time it took the child to complete the task, e.g., 54:1 minute = X:25 minutes.

The purpose for taking rate data is to determine that the child is at an appropriate instructional point. Once a rate signalling proficiency has been reached, the natural decision is to move to the next concept. For children with histories of "poor" learning or "memory problems," you may wish to have them reach the best guess rate 2 or 3 days in a row before moving on to the next concept.

## Error Analysis With Daily Work

How a child completes tasks is also found by examining daily work. Error analysis of daily work can show you very quickly what needs to be reviewed or even retaught on the following days. It is identical in form to an error analysis completed on any specific evaluation measure. An error analysis checksheet kept with the child's folders is a convenient and quick method of record keeping. Table 11.6 gives an example of an error analysis record-keeping sheet for Wayne in multiplication.

**Record-keeping sheets**—Because arithmetic skills can be categorized so easily, a general all-purpose record-keeping error analysis checksheet can be used for most children. The purpose of dating the checksheet is to provide once again an objective and clearly defined record of each child's progress. Types of errors that can be noted in addition, subtraction, and division are presented in Table 11.7.

**Checklists**—Checklists for most areas can typically be found in arithmetic methods texts or even some basal arithmetic series. They can also be developed around the basal text used in the classroom. If, for example, the unit is covering fractions, a checklist can quickly be developed around the objectives associated with that particular unit and the text content for your class. A

**Table 11.6**
Error Analysis Checksheet for Multiplication

### ERROR ANALYSIS CHECKSHEET

Name: _Wayne_                    Teacher: _Mr. Bellow_

Content: _Multiplication_    Date: _Spring 1985_

|  | DATE | | |
|---|---|---|---|
| Error in fact | | | |
| Carried wrong number | | | |
| Error in addition | | | |
| Forgot to carry | | | |
| Error in writing product | | | |
| Used the wrong process | | | |
| Error in algorithm | 2/17 | 2/18 | |
|   Multiplied out of sequence | | | |
|   Forgot to add a carried number | | | |
|   Skipped a number | | | |
|   Improper placement of columns | | | |
| Problems with zero | | | |
|   As a multiplier | | | 2/20 |
|   As a multiplicant | | | |
| No errors | | | 2/19 |

**Table 11.7**
Error Analysis Lists Checksheets

**Addition**
  Errors in facts
  Errors in carrying
    "Lost" carried number
    Forgot to add carried number
    Carried wrong number
    Wrote carried number in columns
    Added the carried number twice
    Carried the wrong number
  Problems with zero
    Carrying zero
    Adding numbers to zero
  Problems with column
    Lost place
    Ignored place value
    Failure to follow algorithm
    Wrote same digit in two columns

**Division**
  Error in facts
  Errors in carrying
    Multiplicative
    Subtractive
  Problems with zero
    In the divisor
    In the dividend
    In carrying/borrowing
  Problems with columns
    Misplaced alignment

**Subtraction**
  Errors in facts
  Errors in borrowing
    Failed to borrow
    Subtracted the top number from the bottom
    Skipped over columns
    Didn't subtract from borrowed number
    Misplaced alignment
  Problems with zero
    Zero at the unit place
    Zero at the tens place
    Zero at the hundreds place
    Zero between two numbers
  Problems with column
    Lost place
    Ignored column
    Failure to follow algorithm
    Misplaced alignment

fractions checklist developed from a third grade text would be very different from one developed for a sixth grade text. Some areas would overlap, e.g., errors in basic number facts. Yet the sixth grade fractions checksheet would be more inclusive and contain much more sophisticated material. Daily or weekly checklists, however unsophisticated, provide a source of informal evaluation that can be compared to class progress and other formal or informal evaluations.

## Informal Tests

**Coding to basal text**—Informal survey or specific math tests are those that provide a sample of problems, but are not formally coded to norms or grade levels. Often informal tests measure specific skill areas or areas associated with texts or kits.

Figure 11.1 shows an informal survey test. This test has been coded directly to the math basal text. In fact, the items have been taken from the text itself. Questions 1 through 3, for example, deal with 2 and 5 as factors and are taken from pages 281, 282, and 284, respectively. The informal survey specifies a particular unit in the text: multiplication of 2 and 5. The items have been coded to topics, i.e., 2 and 5 as factors, number line, commutative property, and name product or factor. The $+/-$ column is a code to indicate correct $(+)$ or incorrect $(-)$. By examining the coded responses, the teacher can get a very quick notion of when to enter the student in the chapter or remediate if necessary. Figure 11.1 provides an example of a coded pre/posttest on Ellis' work. Ellis was in and out of various schools for the first 2 years of his rather spotty academic career. His knowledge of mathematics reflected all this activity. Ellis had learned many concepts in isolation, but he never really had the chance to complete any sequence systematically. He was adept at what he had learned, but he hadn't been exposed to very many concepts. To put Ellis on page 281 on chapter 10 would have been unfair and also might have produced a behavior problem where none had existed before. (Perhaps boredom rather than necessity is the true mother of invention—if not of certain categories of special education classes.) What Ellis needed instructionally was to learn the commutation property. This need was reflected in his informal survey.

What the the informal survey can demonstrate so clearly is the relationship between the child's knowledge and the material at hand. In using an informal survey coded to class materials, the teacher can move directly into instructional activities without initially having to search out teaching material. (Eventually the text may need to be supplemented, but that discovery occurs during instruction.)

**Figure 11.1**
Informal Math Survey Test

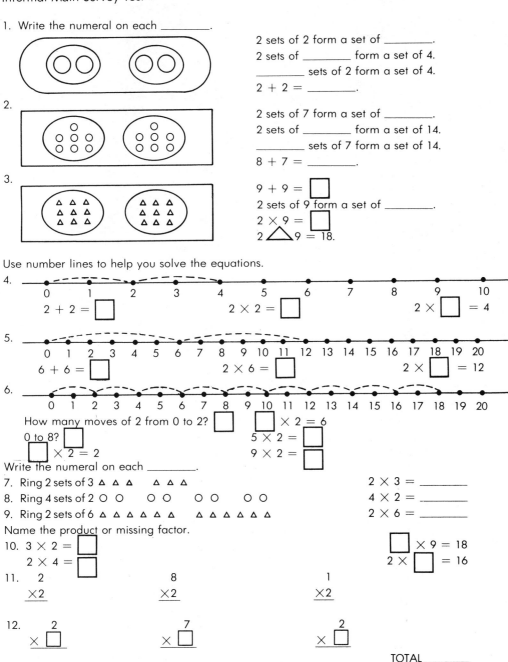

1. Write the numeral on each _____.

2 sets of 2 form a set of _____.
2 sets of _____ form a set of 4.
_____ sets of 2 form a set of 4.
2 + 2 = _____.

2.

2 sets of 7 form a set of _____.
2 sets of _____ form a set of 14.
_____ sets of 7 form a set of 14.
8 + 7 = _____.

3.

9 + 9 = ☐
2 sets of 9 form a set of _____.
2 × 9 = ☐
2 △ 9 = 18.

Use number lines to help you solve the equations.

4.

2 + 2 = ☐          2 × 2 = ☐          2 × ☐ = 4

5.

6 + 6 = ☐          2 × 6 = ☐          2 × ☐ = 12

6.

How many moves of 2 from 0 to 2? ☐          ☐ × 2 = 6
0 to 8? ☐                                     5 × 2 = ☐
☐ × 2 = 2                                     9 × 2 = ☐

Write the numeral on each _____.

7. Ring 2 sets of 3  △ △ △    △ △ △          2 × 3 = _____
8. Ring 4 sets of 2  ○ ○   ○ ○   ○ ○   ○ ○    4 × 2 = _____
9. Ring 2 sets of 6  △ △ △ △ △ △   △ △ △ △ △ △  2 × 6 = _____

Name the product or missing factor.

10. 3 × 2 = ☐
    2 × 4 = ☐                                 ☐ × 9 = 18
                                              2 × ☐ = 16
11.    2          8          1
      ×2         ×2         ×2

12.    2          7          2
      ×☐         ×☐         ×☐

TOTAL_____

**Figure 11.1**
Coded Informal Math Survey Test (Continued)

Book: Modern School Mathematics     Date _____
      Level 2
      Chapter 10; Multiplication 2 and 5    Name _*Ellis*_____
      Teacher's Copy

| Code: | Question | Unit | Page | +/− |
|-------|----------|------|------|-----|
| | 1 | 2 and 5 as factors | 281 | + |
| | 2 | | 282 | + |
| | 3 | | 284 | + |
| | 4 | Number line | 285 | + |
| | 5 | | 286 | + |
| | 6 | | 287 | + |
| | 7 | Commutative property | 288 | − |
| | 8 | | 288 | − |
| | 9 | | 288 | − |
| | 10 | Name product or factor | 289 | + |
| | 11 | | 290 | − |
| | 12 | | 290 | + |

**Student's Form**

Name: _____    Score: _____

Date: _____    Unit: _____

**Comparison with results of formal measures**—Informal surveys can also be compared to more formal achievement tests. The results of the formal and informal tests, combined with teacher evaluation of daily work, can provide a powerful and objective source of information about the child's mathematics needs. The degree to which the comparisons agree may provide the basis for choosing the most appropriate service or combination of services for the child in question. Albert, for example, scored very well on the *KeyMath* and on an informal classroom survey, but his daily work was very poor. Albert's mathematics motivation needed some assistance. This assistance could take place in the regular classroom. Dewey, in contrast, scored poorly on all three evaluative measures. His performance was so consistently low that special services outside of the classroom became the order of the day for him. Finally there was Alec. He scored very low on the *Iowa Math Achievement Subtest*, yet his daily classroom performance and informal test results were among the best in the class. In spite of his formal test results, Alec belonged in the regular classroom. The moral to these three stories is never to make judgments on one data source alone. Albert, Dewey, and Alec, thank you.

### Evaluation and Special Children

Evaluation in mathematics is essentially the same for special children as it is for all other children. The content of arithmetic is constant regardless of the eccentricities or unique characteristics of the learner. Two plus two should equal four whether the child being evaluated is visually impaired, gifted, or normal. The major concern in evaluation is being certain that it is the content that is being evaluated and not some problem unique to the child. Sensory and physically impaired children may need their own testing format. Children with learning or social problems may also need format change, a change that addresses length of evaluation and psychological factors such as stress due to fatigue or fear. Language problems can also be a confounding factor when evaluating math skills. Directions, both written and verbal, need to be clear and sensitive when evaluating all children, but especially when dealing with exceptional ones.

Most formal math tests have not been designed for special populations. As a consequence, both you and the specialist need to carefully monitor both the classroom setting and the format of the test before administering any of these measures. Results of the formal test gain credibility only when the test is delivered with regard for the child's specific needs and compared to teacher observation, informal tests, and daily classwork.

## SUMMARY

In evaluating mathematics, psychological attitudes as well as cognitive knowledge need to be considered. Math anxiety in all its varied forms runs rampant through the schools and is especially vicious for children who already have a low self-concept. For many children, the mathematics problem resides in fear of failure rather than in an actual inability to learn math.

With respect to cognitive mathematics assessment, no single test can be used as the sole criterion for determining an appropriate mathematics program. Teachers have available formal tests, informal tests, and daily records. Error analysis is the basis for comparison for all three measures. The primary purpose of assessment in mathematics is to give the child an appropriate math program. While the format may vary, the content of that math program remains constant and does not recognize handicaps. Two plus two must always result in the answer four—regardless of whether the child sings, points, speaks, or writes the response.

# 12

# Mathematics Instruction

*Virginia Usnick*
*Kathleen McCoy*

Six pairs of eyes dart furtively toward the classroom wall clock. Fingers begin to scratch heads and twirl hair furiously. Coughs seem to increase, keeping time with the slow and steady march of the minute hand. Pencil points snap. Papers are shuffled and the six pairs of eyes plead for a reprieve. As the volume of sighs, sneezes, and hiccups is about to reach an ear-shattering crescendo, a siren reverberates throughout the school. The six pairs of eyes, drooped and dull, suddenly undergo an amazing metamorphosis. The owners of five pairs of eyes go to line up at the door. The sixth pair checks to be sure that all of the 5 plus 20 children in the class are properly prepared for the fire drill. For one more day, both the teacher and her five-member long division group will be able to postpone the continuing and seemingly unending task of learning the long-division algorithm.

This "saved by the bell" mentality is all too common in math instruction. True, the task can be postponed for one more day, but it will be back with the certainty of death and you-know-what come April.

Assuming that the children's mathematical skill needs have been thoroughly assessed, the problem with mathematics classes must involve instruction. Motivation for both teaching and learning math may be less than high for teachers and students, especially remedial students, when both are confronted with a seemingly repetitive no-win (sometimes not even tie) learning situation. Being wedded to the classroom math textbook is one technique that can be guaranteed to produce a dull glaze in the eyes of most children and many teachers. Stressing the use of mathematics in our highly technological age has its merits, as does illustrating the remarkable patterns and unexpected, interesting concepts with which mathematics is replete (Long, 1982). Yet even highlighting the dynamic nature of mathematics will fall short if the teacher does not use proper instructional techniques. For children who have experienced problems learning mathematics, the need for appropriate instruction is even more critical. Children of all types and ages have trouble learning mathematics at one time or another. Mathematics learning problems do not seem to occur instantaneously, but instead seem to develop over an extended period. To complicate matters, the learning difficulty appears to be more severe and more complicated the longer that it remains undetected and untreated (Dunlop, Stoneman, & Cantrell, 1980).

Unfortunately, research in mathematics teaching can generally be interpreted to suggest that there is no one instructional technique able to maximize learning for every child (Sadowski, 1981; Horak & Horak, 1982). Even so, all is not lost. Informal observations of children's progress in remedial instruction suggests that these children need to "learn how to learn" in order to gain from instruction (Sadowski, 1981). Instructional techniques that include strategies for learning may serve as valuable teaching aids for both remedial and first-time mathematics learners, no matter what other material or method is the preferred choice of the teacher or district. Strategies for teaching children to "learn how to learn" mathematics are discussed in this chapter.

# FACTORS TEACHERS CAN MANIPULATE

Teachers have a great deal of latitude in presenting math classes. This allows them to manipulate various instructional factors that affect student learning. Four of the most easily manipulated factors within the instructor's command are time, size of group, reinforcement, and materials. The ways in which the teacher uses these four factors can significantly increase or decrease the amount of math learning that takes place.

## TIME

### Time Spent on Math Tasks

A not-too-surprising fact is that the more time is spent working on a task, the more likely the task is to be mastered. Obviously this statement is somewhat simplistic; factors other than time on-task contribute to learning. Nonetheless, time on-task is critical. In mathematics, the notion of time on-task is very clearly brought home when the amount of time devoted to math instruction is compared to performance.

**Cross-cultural practices**—When the math performance of American children is compared to that of children from countries such as Japan and Taiwan, American children do not fare well. While a very convenient explanation for this performance difference could be chalked up to some inherited predisposition for Asian students to excel in math, this explanation can be quickly and sorely shaken. A fast tally of the amount of time spent on math and math-related activities for American children and Japanese and Taiwanese children provides a more viable explanation of the poor performance of the American children. In short, American children receive less instruction in mathematics than do the other two groups (Stigler, Lii, Lucker, & Stevenson, 1982). In Japan, Taiwan, and the United States (Minneapolis) respectively, first grade children spent an average of 25%, 17%, and 14% of classroom time in mathematics, and fifth graders spent an average of 23%, 28%, and 17% of classroom time. There were also differences in the amount of time spent on mathematics homework. Again, in Japan, first grade students spent an average of 233 minutes each week on mathematics homework (estimated); fifth graders spent 368 minutes. Comparable figures for Taiwan are 496 and 771; for the United States, 79 and 256. If this evidence is too confounded by cultural and educational differences for your taste, here's more.

**Variations within the United States**—Berliner (1980a) analyzed the amount of time children were actively involved in mathematics in four second grade classrooms. He found major differences between classrooms in the amount of time spent on various content areas and in total instruction time. Teachers were clearly providing different types and amounts of instruction in mathematics. Based on these observations, differences in math performance would be expected. The teacher who spends 30 minutes a day in math activities should anticipate a lower level of math achievement for his or her students than the teacher who spends 60 minutes a day in math activities (assuming all other teaching variables are comparable).

## Providing Time for Math Learning

The obvious conclusion is that to increase the level of proficiency of student learning in math, a teacher should increase the amount of time spent working in math. This is one easily manipulated instructional factor. One of the reasons why Johnny can't learn math may be that he's never been given enough time to learn.

## SIZE OF GROUP

Math instruction, like any other content area, can be delivered in a variety of settings. Math can be taught in large groups, small groups, or one-to-one settings. The advantages and disadvantages of each setting have been detailed in other chapters in this book. A quick review should remind you that large-group instruction in which all children are receiving the same information at the same pace is not particularly successful in a classroom that contains children with various levels of skills.

## Uses of Large-Group Instruction

Large-group settings may be useful for brainstorming and aspects of problem solving that are tied more directly to logical deductions than to specific application of specific algorithms. For example, problem-solving questions like "How many showers can you take with a bar of soap?" lend themselves equally to children with low as well as high technical arithmetic skills. In addition, questions of this nature expand a child's ability to think through a problem without the fear of making a skill error. (Some of the answers are: Depends on the size of the soap. Depends on the type of soap being used. Depends on the length of the shower.) Both large- and small-group discussions along the line of thinking just presented allow children to express themselves and at the same time let them hear ideas of others (Knaupp, 1983).

## Small-Group Instruction

**Personal attention**—Small-group instruction can be especially useful when grouping children of comparable skill levels. In the small-group setting, children can get more personal attention while simultaneously benefiting from collaborative work with other members of the group. Discussion is limited to the members of the group, but the group can still support discussion. As long as the members of the group are at approximately the same skill level, small-group instruction may actually be the preferred method of instructional grouping. In a study conducted by Sealey (1985), students actually gave small-group instruction higher ratings than individual work. While small-group instruction didn't actually help the students learn any more math overall, they felt better about the learning environment. Not too startling was the finding that students who worked more slowly than the rest of the group and got too far behind to profit from group discussion gave small-group instruction very unfavorable ratings. These students preferred to work individually.

**Rate variability**—Another advantage of small-group instruction is that it allows those children who are ready to go on in the curriculum to continue and those who are not or who need more time for mastery to continue at their own rate. In a class of 30-plus, the teacher could easily develop six to eight small learning groups.

**Types of groupings**—The groups must have some structure, however, or they are doomed (along with the students) to failure. Fremont (1977) has offered several practical suggestions for small group or cooperative group instruction. Some of the suggestions include voluntary formation of membership, topic selection limited to curriculum or course syllabus, and freedom to choose topical sequence. According to Fremont, the teacher moves from the traditional role of "explainer" to being a skilled organizer of mathematics experiences to assist student learning. Teachers also make judgments that include how much responsibility a student can take, what is needed to improve a student's self-image, and what diagnostic procedures should be used to determine the material or activity that will best improve student progress.

Small-group instruction based upon skill level is often referred to as *diagnostic teaching*. Because a child's skills will fluctuate from topic to topic, a diagnostic grouping is often temporary. Children move from group to group based upon skill need. Flexibility and assessment are the cornerstones of diagnostic skill grouping.

Another kind of small group structure is called *survival grouping* or *co-operative grouping*. Groups of this sort are formed more along the notion of peer tutoring than diagnosed math skill needs. In cooperative math groups, the children teach each other; the learning activity is enhanced by social factors such as friendship and common interests.

## Individualized Instruction

Individualized instruction in mathematics has a valuable place in the classroom, too. The question sparked by the term *individualization* is "How can a teacher provide individualized instruction to a class of 30-plus children in the course of a 45- to 60-minute math period?" If the answer is that individualized instruction means diagnosing the optimum learning experience for a child and providing an environment in which the child can learn, then individualization is not so formidable.

**Within groups**—Individualization of instruction does not mean that one student sits in a classroom all day and interacts with only a teacher or a math worksheet. It allows for grouping several students whose needs are similar (Reisman, 1981). Learners don't need to work alone if their learning is to be individualized.

**Altering formats**—Sometimes a child learns most effectively when working independently and sometimes when working as part of a large or small group (Swenson, 1973). Individualization, then, requires that the teacher take a child or group of children and set up experiences that enhance each child's opportunities to learn math. These opportunities include rate or pace of instruction as well as extra practice materials or materials that reflect present skill level.

## REINFORCEMENT

### "Right Answers"

In addition to the traditional concept of reinforcement as stars for correct responses and checkmarks for incorrect responses, mathematics instruction further demands reinforcement that provides positive feelings. Students can be reinforced for completing various components of a math problem. The "right answer" is just one of the components of the problem. For some students, just initiating the work involved with a problem is worthy of reinforcement. Following directions, completing the work, and being neat and orderly are also praiseworthy accomplishments.

## Process and Product

Since a teacher would want to emphasize mathematics as a process rather than a product, the student's approach to problems and solutions needs to be reinforced just as much as the correct answer. By approaching mathematics as an activity for finding solutions to problems, the teacher can isolate many factors, not just the correct solution, that can be reinforced. The more positive reinforcements or strokes a child receives, the greater the chance the child can develop positive feelings and attitudes.

Art has always been afraid of mathematics. His fear seemed to begin early in the second grade when his teacher casually remarked that math didn't seem to be Art's best subject. The next few times that Art got low marks on his math papers lent more credibility to his teacher's remark. By the time he reached fifth grade, he was a full-blown math-anxious student. He would stall and avoid doing math work in class whenever possible. Art's teacher, recognizing his avoidance behavior and sympathizing with his dilemma, began to slowly improve Art's skills in math by first working on his attitude. The teacher praised all the students in class for their neatness on worksheets. Even though Art didn't have much done, what he did have done was as neat as a CPA's ledger, earning his first bit of praise involving a math activity. Even though his skills have not improved, he seems less reluctant to begin his math assignment. Now that Art has begun to do his work, his teacher can identify skill deficits in order to provide materials and activities to improve his math abilities.

## MATERIALS

### Desensitizing Materials

For children like Art who have had bad experiences in math and developed poor attitudes, the teacher can introduce materials that they do not associate with math failure. The teacher can directly teach math skills through concrete manipulative materials or indirectly teach them by using real-world applications involving math skills. For example, when teaching double-digit multiplication, instead of pulling out the paper and pencil, the teacher can bring out blocks, an abacus, chips, or any other concrete material to illustrate the concept. The teacher guides the student through a problem, allowing the student to work with the manipulative while the teacher records on the symbolic level. So the teacher writes

$$
\begin{array}{r}
53 \\
\times\,12 \\
\hline
\end{array}
$$

on the board. The student, using chips with colors representing place values of tens and ones, would arrange 12 groups of 53, where 53 is represented by 5 blue chips (tens) and 3 yellow chips (ones). While the student manipulates the chips, the teacher records the student's actions through the use of numerical symbols. When the student has had repeated success with the manipulatives, the teacher presents more problems, allowing the student to work the problem with manipulatives and writing down the answers. Next, the student uses the manipulatives to solve numerical problems and records all his or her actions, such as using a "carried" number to indicate that some ones were traded for tens. Finally, the student works the problem using only numbers.

## "Slipped" Into Other Content

Not all classrooms have access to manipulatives, nor do all teachers feel comfortable using them. In situations like these, the teacher can approach instruction in yet another manner. Math can be slipped in under the guise of social studies, science, even art and music. Continuing with the example of $53 \times 21$, the teacher can present a story problem involving these numbers and allow the students to find the answer in nontraditional ways, such as acting the problem out or drawing pictures. For example, if relating this problem to a music class, the teacher might say that she has 53 pieces of music and needs arrangements of each piece for all 21 band members. One student might draw 53 squares to represent the music and repeat this arrangement 21 times. Another student might write 53 in a column 21 times and add them. Through class discussion, the teacher and students can analyze the different ways the problem was solved and relate each way to the traditional math approach. A variation of the traditional story problems is to personalize them by using a child's own name or interests. By personalizing the problem, the student will be more interested and (we hope) more attentive to instruction.

No matter what approach the teacher uses with materials, the main point to remember is that the materials are used to engage the child in active learning. Students with a history of math failure tend to be unwilling to participate in activities associated with their previous failures. By providing new kinds of materials or activities, the teacher lets the students pursue mathematics learning in a nonpunitive fashion.

# INSTRUCTIONAL CONTENT

Mastery of the basic facts is essential for competency in arithmetic skills. Children with learning problems often have difficulty mastering basic arithmetic facts (Myers & Thornton, 1977). Besides being slower in computing basic facts, as a group children with learning problems often make more errors of computation than do their nonhandicapped peers (Fleishner, Garnett, & Sheperd, 1982).

## MAJOR GOALS

A major goal of elementary arithmetic instruction is to have children recall facts rapidly, i.e., know the facts by heart. This requires memorization. But memorization does not have to be burdensome, difficult, or distasteful. It does include the notion of drill activities.

### Principles for Enhancing Basic Fact Recall

When providing drill, you should consider the following principles.

1. Children should have a reasonable understanding of the material they are attempting to memorize (Wood & Dunlap, 1982). They should know the numbers both by the name and quantity they represent, e.g., in addition facts, recognize the " + " sign as the symbol for addition and that equality can be represented with the " = " sign or the line under the vertical problem. For example,

$$\begin{array}{r} 6 \\ +5 \\ \hline \end{array}$$

2. Children should enter drill activities with the intention of memorizing the facts or material. The teacher's responsibility is to alert the students that this is a drill and they need to become quick or proficient with the facts to make other mathematical calculations easier.

3. Drill sessions should be short, varied, and daily (until mastery has been achieved). Drill activities can occur in those spare minutes that arise naturally during the school day, e.g., the 5 minutes spent lining up at the door for lunch or the last 3 or 4 minutes before dismissal. Drill activities need not be restricted to the traditional and ubiquitous flashcards. Problems can be generated through the use of dice rolls, spinners, playing cards, and so forth (Beattie & Algozzine, 1982). Format can be paper and pencil, but may also be board games or oral responses to problems on the overhead projector.

4. The student needs to feel confident in his or her ability to memorize the facts. The teacher needs to encourage the students and praise them for their good efforts, keeping the visual records of each student's progress in order for the student to see growth. These records could include bar graphs and cumulative charts. Figure 12.1 shows such a chart.

5. Each drill session should incorporate only two or three new facts and constantly review previously memorized facts. By only memorizing a few new facts at a time, students will not be overwhelmed by the seemingly monumental task of memorizing all 100 facts.

### Alternative Sequence for Teaching Addition

Once you have applied these four principles and followed the sequence of instruction as provided in your classroom text, you would hope that all the students would have become masters of the basic facts. Alas, this is not always

**Figure 12.1**
Cumulative Graph Showing Progress in Math Facts

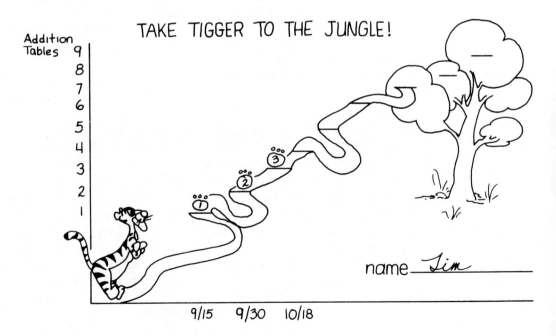

the case. What to do next? According to at least one math educator (Lazerick, 1981), an alternate sequence can be applied. This sequence is comprised of seven steps.

Step 1: The " + 0" facts (e.g., facts like 0 + 3 or 3 + 0). Step 1 covers 19 facts out of the original 100.

Step 2: The " + 1" facts, e.g., facts like 1 + 5 or 5 + 1. Step 2 adds another 17 facts to the student's growing arsenal of basic combinations.

Step 3: The " + 2" facts. Fifteen new facts are added to the student's skills: 51 facts—more than half of all the basic addition facts—have been learned. By pointing out the progress made, you can boost the student's confidence.

Step 4: The "doubles," e.g., 3 + 3, 7 + 7. These facts often don't need to be taught. Most children seem to learn them by osmosis.

Step 5: The "related doubles," e.g., if you know the double (4 + 4 = 8), you apply that knowledge to the fact 4 + 5, and recall that 5 is one more than 4, so if 4 + 4 = 8, then 4 + 5 must equal 9 because 9 is one more than 8.

Step 6: The "9 facts." The best order is to teach "9 + __" before teaching "__ + 9." To teach the 9 + 6 fact, for instance, place 9 markers in one group and 6 in another. Move one marker from the "6" group to the "9" group to make a related fact of 10 + 5. Since many of the " + 9" facts have been learned in steps 1 through 5, there are only 10 new facts to be learned.

Step 7: The "hard facts." There are only 10 facts and their commutative twins to be learned, e.g., 3 + 5 and its twin 5 + 3. There is no evident structure to these 10 facts so they need frequent drill and practice.

## Alternative Sequence for Teaching Subtraction Facts

Learning subtraction facts is often more difficult than learning addition facts, as many primary teachers have commented (Leutzinger & Nelson, 1979). As teachers we must show some students how addition and subtraction are related. If children understand the relationship between addition and subtraction facts, they can use the known addition facts to find the unknown subtraction facts. Sally knows all of her addition tables, but she has problems with her " − 4" subtraction tables. Sally knows that 5 + 4 = 9. She doesn't know that 9 − 4 = 5. Her problem may result from a lack of awareness that addition and subtraction are related. To teach Sally the relationship between the two problems, a sequence of instruction has been proposed. Leutzinger and Nelson (1979) recommend that the teacher first use partitioning activities. These involve separating a group of objects or pictures into two smaller groups, e.g., giving Sally 9 chips and having her form one group of 5 chips and one of 4 chips. The same 9 chips could also be separated into sets of 3 and 6 or 7 and 2. Sally gets to make as many combinations from the 9 chips as she can. After she has demonstrated partitioning skills, she progresses to recording activities.

While forming the groups, the teacher needs to talk with Sally about ways to keep track of the groups she's made. She might have Sally use a chart titled "9" and write down the numbers associated with each of her groups. This can lead to "the way mathematicians record" the groups ... addition and subtraction facts. By writing both addition and subtraction facts for each partition, Sally should begin to see that addition and subtraction are related. She is then ready for Leutzinger and Nelson's (1979) next type of activity, which involves working with missing addends. After giving Sally 5 markers, the teacher asks her how many more she needs to make a group of 9. Sally can count from 5 on (that is, begin counting at 6 and keep track of how many numbers it takes to get to 9) or she can make another group of 9, match her 5 with 5 from the new group, and count how many are unmatched. The teacher shows Sally that these problems can be written as addition facts in the form "5 + __ = 9" or as subtraction facts in the form "9 − 5 = __." Here again the teacher needs to point out that addition and subtraction are related and that knowing the addition facts helps solve the subtraction problems.

The final step in this sequence is to directly apply the known addition facts to solve subtraction problems. Sally's teacher presents her with a written addition fact and has Sally write the subtraction facts that go with it. For example, Sally sees "9 + 5 = 14" and writes "14 − 9 = 5" or "14 − 5 = 9." Given subtraction facts, she writes the related addition facts. When shown "14 − 9 = 5," she writes "5 + 9 = 14" and "9 + 5 = 14." These activities should help Sally realize that since addition and subtraction are related, she can "think addition" when working subtraction problems. That is, when shown "15 − 8 = __" Sally can rely on her addition facts and think "8 plus what equals 15?"

## Alternatives for Teaching Multiplication and Division

Just as addition and subtraction facts are related, so are multiplication and division facts. When the classroom textbook sequence does not work for some of the children, Bolduc (1980) has suggested an alternate sequence. The first step in his sequence is to begin with the 0 and 1 facts. This accounts for 36 of the 100 basic multiplication facts. The next sets are the 2 and 5 facts. Learning the 2's and 5's adds 28 more multiplication facts to the list of learned combinations. The students are now almost two-thirds of the way through learning the multiplication tables. The 9's are then introduced. Nine times tables are fairly easy because we carry them around on our fingers. Samples of finger tables are presented in Figure 12.2. The next set of facts to learn is the squares, e.g., 6 × 6, 7 × 7, 4 × 4. These four sets have covered 80 of the original 100 facts—only 20 facts left to go. The last 20 can be cut to 10 if students know the commutative property, e.g., 4 × 7 = 7 × 4.

Another way of learning the basic multiplication facts is to learn all the facts whose product is less than 10. Next, learn all those combinations whose product is less than 20, and so forth. An example of this sequence is presented in Table 12.1.

Just as subtraction facts can be taught by relating them to addition facts, division facts can be taught by relating them to multiplication facts. The subtraction sequence presented by Leutzinger and Nelson (1979) can be adapted for divison. Using partitioning activities, followed by teacher-and-student recording and finally student recording alone is a useful technique for teaching division facts.

**Figure 12.2**
Samples of Finger Tables

The fingers are numbered as shown.

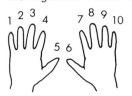

To find 9 × 4, we turn down the fourth finger, and "read" the answer as 36.

9 × 2 = 18          9 × 8 = 72

Source: From E.J. Bolduc, Jr., "The Monsters in Multiplication." *The Arithmetic Teacher* (1980), 28:3, 24-26.

## Table 12.1
### Multiplication Facts Classified by Products

Intervals

| Facts | 0–10 | 10–20 | 20–30 | 30–40 | 40–50 | 50–60 | 60–70 | 70–80 | 80–90 |
|---|---|---|---|---|---|---|---|---|---|
| | 0 × 0 | 2 × 6   6 × 2 | 3 × 7   7 × 3 | 7 × 5   5 × 7 | 5 × 9   9 × 5 | 6 × 9   9 × 6 | 7 × 9   9 × 7 | 8 × 9   9 × 8 | 9 × 9 |
| | 0 × 1   1 × 0 | 2 × 7   7 × 2 | 3 × 8   8 × 3 | 8 × 5   5 × 8 | 6 × 7   7 × 6 | 7 × 8   8 × 7 | 8 × 8 | | |
| | 0 × 2   2 × 0 | 2 × 8   8 × 2 | 3 × 9   9 × 3 | 6 × 6 | 6 × 8   8 × 6 | | | | |
| | 0 × 3   3 × 0 | 2 × 9   9 × 2 | 4 × 6   6 × 4 | 8 × 4   4 × 8 | 7 × 7 | | | | |
| | 0 × 4   4 × 0 | 3 × 4   4 × 3 | 4 × 7   7 × 4 | 9 × 4   4 × 9 | | | | | |
| | 0 × 5   5 × 0 | 3 × 5   5 × 3 | 5 × 5 | | | | | | |
| | 0 × 6   6 × 0 | 3 × 6   6 × 3 | 5 × 6   6 × 5 | | | | | | |
| | 0 × 7   7 × 0 | 4 × 4 | | | | | | | |
| | 0 × 8   8 × 0 | 4 × 5   5 × 4 | | | | | | | |
| | 0 × 9   9 × 0 | | | | | | | | |
| | 1 × 1 | | | | | | | | |
| | 1 × 2   2 × 1 | | | | | | | | |
| | 1 × 3   3 × 1 | | | | | | | | |
| | 1 × 4   4 × 1 | | | | | | | | |
| | 1 × 5   5 × 1 | | | | | | | | |
| | 1 × 6   6 × 1 | | | | | | | | |
| | 1 × 7   7 × 1 | | | | | | | | |
| | 1 × 8   8 × 1 | | | | | | | | |
| | 1 × 9   9 × 1 | | | | | | | | |
| | 2 × 2 | | | | | | | | |
| | 2 × 3   3 × 2 | | | | | | | | |
| | 2 × 4   4 × 2 | | | | | | | | |
| | 2 × 5   5 × 2 | | | | | | | | |
| | 3 × 3 | | | | | | | | |
| Number | 44 | 17 | 13 | 9 | 7 | 4 | 3 | 2 | 1 |

Source: From E.J. Bolduc, Jr., "The Monsters in Multiplication," *The Arithmetic Teacher* (1980), 28:3, 24-26.

## MEANING OF BASIC OPERATIONS

Each basic operation has more than one interpretation. Students need to recognize the type of interpretation required by the math situation or question.

### Addition

Addition has two situations/meanings. The first and most commonly taught is called *joining of sets*. For example: "Two gremlins are on the kitchen counter and four more gremlins join them. How many gremlins are on the counter?" This is a dynamic situation in that students can visualize the motion of the four gremlins joining the two resting on the kitchen counter. The other addition situation, which is less likely to be presented, is *part-part-whole*. In this situation no movement is visualized. Now the two gremlins are still resting on the kitchen counter. The student is told about four other gremlins who are resting on the bathroom counter. The question asked is, "How many gremlins are sitting on counters?" No action has occurred. The gremlins do not leave their respective counters. This kind of problem is static. Teachers should provide students with numerous examples of both kinds of addition situations.

### Subtraction

Subtraction has three meaningful situations: *take away, comparison*, and *missing addend. Take away* is the most easily understood, which is not too surprising since it is typically the only situation presented. An example of a take away problem is: "Peter had eight pies. He ate three of them. How many does he still have?" The second subtraction situation, comparison, is exemplified by this problem: "Peter had eight pies and Simon had three pies. How many more pies does Peter have than Simon?" This is a truly simple comparison because nothing is taken away. The two sets (Peter's pies and Simon's pies) are directly compared.

The third subtraction situation is *missing addend*. This kind of subtraction situation is probably the most difficult for students to understand. However, if the teacher relates subtraction facts to addition facts, this difficulty may be lessened. In this type of problem, the whole and a part of the whole are known. You need to find the missing part. Just as with the meaning of addition, the teacher will need to provide many examples and practice activities using all three types of subtraction problems. Figure 12.3 shows the three types of subtraction problems.

### Multiplication

Multiplication has two meaningful situations. These are *repeated addition* and *Cartesian cross product*, often called an *array*. Both of these meanings of

**Figure 12.3**
Three Subtraction Situations for the Problem "8 − 3"

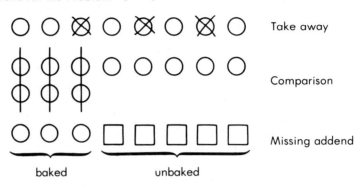

multiplication are commonly taught. Repeated addition is typically used to teach the basic facts, e.g., "Conan captured six wizards. Each wizard had four magic stones. How many magic stones did Conan get?" Figure 12.4 shows Conan's repeated addition approach to multiplication. The other multiplication situation, an array, arranges the problem not in the six separate groups of the repeated addition approach, but rather in an organized group —almost military fashion—with six nice rows of four stones each. Figure 12.5 depicts Conan's array approach to multiplication.

### Division
Division also has two distinct meanings: *partition* and *measurement*. The main differences in these two meanings of division are the way in which the

**Figure 12.4**
Repeated Addition in Multiplication

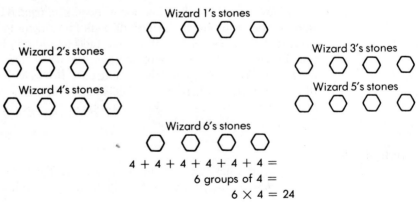

**Figure 12.5**
An Array Approach to Multiplication

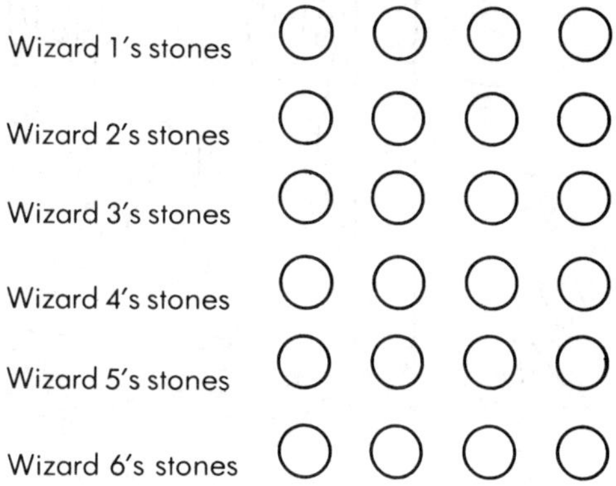

Wizard 1's stones   ○ ○ ○ ○

Wizard 2's stones   ○ ○ ○ ○

Wizard 3's stones   ○ ○ ○ ○

Wizard 4's stones   ○ ○ ○ ○

Wizard 5's stones   ○ ○ ○ ○

Wizard 6's stones   ○ ○ ○ ○

6 groups of 4 =
6 × 4 = 24

situations are visualized and the interpretation of the answer. In a partition situation, the student knows the total number and how many even-sized groups can be made from the total. The problem is to determine how many there are in each group, e.g., "Michael had 15 silver gloves. He has three drawers. How many gloves are in each drawer?" This problem is a real thriller. Students must understand that each group (in this case, group of gloves) must be the same size. Measurement, on the other hand, refers to situations where we already know the size of each group, i.e., "Michael has 15 silver gloves. He puts three in each drawer. How many drawers does Michael need?" Both of these problems can be solved by the division fact 15 ÷ 3, but the visualization and meaning of the answers (five) are totally different. In the partition problem, the answer meant five gloves, while in the measurement problem, the answer meant five drawers. Figure 12.6 shows partition and Figure 12.7 shows measurement. It may be that students have difficulty with division because teachers do not spend enough time helping them interpret the answer.

## Algorithms

Historically, a major goal of elementary education has been to make children proficient in arithmetic computation. A significant portion of children's elementary mathematics training is devoted to mastering computational algorithms. To recap, an algorithm is a routine, step-by-step procedure used in computation (Driscoll, 1980). Algorithms are tools, not educational goals. To be used effectively they must be understood and drilled.

**Figure 12.6**
Partition Approach to Division

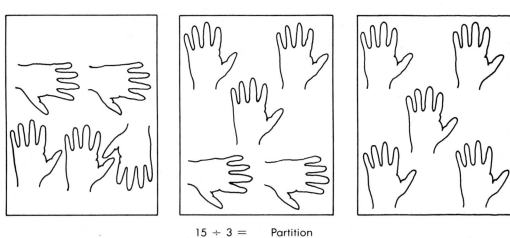

15 ÷ 3 =     Partition

**Figure 12.7**
Measurement Approach to Division

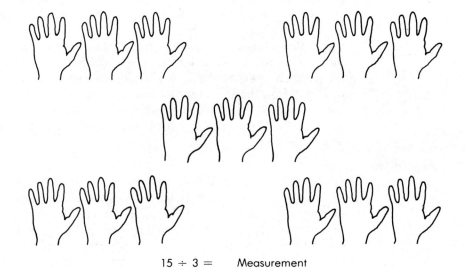

15 ÷ 3 =     Measurement

**Common algorithms**—The most common algorithms are carrying in addition, borrowing in subtraction, and combinations of carrying and borrowing in long division and multiplication. Because algorithms are basically steps or rules to follow in computing an arithmetic problem, they can be likened to the mechanics of composition. A person can complete an operation by following the rules (algorithms) without knowing the meaning of these rules. For example, a person can determine the cost of four new tires, i.e., 4 × $56.00, without understanding why the decimal point must stay after the ones column or why the "20" of the "4 × 6" must be regrouped with the other tens column ($50.00).

**Syntax**—The mechanics or algorithms used in arithmetic have become known as the *syntax* of the operation. While syntax can stand by itself, the ability to use it is greatly enhanced by understanding the meaning associated with it. Meaning in both language and arithmetic is called *semantics*. Together, syntax and semantics provide the learner with the broadest possible knowledge of arithmetic operations.

Prior to the introduction of new math, arithmetic instruction was almost always syntactical, i.e., the rules were learned with little regard to why they worked. After World War II, mathematicians and math educators were concerned that students could compute but did not understand why the rules worked. This lack of semantic knowledge limited the student's ability to solve problems. Reform of curriculum and methodology was demanded from all corners of the country. Enter the "new math" era.

**Semantics**—During the new math era, instructional emphasis was placed on learning or discovering the meaning behind mathematics. The belief was held that knowledge a person discovers (as opposed to being directly taught) would be better understood and retained longer (Skemp, 1971). If a person forgot the process for finding an answer, he or she could regenerate it with a little meaningful reflection. Many mathematics educators put their faith into this system. As a result, students began to understand the structure of mathematics and why algorithms work (semantics). Unfortunately these same students could not compute very quickly, if at all. As would be expected, many educators became concerned that understanding did not mean skill and skill did not mean understanding. Mathematically stated, semantic ≠ syntax, and vice versa. What to do? Syntax and semantics are both necessary for a complete understanding of mathematics (Peck, Jencks, & Chatterly, 1980).

**Educational implications**—Educational implications are clear. Some children may not learn a conceptual knowledge of the algorithm with initial teaching or perhaps ever. Yet most of them can be expected to use the algorithm in a functionally positive manner. Stated another way, many children may learn the syntactic (rules) constraints of a given algorithm without connecting them to the semantic (meaning) information that underlies the algorithm. The lack of a bridge between the syntax and semantics of the algorithm may lead to some serious errors in performance.

Activities have been suggested to help students see the connection between syntax and semantics of basic algorithms (Resnick, 1982; Wirtz, 1974). Presented below is a sequence of activities.

1. Allow students time to explore concrete materials related to mathematical concepts. Exploration activities give learners the opportunity to discover relationships between objects and possibly to generate rules or principles that govern those relationships.

2. Present the students with orally stated problems and allow them to find the answer by manipulating objects.

3. Require students to generate "story situations" and use manipulatives or pictures to arrive at the solution. Use these problems as the basis for demonstrating the appropriate mathematical representation of the problem.

4. Present students with symbolic-level problems (numbers and signs only, with no pictures) and allow them to manipulate objects and record the answer in symbols (numbers).

5. Present students with symbolic-level problems, allow them to manipulate objects, and require recording of manipulatives prior to recording the answer. For example, Thomas is given the problem "34 − 16 = __." He must demonstrate with 34 blocks that he can regroup a 10 to 10 ones, record that regrouping in numbers (symbolically), remove 16 chips, and record the answer.

6. Students begin the sequence again (steps 2 through 5), but this time use pictures or representations of objects rather than actual objects.

7. Students move to mental representation by imagining (visualizing) objects and steps 2 through 5 are again repeated.

8. The final step is to have students work on the symbolic only. No pictures or objects are used—only numbers and signs.

## CONSOLIDATION ACTIVITIES WITH BASIC ALGORITHMS

Once students can associate semantic knowledge with the syntactic aspects of the algorithm, consolidation activities must be presented. Consolidation activities focus upon drill and practice. Even children who have learning problems must take into account the problem-solving aspects of algorithms during drill. Drill without meaning may not permit the child with learning problems to solve even everyday arithmetic problems (Austin, 1982). Research on drill during the last two decades has found that drill must come after meaningful understanding (Cooney, Herstein, & Davis, 1981) and that meaningful development should take up at least half of the class time (Schuster & Pigge, 1965). Research also suggests that students should have knowledge of the basic facts at a stimulus–response level before they begin drilling an algorithm (Driscoill, 1980). Furthermore, different students need different amounts of drill (Gay, 1972) and delayed drill may be more beneficial than drill immediately following instruction on a topic (Horowitz, 1975).

Currently considerable emphasis, at least in some math projects and textbook series, is placed on understanding the relationship between the meaning of algorithms and their respective mechanics. There are several algorithms for each of the basic operations. Some algorithms are more commonly used than others and generally accepted as being quicker. These are usually referred to as *standard* algorithms. Even though standard algorithms are considered quick, they become that way only after development and practice.

## Addition Algorithms

**Carrying**—Although there are several algorithms for addition of multidigit numbers, the most commonly used algorithm in this country is the approach typically called *carrying*. In this algorithm, students begin in the ones place, add the digits, regroup (form groups of 10) if necessary, and indicate that regrouping has taken place by writing above the tens place the digit that indicated how many regroupings were done. The process is then applied to the tens place, etc. (See Figure 12.8.) Children who do not attach meaning to the algorithm might agree with Johnson (1975), who called this algorithm "the addition dance of the digits."

**Figure 12.8**

$$
\begin{array}{r}
1\\
37\\
+\,26\\
\hline
63
\end{array}
$$

According to Riedesel (1980), carrying is the most difficult form of the addition algorithm. Swenson (1973) has stated that it often becomes a stumbling block for students. When students have difficulty with this standard form, alternative methods can be taught. Two common alternatives are *expanded notation* and *partial sums*.

**Expanded notation**—Expanded notation, which is often used when first teaching multidigit addition, requires that students know some place-value concepts. For example, 43 has tens and ones; to be specific, 4 tens and 3 ones. When adding two multidigit numbers, students can use the expanded forms, shown in Figure 12.9.

**Figure 12.9**

```
        48  =  4 tens and 8 ones
      + 37  =  3 tens and 7 ones
```
Step 1: Add the ones and tens.
Step 2: Regroup the ones, if necessary.
Step 3: Put the tens together.
Step 4: Write the tens in a simpler way.
Step 5: Write the answer in number form.

```
        48  =  4 tens and 8 ones
      + 37  =  3 tens and 7 ones
```
| | |
|---|---|
| (Step 1): | 7 tens and 15 ones |
| (Step 2): | 7 tens and (1 ten and 5 ones) |
| (Step 3): | (7 tens and 1 ten) and 5 ones |
| (Step 4): | 8 tens and 5 ones |
| (Step 5): | 85 |

Even though this algorithm is developmental, that is, taught before the standard algorithm, it is useful when the teacher needs to reteach the concept.

**Partial sums**—The partial sums, also a developmental algorithm, shows the sum of the ones and the sum of the tens. (See Figure 12.10.)

**Figure 12.10**

```
        48
      + 37
      ─────
        15 (sum of the ones)
        70 (sum of the tens)
      ─────
        85
```

For some students, these approaches might trigger mental overload, as they must think of more parts than they have before, which causes even more frustration. Yet, for other students, the novelty of these approaches might be just what they need.

**Hutchings' low-stress algorithm**—An approach specifically developed for learning disabled students is Hutchings' low-stress algorithm. In this method, students are not required to keep a running total in their heads but must write down an answer whenever the sum is greater than 9. The power of this algorithm is that students need to know only the basic facts. A step-by-step description of Hutchings' algorithm for finding the following sum can be found in Figure 12.11.

There are several other algorithms for addition. A good math methods text should discuss them.

## Subtraction Algorithms

**Borrowing**—Just as in addition, subtraction has several algorithms. The standard one is decomposition, commonly called *borrowing*. Ikeda and Ando (1974) and Brownell & Moser (1949) all have indicated that the decomposition method was easier to rationalize (make understandable to students) than other algorithms, which probably accounts for its popularity. Yet many teachers express concern that students do not understand it (Driscoll, 1980; Sherrill, 1979).

The most common error with the decomposition algorithm is the reversal of digits within a column, i.e., students take the smaller from the larger, regardless of placement in the column. For example, when working 73 − 29, students often think of "9 minus 3" rather than "3 minus 9," which will produce an answer of 56 instead of the correct answer of 42.

**Figure 12.11**
Modified Hutchings' Low-Stress Addition Algorithm

Problem: 57 + 68 + 76 + 87 + 99 + 58

```
 57
 68    (1) Student adds 7 + 8 and records 15, putting the "1" above the tens.
 76    (2) Student adds 5 + 6 and records 11, putting the "1" above the tens.
 87    (3) Student adds 1 + 7 and records 8, no tens to carry.
 99    (4) Student adds 8 + 9 and records 17, putting the "1" above the tens.
 58    (5) Students adds 7 + 8 and records 15, putting the "1" above the tens.
445    Student proceeds to the tens column and continues in the same manner.
```

**Techniques for LD students**—An approach that has been developed for learning disabled students is to do all the borrowings first. Teachers must caution the students to borrow only when necessary. For example, when solving 3241 − 1736, students need to borow from the tens to the ones and the thousands to the hundreds, but not from the hundreds to the tens. Care must be taken to ensure that students don't overgeneralize the "do all the borrowing first" rule to "borrow in every place." Figure 12.12 shows how this problem should be worked.

While there are many other subtraction algorithms, most of these require math skills beyond entry level.

## Multiplication Algorithms

**Partial products**—When students have problems learning the standard multiplication procedure, you can resort to using the *partial products* algorithm. The partial products approach is quite similar to the partial sums approach in addition. Subproducts in the multiplication problem are found and then totaled, just as subsums in the addition problem are found and then totaled.

**Arrays**—Again, students need to be very familiar with the use of arrays for finding answers to basic multiplication facts. This concept can be expanded to multiplication of multidigit numbers. The use of graph paper for outlining the arrays works well. For example, when working $23 \times 12$, you would outline a rectangle 23 squares long and 12 squares wide. (See Figure 12.13.) The individual squares within the rectangle can be counted to find the total, or the concept of repeated addition can be applied to shorten the counting process.

The partial products algorithm can be used to further shorten the counting process. However, students must understand and be able to write numbers in expanded notation. That is, they must know that 23 can be rewritten as $20 + 3$ and 12 as $10 + 2$. The multiplication problem now becomes

$$\begin{array}{r} 20 + 3 \\ \times\, \underline{10 + 2} \end{array}$$

This form highlights the partial products, which can also be found within the $23 \times 12$ array:

$$
\begin{array}{rcll}
2 \times 3 &=& 6 & \text{(see A in Figure 12.13)} \\
2 \times 20 &=& 40 & \text{(see B in Figure 12.13)} \\
10 \times 3 &=& 30 & \text{(see C in Figure 12.13)} \\
10 \times 20 &=& 200 & \text{(see D in Figure 12.13)}
\end{array}
$$

**Figure 12.12**
Hutchings' Low-Stress Subtraction Algorithm

```
  3 2 4 7      3 2 4 7      3 2 4 7      3 2 4 7       3 2 4 7

 −1 7 3 6          4 7          2 4 7     2 ¹2 4 7      2 ¹2 4 7

              −1 7 3 6     −1 7 3 6     −1 7 3 6      −1 7 3 6
                                                       1 5 1 1
```

**Figure 12.13**
Using Arrays in Basic Multiplication Facts

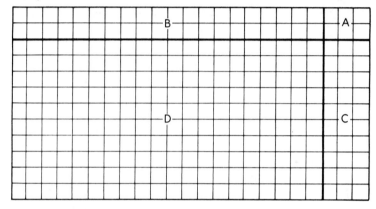

## Division Algorithms

**Myths**—"Long division is the most difficult process taught in the elementary school mathematics program" (Laing & Meyer, 1982, p. 10). A commonly held myth is that children have difficulty learning long division because they lack prerequisite skills in multiplication and subtraction. Recent research findings (Laing & Meyer, 1982) have clearly demonstrated that the majority of errors in long division can be attributed to lack of skill in division and not in subordinate skills. Sylvester's long division problems are incorrect because he doesn't know how to do long division, not because he doesn't know his multiplication or subtraction facts. In all probability, the most effective technique to use with Sylvester is the traditional long division approach in modified form. This form, presented in Figure 12.14, allows Sylvester to clearly attend to the meaning of the process of long division. In solving the problem 64 divided by 3, Sylvester can be taught to realize the 3 means three groups that must be exactly equal in quantity. He has 6 tens. He can distribute 2 tens to each of the 3 groups. No tens are left over, so he moves to the 1's. He has 4 ones and can distribute 1 to each group with 1 left over, i.e., a number that doesn't fit into the three groups. All distributions have been made and each group is the same size—21. The answer would be recorded as 21 with a remainder of 1.

**Figure 12.14**
Modified Long Division Approach

Problem:  64 ÷ 3

Approach:

Step 1: Break 64 into groups of tens and ones
64 = 6 tens and 4 ones

64 = 6 tens                          4 ones

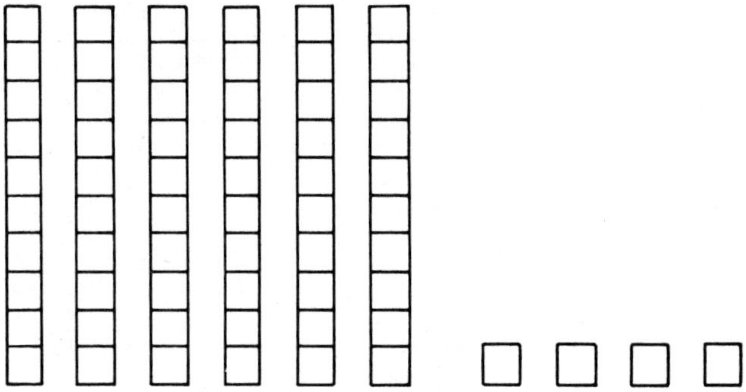

Step 2: Make 3 equal groups

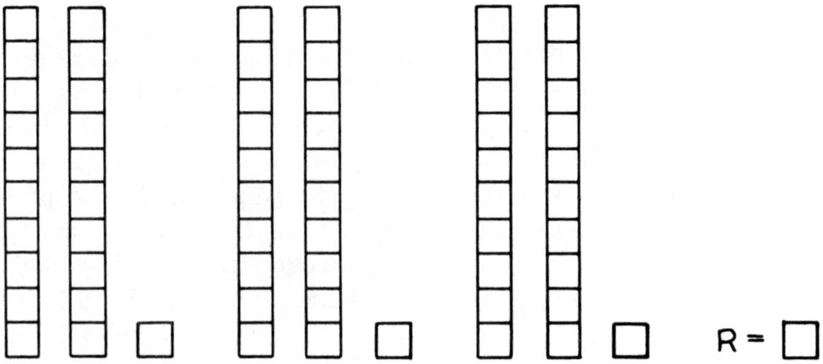

R = ☐

Solution:      tens ¦ ones
              _____
                2 ¦ 1   R 1
             3 ⌐ 6 ¦ 4

Division problems that require regrouping can be solved in much the same manner; for example, in the problem 54 ÷ 4. This means that there are four groups, each of which must be the same quantity. The 5 tens are distributed one to each group, leaving 1 ten over. The leftover ten is regrouped, or broken into 10 ones. These 10 ones are combined with the original 4 ones. Now there are 14 ones. (This combining process is the reason why students "bring down" numbers in the standard long division procedure.) The 14 ones are evenly distributed to the 4 groups, 3 to each group, leaving 2 ones left over. The answer is 13 with a remainder of 2. Figure 12.15 provides a diagram of this process.

**Developmental algorithms**—The two most commonly taught developmental algorithms in long division are *Greenwood* and *Pyramid*. Examples of problems worked with these two algorithms are presented in Figure 12.16. Unfortunately, these two algorithms may actually confuse the students rather than assisting them. One source of confusion lies in the task demand of estimating two-, three-, and sometimes four-digit quotients. This skill in estimation may be too sophisticated for most upper elementary school students. Another source of confusion lies in attempting to transfer from an algorithm based upon measurement (Greenwood or Pyramid) to one based upon partitions (standard algorithm).

## Basic Rules of Thumb

Regardless of which algorithm you are teaching, certain principles of instruction apply. The following is a list that may help you teach algorithms.

1. Identify prerequisite skills. Three prerequisite skills for any algorithm include mastery of the basic facts, understanding of the meaning of the problem (e.g., addition is joining of sets or part-part-whole), and place value.

2. Provide children with prerequisite skills or skill substitutes like number tables, i.e., fact charts found in the back of most folders. Prerequisite skills should be taught prior to teaching the algorithms (Carnine, 1980).

3. Provide a strategy for applying preskills. Simply teaching preskills alone does not ensure that students, especially those with learning problems, will complete the algorithm correctly (Lloyd, Saltzman, & Kauffman, 1981).

4. Make a judgment call as to the relative amount of time spent on the development of meaning and time spent in drill. Even though meaning is the major goal of mathematics instruction, some students may never understand the underlying concepts and may need to learn the mechanics by rote to survive in the academic and real worlds.

**Figure 12.15**

Modified Long Division Approach With Regrouping

Problem:  54 ÷ 4

Approach:

Step 1: Break 54 into groups of tens and ones

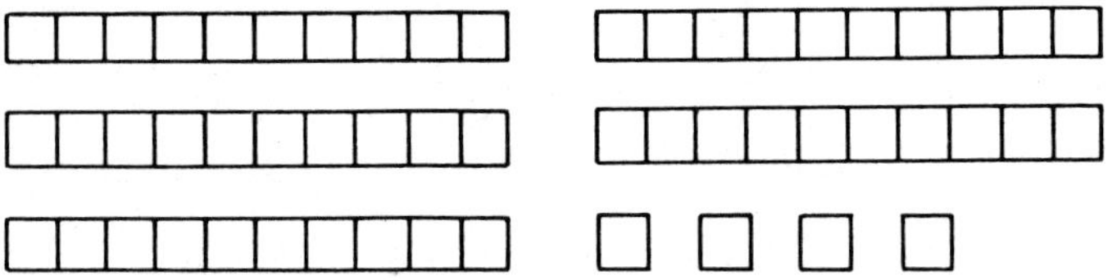

Step 2: Make 4 equal groups out of the tens

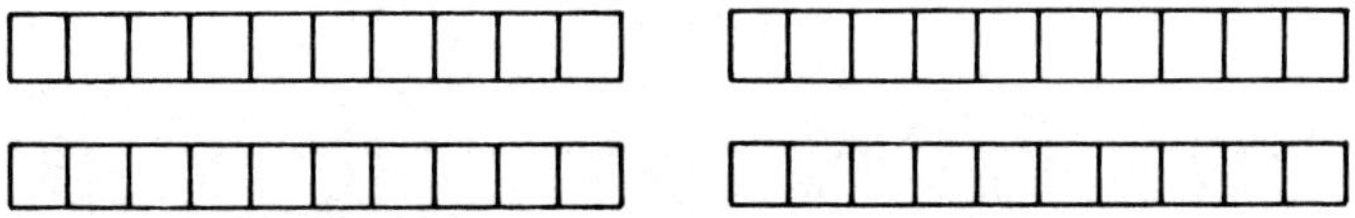

Step 3: Regroup the leftover ten with the ones

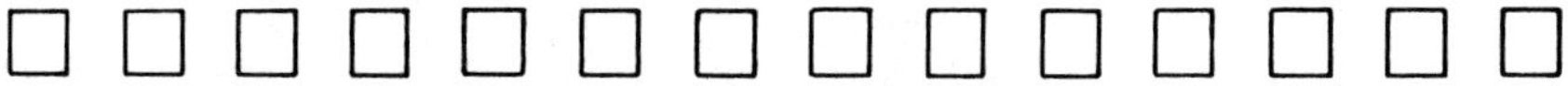

Step 4: Make 4 equal groups out of the ones

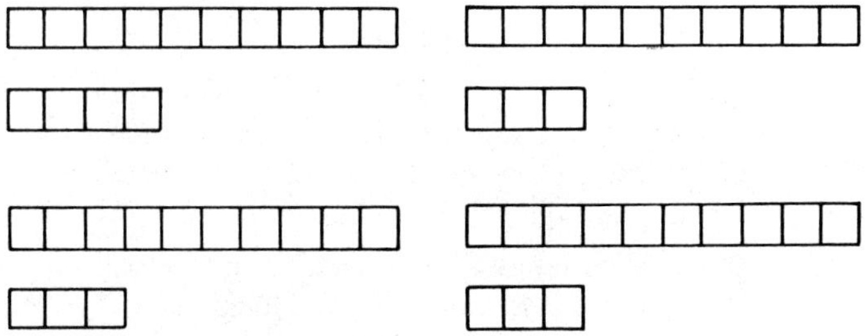

Solution:

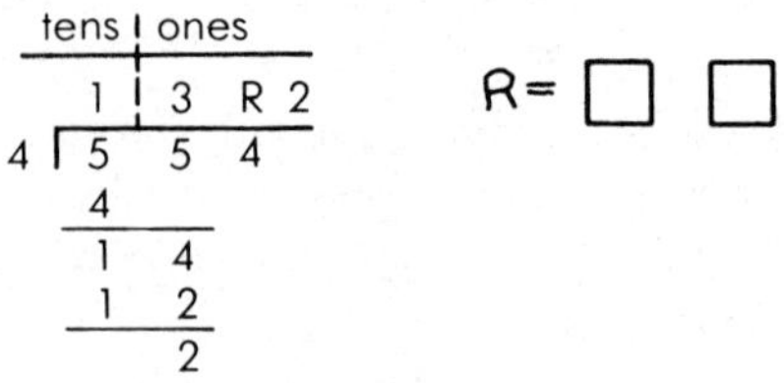

| tens | ones | | |
| --- | --- | --- | --- |
| 1 | 3 | R 2 | |
| 4 ⟌ 5 | 5 | 4 | |
| 4 | | | |
| 1 | 4 | | |
| 1 | 2 | | |
| | 2 | | |

R = ☐ ☐

5. Provide activities that allow for a high success rate. Error rates should be less than 20%; in other words, children should be getting at least 80% of their work correct (Berliner, 1980b).

**Figure 12.16**
Long Division Problems Worked with Greenwood and Pyramid Algorithms

|  | Greenwood |  |  | Pyramid |
|---|---|---|---|---|
|  | 5⌐177̄ |  |  | 35 |
|  | 100 | 20 |  | 5 |
|  | 77 |  |  | 30 |
|  | 50 | 10 |  | 5⌐177̄· |
|  | 27 |  |  | 150 |
|  | 25 | 5 |  | 27 |
|  | 2 | 35 |  | 2 |

**Greenwood**

Solution:

Step 1: Determine the number of times 5 occurs at the **hundreds** level and subtract from 177

```
 5⌐177̄
→100  20
  77
```

Step 2: Determine the number of times 5 occurs at the **tens** level and subtract from 77.

```
 5⌐177̄
 100  20
  77
 —50  10
  27
```

Step 3: Determine the number of times 5 occurs at the **ones** level and subtract from 25.

```
 5⌐177̄
 —100  20
   77
 —50  10
   27
 —25   5
    2
```

Step 4: Add the hundreds, tens and ones and note the remainder.

```
 5⌐177̄
 —100  20
   77
 —50  10
   27
   25 +5
   r2  35 r 2
```

**Figure 12.16**
(Continued)

Pyramid

Solution:

Step 1: Determine the number of times 5 occurs at the **hundreds** level and subtract from 177.

```
   ┌--30
 5 │177
   └-150
      27
```

Step 2: Determine the number of times 5 occurs at the **tens** level and subtract from 27.

```
   ┌-----5
   │   30
 5 │177
   │-150
   │   27
   │ -25
   └--→2
```

Step 3: Add 30 + 5 and note the remainder 2.

```
  + 35 r 2
        5
  + 30
 5│177
  -150
     27
   -25
      2
```

6. Give the students lots of drill and practice. Research indicates that no one form of drill and practice is more effective than any other form. The critical factor is that drill is an integral part of your math program (West, 1980).

## PROBLEM SOLVING

The end goal of mathematics training is problem solving (McGinty & Van Beynen, 1982). All of the energy spent in learning facts and algorithms will be reaped with the student's ability to apply them in problem-solving situations. However, this is not automatic; application of facts and algorithms must be taught.

## Story Problems

Problem solving is often confined to verbal or story problems, typically found at the end of the chapter in the math book. This is the portion of the chapter that the majority of children do the worst on and the part of the chapter that the teacher is most likely to skip. Children often dislike working on word problems because they don't have the strategies to solve them. Sometimes they don't know which operation to perform. An indication of this type of difficulty can be heard in the familiar "Just tell me if I need to add, subtract, multiply, or divide!"

**Math and reading**—For several decades, researchers have been investigating the relationship between math skills and reading ability (Beattie & Schwartz, 1979). Educators used to blame difficulties in problem solving on poor reading skills. Recently we have become aware that reading ability is only one aspect of problem solving (Moses, 1982) and is not necessarily directly related to problem-solving ability (O'Mara, 1981). Even when children understand the process for solving computational exercises and are successful readers, they may have difficulties solving story problems. Learning disabled students often have particular trouble mastering story problems (Dunlap, 1982).

**Necessary skills**—According to Ballew and Cunningham (1982), skills involved in solving story problems include the ability to:

1. Read the problem.
2. Set up the problem so that the necessary computation is ready to be performed.
3. Perform the necessary computation.
4. Integrate reading, interpreting the problem, and computation into the entire solution of a word problem.

The "problem" with solving story problems does not lie in the reading or in the computation, but seems more to be in deciding what to do with the information. Dunlap (1982) has suggested a seven-step procedure for helping students make the correct story problem decisions.

Step 1: Read the story problem.

Step 2: Write the message in the child's words.

Step 3: Draw a picture to illustrate the message.

Step 4: Select relevant numbers.

Step 5: Identify the question.

Step 6: Select the operation indicated by the message and question.

Step 7: Write the number sentence (p. 386).

Yoshi doesn't usually do very well with story problems. Using Dunlap's approach, the teacher presents Yoshi with the following problem: "It's a nice warm day and your cats are outside. Three of the cats are on the porch in the shade. Two of the cats are resting on the branch of a tree. How many cats are there?"

Yoshi and his teacher read the problem together. Yoshi tells the teacher in his own words what the story means: "Two brown cats are up in the tree and three other ones are on the porch out of the sun." He then draws a picture to represent this problem. (See Figure 12.17.) Next Yoshi and his teacher discuss the picture and identify how many cats are in the tree and how many are on the porch. Now they are ready to decide what the problem is asking.

**Figure 12.17**
Yoshi's Picture Representing 2 + 3

They conclude that it wants to know how many cats are in the yard. This means Yoshi has to add the number of cats in the tree to the number of cats on the porch. He writes "2 + 3 = 5." The teacher asks Yoshi what the 5 means. Yoshi answers that it means five cats.

## Strategies for Solving Story Problems

Dunlap's approach seems to be reasonable for helping children solve traditional story problems. However, problem solving encompasses more than story problems. It is the process used when a solution to a situation is sought but is not immediately apparent. This is the part of mathematics that does not rely so much on numbers as on reasoning ability. Krulik and Rudnick (1981) indicate that problem solving is a skill and, like any other skill, can be taught. To enhance students' problem-solving skills, teachers must teach strategies that can help students understand the problem, organize information, and use the information to find a solution. Such strategies include:

1. Looking for patterns
2. Drawing a diagram or picture
3. Using manipulatives
4. Constructing a table or graph
5. Acting it out
6. Working an easier problem of the same type
7. Breaking set/taking a new point of view.

**Looking for patterns**—These problems typically ask "What is the next entry in the series?" and then provide sequences with missing elements, as in: 1, 3, 5, _____ or 0, 1, 3, 6, 10, _____. However, they need not involve numbers, as in the series J, F, M, A, _____, J, _____, A, S, _____, N, _____. Once students have found the next entry, they should be encouraged to verbalize the pattern. In the first example shown, they would state "7" because the series is odd numbers. In the second example, they would say "15" because the series added 1, then 2, then 3, then 4, and now needs to add 5. In the final example, they would choose "M" for the first blank since the series is the first letters of the months of the year. The other blanks would be filled by J, O, and D, respectively.

**Drawing a diagram or picture**—This strategy is included in Dunlap's approach to solving word problems. For example, while driving along the freeway, a driver notices a road sign that reads "Barlow 38 miles, Freemont 105 miles." How far apart are Barlow and Freemont? A diagram would help the child see the relationships within the problem and could suggest the operation needed to solve it. (See Figure 12.18.)

**Figure 12.18**
Using Diagrams to Solve Problems

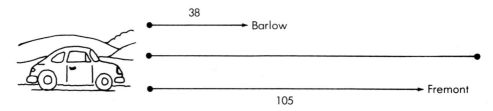

**Using manipulatives**— Manipulatives would be of great help in solving the following problem: "Last Saturday I saw seven cyclists pass my house. I counted 17 wheels. Some riders were on bikes and the rest were on trikes. How many bikers and trikers did I see?" Students could use 17 markers and begin arranging them in groups of 2 (to represent bikes) and groups of 3 (to represent trikes) until they had used all 17 markers, keeping in mind they could have only 7 groups all together. They should discover that there were 4 bikers and 3 trikers.

**Making a table or graph**—This strategy helps students organize any information given in the problem and generate new information to help find a solution, e.g., "Carmen is knitting a sweater. Every seven rows make 1 inch of sweater. How many rows will she have to knit to make the sweater 15 inches long?" (See Figure 12.19.)

**Acting it out**—By becoming actively involved in a problem situation, students may gain a better understanding of the information in the problem and the relationship between the pieces of information. A problem which can be acted out is: "A farmer is taking a goose, a fox, and a sack of grain to the mar-

**Figure 12.19**
Using a Table to Organize Information

| Rows | Inches |
|------|--------|
| 7 | 1 |
| 14 | 2 |
| 21 | 3 |
| ... | ... |
| 70 | 10 |
| ... | ... |
| 105 | 15 |

ket. On the way, he must cross a river. The farmer, who is the only one who can row, finds a boat. But he can only take one commodity at a time with him. If he leaves the fox with the goose, the goose will be eaten. If he leaves the goose with the grain, the grain will be eaten. How does he get all three commodities across the river?" To solve the problem, four students can act out the parts of the farmer, goose, fox, and sack of grain. By trying different actions and discussing what they have done, they will finally decide that the farmer must take the goose across first. He then rows back alone and gets the grain. When he gets the grain across the river, he picks up the goose and brings it back to the original side. He then takes the fox across and comes back alone to get the goose.

**Working an easier problem**—For many students, the stumbling block in problem solving might be the virtual size of the numbers used in a problem. By substituting smaller numbers, students are often able to decide what to do and then reinsert the original numbers. Another use of this strategy is with problems involving fractions. If students substitute whole numbers, the situations are often easier for them to solve. For example, in the problem "What number divided by 1/5 equals 1/5?" (see Figure 12.20), the student could use whole numbers for the 1/5's. The problem then becomes "What number divided by 2 equals 2?" or "What number divided by 7 equals 7?" The pattern is often more evident with the whole numbers than with the fractions: Multiply the two given numbers, since we are looking for a missing product. The original problem could then be solved by $1/5 \times 1/5$ and the solution (1/25) found.

**Breaking set/taking a new point of view**—This strategy is useful for nontraditional problems and often involved in brain teasers. It is probably one of the most useful strategies since real-life problems will not always follow textbook formats. Teachers must choose brain teasers carefully in order to provide enough success experiences that students will continue to participate in problem-solving activities. Students should also be encouraged to use any other known strategies to help them solve these problems. An example of a brain teaser is: "A farmer plants 10 trees in five straight lines, 4 trees to a line.

**Figure 12.20**
Using Substitution to Work Difficult Problems

$$? \div 1/5 = 1/5$$
$$? \div 2 = 2$$
$$? \div 7 = 7$$

How does she do this?" Unless students are taught that some problems cannot be solved with their preconceived ideas, brain teasers and nontraditional problems can cause frustration. In the example given, many students will attempt to order the trees in vertical or horizontal lines and ignore other possibilities, such as diagonal or criss-crossing lines. (Figure 12.21 shows the solution.)

## Employing Strategies

Students need to know that each strategy can be used to solve many different types of problems and that any one problem can be solved by several strategies. Teachers must distinguish between lessons for teaching a strategy and lessons for teaching problem solving. A strategy is like a prerequisite skill in that students need to know it before they can be expected to apply it in a problem-solving situation. Once students know the strategies, teachers must demonstrate how and when to use them. This can be done in problem-solving lessons where everyone, including the teacher, is involved in using learned strategies to solve problems.

## Reading and Problem Solving

Competent problem solvers will need to engage in activities that allow them to gain meaning from written material. They have behaviors common to any competent reader. Listed below are a few of the behaviors associated with competent readers. They:

1. Constantly monitor understanding by using certain strategies, i.e., rereading, skimming, or looking for some easier but related example of the problem, underlining key words, rewording in their own language, or going to another person for a discussion of the topic

2. Stop reading when the information doesn't make sense

3. Find help when clarification is needed

**Figure 12.21**
Solution to Tree-Planting Problem

4. Isolate the key elements and eliminate unnecessary detail
5. Relate information to previously learned concepts
6. Predict what's going to happen next and then confirm or deny information.

Strategies for teaching readers to be competent can best be done through a process developed by Ann Brown called *reciprocal reading instruction.* While reciprocal reading was not specifically designed for teaching problem solving in mathematics, the strategies and teaching techniques can be used quite successfully in math. The four strategies associated with this approach are summarizing, developing questions (i.e., pointing out what is important), analyzing reader problems (difficulties the reader might be having, e.g., "I don't understand what this sentence says" or "How am I going to find out this word?"), and predicting the outcome. These strategies are coupled with a three-step teaching technique.

Step 1 Teacher models.
Step 2 Teacher requests student to summarize.
Step 3 Teacher works with student response.

Students must understand that teachers and other adults go through a thinking process in order to solve problems, that answers do not magically appear in the adult's mind. Teachers can demonstrate these thinking processes by talking out loud as they model the process of solving a problem. Teacher modeling is more than writing the equation and searching for an answer. To model for students effectively, teachers must orally summarize the information from the problem, verbalize questions that would ordinarily be internalized, state the parts needing clarification, and present students with their predictions (Eagle & Watson, 1972). It is extremely frustrating for inexpert problem solvers to be presented with a problem and then have an adult show a nice, clean solution without any evidence of struggle. Students develop the idea that unless they can solve problems quickly, neatly, and precisely, they are mathematics losers.

In trying to solve the problem of the farmer with 10 trees planted in 5 lines, 4 trees to a line, the teacher reads the problem out loud and, using her own words, tells the class what she thinks the problem means. She might say that she knows she can work with 10 trees, 4 in a line and 5 lines. Some questions she might ask of herself are whether the lines cross, whether they all go in the same direction, and whether she can figure out which strategy (such as drawing pictures or using manipulatives) would be best to use. An item that might need clarification could be whether the lines are straight or curved or whether this makes any difference. She then makes some guesses such as "I wonder if it's going to be a rectangle." After trying that shape and seeing that it doesn't work, she makes a new prediction and tests it. This last step might have to be done several times before a solution is located.

The next step is for the teacher and the student to go through the four-strategy process together. Finally, the student assumes the part of the teacher and models the process. The student's first attempts at modeling might not be fully developed or give complete answers; some parts may even be blatantly wrong. The teacher must salvage what is correct and elaborate where necessary.

This three-step processing of teaching modeling, student-teaching cooperation, and student modeling is done over a series of lessons and a number of different problems. Students do not model problems the teacher has already solved, but should have new problems at their level of difficulty.

### Rules of Thumb for Problem Solving

1. Practice translating words from English into mathematical symbols—"seven more than" would be " + 7"; "twice as many as" would be "2 ×."

2. See if relaxation exercises prior to math or problem-solving instruction calms students down and relieves frustration.

3. If students come up with the wrong solution, help them find the question they answered and compare that to the question that should have been asked.

4. Provide students with an equation and solution and have them create a problem that could be solved with it.

5. Give the students credit for having an idea of how to solve the problem, even if the computations do not produce the correct answer (Eagle & Watson, 1972).

6. Since mathematics is a succinct, precise language, encourage students to read carefully so as not to overlook a key word or phrase (Dunlop & Strope, 1982).

7. NEVER EVER SAY "NOW WASN'T THAT EASY?"

## ESTIMATION

Although paper-and-pencil computation has historically been a major portion of elementary mathematics instruction, many real-life problems do not require exact answers. Children often develop reasonable estimation strategies (Ginsburg, Baroody, & Russell, 1982), but these techniques are rarely included in the formal mathematics curriculum.

## Characteristics

Levin (1981) has suggested that any estimation process must include the following characteristics:

1. The computation required in the estimation process can be done mentally. That is, there is no need to resort to calculators, paper and pencil, or other aid.
2. The process produces "partial results" and can be reapplied to produce successively closer approximations. For example, when multiplying 3487 × 2789, the student could estimate the product by solving 3000 × 3000, using only the thousands places; then 3400 × 3000 to get a closer approximation, and so forth.
3. Techniques are simple and easy to use so that students prefer to estimate rather than to ask someone else or to use alternatives such as calculators or paper and pencil.

Students need to be taught that estimation is making an educated guess and so should be done before the paper-and-pencil computation, not afterwards by simply rounding off the answer.

## Techniques

Three common estimation techniques are *front end estimation, rounding off,* and *stating the range. Front end estimation* considers only those digits in the left-most column of the problem and operates with them (that is, adds, subtracts, multiplies, or divides them). (See Figure 12.22.) *Rounding off* is slightly more precise than the front end technique in that each number in the problem is rounded off and operated on. In front end estimation, the estimates might end up being tens, hundreds, or thousands too low since the left-most column might not always be filled. Rounding off can be done to the

**Figure 12.22**
Front End Estimation

|      |        |
|-----:|-------:|
| 2398 |   2000 |
|  846 |      — |
| 3265 |   3000 |
| +1423 | +1000 |
|      |   6000 |

nearest tens, hundreds, thousands, etc., and so provides a more accurate estimate. Figure 12.23 shows the rounding-off technique using the same numbers used in the front end approach. *Stating the range* involves a bit of
rounding off. Numbers are rounded down to the nearest ten, hundred, and
so on, and an estimate is found. Then they are rounded up to the nearest ten,
hundred, and so on, and a second estimate is found. This gives two values between which the actual answer usually falls. (See Figure 12.24.)

**Figure 12.23**
Rounding to the Nearest Thousand

|       |       |
|-------|-------|
| 2398  | 2000  |
| 846   | 1000  |
| 3265  | 3000  |
| +1423 | +1000 |
|       | 7000  |

**Figure 12.24**
Range Estimates, Rounding to 100's

|       | Lower Limit | Upper Limit |
|-------|-------------|-------------|
| 2398  | 2300        | 2400        |
| 846   | 800         | 900         |
| 3265  | 3200        | 3300        |
| +1423 | +1400       | +1500       |
|       | 7700        | 8100        |

# SPECIAL CONSIDERATIONS FOR SPECIAL CHILDREN

## PERCEPTUAL CONSIDERATIONS

There are differences between perceptual aspects and cognitive aspects of
approaching arithmetic. Cognitive aspects refer to processes such as solving problems—problems that are verbally expressed and require logical
thinking. Perceptual aspects refer to such factors as working from up to
down or right to left (Wagner, 1981). Some children with learning problems have directionality problems. Unless assisted, they can have serious
trouble with any kind of columnar work such as regrouping in addition or

subtraction. Using color codes to indicate place value and aides such as graph paper can help a student keep the ones in the ones place and the tens in the tens place. Some students may also have problems with visual perception. They may misperceive a mathematical sign by rotating it, e.g., confusing " × " for " + ." Block (1980) has identified a number of perceptual problem areas that can affect mathematics performance.

1. Reversals, transpositions, rotations, and basic discrimination problems
2. Visual recall—short term or long term
3. Auditory perception, especially in discriminating figure-ground—the child may appear auditorily distractible and have severe problems following oral directions in a class setting
4. Auditory recall—i.e., short-term difficulty remembering digits just heard, and long-term difficulty—sorting number facts
5. Visual–motor integration—i.e., difficulty copying
6. Visual–spatial planning and organizing how and where numbers should go on a page (p. 177)

These kinds of perceptual problems can be found across a wide variety of handicapping conditions, but not all handicapped children suffer from perceptual problems.

## LANGUAGE CONCERNS

Difficulties in understanding mathematics have often been attributed to the difficulty of the vocabulary. While vocabulary is important, the difficulty of the mathematics symbols seems to contribute the most to misunderstandings (Klune, 1973). We cannot assume that a student will simply "pick up" the symbolic material associated with mathematics. Students need to know the meaning of mathematical vocabulary to succeed in problem solving. Unfortunately, direct instruction of mathematical vocabulary appears to influence only performance on tasks involving that vocabulary, i.e., there seems to be very little transfer of learning to mathematical tasks involving other vocabulary (O'Mara, 1981). According to O'Mara (1981),

> Verbal problems can be made easier to read by altering either their syntax (e.g., removing subordinate clauses and providing a series of simple sentences) or the form of the problem (so that the sequence of information in

the problem matches the sequence of information in the equation necessary for the solution), but not by altering the problem verb (using synonyms such as *minus* or *take away* or *less* does not seem to significantly affect pupil performance). (p. 29)

In any event, the language of math seems quite different from that of
prose. Student performance can be improved by eliminating extraneous information and reordering the sequence in which numbers are presented in a
math word problem to conform to the sequence of arithmetic operations
needed to solve the problem (Cohen & Stover, 1981). Complex sentences are
also easier to comprehend when the order of "mention of events directly indicates the temporal order" (Rosenthal & Resnick, 1971).

## SUMMARY

Mathematics instruction has often presented problems for teachers working
with children who find learning math difficult. Teaching math to children who
are slow or who have special instructional needs is compounded when teachers feel that they must cover the text page by page. Strategies for teaching
children to learn how to learn mathematics have been found very useful for
children who have problems in learning basic facts, algorithms, and problem
solving.

Teachers can manipulate instructional factors that have an impact on a
student's learning. Four of the most easily manipulated factors within the
teacher's command are time, size of instructional groups, reinforcement, and
materials. The way teachers use these four factors can significantly increase or
decrease the amount of math learning that takes place.

While most teaching recommendations are similar for any child experiencing math learning difficulties, some special considerations may need to be
made in light of certain handicapping conditions. Children who have perceptual difficulties, e.g, left to right confusion, may need special materials adaptations. Children with language problems may need syntax simplification before math problem solving. Any child with a sensory difficulty, such as a visual
or auditory impairment, will need materials and techniques that account for
these deficits. Instructional emphasis, regardless of handicapping conditions,
should always focus on identification of skills acquired by students and those
skills still needed for a successul mathematics experience.

# References

Adams, M.J., & Collins, A. (1977). *A schema-theoretic view of reading* (Tech. Rep. 32). Urbana, IL: Center for the Study of Reading.

Adams, M.J., & Collins, A. (1979). A schema-theoretical view of reading. In R.O. Freedle (Ed.), *New directions in discourse processing* (Vol. 1). Norwood, NJ: Ablex Publishing.

Adelman, H.S. (1979). Diagnostic classification of LD: A practical necessity and a procedural problem. *Learning Disability Quarterly, 2,* 56-62.

Allington, R.L. (1978). Word identification abilities of severely disabled readers: A comparison in isolation and context. *Journal of Reading Behavior, 10,* 409-416.

Amaria, R.P., Brian, L.A., & Leith, G.D. (1969). Individual vs. cooperative learning: Influence of intelligence and sex. *Educational Research, 11,* 95-103.

Anderson, L.M., Evertson, C.M., & Brophy, J.E. (1979). An experimental study of effective teaching in first-grade reading groups. *The Elementary School Journal, 79,* 193-223.

Anderson, R.C., & Friebody, P.(1979). *Vocabulary knowledge* (Tech. Rep. 136). Champaign-Urbana: University of Illinois, Center for the Study of Reading.

Anderson, R.C., Hiebert, E.H., Scott, J.A., & Wilkinson, I.A.G. (1985). *Becoming a nation of readers: The report of the Commission on Reading.* Washington, DC: National Institute of Education.

Arthur, G. (1950). *The Arthur Adaptation of the Leiter International Performance Scale.* Chicago: C.H. Stoelting.

Ashby-Davis, C. (1981). A review of three techniques for use with remedial readers. *The Reading Teacher, 34,* 534-538.

Ashcroft, S.C., & Zambone-Ashley, A.M. (1980). Mainstreaming children with visual impairments. *Journal of Research and Development in Education, 13*(4), 22-36.

Asher, S.R., Hymel, S., & Wigfield, A. (1978). Influence of topic interest on children's comprehension. *Journal of Reading Behavior, 10,* 35-47.

Austin, J.D. (1982). Children with a learning disability and mathematics. *School Science and Mathematics, 82,* 201-208.

Ausubel, D.P. (1968). *Educational psychology: A cognitive view.* New York: Holt, Rinehart and Winston.

Ausubel, D.P., Novak, J.D., & Hanesian, H. (1978). *Educational psychology: A cognitive view* (2nd ed.). New York: Holt, Rinehart and Winston.

Ayrault, E.W. (1977). *Growing up handicapped.* New York: Seabury Press.

Bailey, E.J. (1975). *Academic activities for adolescents with learning disabilities.* Denver: Learning Pathways.

Baines, H. (1975). *An assessment and comparison of syntactic complexity and word associations of good and poor readers in grades 4, 8, and 12.* Unpublished doctoral dissertation, University of Georgia.

Ballew, H., & Cunningham, J.W. (1982). Diagnosing strengths and weaknesses of sixth-grade students in solving word problems. *Journal for Research in Mathematics Education, 13,* 202-210.

Balthazar, E.E., & Stevens, H.A. (1975). *The emotionally disturbed mentally retarded: A historical and contemporary perspective.* Englewood Cliffs, NJ: Prentice-Hall.

Bank-Mikkelsen, N.E. (1969). A metropolitan area in Denmark: Copenhagen. In R.B. Kugel & W. Wolfensberger (Eds.). *Changing patterns in residential services for the mentally retarded.* Washington, DC: President's Committee on Mental Retardation.

Barraga, N.C. (1976). *Visual handicaps and learning: A developmental approach.* Belmont, CA: Wadsworth.

Bateman, B. (1979). Teaching reading to learning disabled children. In L.B. Resnick & P.A. Weaver (Eds.), *Theory and practice of early reading.* Hillsdale, NJ: Lawrence Erlbaum.

Bean, T.W., & Pardi, R. (1979). A field test of guided reading strategy. *Journal of Reading, 23,* 144-147.

Beattie, J., & Algozzine, B. (1982). Improving basic academic skills of educable mentally retarded adolescents. *Education and the Training of the Mentally Retarded, 17,* 255-258.

Beattie, J.R., & Schwartz, S.E. (1979). Readability of special education math books. *Pointer, 23,* 43-46.

Beattie, L.S., Madden, R., Gardner, E.G., & Karlesen, B. (1976). *Stanford Diagnostic Mathematics Test.* Cleveland: The Psychological Corp.

Beck, I.L., Omanson, R.C., & McKeown, M.G. (1982). An instructional redesign of reading lessons: Effects on comprehension. *Reading Research Quarterly, 17,* 462-481.

Becker, W.C., & Englemann, S. (1977). The direct instruction model. In R. Rhine (Ed.), *Encouraging change in America's schools: A decade of experimentation.* New York: Academic Press.

Beebe, M.J. (1980). The effect of different types of substitution miscues on reading. *Reading Research Quarterly, 15,* 324-336.

Belmont, J.M., Butterfield, E.C., & Borkowski, J.G. (1978). Training retarded people to generalize memorization methods across memory tasks. In M.M. Gruneberg, P.E. Morris, & R.N. Sykes (Eds.), *Practical aspects of memory.* London: Academic Press.

Ben-Jacob, M.G. (1981). Innovative mathematics instruction for the new decade: Strategy methods of mathematics pedagogy. *Focus on Learning Problems in Mathematics, 3,* 5-11.

Bennett, R. (1969). Cecil's problem. *Texas Outlook,* 24-25.

Berliner, D.C. (1980). Allocation time, engaged time and academic learning time in elementary school mathematics instruction. *Focus on Learning Problems in Mathematics, 2,* 27-39.

Berliner, D.C. (1980b). Using research on teaching for the improvement of classroom practice. *Theory into Practice, 19,* 302-308.

Betts, E.A. (1957). *Foundations of reading instructions.* New York: American Book.

Bien, E.C. (1974). The relationship of cognitive style and structure of arithmetic materials to performance in fourth grade arithmetic. (Doctoral dissertation, University of Pennsylvania, 1974). *Dissertation Abstracts International, 35,* 2040-2041. (University Microfilms No. 74-22, 809).

Bigge, J.L., & O'Donnell, P.A. (1976). *Teaching individuals with physical and multiple disabilities.* Columbus, OH: Merrill.

Bigge, J., Sirvis, B., & Carpignano, J. (1976). Psychosocial aspects of physical disability. In J. Bigge & P. O'Donnell, *Teaching individuals with physical and multiple disabilities.* Columbus, OH: Charles E. Merrill.

Bigge, M.L. (1976). *Learning theories for teachers.* New York: Harper & Row.

Birch, J.W., Tisdall, W.T., Peabody, R., & Sterrett, R. (1966). *School achievement and effect of type size on reading in visually handicapped children.* Pittsburgh: University of Pittsburgh.

Bishop, A.J. (1980). Classroom conditions for learning mathematics. In R. Karplus (Ed.), *Proceedings of the Fourth International Conference for the Psychology of Mathematics Education.* Berkeley, California.

Bishop, D.V.M. (1982). Comprehension of spoken, written, and signed sentences in childhood language disorders. *Journal of Child Psychology and Psychiatry, 23,* 1-20.

Blackburn, J.E., & Powell, W.C. (1976). *One at a time: All at once: The teacher's guide to individualized instruction without anarchy.* Pacific Palisades, CA: Goodyear.

Block, G.H. (1980). Dyscalculia and the minicalculator. *Academic Therapy, 16,* 175-181.

Bloom, B.S. (1977). Favorable learning conditions for all. *Teacher, 95,* 22-28.

Bloom, L., & Lahey, M. (1978). *Language development and language disorders.* New York: Wiley.

Bolduc, E.J., Jr. (1980). The monsters in multiplication. *The Arithmetic Teacher*, *28*(3), 24-26.

Boucher, C.R., & Deno, S.L. (1979). Learning disabled and emotionally disturbed: Will the labels affect teacher planning? *Psychology in the Schools, 16*, 395-402.

Bransford, J.D., & Johnson, M.K. (1972). Contextual prerequisites for understanding: Some investigations of comprehension and recall. *Journal of Verbal Learning and Verbal Behavior, 11*, 717-726.

Brigance, A. (1977). *Brigance Diagnostic Inventory of Basic Skills*. North Billerica, MA: Curriculum Associates.

Britton, J.N. (1970). Now that you go to school. In R.L. Warren (Ed.), *Children and writing in the elementary school*. London: Oxford University Press.

Brockmiller, P.R., & Coley, J.D. (1981). A survey of method, materials, and teacher preparation among teachers of reading to the hearing impaired. *Reading Teacher, 34*, 526-529.

Brophy, J.E. (1979). Teacher behavior and its effects. *Journal of Educational Psychology, 71*, 733-750.

Brownell, W.A., & Moser, H.E. (1949). Meaningful vs. mechanical learning: A study in grade III subtraction. *Duke University Studies in Education, 8*. Durham, NC: Duke University Press.

Bryan, T.H., & Bryan, J.H. (1978). Social interactions of learning disabled children. *Learning Disabled Quarterly, 1*(1), 33-38.

Bryant, N.D., Fayne, H.R., & Gettinger, M. (1982). Applying the mastery learning model to sight word instruction for disabled readers. *Journal of Experimental Education, 50*, 116-121.

Bulmahn, B.J., & Young, D.M. (1982). On the transmission of mathematics anxiety. *Arithmetic Teacher, 30*, 55-56.

Burdwell, R. (1981). Feedback: How does it work? *The Journal of Experimental Education, 50*, 4-8.

Callaway, B. (1981). What turns children "on" or "off" in readng. *Improving Reading, 18*, 214-217.

Carnine, D.W. (1980). Preteaching versus concurrent teaching of the component skills of a multiplication problem-solving strategy. *Journal for Research in Mathematics Education, 11*, 375-379.

Carnine, D.W. (1981). Reducing training problems associated with visually and auditorily similar correspondences. *Journal of Learning Disabilities, 14*, 276-279.

Carnine, D.W., & Silbert, J. (1979). *Direct instruction reading*. Columbus, OH: Charles E. Merrill.

Carrow, E. (1974). *Carrow Elicited Language Inventory*. Austin, TX: Learning Concepts.

Carter, A., & Stokes, W.T. (1982). What children know about reading before they can read. *Journal of Education, 64*, 173-184.

Carter, R. (1977). *Help! These kids are driving me crazy.* Champaign, IL: Research Press.

Cartwright, G.P. (1969). Written expression and spelling. In R.M. Smith (Ed.), *Teacher diagnosis of educational difficulties* (pp. 95-117). Columbus, OH: Charles E. Merrill.

Cazden, C.B. (1972). *Child language and education.* New York: Holt, Rinehart & Winston.

Ceci, S.J., & Peters, D.J. (1980). Dyscalculia and the perceptual deficit hypothesis: A correlational study. *Focus on Learning Problems in Mathematics, 2,* 11-14.

Chapman, E.K. (1978). *Visually handicapped children and young people.* London: Routledge and Kegan Paul.

Chinn, P.C., Drew, C.S., & Logan, D.R. (1979). *Mental retardation: A life cycle approach* (2nd ed.). St. Louis: C.V. Mosby Co.

Chomsky, C. (1969). *The acquisition of syntax in children from 5 to 10.* Cambridge: MIT Press.

Chomsky, N. (1959). A review of "Verbal Behavior," by B.F. Skinner. *Language, 35,* 26-58.

Christine, R.O., & Hollingsworth, P.M. (1966). An experiment in spelling. *Education, 86,* 565-567.

Christopherson, S.L., Schultz, C.B., & Warren, Y. (1981). The effect of two contextreal conditions on recall of a reading passage and on thought processes in reading. *Journal of Reading, 24,* 573-578.

Clark-Meeks, L.F., Quesenberry, N.L., & Mouw, J.T. (1982). A look at mathematics attitudes of prospective teachers in four concentration areas. *School Science and Mathematics, 82,* 317-320.

Clarke, B.R., Rogers, W.T., & Booth, J.A. (1982). How hearing impaired children learn to read: Theoretical and practical issues. In R.E. Kretschmer (Ed.), *Reading and the hearing impaired individual* (Monograph). *Volta Review, 84,* 57-69.

Claxton, G. (1980). Memory research. In J.J. Tuinman, (Ed.), *The Journal of Reading, 23,* 414-419.

Clay, M.M. (1972). *Reading: The patterning of complex behavior.* New York: International Publishing.

Clay, M.M. (1976). Early childhood and cultural diversity in New Zealand. *Reading Teacher, 29,* 333-342.

Cleek, M.K., Gieber, M., & Mair, C. (1978). *Clarification of P.L. 94-142 for the classroom teacher.* Philadelphia: Research for Better Schools.

Cohen, S.A., & Stover, G. (1981). Effects of teaching sixth-grade students to modify format variables of math word problems. *Reading Research Quarterly, 16,* 175-200.

Conley, J.E. (1976). Role of idiomatic expressions in the reading of deaf children. *American Annals of the Deaf, 121,* 381-385.

Connolly, A., Nachtman, W., & Pritchett, E. (1976). *Manual for KeyMath Diagnostic Arithmetic Test.* Circle Pines, MN: American Guidance Service.

Cooney, T.J., Herstein, J.J., & Davis, E.J. (1981). The effects of two strategies for teaching two mathematical skills. *Journal for Research in Mathematics Education, 12,* 220-225.

Cooper, C.R. (1977). Holistic evaluation of writing. In C.R. Cooper & L. Odell (Eds.), *Evaluating writing: Describing, measuring, judging* (pp. 3-31). Buffalo, NY: National Council of Teachers of English.

Cornett, R., Knight, D., Reynolds, H., & Williams, C. (1979). A theoretical model of the development of reading in hearing impaired children. *Directions, 1,* 43-68.

Cotugno, A.J. (1981). Cognitive controls and reading disabilities revisited. *Psychology in the Schools, 18,* 455-459.

Cox, R.M., & Shrigley, R.L. (1980). Comparing three methods of practicing reading to reduce errors in oral reading. *Reading Improvement, 17,* 306-310.

Craighead, W.E., Kazdin, A.E., & Mahoney, M.J. (1976). *Behavior modification: Principles, issues and applications.* Boston: Houghton Mifflin.

Cromer, W. (1970). The difference model: A new explanation for some reading difficulties. *Journal of Educational Psychology, 6,* 471-483.

Davis, F.B. (1942). Two new measures of reading ability. *Journal of Educational Psychology, 33,* 365-372.

Day, W.F., & Beach, B.R. (1971). Auditory versus visual presentation. In S. Duker (Ed.), *Teaching listening in the elementary school.* Metuchen, NJ: Scarecrow Press.

Denckla, M.B. (1978). Minimal brain dysfunction. In J.S. Chall & A.F. Mursky (Eds.), *Education and the brain.* Chicago: University of Chicago Press (Seventy-seventh yearbook of the National Society for the Study of Education, Part III).

Diveck, C.S. (1975). The role of expectations and attributions in the alleviation of learned helplessness. *Journal of Personality and Social Psychology, 31,* 674-685.

Doehring, D.G., & Aulls, M.W. (1979). The interactive nature of reading acquisition. *Journal of Reading Behavior, 11,* 27-40.

Drass, S.D., & Jones, R.L. (1971). Learning disabled children as behavior modifiers. *Journal of Learning Disabilities, 4,* 418-425.

Driscoll, M.J. (1980a). Algorithms in elementary school mathematics. In *Research within reach: Elementary school mathematics* (pp. 91-98). Washington, DC: National Institute of Education.

Driscoll, M.J. (1980b). Looking beneath and beyond the tests. *Focus on Learning Problems in Mathematics, 2,* 57-63.

Dunlap, W.F. (1982). Readiness for solving story problems. *Academic Therapy, 17,* 581-587.

Dunlop, K.H., Stoneman, Z., & Cantrell, M.L. (1980). Social interaction of exceptional children and other children in a mainstreamed preschool classroom. *Exceptional Children, 47,* 132-141.

Dunlop, W.P., & Strope, G.J. (1982). Reading mathematics: Review of literature. *Focus on Learning Problems in Mathematics, 4*, 39-50.

Dunn, L.M. (1968). Special education for the mildly retarded—Is much of it justified? *Exceptional Children, 35*, 5-22.

Dunn, L.M. (Ed.). (1977). *Exceptional children in the schools.* New York: Holt, Rinehart & Winston.

Dunn, L.M., & Markwardt, F.C. (1970). *Peabody Individual Achievement Test.* Circle Pines, MN: American Guidance Service.

Durkin, D. (1977, October). Comprehension instruction—where are you? *Reading Education Report No. 1.* Urbana: University of Illionois, Center for the Study of Reading.

Durkin, D. (1981). Reading comprehension instruction in basal reader series. *Reading Research Quarterly, 16*, 515-544.

Durrell, D.D. (1955). *Durrell Analysis of Reading Difficulty.* New York: Harcourt Brace.

Dykstra, R. (1974). Phonics and beginning reading instruction. In C. Walcutt, J. Lamport, & G. McCracken (Eds.), *Teaching reading: A phonic/linguistic approach to development reading.* New York: MacMillan.

Eagle, M.R., & Watson, F.R. (1972). On teaching problem solving in mathematics. *Mathematics Teaching, 59*, 8-11.

Eberwein, L. (1982). Do dialect speakers' miscues influence comprehension? *Reading World, 21*, 255-263.

Edwards, L., & DePalma, J. (1982). Emotional disturbance. In E.L. Meyen (Ed.), *Exceptional children in today's schools: An alternative resource book.* Denver: Love.

Ehri, L.C., & Wilce, L.S. (1980). Do beginners learn to read function words better in sentences or in lists? *Reading Research Quarterly, 15*, 451-476.

Elliot, S.N., & Carroll, J.L. (1980). Strategies to help children remember what they read. *Reading Improvement, 17*, 272-277.

Engelhardt, J.M. (1982). Using computational errors in diagnostic teaching. *Arithmetic Teacher, 29*, 16-32.

Engelmann, S. (1969). *Preventing failure in the primary grades.* Chicago: Science Research Associates.

Epstein, M., Hallahan, D., & Kauffman, J. (1975). Implications of the reflectivity-impulsivity dimension for special education. *The Journal of Special Education, 9*, 11-25.

Evans, D.T., & Hall, J.K. (1978). *The delivery of educational services ... and the special child.* Palo Alto, CA: VORT.

Ewaldt, C. (1981). A psycholinguistic description of selected deaf children reading in sign language. *Reading Research Quarterly, 17*, 58-89.

Ferster, C.B., & Perrott, M.C. (1968). *Behavior principles.* New York: New Century.

Fleischner, J.E., Garnett, K., & Sheperd, M.J. (1982). Proficiency in arithmetic basic fact computation of learning disabled and nondisabled children. *Focus on Learning Problems in Mathematics, 4*, 47-56.

Fleisher, L.S., Jenkins, J.R., & Pany, D. (1979). Effects on poor readers' comprehension of training in rapid decoding. *Reading Research Quarterly, 15,* 30-48.

Flesch, R. (1955). *Why Johnny can't read.* New York: Harper and Row.

Flesch, R. (1979). Why Johnny still can't read. *Family Circle, 92,* 26-46.

Fraiberg, S. (1959). *The magic years: Understanding and handling the problems of early childhood.* New York: Charles Scribner.

Fraiberg, S. (1977). *Insights from the blind.* New York: Basic Books.

Fredricksen, C.H. (1979). Discourse comprehension and early reading. In L.B. Resnick & P.A. Weaver, *Theory and practice of early reading.* Hillsdale, NJ: Lawrence Erlbaum.

Freeman, D.J., Kuhs, T.M., Knappen, L.B. & Porter, A.C. (1982). A closer look at standardized tests. *Arithmetic Teacher, 29,* 50-54.

Fremont, H. (1977). Organizing a learning cooperative: Survival groups. *National Council of Teachers of Mathematics Yearbook, 77,* 98-112.

Freudenthal, H. (1981). Major problems of mathematics education. *Educational Studies in Mathematics, 12,* 133-150.

Frostig, M., Lefevre, W., & Whittlesey, J. (1966). *Administration and scoring manual: Marianne Frostig Developmental Test of Visual Perception.* Palo Alto, CA: Consulting Psychologists Press.

Fry, M.A., & Lagomarsino, L. (1982). Factions that influence reading: A developmental perspective. *School Psychology Review, 11,* 239-250.

Gagné, E.E. (1975). Motivating the disabled learner. *Academic Therapy, 10,* 361-362.

Gagné, R. (1983). Some issues in the psychology of mathematics instruction. *Journal for Research in Mathematics Education, 14,* 7-18.

Gallagher, P.A. (1979). *Teaching students with behavior disorders.* Denver: Love.

Gambrell, L.B., Wilson, R.M., & Ganett, W.N. (1981). Classroom observations of task-attending behaviors of good and poor readers. *Journal of Educational Research, 74,* 400-404.

Gaskins, I.H. (1982). Let's end the reading disabilities/learning disabilities debate. *Journal of Learning Disabilities, 15,* 81-83.

Gay, L.R. (1972). Use of a retention index for mathematics instruction. *Journal of Educational Psychology, 63,* 466-472.

Gearheart, B.R., & Weishahn, M.W. (1980). *The handicapped student in the regular classroom* (2nd ed.). St. Louis: C.V. Mosby.

Gentile, L.M. (1981). Dyslexia: A letter to the media. *Journal of Reading, 24,* 565-567.

Gessell, J.K. (1977). *Diagnostic Mathematics Inventory.* Monterey, CA: CTB/ McGraw-Hill.

Gibson, E.J., & Levin, H. (1975). *The psychology of reading.* Cambridge: MIT Press.

Ginsburg, H. (1976). Learning difficulties in children's arithmetic: A clinical cognitive approach. In A.R. Osborne (Ed.), *Models for learning mathematics.* Athens: University of Georgia, Department of Mathematics Education.

Ginsburg, H.P., Baroody, A.J., & Russell, R.L. (1982). Children's estimation ability in addition and subtraction. *Focus on Learning Problems in Mathematics, 4*, 31-46.

Giordano, G. (1982). Does episodic memory influence initial reading instruction? *Journal of Learning Disabilities, 15*, 467-469.

Gipe, J. (1978-79). Investigating techniques for teaching word meanings. *Reading Research Quarterly, 14*, 624-644.

Gipe, J.P., & Arnold, R.D. (1979). Teaching vocabulary through familiar associations and contexts. *Journal of Reading Behavior, 11*, 281-285.

Glass, R.M., Christiansen, J., & Christiansen, J.L. (1982). *Teaching exceptional students in the regular classroom*. Boston: Little, Brown.

Goldstein, K. (1939). *The organism: A holistic approach to biology derived from pathological data in man*. New York: American Book.

Gonzales, R. (1980). Mainstreaming your hearing impaired child in 1980: Still an oversimplification. *Journal of Research and Development in Education, 13*, 15-21.

Good, T.L. (1979). Teacher effectiveness in the elementary school. *Journal of Teacher Education, 30*, 52-64.

Goodman, K.S., & Burke, C.L. (1973). *Theoretically-based studies of patterns of miscues in oral reading performance* (U.S. Office of Education project No. 9-0375). Washington, DC: U.S. Government Printing Office.

Goodman, K.S., & Goodman, Y.M. (1979). Learning to read is natural. In L.B. Resnick & P.A. Weaver (Eds.), *Theory and practice of early reading*. Hillsdale, NJ: Lawrence Erlbaum.

Gormley, K.A. (1981). On the influence of familiarity on deaf students' text recall. *American Annals of the Deaf, 126*, 1024-1030.

Gormley, K.A. (1982). The importance of familiarity in hearing impaired readers' comprehension of text. *Volta Review, 84*, 71-80.

Gormley, K.A., & Geoffrin, L.D. (1981). Another view of using language experience to teach reading to deaf and hearing impaired children. *Reading Teacher, 34*, 519-525.

Gottlieb, J., Semmel, M.I., & Veldman, D.J. (1978). Correlates of social status among mainstreamed mentally retarded children. *Journal of Educational Psychology, 70*, 396-405.

Graham, S. (1982). Comparing the SQ3R method with other study techniques for reading improvement. *Reading Improvement, 19*, 44-47.

Graham, S., & Miller, L. (1980). Handwriting research and practice: A unified approach. *Focus on Exceptional Children, 13*(2), 1-16.

Greer, B.B., Allsop, J., & Greer, J.G. (1980). Environmental alternatives for the physically handicapped. In J.W. Schifani, R.M. Anderson, & S.J. Odle (Eds.), *Implementing learning in the least restrictive environment* (pp. 128-129). Baltimore: University Park Press.

Gresham, F.M. (1982). Misguided mainstreaming: The case for social skills training with handicapped children. *Exceptional Children, 48*, 422-433.

Gronlund, N.E. (1973). *Preparing criterion-referenced tests for classroom instruction.* New York: Macmillan.

Grossman, H.J. (1977). *Manual on terminology and classification in mental retardation.* American Association on Mental Deficiency Special Publications Series No. 2.

Guthrie, J.T. (1982). Effective teaching practices. *The Reading Teacher, 35,* 766-768.

Guttentag, R.E., & Haith, M.M. (1980). A longitudinal study of word processing by first-grade children. *Journal of Educational Psychology, 72,* 701-705.

Haladyna, T., & Thomas, G. (1979). The attitudes of elementary school children toward school and subject matters. *Journal for Experimental Education, 48,* 18-25.

Hall, J.E. (1971). Effect of response bias of mental retardates upon oddity learning. *American Journal of Mental Deficiency, 75,* 579-585.

Hallahan, D.P., & Kauffman, J.M. (Eds.). (1976). *Teaching children with learning disabilities.* Columbus, OH: Charles E. Merrill.

Halliday, M.A.K. (1969). Relevant models of language. *Education Review, 22,* 1-128.

Hammill, D.D., & Bartel, N.R. (1978). *Teaching children with learning and behavior problems.* Boston: Allyn and Bacon.

Hanninen, Kenneth A. (1975). *Teaching the visually handicapped.* Columbus, OH: Charles E. Merrill.

Hansen, C.L. (1978). Writing skills. In N.G. Haring, T.C. Lovitt, M.D. Eaton, & C.L. Hansen (Eds.), *The fourth R: Research in the classroom* (pp. 93-126). Columbus, OH: Charles E. Merrill.

Harber, J., & Bealty, J. (1978). *Reading and the Black English speaking child.* Newark, DE: International Reading Association.

Haring, N.R., Lovitt, T.C., Eaton, M.D., & Hansen, C. (1978). *The fourth R: Research in the classroom.* Columbus, OH: Charles E. Merrill.

Harris, A.J. (1978-79). A reaction to Valtins' "Dyslexia: Deficit in reading or deficit in research?" *Reading Research Quarterly, 14,* 222-225.

Harris, A.J. (1982). How many kinds of reading disabilities are there? *Journal of Learning Disabilities, 15,* 456-460.

Harris, V.W., & Sherman, J.A. (1973). Effects of peer tutoring and consequences on the math performance of elementary classroom students. *Journal of Applied Behavior Analysis, 6,* 587-597.

Hart, J.T., Guthrie, J.T., & Winfield, L. (1980). Black English phonology and learning to read. *Journal of Educational Psychology, 72,* 636-646.

Hashimoto, I.Y. (1982). An assessment of controlled composition as a teaching technique for basic writing. *The English Record, 33,* 17-20.

Hayes, D. (1982). Handwriting practice: The effects of perceptual prompts. *Journal of Educational Research, 75,* 169-172.

Hayes, D.A., & Diehl, W. (1982). What research on prose comprehension suggests for college skills instruction. *Journal of Reading, 25,* 656-661.

Hayes, J. (1977). Annual goals and short-term objectives. In S. Toors (Ed.), *A primer on individualized education programs for handicapped children*. Reston, VA: Foundation for Exceptional Children.

Head, J. (1981). Personality and the learning of mathematics. *Educational Studies in Mathematics, 12*, 339-350.

Heil, H.F. (1976). *The relationship of certain written language variables to measures of reading comprehension in the primary grades*. (Unpublished report). Hofstra University. (ERIC Document Reproduction Service No. ED 145 457)

Heward, W.L., & Orlansky, M.D. (1980). *Exceptional children*. Columbus, OH: Charles E. Merrill.

Heydorn, B.L., & Cheek, E.H., Jr. (1982). Reversals in reading and writing: Perceptual, developmental, diagnostic, and remedial aspects. *Reading Improvement, 19*, 123-128.

Hiebert, J., & Carpenter, T.P. (1982). Piagetian tasks as readiness measures in mathematics instruction: A critical review. *Educational Studies in Mathematics, 13*, 329-346.

Hieronymous, A.N., Lindquist, E.F., & Hoover, H.D. (1982). *Iowa Test of Basic Skills*. Chicago: Riverside.

Hirsch-Pasek, K., & Treiman, R. (1982). Recoding in silent reading: Can the deaf child translate print into a more manageable form? In R.E. Kretschmer (Ed.), *Reading and the hearing impaired individual* (Monograph). *Volta Review, 84*, 57-69.

Hodgkinson, J. (1979). What's right with education. *Phi Delta Kappan, 61*, 159-162.

Horak, V.M., & Horak, W.J. (1982). Let's do it: Collecting and displaying the data around us. *Arithmetic Teacher, 30*, 16-20.

Horn, T. (1969). Spelling. *Encyclopedia of Educational Research* (4th ed.). New York: Macmillan.

Horowitz, S. (1975, April). *Effects of amount of immediate and of delayed practice on retention of mathematical rules*. Paper presented at the annual meeting of the American Educational Research Association, Washington, DC (ERIC Document Reproduction Service No. ED 120 010)

Howell, K.W., & Kaplan, J.S. (1978). Monitoring peer tutoring behavior. *Exceptional Children, 45*, 135-137.

Howell, S., & Riley, J.D. (1978). Words for positive teacher–student interaction in reading instruction. *The Reading Teacher, 31*, 620-623.

Hoyles, C. (1982). The pupil's view of mathematics learning. *Educational Studies in Mathematics, 13*, 349-372.

Hresko, W.P., & Reid, D.K. (1981). Five faces of cognition: Theoretical influences on approaches to learning disabilities. *Learning Disabilities Quarterly, 3*, 238-243.

Hudson, F.G., & Graham, S. (1978). An approach to operationalizing the I.E.P. *Learning Disability Quarterly, 1*, 13-32.

Hughes, T. (1978). *What the British tell the U.S. about writing and reading*. Paper presented at the Great Lakes Regional Conference of the International Reading Association, Cincinnati. (ERIC Document Reproduction Service No. ED 175 020)

Hull, R.H. (1973). Group vs. individual screening in public school audiometry. *Colorado Journal of Educational Research, 13*, 6-9.

Hunt, K.W., & O'Donnell, R. (1970). *An elementary school curriculum to develop better writing skills* (Project No. 8-0903) Tallahassee: Florida State University. (ERIC Document Reproduction Service No. ED 050 108)

Idol-Maestas, L. (1983). *Special educator's consultation handbook.* Rockville, MD: Aspen.

Ikeda, H., & Ando, M. (1974). A new algorithm for subtraction? *The Arithmetic Teacher, 21*, 716-719.

Jan, J.E., Freeman, R.D., & Scott, E.P. (Eds.). (1977). *Visual impairment in children and adolescents.* New York: Grune & Stratton.

Jastak, J.E., & Jastak, S.R. (1978). *Wide Range Achievement Test.* Wilmington, DE: Jastak Associates.

Jenkins, J.R., Mayhill, W.F., Peschka, C.M., & Jenkins, L.M. (1974). Comparing small group and tutorial instruction in resource rooms. *Exceptional Children, 40*, 245-250.

Jenkins, J.R., Stein, M.L., & Osborn, J.R. (1981). What next after decoding? Instruction and research in reading comprehension. *EEQ, 1*, 27-38.

Johnson, D.D., Toms-Bronowski, S., & Pittelman, S.D. (1982). Vocabulary development. In R.E. Kretschmer (Ed.), *Reading and the hearing impaired individual* (Monograph). *Volta Review, 84*, 11-24.

Johnson, M., & Bailey, J.S. (1974). Cross-age tutoring: Fifth graders as arithmetic tutors for kindergarten children. *Journal of Applied Behavior Analysis, 7*, 223-232.

Johnson, P.B. (1975). *From sticks and stones: Personal adventures in mathematics.* Chicago: Science Research Associates.

Johnson, S.W. (1979). *Arithmetic and learning disabilites.* Boston: Allyn and Bacon.

Jones, J.W. (1969). *The visually handicapped child.* Washington, DC: U.S. Government Printing Office.

Juel, C. (1980). Comparison of word identification strategies with varying context, word type, and reader skill. *Reading Research Quarterly, 15*, 358-376.

Kagan, J. (1966). Reflection-impulsivity: The generality and dynamics of conceptual tempo. *Journal of Abnormal Psychology, 7*, 17-24.

Kameenui, E.J., Carnine, D.W., & Freschi, R. (1982). Effects of text constructive and instructional procedures for teaching word meanings on comprehension and recall. *Reading Research Quarterly, 17*, 367-388.

Kane, B.J., & Alley, G.R. (1980). A peer-tutored, instructional management program in computational mathematics for incarcerated, learning disabled juvenile delinquents. *Journal of Learning Disabilities, 13*, 148-151.

Karlsen, B., Madden, R., & Gardner, E.F. (1976). *Stanford Diagnostic Reading Test.* New York: Harcourt Brace Jovanovich.

Katz, L., & Mathis, S.L., III (1978). *The deaf child in the public schools: A handbook for parents of deaf children* (2nd ed.). Danville, IL: Interstate Printers & Publishers.

Katz, L., Mathis, S.L., & Merrill, E.C., Jr. (1978). *The deaf child in the public schools*. Danville, IL: Interstate Printers and Publishers.

Katz, R.B., Shankweiler, D., & Libermen, I.Y. (1981). Memory for item order and phonetic recoding in the beginning reader. *Journal of Experimental Child Psychology*, 32, 474-484.

Kaufman, M.E., & Alberto, P.A. (1976). Research on efficacy of special education for the mentally retarded. In N.R. Ellis (Ed.), *International review of research in mental retardation* (Vol. 8). New York: Academic Press.

Kendall, J.R., & Hood, J. (1979). Investigating the relationship between comprehension and word recognition: Oral reading analysis of children with comprehension or word recognition disabilities. *Journal of Reading Behavior, 11*, 41-46.

Kibby, M.W. (1979). The effects of certain instructional conditions and response modes in initial word learning. *Reading Research Quarterly, 15*, 147-171.

Kirk, S.A., & Elkins, J. (1975). Characteristics of children enrolled in the child service demonstration centers. *Journal of Learning Disabilities, 8*, 630-637.

Kirk, S.A., Kliebhan, J.M., & Lerner, J.W. (1978). *Teaching reading to slow and disabled learners*. Boston: Houghton Mifflin.

Kirp, D. (1974). Student classification, public policy, and the courts. *Harvard Educational Review, 44*, 6-52.

Kitagawa, M.M. (1982). Expressive writing in Japanese elementary schools. *Language Arts, 59*, 18-22.

Klune, G. (1973). Sources of reading difficulty in elementary algebra textbooks. *The Mathematics Teacher, 66*, 649-652.

Knaupp, J. (1973). Are children's attitudes toward learning arithmetic really important? *School Science and Mathematics, 73*, 9-15.

Koch, L. (1974). Developmental dyscalculia. *Journal of Learning Disabilities, 7*, 164-167.

Kosc, L. (1980). To the problem of diffuseness in terminology in the field of disturbances and disorder of mathematical abilities. *Focus on Learning Problems in Mathematics, 2*, 79-83.

Kraner, R.E. (1980). Math deficits of learning disabled first graders with mathematics as a primary or secondary disorder. *Focus on Learning Problems in Mathematics, 2*, 7-27.

Krulik, S., & Rudnick, J.A. (1981). Suggestions for teaching problem solving—A baker's dozen. *School Science and Mathematics, 81*, 37-41.

Lagrow, S.J. (1981). Effects of training on CCTV reading rates of visually impaired students. *Journal of Visual Impairment and Blindness, 75*, 368-372.

Laing, R.A., & Meyer, R.A. (1982). Transitional division algorithms. *The Arithmetic Teacher, 29*, 10-12.

Lance, W.D. (1976). What you should know about PL 94-142. *Educational Communications and Technology, 21*, 14.

Larrivee, B., & Cook, L. (1979). Mainstreaming: A study of the variables affecting teacher attitude. *The Journal of Special Education, 13*, 315-324.

Lazerick, B.E. (1981). Mastering basic facts of addition: An alternate strategy. *The Arithmetic Teacher, 28*(7), 20-24.

Leeding, R.T., & Gammel, C. (1982). Reading in the preschool. *Volta Review, 84*, 166-170.

Lernhardt, G., Zigmond, N., & Cooley, W.W. (1981). Reading instruction and its effects. *American Educational Research Journal, 18*, 343-361.

Lester, F.K., Jr. (1980). A procedure for studying the cognitive processes used during problem solving. *Journal of Experimental Education, 48*, 323-327.

Leutzinger, L.P., & Nelson, G. (1979). Using addition facts to learn subtraction facts. *The Arithmetic Teacher, 27*(4), 8-13.

Levin, J.A. (1981). Estimation techniques for arithmetic: Everyday math and mathematics instruction. *Educational Studies in Mathematics, 12*, 421-434.

Lewkowicz, N.K. (1980). Phonemic awareness training: What to teach and how to teach it. *Journal of Educational Psychology, 72*, 686-700.

Liddle, W. (1970). *Reading for concepts—Book A.* New York: McGraw-Hill.

Lippit, G. (1969). Looking at our use of time. *Training and Development Journal, 23*, 3-6.

Lloyd, J., Saltzman, N.J., & Kauffman, J.M. (1981). Predictable generalization in academic learning as a result of preskills and strategy planning. *Learning Disability Quarterly, 4*, 203-216.

Long, C.T. (1982). Mathematical excitement—The most effective motivation. *Mathematics Teacher, 75*, 413-415.

Lorenz, J.H. (1982). On some psychological aspects of mathematics achievement assessment and classroom interaction. *Educational Studies in Mathematics, 13*, 1-19.

Lovaas, O.J., Schaeffer, B., & Simmons, J.Q. (1975). Building social behavior in autistic children by use of electric shock. *Journal of Experimental Research in Personality, 1*, 99-109.

Love, H.D. (1978). *Teaching physically handicapped children: Methods and materials.* Springfield, IL: Charles C Thomas.

Lowenfield, B., Abel, G.L., & Halten, P.H. (1969). *Blind children learn to read.* Springfield, IL: Charles C Thomas.

MacKennin, D.W. (1962). The nature and nuture of creative talent. *American Psychologist, 17*, 484-495.

MacMillan, D.L. (1977). *Mental retardation in school and society.* Boston: Little, Brown.

Madden, N.A., & Slavin, R.E. (1983). Mainstreaming students with mild handicaps: Academic and social outcomes. *Review of Educational Research, 53*, 519-569.

Madden, R., Gardner, E.F., & Collins, C.S. (1983). *Stanford Early School Achievement Test* (2nd ed.). Cleveland: Psychological Corp.

Marcus, M. (1977). *Diagnostic teaching of the language arts.* New York: Wiley.

Malicky, G., & Schiebein, D. (1981). Inferencing behavior of good and poor readers. *Reading Improvement, 18,* 335-338.

Manzo, A.V. (1975). Guided reading procedure. *Journal of Reading, 18,* 287-291.

Martin, C.J. (1978). Mediational processes in the retarded: Implications for teaching reading. In N. Ellis (Ed.), *International review of research in mental retardation* (Vol. 9). New York: Academic Press.

Martin, G.G., & Hoben, M. (1977). *Supporting visually impaired students in the mainstream.* Minneapolis: Leadership Training Institute/Special Education.

McDowell, R.L., Adamson, G.W., & Wood, F.H. (1982). *Teaching emotionally disturbed children.* Boston: Little, Brown.

McGinty, R., & Van Beynen, J. (1982). Story problems: Let's make them just that. *School Science and Mathematics, 82,* 307-310.

McLeod, D.B., & Adams, V.M. (1979/80). The interaction of field independence with small group instruction in mathematics. *The Journal of Experimental Education, 48,* 118-124.

McLeod, D.B., & Adams, V.M. (1980/81). Locus of control and mathematics instruction: Three exploratory studies. *Journal of Experimental Education, 49,* 94-99.

Meece, J.L. (1981). *Development of math anxiety during middle childhood.* Unpublished doctoral dissertation, University of Michigan.

Mehan, H., Meihls, J.L., Hertweck, A., & Crowdes, M.S. (1983). Identifying handicapped students. In S.B. Barharach (Ed.), *Politics and administration: Organizational analysis of schools and school districts.* New York: Praeger Press.

Mellon, J.C. (1969). *Transformational sentence-combining: A method for enhancing the development of syntactic fluency in English composition.* Champaign, IL: National Council of Teachers of English.

Mercer, C.D., & Mercer, A.R. (1981). *Teaching students with learning problems.* Columbus, OH: Charles E. Merrill.

Mercer, C.D., & Mercer, A.R. (1985). *Teaching students with learning problems* (2nd ed.). Columbus, OH: Charles E. Merrill.

Meyer, B.F., Brandt, D., & Bluth, G. (1980). Use of top level structure in test: Key for reading comprehension of ninth grade students. *Reading Research Quarterly, 16,* 72-103.

Meyer, C.L. (1966). The relationship of early special class placement and the self-concepts of mentally handicapped children. *Exceptional Children, 33,* 77-81.

Meyerowitz, J.H. (1962). Self-derogations in young retardates and special class placement. *Child Development, 33,* 443-451.

Micklas, J. (1980). The facts, please, about reading achievement in American schools. *Journal of Reading, 6,* 41-45.

Milofsky, C.D. (1974). What special education isn't special. *Harvard Educational Review,44*, 437-458.

Misbach, D.L., & Sweeney, J. (1970). *Education of the visually handicapped in California public schools.* Sacramento, CA: Department of Education.

Mittler, P., Jeffree, D., Wheldall, K., & Berry, P. (1977). Assessment and remediation of language comprehension and production in severely subnormal children. *Collected Original Resources in Education, 1*(2), 2572-2799.

Montessori, M. (1964). *The Montessori method* (A.E. George, trans.). New York: Schocken Books.

Montgomery, M.A. (1957). *The test-study method versus the study-test method of teaching spelling in grade two: Study II.* Unpublished master's thesis, University of Texas, Austin.

Moores, D.F. (1978). *Educating the deaf: Psychology, principles, and practices.* Boston: Houghton Mifflin.

Morse, W.C. (1981, April). *Diagnosis and prescription: The affective half.* Paper presented at the Eighth Annual Conference of the Research Council for Diagnostic and Prescriptive Mathematics, Hershey, PA.

Moses, B. (1982). Individual differences in problem solving. *The Arithmetic Teacher, 30*, 10-14.

Moskowitz, B.A. (1982). The acquisition of language. In H.B. Allen & M.D. Linn (Eds.), *Readings in applied English linguistics* (pp. 164-180). New York: Knopf.

Mueller, D.J. (1976). Mastery learning: Partly boon, partly boon-doggle. *Teachers College Record, 78*, 41-52.

Myers, A.C., & Thornton, C.A. (1977). The learning disabled child: Learning the basic facts. *The Arithmetic Teacher, 25*, 46-50.

National Council of Teachers of Mathematics. (1981). *Priorities in school mathematics.* Reston, VA: Author.

Neuman, S.B. (1981). A comparison of two methods of teaching vowel knowledge. *Reading Improvement, 18*, 264-269.

Newell, V.K. (1983). Problem solving: If now now—then when! *Arithmetic Teacher, 30*, 4.

Newland, T.E. (1969). *Blind Learning Aptitude Test.* Champaign, IL: T. Ernest Newland.

Niles, J.A., Graham, R.T., & Winstead, J.C. (1979). Teacher feedback as a factor in oral reading. *Reading in Virginia*, 16-18.

Noble, E.F. (1981). Self-selection: A remedial strategy for readers with a limited reading vocabulary. *The Reading Teacher, 34*, 386-388.

Northcott, W.H. (Ed.). (1980). *The hearing impaired child in a regular classroom: Preschool, elementary, and secondary years: A guide for the classroom teacher and administrator* (1st ed. rev.). Washington, DC: Alexander Graham Bell Association for the Deaf.

O'Mara, D.A. (1981). The process of reading mathematics. *Journal of Reading, 25,* 22-29.

Otis, A., & Lennon, D. (1979). *Otis-Lennon Mental Ability Test.* Cleveland: Psychological Corp.

Otto, W., McMenemy, R.A., & Smith, R.J. (1973). *Corrective and remedial teaching* (2nd ed.). Boston: Houghton Mifflin.

Pany, D., & McCoy, K.M. (1983, April). *Effects of corrective feedback on word accuracy and reading comprehension of learning disabled and average readers.* Paper presented at Annual Meeting of American Educational Research Association, Montreal, Canada.

Pany, D., McCoy, K.M., & Peters, E. (1981). Effects of corrective feedback on comprehension skills of remedial students. *Journal of Reading Behavior, 13,* 131-144.

Paolitto, D.P. (1976). The effect of cross-age tutoring on adolescence: An inquiry into theoretical assumptions. *Review of Education Research, 46,* 215-237.

Pascarella, E.T., & Pflaum, S.W. (1981). The interaction of children's attributive and level of control over error correction in reading instruction. *Journal of Educational Psychology, 73,* 533-540.

Payne, J.S., & Patton, J.R. (Eds.). (1981). *Mental retardation.* Columbus, OH: Charles E. Merrill.

Payne, J.S., Polloway, E.A., Smith, J.E., & Payne, R.A. (1977). *Strategies for teaching the mentally retarded.* Columbus, OH: Charles E. Merrill.

Pearson, D.P., Hansen, J., & Gordon, C. (1979). *The effect of background knowledge on young children's comprehension of explicit and implicit information.* (Tech. Rep. No. 116). Urbana: University of Illinois, Center for the Study of Reading.

Peck, D.D., Jencks, S.M., & Chatterly, L.J. (1980). How can you tell? *The Elementary School Journal, 80,* 179-183.

Pehrsson, R.S.V. (1974). The effects of teacher interference during the process of reading. *Journal of Reading, 17,* 617-621.

Pelosi, P.L. (1981). The disabled reader in years past. *Journal of Research and Development in Education, 14,* 1-10.

Peng, C., & Levin, J.R. (1979). Picture and children's story recall: Some questions of durability. *Educational Communication and Technology Journal, 27*(1), 39-44.

Perfetti, C.A., & Lesgold, A.M. (1979). Coding and comprehension in reading skills and implications for reading instruction. In L.B. Resnick & P.A. Weaver, *Theory and practice of early reading.* Hillsdale, NJ: Lawrence Erlbaum.

Perron, J.D. (1974). *An exploratory approach to extending the syntactic development of fourth-grade students through the use of sentence-combining methods.* Unpublished doctoral dissertation, Indiana University, Bloomington.

Peterson, P.L., Janicki, J.C., & Swing, S.R. (1981). Treatment interaction effects on children's learning in large-group and small-group interactions. *American Educational Research Journal, 18,* 453-473.

Petty, W. (1978). The writing of young children. In C.R. Cooper & L. Odell (Eds.), *Research on composing: Points of departure* (pp.73-83). Urbana, IL: National Council of Teachers of English.

Petty, W., & Green, H. (1968). *Developing language skills in the elementary schools* (3rd ed.). Boston: Allyn & Bacon.

Pflaum, S.W., & Pascarella, E.T. (1981). Interactive effects of prior reading achievement and training in context on the reading of learning disabled children. *Reading Research Quarterly, 16,* 138-157.

Phelps-Gunn, T., & Phelps-Terasaki, D. (1982). *Written language instruction: Theory and remediation.* Rockville, MD: Aspen.

Polloway, E.A., & Smith, J.E., Jr. (1982). *Teaching language skills to exceptional learners.* Denver: Love.

Polyson, J.A. (1979). Toward a better view of children's problem behavior. *Psychology, 16,* 33-37.

Prehm, H.J. (1976). Learning performance of handicapped students. *The High School Journal, 59,* 275-281.

Prescott, G.A., Balow, I.H., Hogan, T.R., & Farr, R.C. (1978). *Metropolitan Achievement Tests: Survey Battery.* Cleveland: Psychological Corp.

Quigley, S.P. (1982). Reading achievement and special reading materials. In R.E. Kretschmer (Ed.), *Reading and the hearing impaired child* (Monograph). *Volta Review, 84,* 95-106.

Quigley, S.P., & Kretschmer, R.E. (1982). *The education of deaf children: Issues, theory, and practice.* Baltimore: University Park Press.

Quinn, L. (1981). Reading skills of hearing and congenitally deaf children. *Journal of Experimental Child Psychology, 32,* 139-161.

Radatz, H. (1980). Students' errors in the mathematical learning process. *For the Learning of Mathematics, 1,* 16-20.

Readence, J.E., & Harris, M.M. (1980). False prerequisites in the teaching of comprehension. *Reading Improvement, 17,* 18-21.

Reifman, B., Pascarella, E.T., & Larson, A. (1981). Effects of word bank instruction on sight word acquisition: An experimental note. *Journal of Educational Research, 74,* 175-178.

Reisman, F. (1981). Performance on Torrance's thinking creatively in action and movement as a predictor of cognitive development of young children. *Creative Child and Adult Quarterly, 6,* 205-209, 233.

Resnick, L.B. (1979). Toward a usuable psychology of reading instruction. In L.B. Resnick & P.A. Trever (Eds.), *Theory and practice of early reading.* Hillsdale, NJ: Lawrence Erlbaum.

Resnick, L.B. (1980). *The role of invention in the development of mathematical competence.* University of Pittsburgh, Learning Research and Development Center.

Resnick, L.B. (1982). Syntax and semantics in learning to subtract. In T.P. Carpenter, J.M. Moser, & T.A. Romberg (Eds.), *Addition and subtraction: A cognitive perspective* (pp. 136-155). Hillsdale, NJ: Lawrence Erlbaum.

Resnick, L.B., & Ford, W.W. (1981). *The psychology of mathematics for instruction.* Hillsdale, NJ: Lawrence Erlbaum.

Reynolds, M. (1978). *Teaching exceptional children in all America's schools.* Reston, VA: Council for Exceptional Children.

Riedesel, C.A. (1980). *Teaching elementary school mathematics* (3rd ed.). Englewood Cliffs, NJ: Prentice-Hall.

Rittenhouse, R.K., & Stearns, K. (1982). Teaching metaphor to deaf children. *American Annals of the Deaf, 127,* 12-17.

Rogers, C.M., Smith, M.D., & Coleman, G.S. (1978). Social comparison in the classroom: The relationship between academic achievement and self concept. *Journal of Educational Psychology, 70,(1),* 50-57.

Rosamond, F. (1982). Listening to our students. *For the Learning of Mathematics, 3,* 6-11.

Rosenshine, B.V., & Berliner, D.C. (1978). Academic engaged time. *British Journal of Teacher Education, 4,* 3-16.

Rosenthal, D.J., & Resnick, L.B. (1971). *The sequence of information in arithmetic word problems.* (ERIC Document Reproduction Service No. ED 040 909)

Ross, A.O. (1976). *Psychological aspects of learning disabilities and reading disorders.* New York: McGraw-Hill.

Rosso, B.R., & Emans, R. (1981). Children's use of phonic generalizations. *The Reading Teacher, 34,* 653-658.

Rotter, J.B. (1975). Some problems and misconceptions related to the construct of internal versus external control of reinforcement. *Journal of Consulting and Clinical Psychology, 43(1),* 55-66.

Rubin, R.A., & Balow, B. (1978). Prevalence of teacher identified behavior problems: A longitudinal study. *Exceptional Children, 45(2),* 102-111.

Rudloff, J.S. (1966). The hearing handicapped retarded reader. *Volta Review, 68,* 567-571.

Rummelhart, D.E. (1977). Toward an interactive model of reading. In S. Dornic (Ed.), *Attention and performance VI.* Hillsdale, NJ: Lawrence Erlbaum.

Sadowski, C.J. (1981). Relationship between origin climate, perceived responsibility and grades. *Perceptual & Motor Skills, 53,* 259-261.

Salvia, J., & Ysseldyke, J.E. (1978). *Assessment in special and remedial education.* Boston: Houghton Mifflin.

Samuels, J. (1981). Some essentials of decoding. *EEQ, 2,* 11-25.

Samuels, J.S., & Turnure, J.E. (1974). Reading achievement in first grade boys and girls. *Journal of Educational Psychology, 66,* 29-32.

Samuels, S.J. (1970). How your mind works when reading: Describing elephants no one has ever seen. In L.B. Resnick & P.A. Weaver (Eds.), *Theory and practice of early reading* (Vol. 1). Hillsdale, NJ: Erlbaum.

Santosstefano, S. (1978). *A biodevelopmental approach to clinical child psychology: Cognitive controls and cognitive therapy.* New York: Wiley.

Sapon-Shevin, M. (1979). Mainstreaming: Implementing the spirit of the law. *Journal of Negro Education, 48,* 364-381.

Schmid-Schönbein, G. (1979). Language learning at preschool age. In R. Freudenstein (Ed.), *Teaching foreign languages to the very young: Papers from seven countries on work with 4- to 8-year-olds.* Oxford: Pergamon Press.

Schofield, H.L., & Start, K.B. (1979). Product variables as a criteria of teacher effectiveness. *Journal of Experimental Education, 48,* 130-136.

Scott, Foresman and Co. (1981). *D'Nealian handwriting.* Glenview, IL: Author.

Sealey, J. (1985). Remediation. *R & D Interpretation Service Bulletin: Mathematics.* Charleston, WV: Appalachia Educational Lab.

Seward, C. (1982). Hearing impairments. In E.L. Meyens (Ed.), *Exceptional children in today's schools: An alternative resource book.* Denver: Love.

Shankweiler, D., & Liberman, I. (1972). Misreading: A search for causes. In J.V. Kavanaugh & I. Mattingly (Eds.), *Language by ear and by eye: The relationships between speech and reading.* Cambridge: MIT Press.

Sharan, S., Ackerman, Z., & Hertz-Lazarowitz, R. (1979). Academic achievement of elementary school children in small-group vs. whole-class instruction. *The Journal of Experimental Education, 48,* 125-129.

Sharan, S., & Sharan, Y. (1976). *Small group teaching.* Englewood Cliffs, NJ: Educational Technology Publications.

Shaughnessy, J., Haladyna, T., & Shaughnessy, J.M. (1983). Relations of student, teacher, and learning environment variables to attitude toward mathematics. *School Science and Mathematics, 83,* 21-36.

Shepard, L.A., & Smith, M.L. (1983). An evaluation of the identification of learning disabled students in Colorado. *Learning Disability Quarterly, 6,* 115-117.

Sherrill, J.M. (1979). Subtraction: Decomposition versus equal addends. *The Arithmetic Teacher, 27,* 16-17.

Shuman, R.B. (1982). Reading with a purpose: Strategies to interest reluctant readers. *Journal of Reading, 25,* 725-730.

Shuster, A., & Pigge, F. (1965). Retention efficiency of meaningful teaching. *The Arithmetic Teacher, 12,* 24-31.

Silbert, J., Carnine, D., & Stein, M. (1981). *Direct instruction mathematics.* Columbus, OH: Charles E. Merrill.

Simner, M.L. (1981). The grammar of action and children's printing. *Developmental Psychology, 17,* 866-871.

Singer, H. (1980). Sight word learning with and without pictures: A critique of Arlin, Scott, and Webster's research. *Reading Research Quarterly, 15,* 290-299.

Sister Barbara Louise (1982). The magic carpet: Language drama in everyday life. *American Annals of the Deaf, 127,* 10-11.

Skemp, R.R. (1971). *The psychology of learning mathematics.* Baltimore: Penguin Books.

Skemp, R.R. (1981). What is good environment for the intelligent learning of mathematics? Do schools provide it? Can they? *Psychology of Mathematics Education, 2,* 47-55.

Slesnick, T. (1982). Algorithmic skill vs. conceptual understanding. *Educational Studies in Mathematics, 13,* 143-154.

Sloane, H.N., Buckholdt, D.R., Jenson, W.R., & Crandall, J.A. (1979). *Structured teaching: A design for classroom management and instruction.* Champaign, IL: Research Press.

Smart, R., Wilton, K., & Keeling, B. (1980). Teacher factors and special class placement. *The Journal of Special Education, 14,* 217-229.

Smead, V.S., & Chase, C.I. (1981). Student expectations as they relate to achievement in eighth grade mathematics. *Journal of Educational Research, 75,* 115-120.

Smith, D.D. (1981). *Teaching the learning disabled.* Englewood Cliffs, NJ: Prentice Hall.

Smith, F. (1971). *Understanding reading: A psycholinguistic analysis of reading and learning to read.* New York: Holt, Rinehart and Winston.

Smith, R.M., & Neisworth, J.T. (1975). *The exceptional child: A functional approach.* New York: McGraw-Hill.

Smith, S.C. (Ed.). (1978). *Clarification of P.L. 94-142 for the classroom teacher.* Philadelphia: Research for Better Schools.

Spache, G.D. (1972). *Diagnostic Reading Scales.* Monterey, CA: McGraw-Hill.

Spearritt, D. (1979, July). *Relationships among the four communication skills during the primary school years* (Paper presented at the Conference on Developing Oral Communication Competence in Children, Armidale, Australia). (ERIC Document Reproduction Service No. ED 180 025)

Spiegel, D.L., & Rogers, C. (1980). Teacher responses to miscues during oral reading by second grade students. *Journal of Educational Research, 74,* 8-12.

Spitz, H.H. (1973). Consolidating facts into the schematized learning and memory system of educable retardates. In N.R. Ellis (Ed.), *International review of research in mental retardation* (Vol. 6). New York: Academic Press.

Stevens, K.C. (1981). Chunking material as an aid to reading comprehension. *Journal of Reading, 25,* 126-129.

Stevens, K.C. (1982). Can we improve reading by teaching background information? *Journal of Reading, 25,* 326-329.

Stigler, J., Lii, S., Lucker, G.W., & Stevenson, H.W. (1982). Curriculum and achievement in mathematics: A study of elementary school children in Japan, Taiwan, and the United States. *Journal of Educational Psychology, 74,* 315-322.

Stott, D.H. (1981). Behavior disturbance and failure to learn: A study of cause and effect. *Educational Research, 23*, 163-172.

Stowitschek, J.J., Gable, R.A., & Hendrickson, J.M. (1980). *Instructional material for exceptional children.* Germantown, MD: Aspen.

Straw, S.B. (1981). Grammar and the teaching of writing: Analysis versus synthesis. In V. Froese & S.B. Straw (Eds.), *Research in the language arts: Language and schooling* (pp. 147-161). Baltimore: University Park Press.

Strong, W.S. (1983). *Sentence combining: A composing book* (2nd ed.). New York: Random House.

Suydam, M.N. (1982). Update on research on problem solving: Implications for classroom teaching. *Arithmetic Teacher, 29*, 56-60.

Swan, D.K. (1968). *English now: Drill book.* London: Longman.

Swenson, E.J. (1973). *Teaching mathematics to children* (2nd ed.). New York: Macmillan.

Swing, S.R., & Peterson, P.L. (1982). The relationship of student ability and small-group interaction to student achievement. *American Educational Research Journal, 19*, 259-274.

Tamor, L. (1981). Subjective text difficulty: An alternative approach to defining the difficulty level of written text. *Journal of Reading Behavior, 13*, 165-172.

Taylor, H.G., Satz, P., & Friel, J. (1978). *Developmental dyslexia in relation to other childhood reading disorders: Significance and clinical utility.* Unpublished paper. Gainesville: University of Florida, Neuropsychology Laboratory.

Taylor, H.G., Satz, P., & Friel, J. (1979). Developmental dyslexia in relation to other childhood reading disorders: Significance and clinical utility. *Reading Research Quarterly, 15*, 84-101.

Taylor, W.F., & Hoedt, K.C. (1966). The effect of praise upon the quality and quantity of creative writing. *Journal of Educational Research, 60*, 80-83.

Telford, C.W., & Sawrey, J.M. (1981). *The exceptional individual: Psychological and educational aspects* (4th ed.). Englewood Cliffs, NJ: Prentice Hall.

Templin, M.C., & Darley, F.L. (1960). *The Templin-Darley Tests of Articulation.* Iowa City: University of Iowa, Bureau of Educational Research and Service.

Terman, L., & Merrill, M. (1973). *Stanford-Binet Intelligence Scale.* Chicago: Riverside.

Thomas, J.W. (1980). Agency and achievement: Self-management and self-regard. *Review of Educational Research, 50*, 213-240.

Thomas, M.A. (1980). Most productive environments for mentally retarded individuals. *Journal of Research and Development in Education, 13*, 7-14.

Thorndike, E.L. (1913). *Educational psychology* (Vol. 1). New York: Teachers College, Columbia University.

Thurman, S.K., & Fiorelli, J.S. (1980). Perspectives on normalization. *The Journal of Special Education, 13*, 340-346.

Thurman, S.K., & Lewis, M. (1979). Children's response to differences: Some possible implications for mainstreaming. *Exceptional Children, 45,* 468-470.

Torgeson, J., & Kail, R.V. (1980). Memory processes in exceptional children. In B. Keogh (Ed.), *Advances in special education* (pp. 55-99). Greenwich, CT: JAI Press.

Travers, R.M.W. (1967). *Essentials of learning: An overview of students of education.* New York: MacMillan.

Trovato, J., & Bucher, B. (1980). Peer tutoring with or without home-based reinforcement for reading remediation. *Journal of Applied Behavior Analysis, 13,* 129-141.

Trybus, R.J., & Kerchmer, M.A. (1977). School achievement scores of hearing impaired children. National data on achievement status and growth patterns. *American Annals of the Deaf Directory of Programs and Services, 122,* 62-69.

Tuinman, J.J. (1980). The schema schemers. *Journal of Reading, 23,* 414-419.

Turnbull, A.P., & Schulz, J.B. (1979). *Mainstreaming handicapped students: A guide for classroom teachers.* Boston: Allyn & Bacon.

Vaidya, S., & Chansky, N. (1980). Cognitive development and cognitive style as factors in mathematics achievement. *Journal of Educational Psychology, 72,* 326-330.

Valtin, R. (1978-79). Dyslexia: Deficit in reading or deficit in research. *Reading Research Quarterly, 14,* 207-221.

Van de Walle, J.A., & Thompson, C.S. (1981). Fitting problem solving into every classroom. *School Science and Mathematics, 81,* 289-297.

Van Riper, C.G. (1963). *Speech correction: Principles and methods* (4th ed.). Englewood Cliffs, NJ: Prentice-Hall.

VanderVolk, C. (1981). *Assessment and planning with the visually impaired.* Baltimore: University Park Press.

Vaughan, J.L., Jr. (1982). Use the construct procedure to foster active reading and learning. *Journal of Reading, 25,* 412-422.

Veatch, J. (1966). *Reading in the elementary school.* New York: Ronald Press.

Vygotsky, L.S. (1962). *Thought and language.* Cambridge: MIT Press.

Wagner R.F. (1981). Remediating common math errors. *Academic Therapy, 16,* 449-453.

Wallbrown, F., Vance, H.B., & Blaka, J. (1979). Developing remedial hypothesis from ability profiles. *Journal of Learning Disabilities, 8,* 557-561.

Wanberg, E.G., & Thompson, B. (1982). Miscue and cognitive development patterns of differentially skilled readers. *Reading Improvement, 19,* 98-103.

Ward, M., & McCormick, S. (1981). Reading instruction for blind and low vision children in the regular classroom. *The Reading Teacher, 34,* 434-444.

Warncke, E.W. (1981). Can disabled readers with emotional problems win? *Journal of Research and Development in Education, 14,* 35-40.

Weaver, P.A., & Resnick, L.B. (1979). The theory and practice of early reading: An introduction. In L.B. Resnick & P.A. Weaver (Eds.), *Theory and practice of early reading.* Hillsdale, NJ: Lawrence Erlbaum.

Webb, N.M. (1982). Student interaction and learning in small groups. *Review of Educational Research, 52,* 421-445.

Wechsler, D. (1974). *The Wechsler Intelligence Scale for Children–Revised.* New York: The Psychological Corp.

Wellman, M.M. (1983). Teaching handwriting: Implications of neuropsychological research. *Reading Improvement, 20,* 54-57.

West, T.A. (1980). The effectiveness of two drill strategies (paper-and-pencil, electronic calculator) in facilitating the learning of basic multiplication combinations with factors of 7, 8, or 9. *School Science and Mathematics, 80,* 97-102.

Whitfield, P., & Stoddart, D.M. (1984). *Hearing, taste, and smell: Pathways of perception.* New York: Torstar Books, 17-18.

Widmer, C.C. (1980). Math anxiety and elementary school teachers. In R. Karplus (Ed.), *Proceedings of the Fourth International Conference for the Psychology of Mathematics Education.* Berkeley, California.

Wiig, E.H., & Semel, E.M. (1976). *Language disabilities in children and adolescents.* Columbus, OH: Charles E. Merrill.

Williams, J., (1979). The ABD's of reading: A program for the learning disabled. In L.B. Resnick & P.A. Weaver (Eds.), *Theory and practice of early reading* (Vol. 3). Hillsdale, NJ: Lawrence Erlbaum.

Wirtz, R.W. (1974). *Drill and practice at the problem solving level: An alternative.* Washington, DC: Curriculum Development Associates.

Wolfensberger, W. (1972). *The principle of normalization in human services.* Toronto: National Institute on Mental Retardation.

Wood, M., & Dunlap, W.P. (1982). Application of drill and practice. *Focus on Learning Problems in Mathematics, 4,* 15-21.

Wright, C.D., & Wright, J.P. (1980). Handwriting: The effectiveness of copying from moving versus still models. *Journal of Educational Research, 74,* 95-98.

Wyne, M.D., & Stuck, G.B. (1979). Time on-task and reading performance in underachieving children. *Journal of Reading Behavior, 11,* 119-128.

Yap, K.O. (1979). Vocabulary—Building blocks of comprehension? *Journal of Reading Behavior, 11,* 49-59.

Ysseldyke, J.E., Algozzine, B., Richey, L., & Graden, J. (1982). Declaring students eligible for learning disability services: Why bother with the data? *Learning Disability Quarterly, 5,* 37-44.

Ysseldyke, J.E., Thurlow, M., Graden, J., Wesson, C., Algozzine, B., & Deno, S. (1983). Generalizations from five years of research on assessment and decision making: The University of Minnesota Institute. *Exceptional Education Quarterly, 4,* 75-94.

Zweng, M.J. (1979). The problem of solving story problems. *Arithmetic Teacher, 27,* 2-3.

# Index